P9-BJU-664

Greek Thought

Greek Thought
and the Origins of the
Scientific Spirit

By
LÉON ROBIN
Professor at the Faculty of Letters of the University of Paris

WITH A MAP

NEW YORK / RUSSELL & RUSSELL

Translated from the new revised and corrected French edition
by
M. R. DOBIE

FIRST PUBLISHED IN 1928
REISSUED, 1967, BY RUSSELL & RUSSELL
A DIVISION OF ATHENEUM PUBLISHERS, INC.
BY ARRANGEMENT WITH
ROUTLEDGE & KEGAN PAUL LTD., LONDON
L. C. CATALOG CARD NO: 66-27142
ISBN: 0-8462-0906-3
PRINTED IN THE UNITED STATES OF AMERICA

CONTENTS

v

CONTENTS

BOOK THREE

HUMAN CULTURE

CONTENTS

FOREWORD

PURE THOUGHT

*At the beginning of the present volume we may be permitted
to observe that there is no history of the world in existence which
gives to the history of ideas the place which it will have in this
series or makes it so completely and profoundly a part of the
history of man.*

*We are not speaking of the world-histories which present a
positive character, for we have not forgotten that there are such,
in which the Idea more than holds a great place in history, since
it is given* a priori *as the very foundation of history. There
are theologians who have known the designs of God, gesta Dei
per homines, and metaphysicians who have constructed the
philosophy of history dialectically, by the omnipotence of their
Reason. But in this synthesis in which we gather together all
explanatory factors, and try to credit each with its true share,
our aim is to inquire what is the share, not of the Idea, but of
pure ideas. " Historical idealism must turn experimental. It
must take root in positive psychology, to become exact and to
ramify in the history of ideas."* [1] *So we shall here follow the
evolution of the psychism whose humble beginnings we have
related,* [2] *at the stage where, not content with thinking itself,
thought enjoys itself and expands in speculation which in
appearance is wholly disinterested.*

*Now, the problem presented by the whole of the period of
history which we have entered with Greece is twofold. For one
thing, we have to inquire to what extent Thought, in the succession of time and in all the multitude of men, schools, and peoples
who have speculated, possesses a unity, represents a* logic. *We
must also inquire what active influence that pure thought had—
to what extent the knowledge, to which it tended, transformed, with*

[1] See our *Synthèse en histoire*, p. 212.
[2] See Forewords to *Prehistoric Man*, pp. v ff., xii, and *Language*, pp ix ff.,
xv ff., both in this series.

the conception of life, the conduct of men and the organization of societies.

Our own belief—and it is a hypothesis which animates this series—is that there is a human Thought, *that, in the millions of facets in which the Real is reflected throughout time and space, one single endeavour is being accomplished. And we believe that the power of ideas is immense, that even the most abstract ideas always have some secret relationship with life, some indirect action upon it, and that the search for truth, therefore, is essentially the task of man. To know is to adapt oneself with method.*[1]

But our admirable fellow-workers have not accepted any theoretical conditions and are not subject to any pressure. As this series develops, it will check experimentally—let us say it once again—the hypotheses which give the work its full import.

Now, Professor Robin is one of those historians of philosophy who, in the fullness of their knowledge, by the very suggestion of the subject which they are studying, have understood that philosophy cannot be shut off from life, but is connected with the fundamental needs of mankind. The practical and collective origins of thought are well brought out in the first chapters of his book.

Greek philosophy arises from morality and religion. Between the " moral demands of common thought" and the various views about the past or present history of the universe " which religious beliefs contain," on the one hand, and the original and free attempt of Greek thinkers " to organize a system of reflections on the order of nature or on that of conduct" on the other, Professor Robin perceives a preliminary work of reflection on popular, spontaneous notions, by way of which reflection men advance from religion to philosophy. And this work is " a social thing," he says. " It is effected in an impersonal, obscure, continuous fashion, accompanying and expressing the progress of manners and religious sentiment" and, likewise, " of the craftsmanship which labours to master nature" (p. 17). So he distinguishes between three stages. After

---

[1] " From the evolutionary point of view, consciousness is above all a means placed at the disposal of an organism in order that it may react more appropriately," D. Roustan, " La Science comme instrument," in *Rev. de Métaph. et de mor.*, Sept., 1914, p. 614. Cf. Piéron, " L'Évolution du psychisme," in *Rev. du Mois*, March, 1908, p. 291 ; Mach, *La Connaissance et l'erreur*, pp. 12, 387.

the " common " or " collective " thought of the beginning come a " social " thought, which takes up the results of that spontaneous creation, and then individual thought, which criticizes those results. With great discernment, he observes that moral reflection, in consequence of the demands of life lived in common, precedes reflection about nature, whereas critical reflection on the principles of conduct, on account of the same demands, only begins late.

In this evolution, it might, perhaps, be interesting to determine more exactly the part played by the individual and that played by the society, to make a clear distinction between the social and the collective.

Morality, without any doubt, answers to a need of the society. It is specifically and originally social. Yet it is only created by individuals, special beings, and especially thanks to certain individuals, who are social agents. In general, a society is made by individuals, and then it thinks itself *in individuals, before being transformed by their criticism. But at no step in the social development, and particularly of the moral development, even when the work is* anonymous, *can one say absolutely that it is* impersonal.

Still less can one say it of the work which culminates in a systematic view of the universe. Psychism develops in society, but it is anterior to society—it is even anterior to humanity. It is constituted in the brain of the individual. It is the most contingent part of the acquisitions and creations of the mind which is communicated and handed down ; so a collective *mentality, in the strict sense of the word, arises.[1] They take the form of institutions ; and we know that by the tyranny of the institution society keeps the intelligence immobile in myths and arbitrary concepts.[2] But they also form a thread of logic, and that is* human thought, *the impersonal effort of the personality.*

Regarding the earliest schools of Greek thinkers, Professor Robin says, " For a long time the collective work of the association hid the personal contribution of individuals *in an obscurity which the historian has great difficulty in piercing " (p. 34).*

---

[1] The *collective* is what answers, not to a social necessity or to a logical effort, but to the contingent characteristics of a collectivity. See *La Synthèse en histoire*, pp. 77 ff.

[2] See Forewords to *Language*, pp. xix-xx, and *From Tribe to Empire*, pp. xx ff., in this series.

This remark applies equally well, mutatis mutandis, *to the earliest development of reflection and even to the spontaneous elaboration of morality and speculation on nature. If, in the case of the old schools, " a few great names, almost symbolical, emerge from the darkness," these names—for example, those of the Seven Sages, the list of whom is given variously—seem to us not so much to sum up the efforts of groups as to assert individualities.*

In short, the subject, and the great interest, of this book is to show the strengthening of critical thought and the increasing importance of the thinker, who appears in the foreground of Greek history. And since, as we have said, Professor Robin does not shut thought off from life, neither from the various modalities of life nor from its profound and permanent needs, he shows us how philosophy, going over from Ionia into Greece Proper and then into the colonies, comes under the influence of institutions and manners, and reflects the very contingencies of the individual temperament and of the profession ; but he chiefly devotes himself to following, in the luminous field of the reflective consciousness, the internal organization and continuous progress of knowledge.[1]

That thought in Greece should have assumed this new character—that it should have become speculative—is one of the aspects of the Greek *miracle. It would not be just to reject this term on the ground that Greece received much of its intellectual material from the East—religious myths, practical knowledge, technical processes. Nothing is born of nothing ; as Lange has said, " the crude opposition of originality and tradition can no longer be employed. Ideas, like organic germs, fly far and wide, but the right ground alone brings them to perfection. . . . The true independence of Hellenic culture rests in its* perfection, *not in its beginnings."* [2] *And A. Lalande, who quotes the passage, adds : " A distinct thought is never anything but the last link of a long chain of obscure thoughts, of needs and actions which have led to it. Everything begins in the unconscious ; and if it is wrong to maintain that without a consciousness man would not be a worse intellectual machine, it is at least certain that it appeared late, and that in its first*

[1] See especially pp. 33-4, 70, 86, 90-1, 127-8, 131-2, 134, 369.
[2] *History of Materialism,* Eng. trans., vol. i, p. 10, n. 5.

steps it had to take up, in so far as it was profitable, an immense inheritance which it had not accumulated." [1]

Greece created human reason. *In the East, the man who "knows" is he who holds divine secrets ; he is a priest, a prophet, a Magus, a wonder-worker.*[2] *The* thinker *is a novelty— that is, the man who makes a profession of thinking on his own account, who places his own name even on the ideas which he takes over because the quality of his intellectual instrument gives him authority and inspires confidence. This ideal of the Greek thinker, " disinterested love of the eternal order of things " (Milhaud) or " the need to explain logically " (Lalande)—that is something which we did not find before the flowering of Greek civilization.*

Here the play of the speculative faculties goes together with the play of the æsthetic faculties ; the " abstract world of the thinker " is built up by the side of the " coloured, living world of the poet " (Ouvré), and the pleasure of understanding complements or corrects the art of enjoying. Men have reached a stage of evolution where the mind no longer serves only the elementary needs of humanity, but by its own needs and its own exercise creates a new humanity.

This play of the mind will go through two quite distinct phases. In the phase of naturalism, *mind opposes nature and tries to take possession of it ; or it tries every hypothesis which may explain the becoming of things, not without relying on certain positive observations and profiting, at each new hypothesis, by earlier hypotheses. In the phase of* humanism, *the individual is contrasted with society, and thenceforward man, taking more interest in himself, analyses the processes of which he made use in his various activities. He will develop the technique of techniques, methods for conducting oneself well in all things— working well, speaking well, thinking well. Logic, in the wide sense, will rise to the second power, and, as the mind takes itself as an object of study, logic, in the restricted, epistemological sense, will be created.*[3]

The Sophists, whose originality in intellectual history is considerable, inaugurate this second phase. They teach men to

---

[1] General review on ancient physics, in *Rev. de Synthèse historique*, ii (1901), p. 205. Cf. G. Rodier, general review on the history of Greek philosophy, *ibid.*, xiii (1906), p. 209 ; T. Gomperz, *Greek Thinkers*, beginning of Book III.

[2] Ouvré, *Les Formes littéraires de la pensée grecque*, p. 166.

[3] See below, pp. 131-3, 147.

handle the λόγος, *which is the word, the formula, but is also reasoning, thought. But it is the* Γνῶθι σέαυτον *of Socrates which really opens a new world. It not only calls for reflection on the creations of life ; it bids the internal gaze to descend into the deep abysses of being.*

One might well expect that there would be a Socratic problem, as there is a Homeric problem or a Shakespearean problem, and that Plato's hero might be a kind of legendary personage ; but Socrates survives the test and remains the author " of a revolution without its like in the whole history of philosophy, of which the Cartesian and Kantian revolutions are merely the renewal or the development." [1]

Plato, for his part, synthetizes the previous efforts of thought. He unifies nature and man, mechanism and dynamism, by belief in the reality of Ideas—which are revealed in man. He gives a first example of construction following upon criticism, in which the ambition of the mind is displayed by a powerful dialectic. He has every audacity and every charm ; he manifests in full the Greek spirit, " at once bold and moderate, intuitive and rational, mystical and positive, artistic and geometrical." [2]

The Greeks intoxicated themselves with dialectic. Professor Robin offers us a wonderfully fascinating spectacle, when he makes that multitude of philosophers pass before us, some deep and sincere thinkers, others jugglers with ideas and conjurers with words ; when he draws portraits of the Scholarchs, some tied to a city and others travelling about, seeking at the same time to recruit disciples and to extend their knowledge of men and things ; when he calls up the groups and the schools, some true brotherhoods (the Pythagoreans and Epicureans) and some true universities (the Academy and Lyceum). He shows us Greece, arguing and argumentative, giving itself up to the intoxication in which the young reason discovers its powers without recognizing its limitations.

But a time will come, that of moralism, in which interest in conduct (which is implied even in the apparently most disinterested speculation) will take front place ; when, as a result of intellectual lassitude and also of political circumstances, [3] *the Wise Man will work, not for the organization of the City,*

---

[1] See H. Carteron, " Un Nouveau Point de vue sur l'hist. de la philosophie grecque " (with reference to Dupréel, *La Légende socratique et les sources de Platon*), in *Rev. Philosophique*, July-Aug., 1923, p. 122.
[2] Below, p. 235.   [3] Pp. 313-14.

but for the best use of his own life. On the Scepticism produced by all the pullulation of systems, or on some eclectical doctrine, a law of the sovereign good is grafted. This goes on until the day when the moral crisis becomes acute. Then Oriental mysticism, which has already filtered into certain sects of Greece, extends its influence; and we are in the Hellenistic age. At last, at the beginning of the Christian era, the rising flood of faith sweeps away the work of Greek reason, for many centuries to come. " The infinite, which for Plato or Aristotle or the Stoics was a sign of unreality or of resistance to the order of reason, becomes for Plotinus the fullest and most perfect power of the Ego." [1]

But Greek thought will be " reborn." " The problems which the old thinkers of Greece set themselves," Professor Robin rightly says, " are eternal problems " (p. 4). Κτῆμα εἰς ἀεί— *the phrase of Thucydides applies to them too.*

In this intellectual evolution, what was the part played by science ? At the beginning, philosophy and science were intermingled. The philosophers tried to solve their problems by collecting, more or less consciously, the knowledge of their time ; but they went beyond that knowledge in their desire to explain everything. In consequence of the excessiveness of their pretensions and the difficulties of their contradictions, thought came in the end either to the abdication of reason in the face of faith, or to a prudent submission of reason to experience. One cannot, it seems to us, overestimate the importance of the Greek Sceptics (who denied science, chiefly because they formed too high an idea of it), and in particular of the empirical Sceptics, who were, as Brochard has shown, the Positivists of antiquity. " If the ancient Sceptics could return," says their historian, " they would be ardent apostles of progress." [2]

Although Professor Robin presents philosophy and science in their constant relationship, he draws a distinction between the history of the one and that of the other in which he shows himself a philosopher. " The history of philosophy," he declares, " is philosophy. It has for the philosopher an ever-living interest. . . . The history of science, on the contrary, is not science ; it is the

---

[1] Below, pp. 369-70.

[2] *Les Sceptiques grecs*, p. 416. On the rôle of Scepticism, see H. Berr, *La Synthèse des connaissances et l'histoire*, p. 25, and *An jure inter scepticos Gassendus fuerit numeratus*, p. 89.

past of science, the dead part of its effort towards truth, or the effort forgotten when the end has been reached. This history, therefore, satisfies the curiosity of the erudite, but not, like that of philosophy, the most general and deepest needs of thought " (p. 4). *We believe that, from our point of view—the evolution of humanity, and, in particular, the progress of psychism in human evolution—the history of science is not a dead thing, a matter for the curiosity of the erudite. Not only does it show the mind adapting itself to things and man taking possession of his environment, but it makes us follow the constitution of a method intended to solve the problems which the mind sets itself, which it formerly tried to decide in religion, and then in meta-physics. Science gradually accumulates positive material which makes it possible to put the a priori views of the mind to the test. It is indeed an organon, an instrument for solving philosophic problems. The history of science is necessary to the history of thought, because the instrument of the progress of thought is science.*[1]

In the preceding volumes, we have seen the need for being, the logical principle, inherent in life, feeding itself with representa-tions of things, making it possible to anticipate phenomena, creating an initial knowledge, knowledge gained by living. We have seen the constitution of the various crafts, which imply an increased knowledge, but a practical knowledge. Here we shall see, as we have said, the Greeks reflecting on technical processes, creating methods, *rising to the general method of deduction, and at length applying it—because it involved a play of the pure reason, which they enjoyed—to number and figure.*

The Greeks are essentially geometricians, in the sense which the word finally took on, as against its etymology. The original " land-measurer " changed his name to that of " land-divider," geodaites,[2] *while the geometrician became the virtuoso of reason, of the reason which constructs by internal necessity and not by statement pure and simple. " In every domain of knowledge, the peoples of the East and Egypt had handed on to the Greeks a great number of data, rules, and processes useful to everyday*

---

[1] See our *Synthèse en histoire*, pp. 188 ff. ; *Peut-on refaire l'unité morale de la France ?* p. 104 ; A. Georges-Berthier, " L'Histoire des sciences en France," in *Rev. de Synth. hist.*, xxviii (1914).

[2] See P. Tannery, general review of the history of geometry, in *Rev. de Synth. hist.*, ii (1901), p. 284.

life. The Greeks did not confine themselves simply to recording them, with the intention of adding to the list indefinitely. . . . *They wanted to understand the reason of what was given to them as a total of empirical processes ; they wanted to justify, by the resources of their intelligence alone, the rules to which men had been led by a long process of observation." In its " abstract dreaming," the mind strengthened itself by the dazzling results of its efforts. " The Greek geometrician's disinterestedness, his remoteness from all practical considerations, may have been one of the profound causes of the advance of his science, and, at the same time, of its future fruitfulness in respect even of applications."* [1]

It may be said that here the scientist is not completely distinct from the philosopher, in the sense that he, too, moves in the world of ideas, and has for his object, as has been observed, the λόγος *rather than the* πρᾶγμα, *the intelligible rather than the fact.* [2] *Their gaze being bent on eternal forms, the Greeks turned away from matter. They considered it a degradation of being, and regarded the activities applied to it as servile.* [3] *Furthermore, " in their eyes the idea of experiment was associated with sorcery, superstition, and charlatanism."* [4] *Lastly, these prejudices, which lasted long, were supported by moral preoccupation, which reinforced the contempt for all kinds of*

---

[1] See G. Milhaud, *Les Philosophes géomètres de la Grece*, p. 368 ; " La Pensée mathématique : son rôle dans l'histoire des idées," in *Rev. Philosophique*, Apr., 1909, p. 350 ; *Le Rationnel*, chap. iii, on Greek geometry, p. 81. Cf. Weber, *Le Rythme du progres*, p. 222 ; D. Roustan, art. cit., p. 626 ; L. Brunschvicg, *Les Étapes de la philosophie mathématique*, bk. ii, ch. iv, note. For the psychology of pure mathematics, see P. Chaslin, in *Journal de Psychologie*, Oct., 1922.

[2] See Weber, op. cit., p. 291. Höffding, in *La Pensée humaine*, expresses the same idea in the following terms : " Ancient thought believed in apotheoses, but not in incarnations " (Fr. trans., p. 129).

[3] See Gina Lombroso-Ferrero, " Pourquoi le machinisme ne fut pas adopté dans l'antiquité," in *Revue du Mois*, 10th Nov., 1920 : " Archimedes, Plutarch says . . . regarded mechanics in general and all practical operations as a vile and obscure art. So he devoted himself only to the sciences connected with beauty and perfection, to those not connected with any necessity of life. And Aristotle apologizes for speaking of such things, which are rightly despised by wise men and philosophers " (p. 459). Cf. Meyerson, " Y-a-t' il un rythme dans le progres intellectuel ? " in *Bull. de la Soc. fr. de Philosophie*, Feb.-March, 1914, pp. 100–2 : " Plato, speaking of mathematical demonstrations into which mechanics were introduced . . . declares that that is ' corrupting geometry ' and ' robbing it of its dignity,' by making it go ' like a runaway slave from the study of incorporeal, intelligible things to that of objects which come under the senses and by using, in addition to reasoning, bodies which have been fashioned, slowly and slavishly, by manual labour." See also J. Burnet, " L'Expérimentation et l'observation dans la science grecque," in *Scientia*, Feb., 1923, pp. 93–102.

[4] Egger, *Science ancienne et Science moderne*, p. 22. For magic, see the volume in this series on Greek religion.

industry.[1] *Experimental science long lacked a sympathetic environment, an organization, laboratories.*[2]
But one must not exaggerate this " inattention to matter."
Paul Tannery has ingeniously called attention to the mechanical toys (θαύματα) which were meant to amuse the public and amused the inventor himself. " Like a child in its cradle, man, in the presence of the natural forces, began to play with them. He learned his power in amusing himself. The idea of using it in another way, of making nature subject to himself for useful ends, by multiplying the effects obtained on a small scale, germinated very slowly. . . . The part played by this motive of amusement in the development of the sciences appears very much obliterated to-day. But if one were to study, underneath the accepted externals, the innermost psychology of the scientific inquirer, one would no doubt recognize that . . . the same impulse still works in the bottom of our souls."[3]

But this play of the mind, this activity which takes possession of nature, are exercised in a higher and more profitable manner. The needs of life, in spite of prejudice and the force of tradition, led to progress in certain branches, such as medicine (Hippocrates and the Asclepiads),[4] *and the genius of certain individuals (Straton, Euclid, Archimedes, Ctesibios, Heron, Thucydides)*[5] *enriched positive knowledge.*

Aristotle had very lofty ambitions as a scientist, but his influence is disputable. He wanted to be an encyclopaedist; but his systematic mind, in spite of a very keen care for information and method, was necessarily inclined to impose solutions where he should have left problems open. On the other hand, even better than Plato, he established a general framework for the specialists. He inaugurated the conception of synthetic science, of science as one single whole, to which the Sceptics were to give a new character—since they prudently made it an inaccessible or distant ideal.[6]

---

[1] G. Lombroso-Ferrero, art. cit., pp. 461–3.
[2] See Egger, op. cit., and Lalande, art. cit. in *Rev. de Synth. hist.*
[3] Tannery, general review of the history of mechanics, in *Rev. de Synth. hist.*, iv (1902), p. 198.
[4] See Ouvré, *Les Formes littéraires de la pensée grecque*, p. 457 ; Meyerson, in *Bull. de la Soc. fr. de Phil.*, quoted above, pp. 95–7 (invention of the pulley, screw-press, astrolabe, water-clock, etc.).
[5] T. Gomperz in his great work lays stress on the contribution of the historians to the formation of the critical spirit and of positive knowledge. On the philology and, in general, the scientific spirit of the Alexandrians, see A. Croiset, *L'Hellénisation du monde antique*, p. 270.
[6] For Aristotle's science, see Gomperz, op. cit., vol. iv, pp. 62, 108, etc.

We shall resume, much later, the history of the progress of knowledge and shall again come upon the problem of the part played by science.[1] *It has been necessary here to underline the origins of scientific thought, to mark the importance of the history of the sciences, and to put it in its place in the history of human thought, in the general history of civilization.*[2]

That history of thought, in its various aspects, and in particular the history of ancient thought, is singularly difficult to reconstruct. One of the great merits of this book—wherein it is in harmony with one characteristic of the series—is that it does not disguise difficulties, but emphasizes the uncertainties and lacunae.

In the presence of contradictory texts and divergent interpretations, the best historians of philosophy, like Professor Robin, sometimes display a kind of coquetry in their attitude of reserve. But many contradictions are explained, as soon as one does not try " to make a philosopher more systematic than he was " ; many interpretations are reconciled, when one considers that the thought of the masters, of Plato and Aristotle, " has depths which they themselves did not perceive "—" Is it not just the obscure tendencies, which they obeyed without being clearly aware of them, that explain the influence of their doctrines and their later developments ? "[3] *In fact, this book proves that the history of Greek thought is possible and that it has made great progress.*

At the end of an excellent general review of ancient philosophy, G. Rodier complained that the immense effort of philology had not yet produced its full effect on the history of thought. " The

---

[1] *Science in the Middle Ages.* Weber has an interesting, but very exaggerated theory, according to which the Graeco-Roman, mediaeval, and modern civilizations " belong to one same great phase in evolution," which is speculative, in contrast to the earlier period and the contemporary period, in which technique and experience develop. See op. cit., p. 292, note, and the discussion in *Bull. de la Soc. fr de Phil.* quoted above. On the periods of the history of the sciences, see Mentré, " Une Thèse de Cournot," in *Rev. de Synth. hist.*, xi (1905), p. 1.

[2] Even mathematics can be claimed as part of the history of civilization. Moritz distinguishes between the history of *Mathematics*, which is special and abstract (*fachmässige Entwickelungsgeschichte*), and the *History* of mathematics, in which " the picture of civilized life (*Kulturleben*) serves as a foundation, and on that foundation the mathematical features which characterize it stand out in full light." See Paul Tannery, on the general history of the sciences, in *Rev. de Synth. hist.*, viii (1904), p. 8. On the relations between the development of the sciences and economic development, see G. Richard, " Unité de l'histoire des sciences et de l'histoire économique," *ibid.*, xiii (1906), p. 1.

[3] G. Rodier, art. cit., in *Rev. de Synth. hist.*, xiii (1906), pp. 214, 362.

materials, carefully checked, accumulate on the ground, while the building hardly seems to advance. This is doubtless because the task of the architects is the hardest, and their constructions are often hasty and provisional. But it is chiefly because, by giving all their attention to the choice of the stones, they no longer have time to put them together in layers." [1] Here we have the complete building ; the architect has known how to use and master his immense erudition. Discerning and cautious interpretation of doctrines, vigorous characterization of systems and schools, which makes the beginnings and ends of chapters valuable and illuminating connecting-links, the quotations which are necessary and no more, being the text of the thinkers forming the very substance of the exposition—here we have a combination of qualities which would fulfil the aspirations of Léon Robin's predecessor at the Sorbonne.

HENRI BERR.

[1] *Ibid.*, p. 361.

INTRODUCTION

CHAPTER I

SUBJECT AND DIVISIONS

THE historian of philosophy has the very great advantage of having to deal, as a rule, not with mere facts of all kinds, but with facts which speak to the intelligence. For the facts which he must discuss are chiefly thoughts, and, indeed, thoughts which pretend to express truths, or Truth.

But he has a corresponding disadvantage as well. For, however strictly a thinker may define his ideas and explain their connexion, he cannot help leaving some play to the subjective interpretations of the historian. The latter tries to enter into communion with another's thoughts, but that indispensable effort of intellectual sympathy inevitably obliges him to draw upon his own resources for what seems to him necessary for complete intelligibility. Is there perfect agreement among the historians of modern philosophy, even on essential questions, regarding such highly organized systems as those of Descartes, Spinoza, Leibniz, and Kant ? There is all the more danger of the interpreter's ideas intruding into those of the author whom he is discussing when he undertakes to write a history of ancient thought.

Let us imagine the most favourable case possible, where we possessed a thinker's complete philosophical works, and the text, as handed down to us, gave rise to no doubts as to the meaning of his ideas, and the authenticity of every passage and its position in the whole work were beyond dispute. Even then it would be very difficult for the historian to achieve the sympathetic communion expected of him without his own personality coming into the resurrection of thought which should be the result—both his own individual ideas and those which he takes from his age. Suppose, for example, that he

1

tries to make the author live again, in himself and in his social environment. Our knowledge of both is fragmentary and uncertain ; who would venture to think that he can make Plato and Aristotle live again in their true light ? Suppose that he leaves that external element alone, and confines himself to considering their ideas and their logical relationship. Then he is in danger of arbitrarily imposing on them the form in which later elaboration has clad the same conceptions ; for example, he may try to understand Plato through Kant. If he is not to modernize ancient thought involuntarily, he should be able to make himself a new soul, and caution in interpretation becomes all the more difficult, the more one strives to elucidate the obscurities of that thought, for oneself and for others.

Now, as a fact, the historian's path is far from being free of other obstacles created by the circumstances in his adventurous voyage in quest of ancient thought. The texts at his disposal are the outcome of a manuscript tradition ten centuries old and older, and during that time they have undergone many distortions—mistakes in copying, arbitrary corrections, omissions, and interpolations of marginal glosses. Sometimes papyri or inscriptions furnish him with older texts, but as a rule these are miserable scraps, so dilapidated that their restoration is often very doubtful. In every case, the text must be subjected to a delicate exegesis, which can never be accepted as absolutely authoritative. Nor is that all : there are problems of authenticity, which the testimony of the ancient catalogues does not enable us to settle with certainty, for our scruples regarding the attribution of literary works were the exception in antiquity. We know, too, the stimulus which the art of the forger received from the eager curiosity of book lovers. Lastly, since the date of any writing, or even its position in the whole of the author's works, can very seldom be exactly determined, it is almost impossible to establish with certainty the relationship between various expressions of the thought of a single philosopher.

The difficulties are greater and more numerous when one has nothing but fragments and external evidence. This is the case, not only with all philosophers earlier than Plato, but with most of those who lived after Aristotle. Only rarely, for example, have we information regarding the order of the fragments in the whole work, so that it is hard to say what place each holds in the development of the author's thought. Moreover, many books, which no philosophic school considered itself beholden to preserve, had already disappeared ; later writers spoke of them and quoted them without having them before their eyes. As for external testimonies, very few concerning the earlier philosophers come from contemporaries. Most of them come from erudite compilers, makers of handbooks, who lived centuries later. One has, therefore, to find out who were their authorities—a laborious undertaking which, even when it seems crowned with success, does not always wholly satisfy the critical spirit, unable to go back with certainty to the original authority or to compare him with the late statements which are derived from him through so many intermediaries. There is, indeed, one case—that of Socrates—where we have to be content with external evidence alone, and nowhere else is the burden of proof harder for the historian of Greek thought.

Nor is he in any better case when he tries to establish the dates of philosophers, especially of the earlier ones. Yet this is a task of the first importance in a study in which it is proposed to arrange facts in order of succession and especially to determine the mutual influence of doctrines. In addition, the lives of many of these ancient teachers were very early wrapped in such a thick haze of religious legends that they begin and end in the mystery of a divine existence.

An exact and ever-present sense of these difficulties, therefore, compels one both to caution and to modesty. It also makes one understand what is the task to which one must constantly apply oneself. In great part, this task concerns both social or political history, with its ancillary subjects, and philology. The latter, above all, must supply the materials, without which the historian of thought would be working in the air and would waste his energies in trying to reconstruct a whole of which too many portions were lacking. These materials are often slight and apparently of no great significance. But they constitute an indispensable foundation. Does this mean that, in the kind of subject with which we are dealing, the direction of the work should be entirely left to the philologists, as has been done, in particular, in Germany ? They have shown a patience and often a discernment which are admirable. But a historian of thought must have something more than erudition, for his endeavour is to rediscover methods of arriving at the truth, to reconstruct systems of ideas ; so he is a philosopher as much as a historian. His object is not so much to determine the individual or collective influences which may have contributed to the formation of a body of thought, as to understand that thought by setting it in its place and underlining the potentialities which it contains. Philosophic and scientific thought is doubtless a product and part of a development ; but that product can be studied for itself and as a complete part.

A last question arises : what, exactly, is the subject of our study, and what are its divisions ? First of all, I have spoken so far of the history of Greek thought. It would be more correct to speak of Graeco-Roman thought. Certainly, the Latins were not inventors, in science or in philosophy. But, if one thinks of what our knowledge of Greek thought owes to Lucretius, to Cicero, to Seneca, and to yet others, it would be unjust not to recognize the contribution of Rome. Secondly —and this is more important—the very word " thought " is most equivocal : thought exists in literature, in history, in common opinions, in religious beliefs, no less than in science or philosophy. But there it exists in a form which is not systematic, or which is not reflective. It would not even be enough to speak of rational thought ; does that mean philosophy alone, or science and philosophy together ? The two were indissolubly united in the earliest days of Greek thought, and they remained closely connected all through its development. But the history of the two cannot be studied in the same spirit. The history of philosophy is philosophy. It has for the philosopher an ever-living interest, which goes beyond that of pure erudition. The problems which the old thinkers of Greece set themselves as philosophers are eternal problems ; their terms have not changed, but the discussion of them has been fed with new material. The history of science, on the contrary, is not science ; it is the past of science, the dead part of its effort towards truth, or the effort forgotten when the end has been reached. This history, therefore, satisfies the curiosity of the erudite, but not, like that of philosophy, the most general and deepest needs of thought.[1]

[1] Besides, the history which I have undertaken to relate is not that of the *whole* evolution of Greek science, a vast subject extending far beyond the field assigned to me, but only, as the title says, that of the *origins* of the scientific *spirit*. See L. Brunschvicg's preface to Arnold Reymond's work, **XXXVa**, p. 6.

What are to be the limits and divisions of our study ? In the region of beginnings, it will exclude the form and content of the collective conscience, and will begin with the first literary expressions of moral, philosophic, or scientific thought. At the other end, it will exclude patristics,[1] or the development of Christian thought, which, being derived from other tendencies and opposed to properly Hellenic philosophy, belongs to another setting ; and it will end with the closing of the School of Athens in 529 by the Edict of Justinian. In this organic development, lasting about fourteen centuries, it is perhaps sufficient to distinguish between a period of formation, a period of maturity, and a period of old age, but an old age which is not mere decrepitude. Each of these periods, as is natural in an organic development, contains the germs of the characteristics which will mark the next.

In the first there are two phases. The main feature of the first is the intimate union of science and philosophy ; this, which is improperly called the " pre-Socratic " period, extends into the time of Socrates and later still. The second phase, that of the Sophists and Socrates, tends to disengage the notions of general culture and philosophy, but in opposite directions.

There are two phases in the second period also. On the one hand, there is the constitution, by Plato and Aristotle, of philosophy as a science superior to the other sciences, a greater number of which are organized as distinct specialities, connected, however, with the teaching of philosophy. On to this trunk, on the other hand, critical and epistemological developments and practical applications are grafted ; this work was commenced in the school of Socrates himself in the preceding phase, and was continued by the great post-Aristotelian schools. For these latter, we must be content to draw their main lines, accurately but without detail. Since we have to make sacrifices, it must not be at the expense of the vigorous tree of which these schools were offshoots.

With still greater reason, the last period, which covers about six centuries, will not be treated on the same scale as the others. It is true that it is partly, in its second phase, a period of renovation, but otherwise it is mainly one of restoration and erudition. While in the schools of Plato and Aristotle an

[1] Unlike X.

immense labour of exegesis is performed on the work of those two masters, the tendency—eclectic or syncretic—to reconcile and combine opposed philosophies becomes general. Hellenized by the conquests of Alexander, the East exercises a new influence on the Greek mind. It gives to the revival of the ancient doctrines a colouring which they did not originally possess. With Plotinus and his school, mystical irrationalism is erected into a method for uniting oneself with the absolute real. Out of the confused mass of mythical representations and purely utilitarian or purely magical practices furnished by the East, the Greek genius had in the past produced the rational achievement of science and philosophy. In its decline, it was again from the unsteady flame of Oriental thought that its last rays took their light. Yet those rays were the dawn of a new thought—but one which belongs to another phase in history. It was Greek thought no longer.

SOURCES

THE sources from which the history of Graeco-Roman thought
is drawn, and their relative value, present a preliminary
question of great importance.

First of all, for doctrines and ideas, it is clear that we must,
as much as possible, go to the philosophers themselves.
Unfortunately, the possession of an author's whole works, or
even of a single complete and really original work, is an
advantage which we are usually denied. It cannot be recalled
too often that the knowledge which we can obtain *immediately*
of the philosophic and scientific thought of Graeco-Roman
antiquity is very limited and very disconnected.

Usually, therefore, we have to depend on *mediate* sources.

First, it may happen that, without any definite historical
intention, a philosopher gives us, accidentally or apropos of
some discussion, some information about his predecessors or
contemporaries. Plato and Aristotle were in this sense
historians of philosophy. The greater part of the former's
work is we shall see later to what extent—a testimony regarding Socrates. In general, Plato would tell us much, if he did
not so often distort or wrap up his testimony, again and again
refusing to name the men of whom he is speaking, especially
in the case of contemporaries, so that the problem of identification is usually extremely knotty. Aristotle is more explicit.
But he is too much concerned with bringing out anything in
his forerunners which is a presentiment of his own teaching;
his attitude towards them, and especially towards Democritos
and Plato, is too obviously polemical for the trustworthiness
of his evidence—precious as it is—to be accepted without
discrimination or criticism. The same tendency to take one's
stand in the heart of one's own doctrine, in order to assimilate
other doctrines to it or to prove their hopeless impotence,

seems to have been characteristic of all the writings about philosophers and their sects which, after Aristotle's time, were produced abundantly in every school. The Stoics and Sceptics were either out-and-out " accommodators " or pamphleteers. Philon the Jew is a mine of information, but his anxiety to understand Greek philosophy as a version of the Bible inclines him to involuntary distortions. In the eyes of the Neo-Platonists, Plato, properly interpreted, contains in himself the whole of previous philosophy.

But, by the side of these occasional historical studies, there are other works, in which history is the chief concern—a monograph, a comparative history, a philosophical exegesis, or the history of a special doctrine. Even here we cannot hope for the objectivity which we demand of a historian, and the author always remains the man of a school. It is, nevertheless, in this group that we must recognize the true origins of the history of philosophy and science. In virtue of all the special tracts, unfortunately lost,[1] which he wrote about his predecessors and contemporaries, Aristotle belongs to this group no less than to that mentioned above. Moreover, in his school he gave a remarkable impulse to historical writing, as we shall see. Connected indirectly with these studies is a little work which has caused much ink to flow and will be discussed later —*On Xenophanes, Zenon, and Gorgias*, or, as it is now called, *On Melissos, Xenophanes, and Gorgias*.

Furthermore, the writings of Plato and Aristotle were, from the Ist century B.C. onwards, the subject of commentaries of professors, some of whom had powerful and penetrating minds and possessed remarkable erudition. Now, in their work of exegesis they found occasion to compare doctrines and to collate the historical data which they encountered in their explanations with such texts as they still possessed or with earlier expositions.

Plato was thus treated by Poseidonios, whose commentary on the *Timaeos* is known by some quotations or analyses ; by the anonymous writers of the IInd century after Christ who wrote on the *Theaetetos* and *Timaeos* (a fairly long fragment of the former commentary was found on an Egyptian papyrus, and the other was probably the foundation of the Latin

---

[1] See the fragments of Aristotle published by V. Rose, sec. v, *Philosophica* (cf. below, Bibliography, relative to Aristotle).

commentary of Chalcidios, of the IVth century, which had
such an influence on Mediaeval thought) ; and, in the same
period, by Albinus, who was a pupil of the famous Gaius and
wrote an *Introduction to the Teaching of Plato*, with a résumé
of it, and by Theon of Smyrna and his valuable little book,
*On the Mathematical Knowledge required for an Understanding
of Plato.* From the Vth and VIth centuries we have the Neo-
Platonic commentaries of Proclos and Olympiodoros the
Younger.

Far more complete and important for the historian is our
collection of commentaries on Aristotle. Aspasios (first half
of the IInd century after Christ) is the oldest of whom anything remains. But those to whom we owe most are Alexander
of Aphrodisias, at the end of the IInd century and beginning
of the IIIrd, whose master, Aristocles of Messana, is often one
of our best informants, and, in the VIth century, the Neo-
Platonist Simplicius, who lavished the treasures of his
wonderful erudition upon his commentaries. Almost all our
pre-Socratic fragments come from Simplicius. So, too, a great
part of what we know of Stoic logic is derived from such of
these commentaries as are devoted to the various books of
Aristotle's *Organon*, among which one must mention also the
works of the Neo-Platonists Dexippos (IVth century), Ammonios (end of the Vth), and others. To the Greek commentators we should add the Roman Boëthius, Theodoric's
minister, by whom a great part of the logic of Aristotle and
ancient philosophy was transmitted to the Christian Middle
Ages.

In another subdivision of the same class we must place
those writers whose historical curiosity is not pure of all alloy,
and whose common characteristic is the desire to make various
doctrines known, only in order to compare them with a view
to contrasting or combining them. They have the mind of
the historical reviewer.

In the first rank one must mention Cicero, whose philosophical works are a most precious source, in spite of the haste
with which they were written and in spite of their incoherence
and too frequent marks of their author's lack of philosophical
understanding and frivolity of mind. They are translations
or résumés of Greek works which we have lost, and have
preserved for us something of the thought of Middle Stoicism,

of the New Academy and even of the last representatives of the Old, of the eclecticism of Philon of Larissa and of Antiochos of Ascalon, of Philodemos, the most learned of the Epicureans, and, through him, an echo of Phaedros.

Like Cicero, Plutarch of Chaeroneia, though he declares himself a Platonist, is an eclectic, but of another stamp ; if he is lacking in strength and strictness, at least he knows much, and knows it well ; he understands the things of which he speaks. The *Morals* is a mine which has not yet been sufficiently explored and worked. To Galen, the philosophic physician, we are indebted for a mass of valuable information, often accompanied by extensive quotations, on the first Peripatetics and the Old Stoa. The erudition of the Sceptic Sextus Empiricus is perhaps more indirect than that of Plutarch, but it is hardly less abundant, and his book, *Against the Dogmatists*, is a prodigious historical compendium. There is more philosophical indifference in such compilations, intended for entertainment, as the *Attic Nights* of the Latin Aulus Gellius or the *Deipnosophistae* of the Greek Athenaeos (IInd century), in which an immense variety of information is to be found. The *Florilegium* and *Eclogae physicae et ethicae* of John of Stobi or Joannes Stobaeos (Vth century) are a still richer and more instructive collection. And the analyses of lost texts, the precious bits of information which one finds in the *Bibliotheca* and *Lexicon* of the Patriarch Photios (middle of the IXth century), one of the most illustrious representatives of Byzantine learning ! Lastly, as others had placed their erudition at the service of their philosophy, the Christians used theirs against philosophy and in the service of their faith—Justin Martyr, Clement of Alexandria, who wrote the *Stromateis*, Origen, who, to refute Celsus, followed the apologist of Pagan philosophy on to his own ground, Eusebios, Bishop of Caesareia, with his *Evangelical Preparation*, Arnobius, Lactantius, St. Augustine, and the rest.

Another class of sources, to which many of the writers just mentioned are linked, and of which we knew little before the researches of Hermann Diels, forty years ago, is that of the " Doxographers." This is the name given to the writers who devoted themselves to collecting and classifying under subjects the " opinions " (*doxai, placita*) of the ancient philosophers. The works of this kind which we have preserved are : the

Placita attributed to Plutarch, the *Philosophic History* ascribed to Galen, the *Philosophumena* (first book of the *Refutation of All Sects*) of St. Hippolytos (beginning of the IInd century), formerly attributed to Origen, the treatise of Bishop Nemesios of Emesa (end of the IVth century) *On the Nature of Man*, and the *Treatment of the Affections of the Greeks* of another bishop, Theodoret (first half of the Vth century), to which one may add the satire of Hermeias on the pagan philosophers (IInd or IIIrd century) and certain parts of Epiphanios's book *Against the Sects* (second half of the IVth century). In particular, careful examination of the works of Eusebios and Stobaeos has made it possible to find traces in both of an abridgement of the history of philosophy compiled by Arios Didymos, an Alexandrian grammarian who was intimate with Augustus, the surviving fragments of whose writings deal only with Plato, Aristotle, and the Stoics. Furthermore, the comparison of the Pseudo-Plutarch's *Placita* with the *Eclogae physicae* of Stobaeos and chapters V and following of the IVth Book of Theodoret has shown that these authors must have drawn from a common source. Now Theodoret tells us that, besides some other books which cannot have been his principal source, he used the *Collection of the Opinions of the Philosophers* composed by Aëtios. The latter seems to have been an eclectic Peripatetic like Arios Didymos, and probably lived at the end of the Ist century and the beginning of the IInd. The author of the *Placita* was content with abridging his writings, and Nemesios with making a compilation of them. This exhumation, as it were, of a witness long buried in profound oblivion is of great importance, for his work, like that of Arios Didymos, has the merit—a novelty to us—of a certain philosophic impartiality.

On another side, scholars had long before picked out of Simplicius's commentary on Aristotle's *Physics* a fair number of extracts, all regarding the "principles," from a work of Theophrastos in eighteen books, entitled *Opinions of the Physicists* (Φυσικῶν δόξαι). As early as the Alexandrian period, a fragment of the same work—the last book or part of it—had been extracted, and two copies of this have come down to us. Now, there is a remarkable similarity between this writing of Theophrastos and all the doxographical writings subsequent to our era. Might not all this doxography, therefore, have come from the *doxai* of Theophrastos, from his history of physics ? But the difficulty was to establish the provenance of each of these writings, their mutual relationship, and their derivation. This is the task which Diels undertook in the *Prolegomena* to his *Doxographi Graeci*, and carried to success with rare insight. The concordance of the *Placita* with Stobaeos, and what Theodoret and Nemesios also drew from the original source, namely, the book of Aëtios, make it possible almost to reconstruct that book, and to establish the plan of it, which was a division of the opinions under questions —the principles and the universe, celestial things and terrestrial things, soul and body, each of these big questions being further subdivided into more particular problems.

But Aëtios seems in his turn to have been inspired by an older collection, to which Diels gives the name of *Vetusta placita*. For we observe a remarkable concordance of our *Placita* with certain fragments of Cicero's *Prior Academics* and *On the Nature of the Gods*, and with what Censorinus, in his *On the Natal Day*, has preserved of Varro's *Loghistorici*. These unknown *Vetusta placita* would, therefore, belong to the first half of the Ist century B.C., and probably came from the school of Poseidonios. So, by degrees, it has come to be supposed that these successive works of doxography all derive, in the end, from the great work of Theophrastos. From him comes the method followed by the doxographers, and it is the method of Aristotle himself, which consists in studying the philosophers with reference to a question.

Moreover, it is not only through Aëtios that one goes back thus indirectly to the archetype of doxography ; traces of it are likewise found, in Hippolytos chiefly, but also in the fragments of *Stromateis* which Eusebios attributes, certainly wrongly, to Plutarch, and, lastly, in Diogenes Laërtios, whom we shall discuss presently. It is possible, too, that it served as a model for the historical handbooks which, as we have seen, every school composed for the use of its followers, like those of the Stoic Panaetios, the Academician Cleitomachos, or the Epicureans Apollodoros and Philodemos.[1] To have done with doxography, let us simply add that the *Philosophic History*, wrongly ascribed to Galen, being probably of about the VIth

---

[1] That of Apollodoros is sometimes known under the title of Συναγωγὴ τῶν δογμάτων.

century, puts us on the track of an abridgement, perhaps composed by an eclectic Stoic between the time of Seneca and that of the Antonines, which appears to have been utilized by Sextus Empiricus.

All this critical analysis gives a good example of the help which the historian of philosophy may expect from philology ; it enables him to have a clear view of his means of information, to discern the relations between them, and to appreciate their relative worth.

A last class of evidence, closely connected with the foregoing, presents a new characteristic. Here doxography, the collection and classification of opinions, yields place to history properly so called, in the form of bibliographical tables, of researches into the chronology of the philosophers, their order, and their lives.

The importance of the work of the ancient bibliographers for the historian of philosophy is manifest. Now, this work, to which we owe our knowledge of the texts and that of the titles of so many lost books, was peculiarly favoured by the socialization of the library, by the formation of public collections by the side of private collections and those of schools. It was, we are told, on the advice of Demetrios of Phaleron, when, driven from Athens, he took refuge with Ptolemy Soter, that that prince founded the Library of Alexandria. So the honour of this fruitful innovation falls to the Peripatetic school, of which Demetrios was a zealous friend, and this is yet another evidence of what the organization of historical studies owes to that school. Callimachos of Cyrene, who succeeded Zenodotos as director of the Library, wrote *Pictures* (πίνακες) of the writers " who had made a name for themselves in every kind of study." The well-known classification of the dialogues of Plato in trilogies, with which the name of Aristophanes of Byzantion, a pupil of Callimachos, is associated, may doubtless give one some idea of the lines on which these lists were arranged. The same is true of the tetralogical classification of the works of Democritos, which is ascribed by Diogenes Laërtios to Thrasyllos and is probably earlier. Such, too, may be the origin of the list of works contained in each of Diogenes' lives of philosophers.

Catalogues of philosophers were also drawn up. The papyri of Herculaneum have preserved for us two precious specimens, both from the hand of the Epicurean Philodemos, one giving the philosophers of the Academy and the other those of the Porch, the latter being derived from an earlier Stoic source. There are also some remains of a similar work by the Stoic Apollonios of Tyre, *Picture of the Philosophers of the School of Zenon and of their Works*. These lists were drawn up by certain scholars in accordance with another idea, which, in spite of the errors and exaggerations to which it certainly gave rise, is first and foremost historical—the idea of successions or *diadochies*. For the object then was to establish chronologically the relationship of philosophers as teachers and pupils. The first to write " successions " appears to have been Sotion, a grammarian of Alexandria (end of the IIIrd century B.C., beginning of the IInd), whose work was abridged, about the middle of the IInd century, by one Heracleides Lembos. This abridgement was used by Diogenes Laërtios, as were the works of certain other writers of " successions " of that century and the next—Antisthenes, perhaps the same as Antisthenes of Rhodes, the Academician Sosicrates, Alexander Polyhistor, Nicias of Nicaea, Diocles of Magnesia, and a man whom Diogenes does not cite, Jason of Rhodes, the nephew of Poseidonios.

Among chronological studies we again come upon the activity of the Alexandrian librarians as historians. For Eratosthenes, the keeper of books under Ptolemy Euergetes, and famous also as an astronomer and as a geographer, wrote the *Chronographies*, which seem to have served as a model for the *Chronicles* of Apollodoros of Athens (IInd century B.C., second half). It has been possible to extract from Diogenes Laërtios sufficient fragments of this work, written in iambic trimeters, to obtain an idea of Apollodoros' method. The fall of Troy, which he places at a date corresponding to 1184–3 B.C., is the beginning of the historical era ; subsequent years are designated by the number of the Olympiad and by the name of the Eponymous Archon of Athens, and certain great events, such as the fall of Sardis (546–5) or the foundation of Thurion (444–3), are mentioned as landmarks.[1] The chief object of his chronology is to determine the *akme* of every philosopher, the *culminating point* of his existence, his *floruit*,

---

[1] These double dates are explained by the fact that the Greek year, beginning at the summer solstice, does not correspond to our own.

about his fortieth year. He makes this date coincide with the most important fact that he knows about each, or with some notable contemporary event, and from it he calculates the date of birth and, when he knows the length of a man's life, that of his death. Lastly, so far as he can, he combines these dates so as to bring out significant sequences and synchronisms. Thus, he places the birth of Anaximenes, the third philosopher of the Milesian school, in the year of the *akme* of Thales, the founder of that school, and the death of Anaximandros, Thales' successor, in or near the year of the *akme* of Anaximenes.

Finally, we must speak of biographical works, with which doxography was fairly often mingled, but this time in order of date, not of subject.

Many of these were used, more or less directly, by Diogenes Laërtios—those of Neanthes of Cyzicos, who lived at the court of Attalos I, King of Pergamon, in the second half of the IIIrd century B.C., and wrote *Lives of Illustrious Men ;* of the physician Antigonos of Carystos, a young contemporary of the foregoing, whose contribution to the lives of Menedemos, Timon the Sceptic, Zenon, Lycon, and the Academicians Polemon, Crates, Crantor, and Arcesilaos has been made clear by a methodical collection, similar to that effected for Apollodoros ; of the Peripatetic Satyros (end of the IIIrd century), of whom Heracleides Lembos made an abridgement, distinct from that which he made of Sotion ; and of another Peripatetic, of about the same time, Hermippos of Smyrna, who was a pupil of Callimachos and, in spite of his weakness for fabulous tales and his lack of critical spirit, has given us many useful indications. Diocles of Magnesia, whom we have already mentioned, also wrote *Lives* of philosophers, and in the Ist century B.C. Hippobotos combined the study of successions with biography. Lastly, the *Memoirs* and *Varied History* of the Sceptic Favorinus of Arelate, who taught rhetoric in Rome with brilliant success under Hadrian and Antoninus Pius and was the master of Aulus Gellius, appear to have been collections of anecdotes and apophthegms.

It is chiefly through Diogenes Laërtios (middle of the IIIrd century) that we know all this work ; it is in him that it is presented to us, blended with doxography, but in a singularly corrupt form. Yet his compilation in ten books, *The Lives,*

Teachings, and Apophthegms of the Celebrated Philosophers, is of infinite value. First, it has given us a means of going back, by careful criticism, to earlier sources. Moreover, it has preserved quantities of fragments, and even complete texts—three letters of Epicuros and the *Principal Thoughts*. Lastly, it is a complete work. Curiously enough, the history of every school is not brought down to the same point. The Porch is described down to the end of the IIIrd century (Chrysippos) and so is the Lyceum (Lycon), Epicureanism to the middle of the IInd (surprising if Diogenes was himself an Epicurean), and the Academy to the end of the same century (Cleitomachos), while in the case of Scepticism he takes us to the beginning of the IIIrd century of our era, since he speaks of Sextus and Saturninus (not that that is sufficient reason for regarding him as a Sceptic). It is impossible here to enter into the very controversial and difficult question of the sources of Diogenes and the principles which may have governed his compilation. It ranges from extreme brevity to extreme prolixity, and the incoherence of our text sometimes makes it wholly baffling.

We should also mention, in the same class, two very different groups of documents. First, there are all the Neo-Pythagorean and Neo-Platonic biographies, of which we shall speak later, which are full of fiction and superstition, but contain a great many useful indications, and, besides, are in themselves evidence of a state of mind. Secondly, there are the dictionaries, the articles in which often give interesting details, although the sources are not sufficiently known—the *Lexicon* of the Byzantine Suidas (Xth century), who may have used Diogenes Laërtios, and another similar lexicon, of uncertain date (between the Xth and XIIIth centuries), which has been wrongly identified with the *Onomatologos* of Hesychios (VIth century) and seems to be derived from Diogenes Laërtios and Suidas.

Such, incompletely enumerated and briefly appraised, is the scanty material, full of gaps and often dilapidated, at the disposal of the historian of the philosophical and scientific thought of Graeco-Roman antiquity.

BOOK ONE

ORIGINS

Chapter I

BEGINNINGS OF MORAL REFLECTION

The history of Greek thought does not start only at the moment at which an original and free attempt to organize a system of reflections on the order of nature or on that of conduct first becomes marked. It begins with the attempt to ascertain the moral demands of common thought, or to extract from religious beliefs the various views which they contain regarding the past or present history of the universe.

That primitive attempt at reflection is a social thing ; for it is effected in an impersonal, obscure, continuous fashion, accompanying and expressing the progress of manners and religious sentiment and that of the craftsmanship which labours to master nature. But the success of the attempt differed greatly, according as it dealt with the order of conduct and with that of external things. As early as the end of the VIIth century, the collective endeavour to obtain an intelligible view of nature was transformed, in spirit and in methods, by attempts at personal criticism, which gave birth to a science and a philosophy. But it is not until the second half of the Vth century, with the exception, perhaps, of Xenophanes, that we find a truly critical analysis of traditional principles of conduct, an attempt to justify the abandonment or preservation of them. Before that, " scientists " and philosophers had hardly done more than reflect the conceptions of popular wisdom, or, more usually, the beliefs of a society of initiates ; the interpreters of moral reflection were chiefly poets and lawgivers. For the demands to which that reflection responded were the deepest and most immediate demands of life lived in common ; so long as those demands acted on the conscience definitely and imperatively, it was hardly asked what they were worth. That is why moral reflection must be considered first and sketched in its essential features, pending the day when it will become a matter of philosophy.

The earliest literary expressions known to us of an attempt of Greek thought to co-ordinate the dictates of the collective conscience regarding the life and conduct of men and to formulate them in conceptions of general application, are found in the Homeric poems and in Hesiod. One can understand the important place which these works held in the education of the young ; later they were to serve as the basis of all discussion on moral problems.

In the Homeric poems, to tell the truth, moral reflection is hardly separated from epic narration. But, first of all, the narrative cannot have failed to inspire the hearers with preferences for one hero or another—for Achilles or Odysseus, for Nestor or Ajax—and consequently to stimulate moral appreciation. Moreover, the weakness of religious sentiment in Homer betrays the tendency of moral reflection towards independence, a favourable condition for what may be called its " lay-ness." Already, especially in the *Odyssey*, we find, here and there, statements which are like universal judgments on conduct, and express a general view on the destiny of man. But, although the idea of a justice of Zeus, before which violence and deceit must bow in the end, appears incidentally, we more often find a resigned acceptance of all that is unjust and arbitrary in the " lot " ($\mu o \hat{\iota} \rho a$ $\theta \epsilon \hat{\omega} \nu$) which the gods give to men, regardless of the moral worth of their deeds.[1]

The moral conception which, about the middle of the IXth century, inspires Hesiod's poem, the *Works and Days*, deserves deep and careful study. For it bears witness to a remarkable advance in the determination of moral ideas. It is not certain that this advance is due to Hesiod himself ; doubtless he drew upon an old store of popular wisdom, to the formation of which the East may possibly have contributed, and which was already expressed in proverbs and myths. But he could not have done so without an amount of personal elaboration and even criticism, by which the old store of wisdom was transformed and made to produce fruits which are entirely

---

[1] Cf. *Od.*, xvi. 386 ff., with vi. 188 ff., xviii. 129 ff. Cf. *Il.*, xxii. 413 ; xxiv. 527 ff.

new to us. We shall not find a philosophic doctrine in Hesiod. But there is reflection, none the less, virtually rational, regarding the content and the aspirations of Greek civilization, in a given society and at a given time.

The whole poem is full of precepts about the guarantees of well-regulated labour, in accordance with the order of nature, and the fair exchange of services in the social world. But these precepts are subordinated to a general conception of justice as the law of Zeus, which is truly the soul of Hesiodic morality. The fable of the hawk and the nightingale sets forth the problem in striking language : " He is a fool, who would match himself against those stronger than himself," the bird of prey cries to its victim. " He is defeated, and suffers pain as well as shame." [1] This is the language of ὕβρις, of the spirit of immoderateness, of the pride of mastery. But it is as fatal to the mighty as it is to small men. It is better to listen to the voice of Justice, and to forget violence. " For this is the law which the son of Cronos set up for men. To fish and beasts and birds he allotted that they should devour one another, for there is no justice in them ; but to men he gave justice, which is far the best." [2] With the " crooked justice " of kings, " devourers of gifts," the poet contrasts the " straight judgments " which come from Zeus. Since, too, the law which comes from him bears its own sanction, the principle of retaliation is imbued with justice. " He who works ill for another works ill for himself. . . . The eye of Zeus, seeing all and observing all, scans these things when he pleases, nor is he blind to the kind of justice which a city holds within itself. . . . It is bad to be a just man, if the less just man wins the lawsuit ; but I do not think that that is the work of all-wise Zeus." [3] The hour of deserved chastisement always comes. The Oath hastens after the perjured judge. Banished from cities, and weeping over the misfortune of the peoples, Justice " takes her seat beside her father Zeus, son of Cronos, and complains to him of the unjust minds of men." [4]

In the Homeric poems, the power of Zeus was the instrument of a capricious, irritable will, or else of the Fate whose incomprehensible activity consisted in opposing or disappointing our desire to be just. In Hesiod, it is the decree of a conscience which judges rightly and without partiality,

---

[1] 202–12. [2] 213–18, 275–80. [3] 265–73. [4] 249–60.

according to the rule or measure which it has laid down, and deals out terrible punishments to those who have transgressed or exceeded it, and also to those who have slavishly made themselves accomplices of the crime. That is what has brought about the downfall of the " Silver Races " ; that is what will undo the " Iron Race." Now, the principle underlying all the crimes which that race commits against the supreme law is lack of measure or moderation, or the desire to set oneself above order and above the rule. To want to be more than others and to upset, for one's own advantage, by violence or deceit, the equilibrium of persons, to prefer crooked ways to the straight road, and quick and easy profits to those which the gods grant to patient labour and slow economy—that is always, in the vigorous words of the poet, " placing justice in the fist " ($\delta i \kappa \eta$ $\dot{\epsilon} \nu$ $\chi \epsilon \rho \sigma i$). But Hesiod believes ardently in the existence of a right of the weak, and the special work of almighty Zeus is to restore rectitude and measure. " Easily he gives strength and easily he humbles the strong. Easily he diminishes the conspicuous and exalts the obscure. Easily he straightens the crooked and withers up the arrogant." [1]

Without any doubt, Hesiod's morality is inspired by the consideration of experience. Many of his precepts are simply practical counsels, which may be compared to the " morals " of fables, or, as Sainte-Beuve has said, " to the wisdom of honest John (Bonhomme Richard)." But it is none the less indisputable that his profound intention is to set up right against fact, and to replace the animal reign of brute force by the human reign of justice, by willing, hard-working obedience to the divine law. So we find in him, still vague, but already very strong, the sense of an ideal rule, according to which existing moral conditions are to be valued, and which definitely sets right high above fact.

In all that was afterwards produced in the same domain by Greek thought in the early centuries, in which many historians see an advance, I do not think that there were many new ideas, nor anything rising above the sober, vigorous precision of Hesiod. What changed was social conditions. They became more complex, and the growing importance of city organization helped to bring the idea of " good legislation " ($\epsilon \dot{\upsilon} \nu o \mu i a$) and its benefits to the fore. That idea was, in par-

[1] 5–8.

ticular, characteristic of the moral tendencies of Solon, and shows their definitely political aim.

The ancient tradition of the Seven Sages is of peculiar interest to the study of moral reflection. Regarding their names, as we know, the ancients were hardly agreed. One list of the classical period [1] gives Thales of Miletos, Pittacos of Mitylene, Bias of Priene, and Solon (who appear in all lists), with Cleobulos of Lindos, Chilon of Lacedaemon, and Myson of Chenae, who is often replaced by Anacharsis or Periandros. According to Plato, their common characteristic was the " Laconian brevity " with which they expressed their ideas in memorable maxims, such as " Know thyself," " Nothing too much," and so on. They were said to have met one day at Delphi, and to have dedicated these aphorisms to Apollo as first-fruits of their wisdom, causing them to be engraved at the entrance to the temple. In later times collections of these maxims were composed ; [2] but these catalogues and their attributions of particular sayings are highly suspect.

But in the tradition which makes the Seven Sages all live at one time, and, by many anecdotes, supposes a kind of collaboration among them, we perceive at least a vague feeling that the work ascribed to them was collective in character. Many of their maxims are the kind of proverb in which traditional rules or experiences gradually come to be condensed in a striking form. The same is true of the fables of Æsop, a late compilation of very ancient stories, which presented practical observations and teachings in a form which should strike the imagination. But men could not accept these tales as impersonal, and it was just in the second half of the VIIth century that the ancients placed the legendary Æsop, whom, moreover, tradition brought into connexion with one of the Seven Sages. His servile condition and Phrygian nationality may, perhaps, be a symbolic recollection of the popular character and partly Eastern origin of the stories. Similarly, the legend of the Seven Sages shows that it was felt necessary to have definite individuals to whom to ascribe collective, anonymous judgments, as soon as these were expressed in a form which made it possible to reflect upon them.

Furthermore, since these judgments were a kind of

---

[1] Plato, *Protag.*, 343 a-b. [2] **LXVIII**, ch. 73 a.

decrees, it was thought that they must have been uttered by
lawgivers or by men who had played the part of councillors
or arbiters in their cities. This is true of Solon, of Bias, who
was famed for the integrity of his judgments, of Periandros,
the tyrant of Corinth, and of Pittacos, who was Æsymnetes [1]
at Mitylene ; and if Thales appears among them, it is probably
not as a scientist but rather on account of his political activity
in Ionia. " They are not scientists," said the Peripatetic
Dicaearchos, " nor philosophers, but men of common sense
and lawgivers." [2]

So the crystallization of ethical rules ascribed by tradition
to the Seven Sages and the homely moral epic attributed to
Æsop were a work which had been going on for a long time,
as is plain if one reads Hesiod. But the VIIth and VIth
centuries were an age in which relations between peoples
became more active and more penetrating, and also an age
of tremendous internal fermentation and burning political
strife, an age of expansion and political organization, of
colonization and the founding of cities. Then the individual
had the illusion of being emancipated from the old religious
discipline of the city, of holding the guidance of his conduct in
his own hands. Yet, in the midst of all these upheavals and
all this unloosing of passions, he also felt that that guidance
must not be left to the caprice of each, but must be based on
tried norms. He needed a code of conduct. But that could
only be the reflection of the collective conscience in its most
general and most stable acquisitions.

So it is in the same time and in connexion with the same
conditions that there appears, in the middle of the VIth
century, with Phocylides of Miletos and Theognis of Megara,
the form of lyric poetry which is called " Gnomic " or sen-
tentious poetry. In the former writer [3] there is no originality
of thought whatever ; he is interested only in coining phrases
which will express observations or maxims briefly, so that they
shall be easy to remember and to handle in conversation.
But this didactic intention is in itself significant of the interests
of the period. Theognis, on the other hand, though obviously

---

[1] A president who put an end to civil discord by arbitration.
[2] LXVIII, loc. cit., near beginning.
[3] Not the author of the longish poem, the *Sentences of Phocylides*, which was
written by some Jewish forger between the IInd century B.C. and the Ist century
of our era.

under the influence of Hesiod and Solon, is often an original
and daring thinker. Intelligent and passionate, discontented
and argumentative, he invests his reflections on traditional
ideas with a bitter, tragic note, and also with a dialectical,
critical turn which by its bold, urgent vigour anticipates
Xenophanes. He is indignant that, among men, wealth out-
weighs the merits of blood, confounds the good and the bad,
and decides marriages, whereas one should copy the stock-
breeders, who pick out the best specimens for mating. The
strange inconsequence of Zeus bewilders him. Why, when he
knows the heart of every man, does the all-powerful lord of
all things give the same lot to the just and to the unjust ?
Why does he sometimes give prosperity to the latter, while
the former is overcome by poverty ? Why does he make
children pay for the faults of their fathers ? [1] Even if, as has
been thought, these recriminations should be ascribed to Solon
and not to Theognis, they none the less indicate a great novelty:
the will of Zeus is no longer, as it was for Hesiod, absolute
justice ; the moral ideal, without changing in content, has
risen higher. Instead of human morality being judged in the
name of divine justice, divine justice is itself questioned in
the name of a higher principle. So, at least in a sense, reflection
has already risen to the idea that morality has a value of its
own, independent of religious belief.

That is, in its main lines, the development of moral
reflection in the Greek world, from the earliest literary evidence
down to about the middle of the Vth century. As social and
political conditions changed, it gradually set apart and for-
mulated with increasing precision the idea of justice and right
—that is, of the exact and right measure, of balance and
rectitude, in opposition to brutal passion, deceit, and the
ambition to dominate.

[1] 183–92, 373–80, 382–92, 731–52.

CHAPTER II

BEGINNINGS OF A SYSTEMATIC REPRESENTATION
OF THE UNIVERSE. THEOGONIES AND COSMO-
GONIES. INFLUENCE OF THE EAST

WHEN we begin to study the first expressions of the attempt
of Greek thought to obtain a more or less systematic representation of the universe and of the relationships which it
embraces, there is one thing which we must not forget. That
is the fact that we are in the presence of the products of a
collective elaboration, and that that elaboration is not expressed in literature, and therefore does not begin to belong
to history, until it has come to an end and is ready to yield
place to other forms of thought. Our earliest literary documents of this kind are later, from four to perhaps twenty
centuries later, than the evidences of a wealthy and varied
civilization which have been brought to light, for example, by
the discoveries at Troy and Mycenae and in Cyprus, the
Cyclades, and Crete. With these evidences we are already a
long way from what may be called a state of racial childhood.
So what we positively reach is not the age in which the
representation of the universe is still implied in the ritual
practices which ensure the communion of the social group
with the mysterious forces of nature. It is, on the contrary,
the age in which they have become detached and organized
into a system of definite representations, partly affective and
partly intellectual.

These representations, as we know, are given in the form
of myths, that is, of *stories*, which, in telling the genealogy or
certain features in the life of divine personages, express the
natural relations of things by means of images taken from
human generation and action. What is the ultimate foundation of these imaginative constructions ? This is not the place
in which to set forth the animistic and sociological hypotheses,

24

nor to take sides on that difficult question. It is at least probable that myths are the result of the need to make the mystery contained in the rites of an existing cult intelligible. In consequence, for every local cult instituted in the little groups which had divided the soil of Greece among them, there was a distinct myth. But there must have been resemblances between these myths, first, in so far as the groups had a common origin, but chiefly because the myths arose from very general conditions, psychological or social, and, moreover, always referred to the same content—the most remarkable aspects of nature and their most apparent relationships, the most regular phenomena or those most alarming by their suddenness or their effects. Without these two last causes, could we understand the similarity of certain myths of peoples between whom no relationship, direct or indirect, can be assumed ? So, too, the material improvement of communications, by bringing peoples together, must have helped to modify differences. Lastly, the tendency of myths to become unified was necessarily accomplished by an attempt to simplify them, to eliminate inconsistencies as much as possible, and to detach them from the cults to which they were bound. This would be the explanation of the gradual formation of a physical mythology, already possessing a certain universality and a value of its own, independent of religion.

This last characteristic is to be seen in the Homeric poems, where the histories of the gods are already formed into secular legends and shorn of the majesty proper to sacred things. But in societies in which the horizon remained more limited and life was less amiable, myths were envisaged with a seriousness unknown in the Ionian society to which the Homeric poems were addressed. This is to be seen in the *Theogony* which is ascribed to Hesiod but, although it belongs to the Boeotian school of which he is the most distinguished representative, is probably, in its greater part, later than that poet by nearly a century, if not more. The author is interested in myths for their own sake and as a subject of knowledge. He tries to systematize all that is comparatively rational in the various mythical traditions, to compile methodically a complete body of knowledge with a view to education. Since his object is simplicity and universality, his work is already, in that sense, scientific. And this theogony is also cosmogony ; the interest taken in the generations of the gods is dominated by the desire to explain the action of natural forces. Moreover, in the *Works and Days* the direct observation of nature already held a large place, and the *Astronomy* [1] ascribed to Hesiod is, no doubt, a very early product of the Boeotian school.

It is to the Muses that the poet turns for patronage. They know true things, and even their lies are related to truth. They speak to the intelligence and declare what is, what was, and what will be. They sing the " rules " or laws " of all things," going back to the very first principle.[2] " Tell," he bids them, " of the sacred race of the immortals who are for ever, those who were born of the earth (Ge) and of the starry sky (Uranos) . . . and those whom the salt sea (Pontos) reared. And say how first the gods and earth came into being, and the rivers and the boundless sea, with its rushing billows, and the shining stars and the broad sky beyond. . . . And say how they divided their possessions and shared honours among them." [3] The answer to the question, which bears the stamp of scientific curiosity, is well known.[4] At the beginning Chaos appeared ; then, " at once," Earth (Gaia), " the sure foundation of all things," and, in the depths of Earth, misty Tartaros ; and lastly Love (Eros), " fairest among the immortal gods." From Chaos, Erebos (darkness) and Night were born. Then Night gave birth to Ether (the upper air) and Day (Hemera), whose father was Erebos. Earth, in her turn, gave birth first to the starry sky (Uranos), " equal to her, that he may cover her altogether," and then to the great Mountains and the Sea (Pontos), " without any desired love." Lastly, of her union with the Sky the river Ocean was born. Cronos and Rheia, the children of Earth and Sky, were the parents of Zeus. So the Olympian gods were the last born ; the natural forces, as Aristotle observed,[5] were earlier than the powers whose function it was to govern them.

Though still incapable of rising to abstractions without personifying them, the poet nevertheless distinguishes more or less between these personifications and real forces. He may represent nature in a social aspect, as a domain or body of wealth which is apportioned, and its forces as offices or

---

[1] **LXVIII**, ch. 68a.   [2] 27 ff., 32, 37-8, 45, 66 ff.   [3] 105–13.
[4] 116 ff.   [5] *Metaph.*, N. 4, 1091 b 4 ff.

honours, he may speak of the " lot " (μοῖρα) and the fate of things, but in this there is at least the sense of a distribution by classes and a well-regulated order. Lastly, in seeking out filiations from the original stock downwards, he is trying to perceive a relationship of subordination among realities, to discover a common foundation of things which shall serve as a basis for all later becoming, an inner principle of production whereby things shall preserve their properties by heredity, and which shall be permanently organized into a system of stable relationships. Afterwards rational thought did no more than continue this endeavour of mythical theogony and cosmogony ; in transforming it by a change in direction, it gave the illusion of an entirely new and almost spontaneous creation, whereas it merely developed a germ already existing.

Even more justly than in the case of the Hesiodic *Theogony*, we may be content with quite a brief survey of the other cosmogonies. They do not differ from it in their general tendencies, and it is these which especially interest us. Besides, the evidence by which we know them is very incomplete, or belongs to a time very distant from that in which they were composed.

What we know of the cosmogony expounded in the VIth century by Pherecydes of Syros,[1] in a prose work entitled *Theology*, or, more enigmatically, the *Five Secret Places* (πεντέμυχος), comes mainly from Eudemos, that is, from a good Peripatetic source, and from an Egyptian papyrus of the IIIrd century with which a quotation of Clement of Alexandria agrees. It contains an original novelty—above Chthonia, who will become the earth, and Chronos, who appears to be, not time, but the lower part of the sky, from which fire, wind, and water are born, it places Zas or Zeus, the principle of life, the organizer and craftsman of the universe. To accomplish his demiurgic work, he changes himself into Eros, and, on a winged oak, perhaps the osseous framework of the world floating in space, he spreads the nuptial veil on which he will embroider the plan of the earth and that of Ocean, with its dwellings. In the end, Zas must triumph over the evil forces of nature, and the five families of gods born of the three eternal beings, under the leadership of Chronos, fight a battle against the serpent Ophioneus and his army ;

[1] **LXVIII**, ch. 71.

by their victory they secure possession of the sky, and the monsters are hurled into Ocean. Evidently it was not these stories which caused Aristotle to count Pherecydes among the " theologians " in whom all is not mythical.[1] But, if one remembers that he was a contemporary of Anaximandros, it is possible that he accompanied his myths with explanations taken from science. Except in the case of Acusilaos, whose prose *Genealogies* seem to have been a mere copy of Hesiod, this hypothesis may apply also to the cosmogonies which tradition attaches to the names of Epimenides [2] (probably Solon's celebrated Cretan contemporary) and the poet Musaeos,[3] but which were probably composed in the second half of the VIth century by Onomacritos, the court poet of the Peisistratids. It was natural that the compiler should be tempted to adapt them to new tendencies, and, indeed, the part played by Air in Epimenides' system betrays the influence of Anaximenes.

The same is probably true of the Orphic cosmogonies, which are earlier than Homer according to tradition, but are also said to have been collected and edited by Onomacritos. There are several versions of them : (i) that of Eudemos the Peripatetic, which is already implied in certain passages of Plato and Aristotle,[4] and is very similar to the Hesiodic cosmogony (Night taking the place of Chaos) ; (ii) that which is supposed to be found in the *Argonautica* of Apollonios of Rhodes (i. 494–512), which recalls Pherecydes ; (iii) that ascribed to the logographer Hellanicos of Lesbos (middle of the Vth century), on whom so many forgeries have been fathered, and to a mysterious Hieronymos. In these works Platonic and, still more, Stoic influence is visible, mingled with elements of Ionian physics. The origin of things is water and a muddy matter, from which the earth issued. Of their union a monster was born, Chronos or Heracles, unaging time, to whom is added Adrasteia, necessity, which is incorporeal. Chronos-Heracles manufactures an enormous egg, the two halves of which are the sky and the earth. There is mention of an incorporeal god, winged and monstrous, and of another god, the orderer of things, who is called the First-born (Proto-

---

[1] *Metaph.*, N. 4, 1091 b 9. [2] *Theogony* or *Oracles*, χρησμοί.
[3] *Theogony* or εὐμολπία.
[4] Plato, *Crat.*, 402 b ; *Tim.*, 40 d ff. ; Arist., *Metaph.*, Λ. 6, 1071 b 27 ; *De An.*, i. 5, 412 b 25.

gonos), or Zeus, or Pan ; (iv) that which Damascios, to whom
we also owe a fairly confused account of the first and third,[1]
calls *Customary Orphic Theology* or *Rhapsodies*, often regarded
as the oldest, in spite of all the marks of later influences which
it bears. Here we find the image of the egg again. The god
who comes out of it is sometimes called Phanes, the luminous
god, sometimes Metis, intelligence, and sometimes Ericepaeos.
This obscure denomination perhaps signifies the lot reserved
for Phanes, for he will " soon be devoured " by Zeus, who, by
an act of mystical communion, thus assimilates wisdom.
Thereby he becomes the beginning of a new generation of
gods, the last of whom is Zagreus, who, devoured in his turn
by the Titans, is reborn as Dionysos. It is with this version
that the famous Orphic formulas seem to be connected : " At
the sixth generation stop the order of your hymn," and, again,
" Zeus is the head, the middle, and it is from Zeus that all
proceeds " ; he is " the beginning, the middle, and the end." [2]

To try to interpret these myths is as hazardous an undertaking as to try to date them. They are complex products of
the adaptation of legend to the notions elaborated in a more
or less systematic manner by science and philosophy ; however, they tell us something about the state of mind which
opened the road to these last. The myths, living on by the
side of science and philosophy, preserved, as an object for the
erudite curiosity of the mythographers, some fanciful elements,
which had not yet been assimilated and now had no chance
of ever being assimilated. Lastly, the images which they
contained continued, as we see in Plato and the Stoics, to
supply philosophy with a rich fund of symbolical representations, with which to treat the problems before which science
failed.

With this problem goes that of the historical origins of this
first attempt to explain nature.[3] It involves two questions.
First of all, do the Greek myths come from Oriental myths ?
For a long time resemblances have been pointed out between
the cosmogonic images of the Greeks and those of India (the
Rig-Veda), Babylonia (the *Poem of the Creation*), and Egypt
(the *Book of the Dead*). But similar resemblances are found in
Scandinavian and Polynesian myths, and one must therefore

---

[1] *De Princ.*, 123 (2), 124. [2] **LXVIII**, ch. 66, B. 1 and 6.
[3] See the volumes about the East in the *History of Civilization*.

allow that they need not be explained by direct influence, but rather, as we have seen, by a similar reaction of the collective mind, according to laws which are still but little known, to similar realities of nature. We should have to establish filiation with certainty, and we are a long way from being in a position to do so.

Much more important is the other question : was the change in spirit and methods effected by Greek science due to the influence of an Oriental science already existing ? If we answer in the affirmative, we at once overthrow all that has just been said regarding the evolution of Greek science from the mythical cosmogonies of Greece itself. The question is complex, and particularly delicate.

No doubt, it is chiefly in the Neo-Pythagoreans or the Neo-Platonists, in Philon the Jew or the Christian writers, that we meet with the most definite assertions regarding the debt of Greek philosophy to the East, and especially to the sacred books of the Jews. Plato, said Numenios, was " a Moses who talked Greek," and Clement of Alexandria called him " the Judaizing philosopher." But as early as the time of Herodotos,[1] and, later, in that of Plato and Aristotle, the Greeks spoke readily of the wisdom of Egypt, of Babylon, and even of India. From that wisdom came astronomy ; Egypt, where the priestly class enjoyed the leisure for disinterested study, was, according to Aristotle,[2] the cradle of mathematical teaching. It was generally accepted that the very founders of Greek science, Thales and Pythagoras, merely imported it from Egypt, as Eudemos says of the former and Isocrates of the latter.[3] Pythagoras, according to Aristoxenos, that storehouse of Pythagorean tradition, went to visit Zaratas (Zoroaster, Zarathustra).[4] The encyclopaedic knowledge of Democritos was explained by travels to India, where he met the Gymnosophists (fakirs), to Chaldaea and Egypt, where he met Magi and priests, to Persia, and to Ethiopia.[5]

Whatever truth there may be in these statements, at least it cannot be denied that the Greeks were keen travellers, and that, by seaways and caravan-routes, communications may have been established between Ionia on the one hand and

[1] ii. 4, 109. [2] *Metaph.*, A. 1, 981 b 23.
[3] Fr. 84 (**LXVIII**, ch. 1, A. 11) ; Isocr., *Busiris*, 28 (*ibid.*, ch. 4, A. 4).
[4] *Ibid.*, A. 11. [5] *Ibid.*, ch. 55, A. 1 (35).

Egypt, Phoenicia, and Babylon on the other, as between these latter regions and India or China. But all those who, in antiquity, in the Renaissance, at the end of the XVIIIth century, or in the XIXth, have argued more or less convincingly that such communications existed, have neglected two questions. Does the older civilization necessarily have the more advanced science ? Did not difficulties of understanding inevitably confine exchanges to matters which had nothing at all to do with science ? The only means of judging what the East may have given to Greek science in its infancy is to determine the nature of Oriental science from the monuments of it which have survived.

Let us see some of these monuments. For the Babylonians, there are the cuneiform inscriptions of Senkereh (calculations of squares and cubes), that known as the Hincks inscription, which shows the peculiarities of their system of numeration, on a basis of 60 and on a basis of 10, and the predictions of eclipses, based on the cycle of 223 lunations, the mere relation of which proves how adventurous they were. For Egypt, there is the *Calculator's Handbook* of Ahmes, doubtless dating from the first half of the XVIIIth century B.C. (the Rhind Papyrus), which gives the distribution of rations, problems of pay, the assessment of the food-return of grain, tables of concordance for measures, and some other numerical calculations not connected with their practical application—all processes of calculation revealing a clumsiness which bears witness to the absence of any general conception of the rules. There is, too, the fragment of papyrus from Kahun which goes back, perhaps, to over twenty centuries before our era, and gives calculations probably connected with the properties of the triangle whose sides are in the ratio of 3, 4, and 5. The knowledge of those properties may have been the chief foundation of the science of the mysterious *harpedonaptai* or line-stretchers, mentioned in a text ascribed, perhaps wrongly, to Democritos.[1] For the exact orientation of a temple on the cardinal points, a perpendicular had to be constructed on the north-south line. Now, they had observed that if you pegged out a triangle so that the pegs were at distances from each other in a ratio of 5, 4, and 3, you got a right angle. The Chinese had made the same observation, and so, perhaps, had

[1] *Ibid.*, B. 299.

the Hindus, although the Çulvasutras, in which we find it, are
doubtless less ancient than was supposed.

Now, is there anything in all this beyond observations
suggested by practical problems ? For example, it is observed
from experience that $5^2 = 4^2 + 3^2$, and men even have the
curiosity to make similar calculations on other squares. But
between that observation, with the mathematical games to
which it may have given rise, and a demonstration of the
properties of the right-angled triangle there is a whole abyss.
So there is between the observations inspired in the astrologers
by political interests and the disinterested search for an
explanation of astronomical phenomena. Never, so far as we
know, in all its centuries of existence, and even after coming
into contact with the science of the Greeks, did Oriental
science go beyond utilitarian interest and curiosity about
details, to rise to pure speculation and the determination of
principles. Plato was right when, in an often-quoted passage,[1]
he forcibly contrasted the spirit of the Egyptians or Phoenicians
with that of the Greeks with reference to the same branches
of knowledge—on the one side, desire for gain and a kind of
industrious cleverness, and on the other the desire to know.
What the earliest Greek scientists may have received from
the East, therefore, was the accumulated material of ages of
experience, so many questions for disinterested reflection to
answer. Without these, Greek science might perhaps not
have been constituted, and in this sense one cannot speak of
a Greek miracle. But, on the other hand, instead of aiming
immediately at action, these first scientists sought for the
rational explanation ; it was in that and in speculation that
they found, indirectly, the secret of action. That is the new
point of view from which our science has risen.

[1] *Rep.*, iv. 435 e ff. ; cf. *Laws*, v. 747 b-c.

BOOK TWO

SCIENCE AND PHILOSOPHY

CHAPTER I

THE SCHOOL OF MILETOS

IN several places Aristotle lays stress on the difference between those whom he calls the " theologians," who treat science under the form of myth, and the philosophers or " physiologists," who set forth their reasons " in a demonstrative form," whose wisdom, being of a more human kind, does not, like that of the others, affect an air of lordly solemnity, and seeks less to satisfy itself than to communicate itself to others. On both sides, the thinkers whom he thus contrasts are in his eyes the earliest thinkers. Now, the founder of the philosophy which he ascribes to the first philosophers was Thales.[1] This formal and repeated testimony of Aristotle is not contradicted, but rather confirmed, by Theophrastos.[2] For even though the latter declares that Thales had predecessors whom he merely surpassed, yet by including Prometheus among those predecessors he implicitly recognizes the originality of Thales. So, even if Thales is the continuer of the theogony-writers, even if he did not radically change the direction of their efforts, yet he is at least, for us as for Aristotle, the first who transformed the methods of research and exposition in their spirit.

Moreover, with Thales, it seems, the first succession of philosophers begins. From him to Anaximandros and Anaximenes there is a tradition, all the more manifest that it is maintained in one city. There were in Greece at a very early date schools of sculptors, architects, physicians, and rhapsodes. There may also have been schools of theologians. But the tradition preserved in them was in a way external to

---

[1] *Metaph.*, A. 3, 983 b 7, 20 ; 984 a 2, 28 ff.   [2] **LXII,** 475 (10) and n.

them. On the other hand, the characteristic of the first philosophical schools, which were study-centres and research-groups contemporary with the beginnings of science, seems to have been that community and continuity of effort were not bound by tradition, but merely supported by it, while that effort continued to be personal and free. No doubt, these early schools had none of the complex organization and clearly defined status which we find after the foundation of the Academy. But already we see several men meeting, under the leadership of one of them, to devote themselves to labours which, even if their ultimate object was practical, were none the less speculative. Collaboration made a division of labour possible, without which we could hardly understand certain undertakings on a large scale, which we shall discuss later. There was no danger of discoveries being lost, and free progress became possible without any fear of the same ground needing to be covered twice. We must not, therefore, accuse the doxographers of anachronism when, following Theophrastos, they say of a pre-Socratic philosopher that he was the " companion " (ἑταῖρος), " intimate " (γνώριμος), " pupil," or " successor " of another rather earlier philosopher, or, although it is sometimes chronologically impossible, that he " participated " in his teaching. It should be added that for a long time the collective work of the association hid the personal contribution of individuals in an obscurity which the historian has great difficulty in piercing. Only a few great names, almost symbolical, emerge from that darkness. In this respect there is no example more significant than that of the Pythagoreans. In any case, it is not under the vague denomination of " Ionians " that we must class our first philosophers ; they form the School of Miletos.

That the first of these organized corporations of scientists should have been founded in Miletos is perhaps not mere chance. It was then the busiest and richest city of Ionia, where civilization was already far more advanced than in any part of Greece Proper. Its power extended to the southern shores of the Euxine, where it had founded colonies. Its good relations with the Lydian princes brought it indirectly into touch with the Babylonian and Egyptian civilizations. It had its temple at Naucratis, and the court of Sardis attracted the most distinguished Ionians ; it is probable that Thales played an important part under Croesus. Lastly, Miletos, a very ancient Cretan colony, had a share in the oldest Hellenic civilization, the Minoan.

I

THALES

There are doubts about the origin of the man of bold initiative who founded that first school, Thales of Miletos. Were his ancestors Cadmeians of Boeotia, and so of Phoenician and Semitic stock ? Did they come from Caria or Crete ? In any case, they had long been Hellenized. There is hardly less uncertainty about his chronology. One has laboriously to combine data, each of which is itself the result of similar combinations, effected artificially on materials which have not been subjected to any critical test.[1] His *akme* is marked, according to Apollodoros, by his alleged prediction, so often mentioned from Herodotos onwards, of the total eclipse of the sun which is said to have occurred during a battle between the Lydians and the Medes. But was this the eclipse of the 30th September, 610, or that of the 21st July, 597, or that of the 28th May, 584 ? The last date is generally preferred, but there are still many difficulties. Without going into these discussions in detail, it will suffice to say that Thales seems to have lived somewhere between the last third of the VIIth century and the middle of the VIth.

Plato relates [2] that Thales, walking one day with his eyes upon the sky, fell into a well and so aroused the mirth of a Thracian servant-girl who happened to be near. This is a symbolic anecdote which hardly agrees with our other evidence ; for that presents Thales to us as anything but a purely speculative spirit. He was a statesman, who tried to unite the Ionian cities in a defensive confederacy against the Persians. He was a military engineer in the service of Croesus, and is said to have diverted the course of the River Halys by a loop canal. A story told by Aristotle does honour to his commercial aptitude : in the winter he foresaw, by his science, a big olive-harvest, and accordingly hired all the oil-presses in the district at a low price, to sublet them at a

---

[1] See on the method of Apollodoros, above, pp. 14-15.   [2] *Theaet.*, 174 a.

profit, when the time came, to the landowners who were overwhelmed by their harvest. Lastly, even if the old poem entitled the *Nautical Astrology* is not his, at least tradition seems to admit that he based nautical instructions on his astronomical observations, for the use of the navigators of his country. Was it this practical trend of his speculative activity which prevented him from writing ? It is at any rate remarkable that, even in ancient times, no work was attributed to him without being contested, and that no fragment of him survives, except one forgery hardly earlier than our era. All that Aristotle says about him is based on tradition, and perhaps òne which was more or less reshaped in the Vth century.[1]

What we know of Thales' work has two sides—science and philosophy. As to the first, we are told that he could measure from the top of a tower the distance of ships at sea, and reckon the height of a pyramid from the length of its shadow at a certain moment, or by comparing, wherever the sun might be, two triangles of shadow. But had he a theoretical knowledge of the geometrical propositions on the equality of triangles, which these practical methods pre-suppose ? He is credited, it is true, with several theorems. But it is unlikely that he went beyond the point of view of Egyptian or Babylonian science, or caused geometry to make the decisive advance which it was to owe, rather later, to the Pythagoreans. The same is the case with his astronomy, and especially with his famous prediction of the solar eclipse. It was made, Herodotos says, *for the year*, without mentioning whether the eclipse would be visible at a particular point on the earth, and must have had a purely empirical basis, like the similar predictions of the Chaldaean astrologers. Thales had the luck to be right, and in connexion with a memorable event—that was all.

The philosophical part of Thales' work—that is, his physical theory, his doctrine of the principle which produces things and causes them to develop, *physis*, introduces us, on the other hand, to something quite new, in respect both of Eastern science and of the old cosmogony. First of all, the spirit of inquiry is quite different. The idea of a permanent foundation and a matter which is the origin of becoming,

[1] See, below, the revival of Thales' doctrine by Hippon.

which was already implicitly present in the cosmogonies, is for the first time brought to the fore by Thales in a manner which strikes the mind of Aristotle. In a most important passage, the terms of which really belong to his own vocabulary,[1] he gives a precise definition of the conception of which Thales was the original author : something exists which is the original principle of the generation of everything else, to which everything else returns by corruption, which subsists without change under the diversity and changing of the qualities which affect it, and which is the element or imperishable matter of all things ; for Thales, this " nature " (*physis*) is water. So, instead of explaining the diversity of the real by anthropomorphic representations and linking it in the end with the impenetrable mystery of Chaos or the obscurity of Night, Thales gives it as its foundation and principle a reality of experience. Far from regarding his doctrine as a mere extension of cosmogony or a rejuvenation of the Homeric legend, Aristotle combats those who interpret it so. If one likes, he says,[2] one can make Ocean and Tethys the first parents of generation, and say that the gods swear by Styx and that, since that by which one swears is that which has the most dignity, water is the noblest and most ancient of things ; but what Thales said has quite a different meaning.

His method, too, is different. The cosmogonic legend was a narrative ; Thales wishes to give reasons. That is what Aristotle knows, and what Theophrastos says [3] when he defines his method as an induction which, from the facts given in sensation, rises to the universal proposition. It does not, therefore, much matter that Thales' reasons— moisture of the seed and of the nutriment, warm vapours rising from moisture—are taken by Aristotle from later expositions.[4] Many other reasons as well presented themselves to his observation—for example, the silting up of the rivers of his country and the constant encroachment of the land on the sea, to say nothing of the Delta and the inundations of the Nile. He saw, or thought that he saw, that everything comes from a transformation of water and after-

---

[1] *Metaph.*, A. 3, 983 b 6–21.   [2] *Ibid.*, b 27, 984 a 3.   [3] **LXVIII**, ch. 1, A. 13.
[4] *Metaph.*, 983 b 22–7. Note, too, that he knows what is due to Hippon, and does not ascribe it to Thales (*De An.*, i. 2, 405 b 1).

wards returns to water, and then he extended the results of that observation, by a very bold analogy, to the whole of things.

There remain a few propositions whose connexion with his fundamental proposition is not known to us. The first, however, is, according to Aristotle, a consequence of it ; it was, he says, *because* water is the principle of all things that Thales declared that " the earth is on the water," resting and floating on it like a piece of wood ; hence its stability. A similar representation is to be found in one of the Egyptian cosmological myths. But that is not sufficient ground for supposing a real influence, still less for reconstructing Thales' whole cosmology on that basis.[1]

In the other propositions there are, unless Aristotle has forced the meaning, indications of a general view on the very essence of things. According to some, he says, soul is mingled with the whole world, all through, and " that is perhaps why also " Thales thought that " everything is full of gods." Elsewhere he says, " It seems, from all accounts, that Thales admitted that the soul is a moving power, if it is true that he said of the loadstone that it has a soul because it moves iron." [2] Under the influence of Stoic thought, others went even further than Aristotle in the analogical interpretation of these formulas. But, if they are authentic, we are justified in inferring from them that, in Thales' view, matter is living and animated ; that, through the water which is in all things, an activity of divine nature is always present in matter, although not always manifested by it. For the first formula goes beyond the apophthegms of the Seven Sages, and the second does not imply that the magnet is the only material body which has a soul. It does not matter that, in Thales' time, men were still unable to distinguish between matter and mind. That his doctrine was a protest against the common experience which contrasts life with the apparent inertia of matter is sufficient ground for calling it a form of Hylozoism.

[1] As in **LXX**, 69, 70 ff.   [2] *De An.*, i. 5, 411 a 7 ; 2, 405 a 19.

II

ANAXIMANDROS

After Thales, the direction of the School of Miletos passed, about the middle of the VIth century, into the hands of Anaximandros. Of his life we know nothing which is not suspect of confusion. Of the many works attributed to him, only one seems authentic, and he is said to have been sixty-four years old when he published it. It is entitled *On Nature* ($\pi\epsilon\rho\grave{\iota}\ \phi\acute{\upsilon}\sigma\epsilon\omega s$), but this title was probably given to it after Aristotle's time, like all the similar titles of works ascribed to the pre-Socratic philosophers. This book, of which we have a fragment, seems to have survived fairly late ; if Aristotle and Theophrastos had it before them, we can understand why they spoke more of the doctrine of Anaximandros than of that of Thales.

Of the special contributions to the progress of science ascribed to him, the authority for many is uncertain—the invention, or introduction into Ionia, of the *gnomon* or sundial (the scientific use of which is said to have led him to discover the obliquity of the Zodiac), the construction of a celestial globe, and other things. It is at least probable that he was the first to think of making a map of the world, an idea which must have been the result of preparatory work done collectively in the school. Whatever place this undertaking may hold in the total of his scientific activity, what interests the history of thought is rather his attempt to construct a systematic representation of the universe.

The earth, instead of resting on a support, as Thales supposed, hangs in the middle of the sky, at an equal distance from everything else. It is shaped like a pillar (*i.e.* a cylinder), its height being one-third of its breadth, so that it is stable. We occupy the uppermost section. The stars are circles, or rather flat cylinders like chariot-wheels without spokes, in the air surrounding the earth. Inside they are full of fire. A " felting " of " compressed " air, which envelops this fire, is bored, on the felloe, but in the plane of the wheel, with passages like " pipes," through which the internal fire escapes as if through " mouthpieces," " air-holes," or " bellows." It

is this igneous expiration which we see. Every eclipse of the
light of the stars, including the phases of the moon, is therefore
to be explained either by the total or partial stoppage of the
orifices, or by the revolution of the wheel, which does not
always present them towards us. Anaximandros is said to
have been the first to make researches into the distances and
relative size of the stars, or rather of the circles which constitute the orbits of the sun, the moon, the sky of the fixed
stars, and that of the planets. Whatever uncertainties and
gaps there may be in our evidence regarding this astronomical
system, three things seem to be certain. First, the circle of
the sun was held to be the most distant. Secondly, reckonings
dealt with the ratio of the section of the terrestrial cylinder
to the orifice through which the fire appeared and to the
circumference of the sidereal wheel outside the felloe ; in the
case of the sun, for example, that circumference was twenty-
seven times as great as that of the earth, while the orifice
itself was equal to it. Lastly, the figures obtained were not
based on observation, but were sacred numbers, 3 (the
circumference of the earth), 9, 18, 27, which were, moreover,
held in great honour in the cosmogonies.

Whatever we may think of this coinciding of sacred
numbers and astronomical figures, and uncertain as its exact
signification is, the scientific character of the investigations
of Anaximandros is already apparent, and it is seen again in
his attempt to explain how our world was formed, and what
place it holds in the totality of things. But, since the totality
of things is derived from the principle, we must first speak
of the principle, and therefore consider his philosophical
teaching. His principle is the Infinite (τὸ ἄπειρον), a reality
which cannot, without jeopardizing the existence of everything else, be any particular thing, such as water or fire ; nor
does it seem, in spite of what has been said to the contrary,[1]
to be an *intermediate* substance between one element and
another, since the unknown physicists to whom Aristotle
ascribes this conception describe the process of the derivation
of things from the principle downwards in a manner directly
contrary to the conception of Anaximandros. First, it is an
original principle, " unengendered and imperishable," which
" contains and directs all things," the condition of the " un-

[1] **LXXI**, § 15.

failing perpetuity of generations "—in short, something infinite in size, and at the same time undetermined in quality, but, being an universal container, not to be defined merely as absolute virtuality. It is, in addition, that " from which " all things emanate and " to which " they return " by the eternal movement," [1] which certainly seems, when one considers the oppositions and comparisons established by Aristotle in this matter, to be a process of separation and reunion of contraries, the original form of which must be a whirling chaos. Herein, without any doubt, Anaximandros is on the road which will later lead to a mechanical conception of becoming. But, on the other hand, in so far as his principle is a single substance, infinite in size and destitute of specification, he is dynamic in tendency. A precise distinction and contrasting of these two conceptions of becoming would have required an analysis of concepts from which men were still a long way.

Now let us see how things formed, starting from the Infinite, as from a new Chaos. The first separation which takes place in the bosom of the " eternal " causes Hot and Cold to appear. " Consequently," a " sphere of flame " is formed round the circumterrestrial air, like the bark round a tree. Then this sphere of flame breaks, and the fragments so produced are thereupon enclosed in circles, which are the stars. It is a bold notion, but so fragmentary and based on such scanty knowledge that it cannot be compared to the hypothesis of Laplace, although it reminds one of the part of that hypothesis concerning the rings of Saturn. Moreover, there is much obscurity in the evidence. If the earth and the air surrounding it, which are older than the " sphere of flame," come from Cold, as the sphere of flame comes from Hot, must not water be yet older than they ? This must be the meaning of the statement of a doxographer,[2] that " the eternal movement is more ancient than the water of Thales." The action of Hot must have produced exhalations in the water, from which come the air and the movement of the winds, while the remainder, steadily drying up, forms the earth with the sea.[3] This increasing differentiation in change,

---

[1] Infinity in size being admitted, this cannot be the daily movement, as is supposed in **LIV**, 575 ff., and **LXX**, 88.
[2] **LXVIII**, ch. 2, A. 12.   [3] *Ibid.*, A. 27.

characteristic of a doctrine of evolution, also appears in the remarkable explanation which Anaximandros gives of the origins of life and the process by which living beings have gradually succeeded in adapting themselves to changes in their environment—a distant foreshadowing of transformism. The first living creatures were formed in the primitive moisture in consequence of evaporation, and therefore in a mixture of earth, air, and water. At the beginning, all were like fish and enveloped in a scaly membrane. As they grew older, they rose to the region which was already dry, where, dropping their shells, they continued to live, but not for long. Man, therefore, is descended from animals specifically different from himself. If he had at the beginning been such as we see him now, incapable of providing for his own sustenance, how would he have survived ? Therefore other creatures, of the nature of fish, must for a long time have borne him within them, just as certain dog-fish keep their young in their mouths, until the day when he was able to appear on the earth and live there by his own resources.

In truth, all this evolution concerns only our world, and it is very probable that Anaximandros held that the Infinite gave birth, in the bosom of the eternal movement, to other skies and other worlds, infinite in number and, it seems, co-existent, but separated by such vast distances that they are born and die unknown to one another.[1] If he called them gods, therefore, it was not in the same sense as the Infinite, their unengendered, imperishable principle, the seat of the eternal movement, embracing and governing everything. Being thus incorporated in the principle, as in the doctrine of Thales, the divine power is transformed into a natural necessity. But it does not entirely lose its mythical character, just as the cyclic rhythm of generations and corruptions still has a social aspect, that of the compensations for which injustice calls. " That from which all that exists arises," Anaximandros says in strikingly poetic language, " is also that towards which corruption proceeds, by necessity ; for living beings pay to one another the penalty and reparation of their injustice, following the order of time." In other words, the conflict of the contraries Hot and Cold gives rise to a whole balanced system of compensations. Heat, for

---

[1] Cf. **LXXI**, § 18, where the discussion seems convincing.

example, drinks up the water of the earth, and the vapours give it back in rain. But a day will come when, the earth being completely dry and ceasing to nourish the air with its vapours, Hot will make Cold and Wet pay for the outrages which it has suffered from them. So, after evolution comes dissolution ; the worlds return to the Infinite and, a new compensation, the cycle begins again. It is possible that we have here the mark of the pessimistic and mystical speculations of Orphicism.[1] But there is more than that. The combination of all our data seems too strong for us to be able to deny the profoundly rationalistic spirit of this cosmology, a bold and systematic doctrine, sometimes even prophetic, precise and vigorous in its thought. No doubt, the scantiness of our knowledge about Thales forbids us to estimate exactly the originality of Anaximandros in relation to his master. But, in relation to what we know, it is undeniably very great.

III

ANAXIMENES

The last representative of the School of Miletos known to us is Anaximenes, who succeeded Anaximandros. Of his life, which seems to have ended about twenty years before the close of the VIIth century, we know only one thing—that he wrote, in Ionic prose and, unlike his predecessor, in very simple language, a book of which we have only a very short authentic fragment. What the doxographers say of his teaching seems to come from a special treatise which Theophrastos devoted to him, and in any case is sufficiently consistent to allow of a fairly comprehensive exposition, starting from the principle.

His principle, like that of Thales, is an observable reality, but it is air, and that air is infinite, so that the principle of Anaximandros is placed in the domain of experience. Why air ? Not so much, perhaps, because air is what most easily changes its condition,[2] for water presented the same advantages

---

[1] Cf. **XLII**, 93 ff. Physics seem to have held less place than morality in Anaximandros's works.
[2] Simplicius, *De Caelo*, 273 b 45, Heiberg's ed.

for the hypothesis, but rather, no doubt, because, whereas water falls if it is not supported, air is self-sufficient in this respect, and, moreover, seems to have an unlimited diffusion. Another reason may be that Anaximenes wants the world to be a living thing, subject to birth and death, and, therefore, wants it to breathe. This reasoning by analogy is suggested by a fragment : [1] " Our soul, because it is of air, is in each of us a principle of union " (i.e., it makes the unity of the individual) ; " so, too, breath or air contains the whole world " (and makes its unity). Secondly, it seems [2] that the infinity of this determinate substance can only be infinity of *size ;* it cannot be indeterminate in quality as the Infinite of Anaximandros could. So, when we are told that air manifests itself to our senses only by heat, cold, wetness, movement, etc., and not when it is perfectly homogeneous, we must understand by that an apparent indeterminateness, relative to ourselves.

The originality of Anaximenes does not lie in a more precise assertion of the unity of matter,[3] for that is the whole meaning of the doctrine of his two predecessors. His originality is rather in his conception of the relationship of things to the principle from which they are derived and to which they return. For, according to him, every change is produced by " condensations " or " rarefactions " of the air, according as it " contracts " or " relaxes." So a single cause, by the uniform action of its specific properties, is sufficient to account for every variety of phenomenon. The process of separation asserted by Anaximandros accorded so little with the oneness of matter, that in the end his principle came to be regarded as a complex mixture of everything. The explanation of Anaximenes, on the contrary, made a remarkable advance towards clarity in the conception of change. Perhaps this is the sole reason of the favour which his doctrine won and enjoyed for a long time.

To the condensation of the air he ascribed cold ; to its rarefaction, heat. For when we blow air from our mouths, it is cold if we press it with our lips and make it compact,

---

[1] **LXXI**, §28.
[2] Contrary to the opinion in **LXX**, 146–9. The statement of Pseudo-Plutarch (A. 6, beg.) on which this opinion is based is very difficult to explain, if, instead of τῷ μὲν γένει ἄπειρον, one does not read τῷ μὲν μεγέθει. . . .
[3] **LXX**, 158–63.

and hot if we open our mouths wide and let it expand.[1] Fire is rarefied air ; the winds are the condensation of part of the air, driven by less dense air ; if the air is " compressed " and thickened, it becomes clouds, which, by a process of condensation, turn into rain, etc. ; the most complete condensation of water produces earth, and then rocks. This distension and compression, which cause the consistency of the air to vary in degree, are, in a sense, mechanical phenomena, producing separations and reunions of parts, and the air is, like the Infinite of Anaximandros, moved by an " eternal movement." Moreover, the air is a living power, for it is a god. This is another instance of the absence of any distinction, in the early thinkers, between the mechanical and dynamic points of view.

Without dwelling on the particularly thorny question, whether Anaximenes held,[2] like his predecessor, that there are countless worlds, it will be enough if we consider his opinions on the formation and structure of our own universe. The earth seems to have come first. For it to be stable and able to resist the pressure of the air on which it rests, it must be a vast, absolutely flat surface, like a table. Instead of dividing the air, it lies on it like a lid, compelling its mass to remain compact and motionless. By the increasing rarefaction of vapours as they rise further from the earth, the stars are formed. Yet it seems that they are, in part, of an earthy nature, or at least surrounded by invisible earthy bodies, by which all the interceptions of their light may be explained. It is certain, in any case, that they, too, are supported by the air, like " painted pictures " or " leaves of fire." But the comparison which Anaximenes seems to have used in speaking of the moving stars was that of " millstones," whose revolution round the earth on a horizontal plane was also compared, though the relationship between the two images is not clear, to a cap rotating round a head. Other stars, on the contrary, are like " nails fixed on the crystalline surface " ; the existence of the fixed stars, which, giving no heat, must be the most distant stars, is, therefore, definitely recognized, and moreover, in this conception of a solid, transparent celestial sphere, Anaximenes shows himself the originator of ancient astronomy.

[1] **LXVIII**, B. 1.   [2] As is maintained in **LXXI**, §30.

Did the School of Miletos disappear with Anaximenes ? It may be doubted. Certainly the advance of Persian dominion in Ionia must have created new political conditions which were unfavourable to scientific research, and this would explain the migrations westward which took place at this time. Yet, in days when the influence of books was very small, it is rather difficult to understand the revival, in Hippon and Diogenes of Apollonia, a century later, of the philosophical tendency of which that school had been the source, if it did not survive, at least in a reduced form. But really this is such a singular fact and implies so many factors that it must be studied separately and in its own place.

SCIENCE AS THE INSTRUMENT OF MORAL PURIFICATION. PYTHAGOREANISM AND THE ITALIAN SCHOOL

After the School of Miletos, the first fact which the historian of Greek thought encounters is the appearance of the Pythagorean school. By its founder, this new philosophy was Ionian, but it took shape and developed in the part of Southern Italy which the Romans called Great Greece, where Greek colonists had settled about the beginning of the VIIth century, Achaeans, Messenians, Locrians, and others. It was a comparatively new environment, less subject to tradition and therefore more plastic, intelligent, and passionate, in which culture seems to have followed the advance of material prosperity. At Croton, for example, the cradle of Pythagoreanism, there had long been a celebrated school of medicine.

What causes brought about the shifting of philosophical activity from Ionia to these distant regions, and the birth of an " Italian " school, in Aristotle's happy expression ? What part was played by social factors, and what by individual and accidental factors ? These questions are hard to answer. Altogether, there is no more baffling problem than that of the history of Pythagoreanism.

First, the most copious and precise part of our evidence comes from the revived Pythagoreanism of the last years of the Roman Republic and the first four centuries of the Christian era, and through the Neo-Platonists. Alexander Polyhistor, one of the sources of Diogenes Laërtios, was fairly closely associated with the beginnings of Neo-Pythagoreanism, and Neo-Pythagoreans—Apollonios of Tyana, Moderatus of Gades, Nicomachos of Gerasa—are the immediate authorities of the Neo-Platonists Porphyry, for his *Life of Pythagoras* (with the romance of Antonius Diogenes,

48 SCIENCE AND PHILOSOPHY

Incredible Tales of beyond Thule), and Iamblichos, for his
Pythagorean Life. It cannot be denied that these works show
a singular absence of critical spirit, an excessive love of the
marvellous, and a tendency to enrich ancient Pythagoreanism
by means of symbolical interpretations with all the acquisitions of later philosophy, especially Platonic and Stoic. But
one must remember that, between the *last* Pythagoreans of
the old school, at the beginning of the IVth century, and the
revival of Pythagoreanism in the middle of the Ist century B.C.,
the tradition did not die out. Diodoros of Aspendos and
Heracleides Lembos were Pythagoreans ; there were still
Pythagoreans in the time of Poseidonios ; Baccho-Pythagorean
" orgies " were held. It may, therefore, be possible, by
attentive, cautious criticism, to sort out the successive stages
of this obscure tradition from external accretions.[1] Behind
the immediate authority of Diogenes, Iamblichos, and
Porphyry, we reach witnesses who were probably well-informed
—Timaeos of Tauromenion who wrote the history of Sicily
and Great Greece ; Aristoxenos of Taras who, no doubt before
he entered the school of Aristotle, knew the *last* Pythagoreans
(Xenophilos of Thracian Chalcidice and the Phliuntians
Phanton, Echecrates,[2] Diocles, and Polymnastos, the disciples
of Philolaos and Eurytos), and was the son of a man who
had known Archytas, and himself wrote a *Pythagorean Life*
and a book of *Pythagorean Propositions* ; and the Peripatetic
Dicaearchos who, being a Messana man, may have had special
sources of information

There is another difficulty. Pythagoras, the founder,
whose character and doings it would be so interesting to know,
very soon became a legendary figure. Later we shall note
some allusions of his contemporaries.[3] But about half a
century after his death he had already become a superhuman
being for Empedocles.[4] About the same time, Herodotos,
although he ended his life in Pythagorean circles in Great
Greece and Sicily, associates the name of Pythagoras with
the teachings and miracles of the Thracian Zalmoxis and
Pythagoreanism itself with the religious or magical practices
of the Egyptians. In the IVth century, highly cultivated men,

[1] Cf. **LXXVII**, esp. Studies 1, 2, 6, 8, 9.
[2] Phaedon's interlocutor in Plato's dialogue of that name.
[3] Xenophanes and Heracleitos.
[4] If frag. 129 of Empedocles really refers to him.

not only the Platonist Heracleides of Pontus, who had a strongly romantic bent, but even Aristotle in his book *On the Pythagoreans* and his pupils Dicaearchos, Clearchos, Hieronymos, or Aristoxenos, accepted and accredited the legend— Pythagoras was the son of Apollo or Hermes, he descended into Hades and returned, he had a golden thigh, he could be in two places at once, he made prophecies, and so on. Moreover, the care with which Aristotle almost always avoids mentioning his name and speaks rather of " those who are called Pythagoreans " seems to show that for him Pythagoras was only a nebulous figure.

What is more, if we try to discover, in the historical development of the school after its original homogeneity had been broken up, what is due to each individual member, we find the ground slipping from under us. Plato gives little positive evidence and offers for indirect analysis only a tissue, the original threads of which are impossible to disentangle. Aristotle does not mention Philolaos once ; of his book on Archytas practically nothing remains ; if he happens to quote Archytas or Eurytos, one may well ask whether he is not merely borrowing from them a striking expression of an opinion common to the whole group. Usually one is confronted with the enigmatic phrase, " Certain Pythagoreans say. . . ." [1] So we cannot even arrive at Pythagoras's thought by elimination, referring to him anything which does not certainly belong to any other philosopher of his school.

There are, it is true, the Pythagorean writings, which are immediate sources. Unfortunately, they are most of them very suspect. The *Golden Verses* ascribed to Pythagoras are a clumsy compilation of the IIIrd or IVth century of our era, and his legendary *Three Books* (*Educational, Political, Physical*) are a forgery of the IInd or Ist century B.C. The treatise of Ocellus the Lucanian *On the Nature of the Universe* and that of the pretended Timaeos of Locri *On the Soul of the World* are both forgeries, the former being earlier than the Ist century B.C. and the latter a mere summary of Plato's *Timaeos*, dating from the Ist century of our era. It is, however, sometimes possible to find in these apocryphal works traces of the Pythagorean literature of the Vth century, and still more of the IVth, of which we may have a sample in a letter from

---

[1] This anonymity is patent if one reads the ten pages of **LXVIII**, ch. 45.

Lysis to Hipparchos, even if it is not authentic.[1]   Of the fragments of Philolaos and Archytas, some bear evident marks of later influences, but others may very well contain authentic elements.   The problem is really too complex to be considered here.[2]

In sum, in the present state of the Pythagorean question, I think that it is wise to content ourselves with considering early Pythagoreanism altogether, from the end of the VIth century to the middle of the IV, as one fairly homogeneous doctrine, without attempting, save in certain special cases, to determine the contribution of each philosopher.[3]

Pythagoras was born at Samos, and was about forty years old when, for obscure reasons, he left his city and came to Italy.   Of his life at Samos we know hardly anything.   Among those alleged to have been his teachers, some, such as Anaximandros or Pherecydes, are not unlikely ; others are fabulous persons, such as the healer Aristeas of Proconnesos and Abaris the Hyperboreian, a priest of Apollo.   It is possible, when one remembers Heracleitos's judgment on the contemptible science and disastrous " polymathy " of Pythagoras[4] and the evidence of Herodotos on the religious aspect of his activities, that as a philosopher he already had the complex character which we find in him in Italy.   Of the many voyages scribed to him, for instance to Persia, where he did not fail to meet the Magus Zaratas, and to the Druids of Gaul, those which really took place doubtless happened before he settled in Italy.

He landed at Croton, and, at the request, it is said, of the Assembly of Elders, who had been greatly impressed by his discourses, he there began a labour of preaching and apostleship.   His fame spread ; disciples came to him from all Great Greece, from Sicily, and even from Rome.   Such were the origins of the Pythagorean association, which had an educational and mystical object, namely, initiation to a new rule of life, the association being open to women, as is shown by the famous case of Theano, and to foreigners.   It was only as a

---

[1] Cf. **LXXVII**, Studies 1 and 2.

[2] The problem has been revived by the work of Erich Frank (**LXXIX** b).

[3] Contrary to what has been done in **LXXI**, where Pythagoras and the old Pythagoreans, and then Philolaos and the young Pythagoreans, are studied separately.

[4] Frag. 40 Diels (16 Bywater) ; frag. 129 D. (17 B.) is probably a forgery.

side-line that it became a political club (*hetaireia*) at Croton, in consequence of its love of discipline and its actual recruiting, both of which necessarily made it hostile to democratic instability. Furthermore, outside the mother-society at Croton, the affiliation to it of the rulers of a city or of a large number of its citizens could not fail to affect its political orientation. In this way the spirit of the association became predominant at Sybaris and Rhegion and, in Sicily, at Acragas, Catane, and Tauromenion. The preambles of the laws which Zaleucos gave to Locri and Charondas to Catane and Rhegion, though not directly derived from Pythagoreanism, are good evidence of that spirit.

In the meantime, with all his adherents testifying to their faith in him, the conviction which Pythagoras may already have had of the supernatural character of his person and his mission doubtless grew stronger. The feeling of his followers, at least, is shown fairly clearly in a phrase quoted by Aristotle,[1] which is in harmony with so many marvellous tales : " There is one species of reasonable animal, which is god ; a second is man ; Pythagoras is an example of the third." In short, he was one of the inspired, daemonic men who are intermediate between the divine order and the human.

This enthusiasm, however, was not unanimous. The opposition over which the association had triumphed at Croton had not been extinguished. At last violent revolt broke out, led by Cylon, a wealthy Crotoniat of good family. The house of Milon, where the directors of the society were holding a sitting, was besieged and set on fire, and almost all perished in the flames. According to unanimous tradition, the only ones to escape were Archippos and Lysis, who, towards the end of his life, after staying in Achaea, settled in Thebes and was the beloved and respected master of Epaminondas. About Pythagoras himself, Dicaearchos and Aristoxenos disagree. The latter declares that he had retired to Metapontion, being compelled to leave Croton by the attacks of Cylon, and was dead before the disaster ; according to Dicaearchos, he was not present at the seat of the society at the time of the fire, and, having made his escape to Locri, then went to Taras, and finally to Metapontion, where he died after eating nothing for forty days. So all these events are wrapped

[1] Frag. 187.

in a darkness in which some light can only be thrown by a minute comparison of the contradictory data of tradition.[1] It seems, at least, that Pythagoras reached an advanced age and that his death must be placed about the end of the first third of the Vth century.

Of the Pythagoreans of this first generation some names have survived—in particular, those of Cercops, Petron, Brotinos, and Hippasos. One might perhaps include the celebrated comic poet Epicharmos, a young contemporary of Pythagoras, who spent a great part of his life at Syracuse. In many fragments of his work there are Pythagorean ideas, but with unmistakable marks of the influence of Xenophanes and Heracleitos.

The revolution at Croton was followed by similar movements almost everywhere in Great Greece. However, the Pythagoreans managed to hold their own at Rhegion, under Archippos and Cleinias, and at Taras, which was the abode, in the first half of the IVth century, of the celebrated Archytas, whose relations with Plato are certain, despite the fables with which they are surrounded, and who had enough political power in his city to stand up to the tyrant Dionysios of Syracuse. But other members of the association left Italy for the Greek mainland. Two Pythagorean centres were founded, one at Thebes and one at Phlius. The former was the work of Philolaos, the great man of the second Pythagorean generation, about whom we unfortunately know next to nothing. It is possible that, about the beginning of the IVth century, he returned to Italy, profiting by the conciliatory intervention of the Achaeans, who had obtained the recall of exiles. It was to his school, probably, that the Theban interlocutors of Socrates in the *Phaedon*, Simmias and Cebes, belonged, and Lysis may have carried it on. The school of Phlius, if it is true that its founder Eurytos was the disciple of Philolaos, may have been a daughter of the Theban school; to it, as we have seen, the Pythagoreans whom Aristoxenos knew belonged.

This remarkable effacement of individuals behind the personality of the School, which makes it unnecessary to quote other names, may, perhaps, be explained in the case of Pythagoreanism by special reasons. It was not nearly so

---

[1] Cf. **LXXIX**, pt. 3.

much a philosophical school, even of an embryonic kind, as a sort of religious freemasonry. Now, there was already, and had been for perhaps three centuries, a similar association— Orphicism. The origins of Orphicism are obscure, and, although it certainly affected Pythagoreanism, it is probable that the latter helped considerably to give Orphicism the form in which it is known to us. At a very early date it was connected with the Mysteries of Dionysos. Among the Pythagoreans, on the contrary, Apollinism predominated, but it was mingled with Hyperboreianism and, as we have seen, with the legend of the Getic god Zalmoxis. The descent of Pythagoras into the underworld recalls, no less and even more than that of Zalmoxis, the story of Orpheus, the Thracian magician. Whatever the truth may be of these very difficult questions of influence, the object of Orphicism was the mystical revelation of a rule of life by a secret initiation. This consisted of *rites of purification* (καθαρμοί), by which the soul should, in an ecstasy, be " released " from the body, which was as a tomb to it (σῶμα—σῆμα), and preserved from the dangers awaiting it in Hades.[1] Its aim was not so much to teach something as to put those initiated into a definite emotional state. So Orphicism was an association independent of national groups, a private worship outside the framework of public religion or the other mysteries which the latter recognized, for example at Eleusis, and more efficacious in the eyes of the faithful. Being less subject to old bonds and barriers, the social environment of Southern Italy and Sicily was, we may suppose, favourable to Orphic propaganda, which thus prepared the ground for another institution of the same kind, but more cohesive and better disciplined.

The Pythagorean rule of life, unlike Orphicism, allowed, not only for religious beliefs and practices, but for intellectual speculations, which, as a matter of fact, were themselves religious practices. Pythagoras is said to have invented the word " philosophy," " the effort towards wisdom " being a factor of moral sanctification. When the initiates applied themselves to mathematics, astronomy, music, medicine, gymnastics, and the study of Homer and Hesiod, they did so because they regarded these studies, in different

---

[1] Gold tablets of the IVth and IIIrd centuries B.C., found in S. Italy (Thurii and Petelia), Rome, and Crete. Cf. **LXVIII**, ch. 66, 17–21.

degrees, as a means of purifying souls, and bodies with them.

Of the non-speculative purifications, some were positive, concerning the conduct of members. Every evening they had to examine their conscience on three points : " In what have I failed ? " " What good have I done ? " " What have I not done, of what I ought to have done ? " When they woke, they had to arrange for the good use of their day. The morality of the brotherhood seems to have been set forth in a catechism, written in verse to be more easily remembered (*Holy Words*, ἱερὸς λόγος). Respect the gods and bow to their will, remain steadfastly at the post which they have given you to hold in life, defend the law by force against factious men, be true to your friends and say that among friends everything is common (φιλότης ἰσότης), be moderate and simple in the use of your possessions, feel shame when you have done wrong, avoid vain swearing and honour your oath, and, lastly, do not divulge the teaching which you have received by initiation. This rule of secrecy, which must not be confused with the silence imposed on novices as a preparatory test, probably applied to everything comprised in the initiation, and consequently even to the speculative part of the revelations. In the story of Hippasos, slain for revealing a mystery of geometry, there is doubtless a foundation of truth. The ritual formula of the undertaking which bound the initiates in this respect may have been the famous oath of the Pythagoreans : " No ! I swear by Him who has revealed the Tetractys, which contains the source and roots of eternal nature, to our soul." The mystical character of Pythagoreanism is revealed by yet other indications—the Master speaks to novices from behind a curtain, and the famous " He has said it " (αὐτὸς ἔφα) means, not only that his words must be blindly believed, but that his sacred name must not be profaned.

This fundamental religious character makes the negative prescriptions of the rule even more understandable. We know how full it was of perplexing prohibitions—do not eat beans or mallow, do not eat the flesh of animals (not in all cases, but in certain conditions), shun the butchers and huntsmen who take their lives, do not wear woollen garments or anything but linen, do not sacrifice cocks, or white cocks, do not break bread or eat from a whole loaf, do not poke the fire with a knife, do not pick up what has fallen on the ground, do not help a porter to set down his load, do not leave the mark of the cooking-pot on the ashes, etc., etc. Regarding these taboos there is utter confusion and embarrassment among our witnesses. Some of them argue, look everywhere for utilitarian reasons, and finally reject what they cannot thus explain. Others accept everything, and laboriously discover in every prohibition a moral idea, concealed under the " symbol." [1] We now know what interpretations of that kind are worth. For the object of the present work, it is enough to have pointed out that these curious vestiges of a primitive religious mentality survived in Pythagoreanism.

All these regulations, negative and positive alike, seem to have been contained in a sort of code of the complete Pythagorean.[2] It was in the form of a series of questions and answers. Now, some of the questions did not refer to special obligations. Some began with " What is . . . ? " ($\tau\acute{\iota}$ $\acute{\epsilon}\sigma\tau\iota$;), and led to mystical definitions. "What are the Isles of the Blest?" "The Sun and the Moon " Some began "What is most . . . ?" ($\tau\acute{\iota}$ $\mu\acute{a}\lambda\iota\sigma\tau a$), the answer being something perfect. " What is most just ? " " The act of Sacrifice." The rules of knowledge and conduct were called the a ousmata, the articles of faith; they constituted the " philosophy of the Acusmatics," who were contrasted, it is said, with the " Mathematicians " or " men of science."

This contrast does not seem to have existed at the beginning. It does not correspond to that between the novices, or " Exoterics," and the initiates, or " Esoterics." It was the result of a schism in the society, which doubtless occurred about the end of the Vth century. Although a spiritual association, Pythagoreanism had aspired to temporal power. It had failed, and we may suppose that this failure was the cause of the division of the religious and speculative tendencies, which had at first been so closely united. Some, wishing to preserve for the order a spiritual life parallel to that of Orphicism and endowed with the same power of expansion and resistance, attached themselves with blind enthusiasm to the sacramental and mysterious element of the revelation, to rites and formulas; the Acusmatics set out to be devout believers. The Mathematicians, without formally giving up the creed of the others,

---

[1] " Symbols " is the recognized name for these prohibitions in later Pythagorean literature.
[2] **LXVIII**, ch. 45, C. 4.

considered its horizon too limited. They set out to be, likewise for the spiritual salvation of their order, men of science. But this was only possible if they renounced the obligation of mystical secrecy, and justified doctrinal propositions rationally. In the eyes of the pious, therefore, these " scientists " were heretics. It was they, men of the second Pythagorean generation, who transformed the original religious association into a school of philosophy. But it was the religious association, reduced to its rites and its dogmas, which survived until the Neo-Pythagorean revival, while the errors and discoveries alike of the philosophical school were destined to be lost in the general advance of reflection and science.

" What is wisest ? " " Number." " What is most beautiful ? " " Harmony." These two articles of the doctrine of the Acusmatics state mystically the two dominant ideas of the Pythagorean doctrine.

In numbers, the simplest of mathematical things, according to what Aristotle says in substance,[1] the Pythagoreans thought that they saw, much more than in water, fire, and the like, a great number of resemblances to living beings and phenomena. They therefore held that the elements of the numbers are the elements of all things, and that the whole world is harmony and number. So, like the Physicists, they regarded numbers as that from which things proceed and to which they return, their immanent cause and their substance. By the side of this conception Aristotle mentions, without distinguishing them, another, to the effect that numbers are the patterns imitated by things, without, apparently, the patterns being separated from their copies. This more subtle representation of the relationship between numbers and things seems to have been preferred by the younger Pythagoreans, and there is no doubt that it inspired Plato. It is not impossible, moreover, that both conceptions existed side by side in the original doctrine.

It is a very ancient religious tendency, which we cannot be surprised to find in early Pythagoreanism, to invest certain numbers with a sacred value and a mysterious virtue. But what, according to tradition, led Pythagoras to look to them for the foundation of a systematic explanation of things, was the experimental observation of the fact that the qualities and relationships of musical concords are constituted by

[1] *Metaph.*, A. 5, 985 b 26–9, 986 a 1–3 ; 6, 987 b 10–12, 24–30.

numbers. When hammers strike on the anvil, the pitch of
the sound varies with their weight, and the same is true of
strings stretched by various masses. The obvious inaccuracies
which tradition has accumulated in its efforts to be too
precise are not, perhaps, enough to prove that it is fundamentally untrue. In any case, if number is what constitutes
musical concord, it may be what constitutes other things, by
analogy, and even all things. Thus, 7 will be the " right
time " (καιρός), since, for example, periods of seven days,
months, or years are of very great importance in the development of living beings. Marriage is constituted by 5, which
joins the first even and the first odd (1 being regarded
separately). 4 and 9 are justice, since they are the first
numbers obtained by multiplying the first even and the first
odd by themselves, and in justice there is reciprocity of
remuneration (τὸ ἀντιπεπονθός). Whereas intelligence, being
always motionless in itself, is constituted by 1, opinion will
be 2, because it is oscillating and mobile. Although, according
to Aristotle, the Pythagoreans did not give many examples
of these applications, one must connect with them the quaint
method of graphic representation by which Eurytos claimed
to find the number of Man or of the Horse from the number of
coloured stones which he used to draw diagrammatic representations of them. In sum, " all things which it is given
to us to know have a number, and nothing can be conceived
or known without number." [1] It therefore reveals the essence
of things to us, and that is why it is what is wisest.

As for harmony, the most beautiful of things, it is, perhaps
in the words of Philolaos, " the unification of the composed
manifold and the accordance of the discordant " (Frag. 10 D.).
Each thing is a harmony of numbers, and number is a harmony
of opposites, so that, as we have seen, the elements of numbers
are also the elements of things. The fundamental opposition
is between the Limitless and the Limit. Then come, dependent
on these first two terms respectively, Even and Odd, the
Many and the One. Even and Odd are not only elements of
number, but also *specific qualities* of it, which are manifested
in numbers by the ensuing opposition. But what makes the
numbers alternately even and odd, changing their quality, is
a harmonious unification of those two opposites, arithmetical

---

[1] Philolaos, in **LXVIII**, B. 4 and 11, middle.

unity,[1] which is probably what Philolaos called the Even-Odd (ἀρτιοπέρισσον), or the third quality of number. There was a systematic table of these pairs of opposites, almost certainly drawn up by the Pythagoreans of the second generation, which gave seven other oppositions, set out " in columns " (κατὰ συστοιχίαν) under the first three pairs—Left and Right, Female and Male, Quiescent and Moving, Curve and Straight Line, Darkness and Light, Bad and Good, Oblong and Square.[2] So there are ten pairs of opposites, neither more or less, for 10 is the perfect number. That is why, no doubt, False and True were not put in, although Philolaos placed Error on the side of the Unlimited.[3] This queer symbolism contains many other obscurities, some of which will perhaps be cleared up a little in what follows.

Now, how was number conceived ? From the example of Eurytos's method mentioned above, from the evidence of Aristotle, and from a curious fragment of Speusippos's work, *On the Pythagorean Numbers*,[4] it seems to have been conceived in extension. Numbers are not arithmetical sums, but figures and sizes. 1 is the point, 2, the line, 3, the triangle, 4, the tetrahedron ; numbers are the causes of things in that they are the *limits* or *terms* (ὅροι) which define them, as points determine figures. So a symbolical sign, such as a letter of the alphabet, is not a sufficient representation of a number. Before all, it is necessary to show intuitively, by a construction, how number is a harmony of the Unlimited and the Limit, the latter bounding an undetermined space by its unit-terms. In short, number is not yet conceived in a rigorously abstract form, for, without therefore being considered as something continuous, it is a spatial figurative construction of points separated from one another.

The chief factor in this construction is what the Pythagoreans call the " gnomon," that is, the *set-square* by means of which numbers, and therefore things, are " defined " materially, form homogeneous groups, and so become knowable.[5] Thus, if we set the gnomon round unity, represented by a point, the gnomon will be described by three points.

---

[1] Therefore not the same as the One, the simple term opposed to the Many.
[2] Arist., *Metaph.*, A. 5, 986 a 22–b 4.   [3] **LXVIII**, B. 11, end of § 4.
[4] Texts *ibid.*, ch. 32, A.13 ; ch. 33, A. 3 ; ch. 45, B. 9, 25.
[5] Cf. Philolaos, frag. 11, § 2, end.

If we place the gnomon outside the figure so obtained, five points will now be needed to represent it.

In short, for this setting of the gnomon we shall have, starting from unity, to use in succession a number of points corresponding to the series of odd numbers—3, 5, 7, and so on. Now, at each setting we shall obtain the *same* figure, in which the ratio of the sides is always the same, that is, a square, so that the numbers obtained will have to be called squares themselves, 4, 9, 16, and so on. *Square*, therefore, is in the column under *Odd*, and Odd is under *Limit*, since, in an odd number, the gap between the two equal parts is always filled by an intermediate unity, and, moreover, the series of odd gnomons creates figures which are completely limited. If, on the contrary, we wished to enclose, not one point, but two, in the gnomon, the figure would be *other* every time. The first time the gnomon would be described by four points ; then six would be needed to enclose the figure thus obtained. So it would continue, the gnomons being constituted by the series of even numbers (after 2)—4, 6, 8, etc.

Now, we see that in the figures so obtained the ratio of the sides is never the same ; they are, therefore, *oblong* figures (*heteromekes*), and the numbers constituted by these figures, 6, 12, 20, etc., will also be called oblong. So, for reasons the inverse of those given above, *Oblong* comes on the side of *Even*, and *Even* on that of *Unlimited*.[1] Lastly, it seems certain that the Pythagoreans, by the same method and in the same spirit, distinguished other species of numbers, some plane (such as the rectilinear and the polygonal, the simplest of which are triangular) and others solid. It will suffice to consider the example of the rectilinear numbers, or, as they have been called, the oddly-odd. Being " made of limiters," says Philolaos,[2] they are " fields of work which limit " in their turn ; that means that they are made of odds and are

---

[1] **LXVIII**, ch. 45, B. 2 and 28. Cf. **XXI**, 113–17.
[2] **LXVIII**, ch. 32, B. 2 ; cf. A. 13. See also Theon, *Arithmetic.*

odd themselves, so that they can be measured by no number but themselves or unity ; so, too, a right line is similarly situated in respect of all its points, and *Right* therefore appears in the table on the same side as *Odd* and *Limit.*

It is important to note that all these arithmetical speculations are derived from religious inspiration ; it was by a deepening of this mystical inspiration that speculative arithmetic was finally separated from utilitarian reckonings. Nevertheless, especially in early Pythagoreanism, to discover some property of numbers was always to discover some symbolic quality or some characteristic divine " epithet " in them.[1] Thus, 3 is the first number which has " beginning, middle, and end," the first perfect number, that by which Harmony and the All are defined. But the number which is truly perfect, because, as Philolaos says,[2] it best manifests the " virtue " (δύναμις) of Number, is 10, " for it is large ; it perfects and realizes all things ; it is the principle and guide of divine and celestial life no less than human. . . . Without it, everything is indeterminate, mysterious, obscure." In 10 there are contained, for the first time, an equal number of evens and odds, unity with the first even, the first odd with the first square. It is the " foundation " of all numbers. 7 is Athene, in that it is the only number inside 10 which is not generated by any of the numbers which it contains and generates none of them. Moreover, it and 4 are arithmetical means between 1 and 10.[3] Another favoured number is 9, the first odd square. As for the famous Tetractys, mentioned above,[4] which must not be confused with 4, it is, in principle, the series of the first four numbers, the sum of which makes 10 and is represented by the decadic triangle. It is also two geometrical progressions of four terms, starting with 1, with a ratio of 2 and 3 respectively. Now, the last terms of these, one of which is the first even cube and the other the first odd cube, when

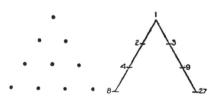

---

[1] Cf. **LXXVII,** Study 4, and, in De Falco's ed. of Iamblichos's *Theologumena* (Teubner), the index of *Epitheta numerorum.*
[2] Philol., frag. 11, beginning.
[3] 1+3=4 ; 4+3=7 ; 7+3=10.
[4] Above, p. 54. Cf. **LXXVII,** 8th Study.

added together and to 1, give the sum of the first eight numbers, four even and four odd.

The contribution of Pythagoreanism to the creation of an independent geometry is stamped with the same character. It is said that when Pythagoras discovered the abstract demonstration of the ratio, already known to the Egyptians (above, p. 31), of the hypotenuse of a right-angled triangle to its sides, he thanked the gods for the revelation by sacrificing a goat to them. Without dwelling on other theorems or problems the demonstrative solution of which is said to have been discovered by the school, or on the terms which it is said to have introduced into the language of geometry, we shall mention only its undoubted studies on at least some of the regular polyhedra, and especially on the tetrahedron and dodecahedron. Now, it was from this figure, cutting it in half into two pentagons, which break up in their turn each into six smaller pentagons, that the Pythagoreans got the famous mystical emblem of the *pentalpha*, or pentagram, which implies the division of the right line in mean and extreme ratio. Lastly, even if there is no truth in the story that Hippasos treasonably divulged the mystery of the incommensurability of the diagonal, it is not impossible that, in their desire to represent the relationship between the hypotenuse and sides of a right-angled triangle in unit-points, when those sides were 1, they were led to reflect upon the surds.

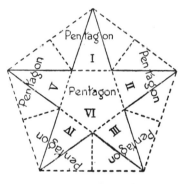

The consideration of musical concords, which may, as we saw, have been the principle of the doctrine, and probably, too, the consideration of the canon of the statuary,[1] gave the Pythagoreans occasion to discover and study *means* or *proportions*, arithmetical, geometrical, and harmonic. Philolaos (frag. 6, § 2) has made a very precise analysis of the octave, which he calls " harmony," that is, the ratio of the length of the four strings of a lyre, bottom, third, middle, and top, represented

---

[1] H. Diels (**LXVIII**, ch. 28) connects the *Canon* of Polycleitos with Pythagorean inspiration

by integers, 6, 8, 9, 12. He calculated the intervals and the various numerical ratios of the consonances—of the *syllabe* (fourth) between the first and second strings or between the last and third, of that " which goes over the high-pitched strings " (the fifth), between the first and third strings or between the second and last, and, lastly, of that " which goes over all the strings " (the octave, ἡ διὰ πασῶν). We then have the " double ratio," 12 : 6, or 4 : 2. Now, this ratio of 12 : 6 is exactly equal to the ratio of the excess of the last string over the second to the excess of the second string over the first, that is, as 12 minus 8 to 8 minus 6. Without pursuing this analysis in detail, we may be content to note two things. The numerical proportions in which the facts of experience are expressed will afterwards make it possible to advance beyond these latter, and, for example, to find the relative length of one string by the study of a proportion. This use of mathematics is of great importance to the progress of science. Secondly, when Philolaos called the cube " geometric harmony, because it has twelve edges, eight corners, and six faces,[1] he showed by a bold analogy how numerical relation, isolated from its matter, becomes capable of being extended to many various things.

We know little of the Pythagorean cosmology, chiefly, no doubt, because our witnesses are more interested in the mathematical speculations of the school, and perhaps also because it was not very different from that of Anaximandros, and, still more, that of Anaximenes. Being a harmony, the world is a thing which has begun, and its generation must be analogous to that of the harmony of number, that is, the determination of an indeterminate empty space. For the world was formed by a kind of aspiration of the unlimited air (πνεῦμα) which is outside the sky ; and the void, having been thus absorbed into the sky, thenceforward separates all the things in it. The agent of this aspiration and the resulting determination is a mysterious central fire, which the Pythagoreans called symbolically " the Mother of the Gods," that is, of the stars, the " hearth " of the universe, the " watch-post of Zeus," his " throne " or his " tower," the " point of attachment " and " unit of measure " of nature. If, therefore, Hippasos regarded fire as the first principle, it is no proof that

---

[1] *Ibid.*, ch. 32. A. 24.

he must have been influenced by Heracleitos. Particular things were then produced by condensations and rarefactions. That implies a vacuum, and the same applies to the theory of Ecphantos, a Pythagorean of the second generation, who regarded the extended units as true atoms. However that may be, the world, thus constituted, and more or less in the manner of a living being, becomes organized progressively, and good is only brought about gradually.[1] But, far from being an endless progress, this evolution comes to an end, at least according to Philolaos, in the " Great Year," to begin once more, perfectly identical with itself.[2] Lastly, there are many worlds, but not infinitely many ; we even hear of a calculation of Petron regarding the number of these worlds, arranged in a triangle.

Round the central fire everything is arranged and the ten celestial bodies revolve in circles. The highest part, the envelope of the universe, was called *Olympos ;* it comprised the sky of the fixed stars, whose own motion from east to west may perhaps have been first recognized by Pythagoras, and also another fire, opposite the central fire, in which the elements exist in all their purity. Underneath is the *Cosmos,* in which the five planets move, in the opposite direction to the sky of the fixed stars, with the sun and moon. Lastly, the *Uranos,* properly so called, is the sublunary, circumterrestrial region, that of unordered becoming and imperfection. Without lingering over the obscure question why this should be so, in spite of the proximity of the directing principle, we shall note only that, if the earth is no longer at the centre, it becomes a star like the other stars, moving round the central fire, so as to produce the succession of days and nights. But what use could the Pythagoreans then see in the daily revolution, which was the proper cause of that succession in the geocentric hypothesis ? This problem, which has long been debated by the historians of astronomy, seems at present inextricable.

What is at least very certain, is that, between the central fire and the earth, turning with the earth on a smaller orbit and facing the hemisphere which we do not inhabit (so as to be invisible to us), they placed a " Counter-earth," so bringing

---

[1] Arist., *Metaph.,* Λ. 7, 1072 b 30–4 ; cf. **CXX**, p. 510, n. 455, i.
[2] As with the Stoics later.

the number of celestial bodies up to ten. The object of this body, and perhaps also of other bodies, equally invisible, seems to have been to explain the eclipses of the moon, and the fact that they are more frequent than eclipses of the sun. For it is from the central fire that the moon and even the sun, like mirrors, receive their light, and the sun its heat, which they then reflect on to us. So one must distinguish between three suns, one being the orb itself, that is, the mirror, one, the rays falling on it from the central fire, and the third the rays reflected towards us. It is said that certain Pythagoreans explained day and night, not by supposing an eastward revolution of the planet earth, by which it received or lost these rays alternately, but by declaring that the earth rotated on its axis, whether, like Hicetas of Syracuse (who is perhaps not merely the fictitious interpreter of the personal opinion of Heracleides of Pontus, in a dialogue of that Platonist), they left the fire in the centre of the universe, or, as Ecphantos is said to have done, placed the earth there.[1] The sun, before the burning of Phaëthon, travelled, not along the Zodiac, but along the Milky Way, which, moreover, some Pythagoreans regarded as the dust of a star which had been burned up and scattered. Lastly, according to Philolaos,[2] the moon, in proportion to its longer days, possessed bigger and more beautiful beasts and plants than those on earth.

It was natural that the mathematical spirit of the school should set its stamp on this cosmology. Each star was the proper place of a number. The central fire being the place of One the principle, the Counter-earth was that of the first 1 of the decad, the earth was that of 2, or Opinion, the sun was that of 7, because, starting from the fixed stars, it held the seventh rank, and also the place of the " right time," since it governed the course of the seasons, and so on.

Nor is there any doctrine more famous than that of the " harmony of the spheres," the foundation of which must have existed, even if, against numerous testimonies, we hold that at least the earliest Pythagoreans adhered to the conception of the stars established by Anaximandros and Anaximenes. That this doctrine was at least very ancient in the tradition of the society, is proved by the fact that in the catechism of

---

[1] **LXVIII**, ch. 37, 1 (cf. below, p 237) ; ch. 38, 1, end, and 5.
[2] *Ibid.*, ch. 32, A 20.

the Acusmatics the Delphic Oracle is identified with the Tetractys and with the harmony " in which the Sirens are." [1] If a body, moving fairly fast, emits a sound, the same must, by analogy, be true of the stars. Now, their speed must vary with their distance, as the speed of vibrations varies with the length of the lyre-string. Therefore there must be in the celestial system the consonances of the lyre. Why do we not hear this harmony ? For the very reason that we have never ceased to hear it, and that a sound is only heard in relation to periods of silence. As a matter of fact, in the presence of our contradictory evidence, it is hard to obtain a precise idea of the details of this musical astronomy.[2]

It is impossible to consider the biological and medical conceptions of the Pythagoreans apart from their relations with the medical school of Croton,[3] and particularly with Alcmaeon.[4] We must, therefore, briefly survey the theories of Alcmaeon regarding physiology and psychology.

Whereas, before his time and even later, the heart was regarded as the common sensorium and seat of thought, he ascribed that function to the brain, to which channels, or " pores," transmitted modifications produced in the organs of sense. For every disturbance in the brain—and Alcmaeon is said to have observed it by dissection, being the first to practise it—affects the sensibility. Each kind of sensation, except perhaps touch, was studied by him, in its organ and in its operation. There is, for example, a sensation of sound when the cavity of the ear, which is empty, resounds at the contact of the outside air. It is said that he studied the course of the optic nerves and recognized three factors in vision [5] —light, or the outside fire, the fire inside the eye, whose existence is made manifest by the fact that when the eye is struck it is illuminated, and, lastly, as a mean between these opposites, the water in the membranes surrounding the eye-ball.

Above sensation, which is common to beasts and men, is intelligence, which man alone possesses. But thought, as science, is for him only the *stable* mode of memory and opinion,

---

[1] **LXXVII**, 132 ff., 260 ff., 276.

[2] It reappears, more or less transformed, in the Myth of Er, in Plato, *Rep.*, x. Cf. below, pp. 197-8.

[3] Milon, one of the heads of the party, married the daughter of Democedes, who was the physician of Darius and cured his wife Atossa.

[4] His book was dedicated to three Pythagoreans, one of whom was Brotinos.

[5] Cf. Plato, *Tim.*, 45 b ff. ; *Soph.*, 266 c.

the basis of which is sensation. The soul is the very principle of life. " Men die," he said (Frag. 2), " because they cannot join the beginning to the end." The soul, on the contrary, is immortal, because, like the stars, whose movement is eternal, in that it is circular and always returns upon itself, it is always moving. His very varied researches in embryogenesis show that he was concerned to know how that principle of life gives birth to an individual being. Death, in his opinion, comes from a reflux of the blood in the veins, chiefly, perhaps, in those of the brain ; it is similar to that which causes sleep, only more complete. Health is the result of the equilibrium (ἰσονομία) and proportionate mixture (κρᾶσις) of qualities (δυνάμεις) which, in accordance with a general law (which may have been first inspired by the Pythagoreans, or by Alcmaeon and the medical school which he adorned ; we do not know which), are opposed in twos—wet and dry, cold and hot, bitter and sweet. Sickness, on the other hand, is the supremacy of one term of one of these pairs. In addition to this determining cause, it is important to know the circumstance which gave rise to it, such as excess or insufficiency of nourishment and the seat of the upset equilibrium, and the external causes, such as the nature of the water or the configuration of the country (Frag. 4).

It was probably under this influence that the younger Pythagoreans, the " scientists," and notably Philolaos,[1] set up a doctrine of medicine very different from what the catechism of the Acusmatics calls " the wisest of human things," which was doubtless merely a religious method of purification. For this new medicine was inspired by the observation of facts, while it tried to interpret them in the light of a general doctrine. By analogy with the world and its central fire, the principle of the human body seems to be the Hot, heat of the seed, heat of the womb, and the desire of that heat to be tempered by cold. It attracts the outer air to itself (that is birth) and returns it by expiration, without which it would destroy itself. Excess and insufficiency of cooling, by acting on the blood, on the humours, on the bile, indirectly cause maladies. Thus normal life is a harmony, a concordance of contraries. Here

---

[1] His ideas on the subject are known to us through Anonymus Londiniensis, the compiler of the *History of Medicine* of the Peripatetic Menon. Cf. **LXVIII**, ch. 32, A. 27

we recognize the thesis maintained by Simmias of Thebes, a pupil of Philolaos, in Plato's *Phaedon*.[1]

But there is something more in that thesis ; namely, that that concord, that harmony of the body, is the soul. The body is like a lyre, the opposition between hot and cold, etc., taking the place of that between high-pitched and low. As contraries, they " stretch " it ; as correlatives, they maintain its unity. If the tension is relaxed or increased too much, the harmony is destroyed and the soul dies, even before the destruction of the body is complete.[2] There is no doubt that the theory is Pythagorean. Plato says that it had the support of Echecrates, who is connected with Philolaos and Eurytos, and it is found in Aristoxenos and, with some differences, in Dicaearchos, both of whom were influenced by Pythagoreanism. Moreover, the remarkable foursome of intelligence and brain, sensibility and heart, embryonic life and navel, generation and sexual organs, mentioned in Fragment 13 of Philolaos, seems to be associated with a similar conception.[3] Yet, how can it be reconciled with another doctrine likewise ascribed to Philolaos (Frag. 14) ? If the soul, as a punishment of its faults, has been buried in the body as in a tomb (σῶμα, σῆμα), it must be a reality independent of the body. And the second Pythagorean of the *Phaedon*, Cebes, also a pupil of Philolaos, adds another theory : the soul is not a result, for it weaves several mortal bodies for itself in succession, at length wearing itself out in the process, and dying before the last of its garments.[4] Lastly, Aristotle, who does not mention the Pythagoreans when he speaks of the harmony-soul, ascribes only two opinions expressly to them. One, whose connexions with Atomism he points out, is to the effect that the soul is dust floating about in the air, made visible to us by a ray of sunlight, and always moving about, even in the calmest weather. According to the other, the soul is the very principle of their movement.[5] If we take the thesis of Simmias together with this last indication, we shall perhaps find the real thought of Philolaos in the proposition, ascribed to him,[6]

---

[1] *Phaedon*, 86 b-c.   [2] *Ibid.*, 86 c-d.

[3] Aristotle's criticism (*De An.*, i. 4, 408 a 10–13) seems to refer to this conception.

[4] *Phaed.*, 86 e-87 e.   [5] *De An.*, i. 4, beginning, and 2, 404 a 16–20.

[6] **LXVIII**, ch. 32, B. 22. That the Περὶ ῥυθμῶν καὶ μετρῶν, from which Claudianus Mamertus gets it, is inauthentic is no proof that the foundation may not be correct. Cf. **II**, 553 (3) (French trans., i. 424).

that the soul is " what brings number and harmony into the body." At least we see how difficult it is to disentangle from all this even the merely probable features of a philosophical theory of the soul.

On the other hand, one can say something more definite about the famous belief of the Pythagoreans in the transmigration of souls, " metensomatosis," not, as it is commonly called, " metempsychosis." Three things only, Porphyry said,[1] are well known of the teachings of Pythagoras—that the soul is immortal ; that it passes into animals of different species and living beings recommence their previous life in accordance with certain cycles (like the world itself) ; and that all animate beings are " of the same kind." Connected with these doctrines, which are probably of Orphic origin, is Pythagoras's declaration that he is the fifth reincarnation of a son of Hermes, to whom his father gave the power, inherited by Pythagoras in his turn, of remembering the whole series of his previous existences. These privileged ones also remember the intervals between their incarnations which they have spent in Hades, where the souls of the dead undergo the penalties to which they have been condemned. So we have the " descents into the underworld " of Pythagoras and many others. This memory, which is for them the sign of the continuity of their existence, also recalls to them the plants and animals through whose bodies their souls have passed. For in any case, even if there is no punishment in Hades, incarnation always means that the soul has not completed the cycle of its purifications ; it is a stage in palingenesia, a means of final redemption. We know the lines in which Xenophanes, a contemporary of Pythagoras, chaffs him for staying the hand of a man who is beating his dog : " Stop ! Do not hit him ! " he says. " It is the soul of a friend of mine. I recognized it when I heard his voice."[2] Aristotle also speaks of these Pythagorean " myths," according to which any soul may enter any body.[3] Now all this is comprehensible only if there is a kinship in species, uniting everything which lives.

It may be that these dogmas, doubtless in connexion with certain traditions of folk-lore, are at the bottom of some of the Pythagorean taboos. One must abstain from beans because

[1] *Life of Pythag.*, 19 (cf. 18), perhaps from Dicaearchos.
[2] Frag. 7 D.   [3] *De An.*, i. 3, end.

the bean-stalk, containing no knots, is a natural passage for souls rising from Hades to the light. Certain animals are more especially sacred because, perhaps, they are more suited than others to receive souls leaving Hades, in virtue of their connexion with the infernal deities.[1] Does this mean that every attack on the body affects the soul, as if it were something of the body ? The reason is rather of the same order as that in the name of which the Pythagoreans forbade men to take their own lives ; [2] we are the " property " of the gods, and it is not for us, except in the religious ceremony of sacrifice, to upset the order which our masters have laid down for the incarnation of souls, with a view to the expiations needed. We see, therefore, that, although some scientific Pythagoreans admitted, by the theory of the soul as a harmony of the body, that the body died by the actual death of its soul, this doctrine must have been a subject of scandal and horror to pious Pythagoreans.

In passing, we have mentioned one of the chief propositions of Pythagorean theology. It is wholly bound up with the moral rule that man " must have commerce with the divine and follow God." This formula raises the question of Pythagorean monotheism. Certainly, reflective thought was at that time tending towards the oneness of the divine, to a complete sovereignty of Zeus. But, with the exception of a very suspect fragment of Philolaos (20), there is no text authorizing us to credit the Pythagoreans with the metaphysical theology which identifies the primitive One with God, as being a transcendent, efficient, organizing cause, in opposition to the Unlimited, which is matter. All that we are told in this sense [3] is simply a Platonic version of early Pythagoreanism. What we find in the probably authentic fragments of Philolaos is, not that God is a first cause, whose efficient power is limited by the resistance of matter, but, on the contrary, that Number and Harmony are first in relation to God, since the Decad lays its law on the divine life as on the human, and the eternal essence ($\dot{a}$ $\dot{\epsilon}\sigma\tau\dot{\omega}$) of things merely allows itself to be penetrated by the divine thought more easily than by ours.[4] All that the Pythagoreans did, then, was to purify popular polytheism and to adapt it to their morality and even to their mathematical theory.

---

[1] On all this, cf. **LXXVII**, 36–8, 289–93.   [2] *Phaedon*, 62 b.
[3] Even by Theophrastos. Cf. **LXVIII**, ch. 45, B. 14.
[4] Frag. 11, § 1, and Frag. 6, beginning.

In sum, Pythagoreanism was at once a religious sect, giving its followers a creed and a rule of life by which to obtain purification and salvation, and a philosophic school, to which thought owes its first successes in its attempt to come at the abstract essence of things and to assign simple and intelligible laws to phenomena. They were physicists, there is no doubt. But in the manner in which they were physicists, by taking number as the principle of things and seeking the supreme law in a harmony of notional oppositions, they went far beyond the physics of the School of Miletos and laid the foundations of a metaphysical philosophy.

CHAPTER III

THE PHILOSOPHY OF BECOMING. HERACLEITOS
OF EPHESOS

THERE is even more philosophy, in the strict sense of the word, in Heracleitos than in the Pythagoreans. Under the name of " polymathy," he condemns the indulgence of Pythagoras and even Xenophanes [1] in particular inquiries which destroys the direct vision of the real. He is a headstrong, haughty genius who wishes to owe nothing save to the purely speculative intuition of the truth. Scornful of details, he develops the various aspects of that original intuition into a philosophy. He has the temperament of an inspired, solitary man, of a " melancholic," as Theophrastos says.[2] In his native town, where his illustrious birth called him to a great part in affairs, he lived cut off from politics. A democratic revolution drove out his friend Hermodoros, perhaps the man who collaborated in the Law of the Twelve Tables. When the Ephesians thus gave the city over " to children," they said, " Let no one be the best among us ! Let any such go elsewhere, and among other men ! " [3] From this indication his book must belong roughly to the end of the first half of the Vth century. It seems to have been a collection of aphorisms in prose, in a language rich in imagery and antithesis, often incomprehensible, which earned Heracleitos his proverbial nickname of " the Dark." This oracular style, which, as he himself says,[4] " neither expresses nor conceals thought, but indicates it," suits a man with a strong, and even excessive, sense of his own superiority. Moreover, it is undeniable that the whole effectiveness of his

---

[1] Frag. 40 D. Cf. above, p. 50.
[2] Diog. Laërt., ix. 6. With this word is connected the legend of the perpetually weeping Heracleitos, amusingly treated by Lucian in his *Auction of the Sects* (14 ; cf. **LXVIII**, ch. 12, C. 5).
[3] Frag. 121 D.   [4] Frags. 92, 93.

ideas is often due to the conciseness of his phrases and the brilliance of his images. But the somewhat charlatanish note in his arrogant tone and Sibylline brevity could not fail to appear in a caricature like that drawn of the Master by the Heracleiteans of the end of the century.

The trend of his thought is marked, first, by the lordly indifference with which he treats special research in physics, being content with popular notions. The sun, for example, is " new every day," for when it sets it is extinguished. " It is a foot wide," as it looks to us (Frag. 6 and 3 D.). All the stars are a kind of basins. In their concave side, which is towards us, bright and dark exhalations accumulate in turn ; hence day and night. If the dark exhalations, which are moist, predominate over the bright, we have winter ; in the contrary case, summer. The phases of the moon are explained by its basin turning partly round. When the basin of a star turns right round, it is eclipsed. Altogether, he seems to have neglected many points in favour of generalities.

The principle from which all things come and to which they return is fire. " This world, which is the same for all things, was made by no god or man. It has always been, it is, and it will be an ever-living fire, kindling with measure and being quenched with measure " (Frag. 30). " There is exchange ($\dot{\alpha}\nu\tau\alpha\mu\omega\iota\beta\dot{\eta}$) of all things against fire, and of fire against all things, as there is exchange of goods against gold and of gold against goods " (Frag. 90). There is no doubt of the dynamic intention : a single substance assumes different forms, on the sole condition that equivalence is maintained among these permutations ($\tau\rho\omega\pi\dot{\eta}$), which are its very life. But, in addition, to give birth to a world, this spontaneous power of changing manifests itself by movement and doubtless gives rise to condensations and rarefactions. For there are, according to Heracleitos, a " way up " and a " way down " ($\dot{\omicron}\delta\dot{\omicron}\varsigma$ $\ddot{\alpha}\nu\omega$, $\kappa\dot{\alpha}\tau\omega$. Frag. 60). These are the two fundamental directions of change. On the downward road, part of the fire thickens and becomes sea, and part of the sea causes land to be born of its " death." On the upward road, moist vapours rise from the land and sea, become clouds, ignite, and return to fire. But if these burning clouds, from which the lightning comes, are extinguished, there is a " whirlwind " ($\pi\rho\eta\sigma\tau\dot{\eta}\rho$) ; once again the fire returns to the sea, and the

HERACLEITOS 73

cycle recommences.[1] The two inverse movements compensate one another, so that, in all the diversity or vicissitude of changes, the quantity of matter exchanged, that is, of fire, remains the same.

Yet it does not seem that it must be so always. For there is not sufficient ground [2] for denying that Heracleitos expected an " universal conflagration " (ἐκπύρωσις). Fire, he said, is " want and satiety " (Frag. 65). " Want " must express the desire which gives rise to the formation of a world, " satiety " the fullness which results from the absorption by fire of all that it had first given away in exchange. " As it advances, fire will judge and convict all things " (Frag. 66). In the course of its successive exchanges, fire always gets back a little more. So, when the Stoics took the essential ideas of their physics from Heracleitos, they did not add this ; they may have given it its traditional name, but nothing more. Besides, Aristotle attributes it to him,[3] without using that name, and agrees with Plato in saying that this total unification of the many takes place in periods, and also in distinguishing its rhythm from that later described by Empedocles. Evolution and involution, while opposing and compensating one another, are continued one into the other, just as a child is continued in the man that he becomes and the man in the child that he begets. It is said that Heracleitos blamed Homer for wishing that Discord might be abolished among men as among the gods ; for this would cause the passing of all things and the annihilation of the universe.[4] For him, on the contrary, this flight is continued in a return. Therefore the death of the world is only apparent ; it is really its life reborn. The cosmic cycles probably balanced one another just as the births and deaths did within each of them, and each day of the " Great Year " of the universe may have been exactly the length of a human generation.[5]

So the main ideas governing Heracleitos's philosophy gradually emerge. First, the opposition and identity of contraries are the condition of the becoming of things. " It is the same in us," he said, " to be what is living and to be what is dead, awake

---

[1] Frags. 31, 36 ; cf. Diog. Laërt., ix. 9 and **LXVIII**, A. 8.
[2] Contrary to the opinion of **LXXI**, § 78.   [3] *Phys.*, iii. 5, 205 a 3.
[4] Plato, *Soph.*, 242 d-e, and, for Aristotle, **LXVIII**, ch. 12, A. 8. Cf. A. 22 (and especially Bywater, 43, which is more complete), and compare the palingenesia based on the succession of contraries in *Phaedon*, 72 b-d.
[5] **LXVIII**, a. 13. Cf. **LXXI**, §§ 75 end, 77.

and asleep, young and old ; for, by change, one is the other, and by change the other, in its turn, is the former " (Frag. 88 ; cf. 57). This perpetual opposition of contraries is, therefore, the principle and the law. " War (πόλεμος) is the father of all things, the king of all things " (Frag. 53), whereas concord and peace are the confusion of all things in the general conflagration.[1] Since warring contraries always tend to substitute themselves for one another, things are in a state of unceasing movement. " Everything flows " (πάντα ῥεῖ), and everything flees ; nothing abides. In one river, the water which washes you is always different ; you will not dip twice in the same water.[2] But this is only one aspect of the universal conflict. In another aspect, it creates a solidarity between the terms which it brings into opposition, for " war is community (ξύνον) and discord is regulation (δίκη) (Frag. 80). So the " course of the contraries " follows " fatal necessity," which seems to constitute both what is fixed and stable in change and what unites pairs of opposites in definite and relatively permanent forms.[3] So discord and instability have their counterpart in agreement and, with it, the necessity of law. " The discordant," he says, " agrees with itself— a harmony of opposite tensions, as in the bow or the lyre " (Frag. 51). The arrow flies, the musical phrase sounds, when the bowman's hands pull the bow and the string in opposite directions, when the musician's fingers draw the strings of the lyre apart from one another. Moreover, the action of these oppositions is regulated and limited ; for example, the straightening of the bow is limited by the rigidity of the bowstring, and the angular tension of the string towards the bowman's body is limited by the limited flexibility of the bow. The same idea is expressed in several vivid phrases. " Things which are cut in opposite directions " (like mortise and tenon) " fit together. The fairest harmony is born of things different, and discord is what produces all things " (Frag. 8). " Let us unite wholes and not-wholes, convergence and divergence, harmony and discord of voices ; of all things, one only, and of one only, all " (Frag. 10).[4] So there is neither confusion

---

[1] Diog. Laërt., 8.
[2] Frags. 12, 49 a, 91. Cf. Plato, Crat., 402 a ; Theaet., 179 d-e.
[3] Diog. Laërt., 7–8 ; cf. LXVIII, A. 5 and 8, and Frag. 84.
[4] Compare the Hippocratic treatise De Victu, i. 17, in which a long passage bears the mark of Heracleitean inspiration (5–24).

nor frittering away, but a varied order of combinations, the agent of which seems to be time ; time is " a child playing at draughts ; the sovereignty of a child ! " (Frag. 52).

But the childish kingship of the player himself cannot be a true kingship ; for that belongs only to the play of contraries and to the harmony which binds them, that is, to God. God is " day and night, winter and summer, war and peace, satiety and hunger " (Frag. 67) ; he is " the invisible Harmony, superior to visible harmony " (Frag. 54). For, according to Heracleitos, there is " one single divine law," which feeds all human laws, but appears to be something other than the unwritten law as opposed to arbitrary decisions, since it is in it that individual thought must " find its strength, as the city in the law " ; it is " something common to everything " which " dominates everything, as much as it pleases, is sufficient in everything, and surpasses everything " (Frag. 114). In short, it is the universal law of the real, identical, it seems, with the " common thought " (ξυνὸς λόγος) which Heracleitos says we must follow (Frag. 2), yet which remains unknown to men, who are blind to what is always before their eyes (Frag. 72). It is a " single wisdom," which " wishes to be called by the name of Zeus," and also " does not wish it," if it is to be in the sense of popular religion, and consists in " knowing the purpose in which everything is ruled in its totality " (Frags. 32, 41). But this single law or thought is an immanent *logos*, the very substance of the exchanges which produce the various things, in other words, fire, that which is most incorporeal, most mobile, most transformable, most active, and most life-giving. In sum, the reaction of the philosophical genius of Heracleitos against popular polytheism is a pantheism, and that pantheism is a physical pantheism.

From this a whole theory of knowledge follows logically. The *logos* is both the divine thought which goes about in nature eternally, and human thought, in so far only as it takes part in that single, eternal movement, and so loses its individuality.[1] Yet men think of nothing but piling up particular bits of knowledge, the abominable " polymathy " ; or else they imagine that the common thought to be followed

---

[1] " Thought," *pensée*, seems to me the best term by which to translate the Greek *logos*, for we designate by it both the content, or object, and the formula which is the intelligible expression of it.

is that of the crowd, and they take their lessons from it. Like asses, " they prefer straw to gold " (Frags. 104 and 9). But it is not his own personal thought that Heracleitos haughtily sets up against the opinions of the learned and of the crowd. It is—and that, too, is the meaning of a solemn declaration which stood at the beginning of his book (Frag. 1) —the Truth, one and eternal, of the divine thought, of which he is the inspired prophet, which is all the real. " Not to me is it wise to lend ear, but to Thought, confessing that all is one " (Frag. 50). On the contrary, individualism in thought, the illusion that " every man has an intelligence of his own " (Frag. 2), is the proper characteristic of knowledge through the senses. Heracleitos vigorously points out how relative it is. Our senses are bad witnesses, if the soul is a " barbarian," unable to penetrate the mystery of their language (Frag. 107). Moreover, whereas thought " gives itself its own growth " (Frag. 115), our senses are dependent on the contraries, without, at the same time, taking harmony into account.

Above the knowledge of the senses, therefore, Heracleitos seems to have placed an absolute truth and a certain kind of scientific knowledge. It is, therefore, hard to understand how Aristotle could say that for Heracleitos there was neither science, because of the perpetual flow of sensible things, nor truth, because he denied the principle of contradiction.[1] But these criticisms are doubtless aimed at those fanatics (whom Plato obviously had in mind) [2] who did not consider Heracleitos's theory of motion sufficiently radical, and held, with the Cratylos under whom Plato is said to have studied before he knew Socrates,[3] that the water of a river is not identical even once. In order to express thought, Cratylos preferred a mere movement of the finger to the words which fix it ! Such excesses can hardly be explained unless they came after Eleaticism, as an exaggerated vindication of multiplicity and change against the exaggerated assertion of unity and immobility. The harmony of contraries was what Heracleitos sought, not the identity of contradictories, which, indeed, as such, were unknown to him. Far from consenting to the dissipation of sensuous knowledge on all the transitory aspects

---

[1] *Metaph.*, Γ. 3, 1005 b 23 ff. ; *Phys.*, i. 2, 185 b 19–23, etc.
[2] *Theaet.*, 179 e ff. Cf. *Crat.*, 334 a.
[3] *Metaph.*, A. 6, beginning, and Γ. 5, 1010 a 7–15.

of becoming, he placed truth in the single substance, whose law serves as a continuous woof and foundation to that ever-changing diversity.

His theory of the soul reflects this general conception. The soul is a hot exhalation; for, in order to know the principle, it must have its mobility, spread everywhere, like it, so that everything is full of souls and geniuses, govern the body as fire governs the world, and transform itself just as fire does. The wisest soul is a dry soul; when it is moistened, as happens in drunkenness, it dies. When we emerge from the torpor of sleep, we begin once more to inhale the thought which is in fire, like embers being rekindled.[1] But the true state of waking is that in which, dead or alive, asleep or not, we see " the unity and community of the cosmos " (Frag. 89). The individuality of life is a death, and immortality consists in setting oneself again, during this life if one can, in the universal stream. " Immortals are mortal; mortals are immortal; our life is the death of the former, and their life is our death " (Frag. 62). This is the Orphic belief, shorn of personal immortality. Hades and Dionysos are one and the same god (Frag. 15), and, as the total conflagration is a new-born life for the world, so is death for man.

This profound sense of the identity of true thought with the law of the universe inspires Heracleitos with a perfectly consequent conception of the moral life. " Wisdom," he says, before the Stoics, " is to say true things and to act according to nature, listening to its voice " (Frag. 112). " It would be no better for men if what they want came to them " (Frag. 110). If passion is to be condemned, it is because it expresses the claim of the individual to raise himself above the natural or divine order and to forget his dependence. " Baby ! So man is called by God, just as the child by a man " (Frag. 79). In consequence, true religion must be the merging of one's thought in the divine thought of the fire which goes about in the universe. To worship images is as foolish as to talk to houses. To hold blood-sacrifices no more serves to purify us than mud can wash away a stain which it has made (Frag. 5).

The thought of Heracleitos, original, vigorous, and profound, left its stamp even on those thinkers who were its

[1] Cf., e.g., Frags. 36, 117 ff., and **LXVIII**, A. 15 and 16 ; Diog. Laërt., ix. 7.

most determined opponents. His conception of the opposition of contraries has a generality not found in Anaximandros or even in the Pythagoreans or Alcmaeon. But, above all, he set in a wholly new light the notion of a law immanent in becoming and serving as an intelligible bond to the contraries, simultaneous or successive. What one must not forget, however, what has been misunderstood both by the ancient philosophers of the concept who opposed Heracleitos and by the Hegelians of our own time who have exalted him, is the fact that he developed his ideas in the field and within the structure of the physics of his age, representing law as a substance of a more subtle kind, and not in the field of a logic which was not yet created, nor, therefore, with a view to breaking down its structure.

CHAPTER IV

THE PHILOSOPHY OF BEING. THE ELEATICS

IT is possible that the School of Elea was founded solely by Parmenides ; it is certain that he represents its fundamental doctrine in its most characteristic form, that Zenon of Elea only illustrated some of its consequences, that Melissos of Samos modified it without changing its spirit, and that, before Parmenides, the germ of the doctrine already existed in Xenophanes of Colophon. There is, therefore, every reason for not breaking up the traditional group of the " Eleatic race," as Plato calls them, and for following the example of Aristotle in this matter. At least morally, Xenophanes is the father of Eleaticism, since he originated the doctrine of the oneness of being.[1]

I

XENOPHANES OF COLOPHON

What he said of Pythagoras and what Heracleitos said of him—that will enable us roughly to place Xenophanes. It is difficult to be more precise, since we lack one piece of information in a bit of biography which we owe to himself. " Sixty-seven years," he writes, " have tossed my weary soul about the land of Hellas, and there were twenty-five more from my birth till it began " (Frag. 8). So he lived ninety-two years at least ; but when did his wandering life begin ? At the fireside, in the winter-time, men ask, " What is your

---

[1] Plato, Soph., 242 d, and Arist., Metaph., A. 5, 986 b 18–28. In **LXXI**, Xenophanes is discussed in chap. ii ("Science and Religion"), Parmenides in chap. iv, Zeno and Melissos, the " Younger Eleatics," in chap. viii. In **XII**, Xenophanes is attached to the Ionians. To dispose of Plato's authority, **LXXI** (140 and n. 3) points out that in Theaet., 179 e, Plato attaches Heracleitos to Homer. But the two cases are in no way parallel.

age, good man ? How old were you when the Mede came ? "
(Frag. 22). One may perhaps find in this question an allusion
to the piece of information which we lack ; he may have
left Ionia when his country was conquered by Harpagus in
the name of Cyrus (545 B.C.), about the time when some
Phocaean emigrants founded Marseilles and others Elea in
Great Greece. His voyages took him to Sicily and then to
Italy, and it is possible that he thereupon settled at Elea. If
his roving existence was, as is not certain, that of a rhapsode,
it at least does not seem to have made him rich, as it should
have done. For the verses which he recited at banquets
were doubtless his own, and, to judge from what remains of
his *Elegies* (in iambics) and his *Parodies* (in hexameters),[1]
his playful vein was too malicious, his thought too free, his
style too full of dignity and moral nobility, and his character
too independent, to attract the custom of the rich and
powerful. To these collections we should, perhaps, add,
among other writings, a poem on Nature (in hexameters),
from which several of our fragments may come. But, whether
Xenophanes wrote a separate philosophic poem or not, he
was a poet who, it cannot be seriously denied, had the soul
of a philosopher.

The most important thing in him is his attempt to
establish an order of values higher than that of sensible
experience, social opinion, and religious tradition, to conceive
of that order by means of highly critical moral reflection,
and to determine the relationship of experience to the moral
realities of which man conceives above himself and his physical
life. His method is no less remarkable ; instead of uttering
dogmatic oracles like Heracleitos, he brings his own views
out in the war which he wages against common opinion.
The dialectical spirit of the other Eleatics is already in him.

Thus, for instance, after attacking with stinging irony his
fellow-countrymen's worship of physical strength, skill, and
beauty, the conceit of Olympic victors, and the honours and
rewards which were heaped on them, which, in some cases,
would be more fairly given to their horses, he adds : " Yet
they are worth less than I. For our wisdom is better than

---

[1] The *Silloi*, from which many of our fragments are said to come, are perhaps
not a separate work, but another title given to the *Parodies* after Timon the
Sceptic wrote his imitations of Xenophanes.

the strength of men and horses. This may be a wild opinion —but it is not right, either, to esteem strength more than good wisdom!" (Frag. 2). So that is the only thing which has value beyond compare. Now, it is in thought that it has its principle; for it consists in a logical attitude, which is that, not of scepticism, but of the critical spirit. Rational knowledge is doubtless superior to sensuous knowledge, since it is able to judge both sensuous knowledge and itself, but it is none the less relative, like the other; we are incapable of absolute knowledge, and " opinion is the lot of all men " (Frag. 34). Truth is not a revelation of the gods, but the hard-won fruit of long research (Frag. 18).

Another example is no less significant. Against the anthropomorphic beliefs of popular religion, Xenophanes directed a criticism which by its eloquent bitterness reveals a singular loftiness of moral sentiment. Men, he says, have given themselves gods in their own image; thus " the Ethiopians say that theirs are black and flat-nosed, while the Thracians say that theirs have blue eyes and red hair." And again, " if oxen and horses and lions had hands and could paint and make works of art with their hands as men do, the horses would make the figures of gods like horses, and the oxen like oxen " (Frags. 14-16). What is more, " all that has been laid upon the gods by Homer and Hesiod is what is a shame and a reproach among men " (Frag. 11 ff.). But this negative criticism has its positive counterpart. If the tales of mythology contain " nothing salutary," there are " religious words " and " pure discourses " for extolling the gods wisely. They may be prayed " to make us able to do the things which are just "; in all this, the rule is " always to have thought for the gods " (Frag. 1, ll. 13 to end), or, in other words, to preserve the true nature of the divine and not to destroy it in its principle by the introduction of elements of sense and passion.

In this sense, Xenophanes comes at length to a remarkable conception of God, which is not monotheistic, as has sometimes been said, but rather pantheistic. This god, in the fragments in which the conception is found, is a single god, who is the highest reality both of the divine order and of the human. Not only does he not have our structure; he has not even our thought. " By the intelligent power of his thought, he sets everything in motion, without toil." " He sees wholly, thinks wholly, hears wholly," so that each of his attributes or acts extends to the totality of his nature. He does not move, and the idea of a change of place at any moment does not even " befit " his nature (which seems to imply that he is eternally everywhere) (Frags. 23-6). Now, Aristotle says [1] that, if Xenophanes was the first, before Parmenides, to " make One," he did not trouble to say whether that oneness is finite or infinite, material or formal ; but, " turning his eyes on the whole universe, he said that the One is God." This testimony of Aristotle, confirmed by the authors whose source is Theophrastos and by Timon the Sillographer,[2] enables us, by fixing the limits of Xenophanes' theory, to do justice to the developments which it receives in chapters 3 and 4 of *On Melissos, Xenophanes, and Gorgias.* The eclectic Peripatetic who, doubtless in the Ist century of our era, composed this little treatise,[3] ascribes to the philosopher-poet a discussion on dialectical antinomies (finite and infinite, movement and rest), which seems as foreign to his age as to the bent of his mind. Yet, in thus conceiving of all that is as one single being, who is wholly in all that is, eternal, motionless, unchangeable, God constituted by a thought higher than our own, Xenophanes was breaking completely with previous physics, and was defining the principle of things in an entirely new way. He was creating a new physical theory, the true name of which is ontology. Its method is one whose plan we have seen gradually becoming more precise—the determination of what attributes logically befit anything that is, or Being itself, without contradicting or destroying its essence.

That being so, we may be surprised that Xenophanes should have had a physical theory, properly so called. It seems to have been of a singular character. It was a late apparition, and there is an airiness about it which has made some regard it as a parody of Ionian physics.[4] But with all that, we find undoubted proofs of skill in observation and a desire to interpret facts, and an amount of research varied enough to be quoted as an example by the foe of " polymathy " yet consistent enough for the same Heracleitos to think it

[1] *Metaph.*, A. 5, 986 b 20–4.
[2] **LXVIII**, ch. 11, A. 31 (2 ff., 8 ff.), 33 (2), 34–6, beginning.
[3] *Ibid.*, A. 28. Cf. **II**, 617–39 (French trans., 2–20) ; **LXII**, 108 ff.
[4] **LXX**, 132.

wise to take over certain theses of a crudely empirical inspiration.[1] Lastly, it contains some assertions, so contradictory of certain principal tenets of the author's philosophy, that one might ask whether we have not here already a physics of appearance, similar to what Parmenides will one day call " the physics of opinion." From this point of view, one might perhaps fairly well reconcile the concrete curiosity which Xenophanes exerted and satisfied on his voyages with his tendency to set up his moral aspirations and the logical demands of pure speculation on an independent and higher plane. Thus, for example, Being, since it is being-everything, is necessarily finite. But it is none the less true that, when a traveller sees the sun go down in a region of the earth which he has not yet reached, and, on arriving there, finds another sun, which will again set far ahead of him, the sun seems to his experience to go on in its course infinitely.[2] So, too, when Xenophanes says that " the limit of the earth on which we tread appears, above, to touch the air, but below it stretches to infinity " (Frag. 28), he means that, in our experience, the sky limits our earthly horizon uniformly, and yet that horizon seems to be able to recede and widen without ceasing. Thus he seems to have been chiefly concerned to translate sensible appearances faithfully, without introducing anything into them which belongs to another domain, and his physical theory is another aspect of his criticism of opinions, and more specially, perhaps, of his religious criticism.

His hypotheses, when he makes any, show the same tendency, for they consist in bringing facts supposed to be mysterious or distorted by mythology down to the level of the facts of present or common experience. Lightning, for instance, is a phenomenon analogous to the St Elmo's fire which appears on the masts of ships on stormy nights.[3] On personal observations he founded a Neptunian theory of the formation of the earth and of living creatures, which is a more precise development of the ideas of Anaximandros. In Paros, Malta, and the stone-quarries of Syracuse, he had seen the impressions of fish and marine plants and shells. Perhaps,

---

[1] That the sun is new every day ; that the stars are burning clouds, alternately extinguished and rekindling ; etc.
[2] **LXVIII**, A. 41 a ; 33 (3, end).
[3] *Ibid.*, A. 39, 45.

therefore, everything was once a mass of marine ooze, and then, under the action of the air, the heat of the sun, and an internal fire, the water of the sea partly evaporated and the earth was partly dried, enclosing marine species in it.[1]

In sum, while, by his theology, Xenophanes is descended from the Ionians, he does not associate himself with their vast syntheses. In this indifference, which Heracleitos had already shown in respect of traditional physics, there is, perhaps, a dim presage of the revolution effected by the Sophists and Socrates in the orientation of thought.

II

PARMENIDES OF ELEA

It is not certain that Parmenides ever came into personal contact with Xenophanes. But if the latter's doctrine is that which I have just described, his influence cannot be denied. It is blended with another influence, that of the Pythagoreans, which Parmenides is said to have received through one Ameinias. It is perhaps to this influence, of which we shall see more certain indications presently, that we must ascribe the activity as a lawgiver and statesman which Parmenides is said to have shown in his native city. To establish his dates, we must decide between the indications of Apollodoros and the famous account of Plato at the beginning of his *Parmenides*,[2] where we are told that at the age of about sixty-five, going to Athens with Zenon, who had just been giving readings of his book in that city, and was then aged about forty, he met Socrates, who was still quite young at the time. Unfortunately, this account gives rise to many difficulties, the chief of which will be seen when we consider the life of Socrates. Plato is therefore suspect of having invented these circumstances in order to emphasize the part played by Eleatic influence in the transformation of a doctrine which he had hitherto declared to be his master's. Apollodoros, in his turn, seems a little too ingenious,

---

[1] *Ibid.*, Frags. 30 ff., 33, and A. 32 middle, 33, middle and end (with the interesting correction of **XI**, i. 174 ff.), 46–8. In this last passage, there is mention of a periodically erupting volcano on the island of Lipara.
[2] 127 a-c. Cf. also *Theaet.*, 183 e ; *Soph.*, 217 c.

when he makes Parmenides' birth coincide with the *floruit* of Xenophanes, and Zenon's birth with the *floruit* of Parmenides. These two sources of information being irreconcilable, we must be content to say that Parmenides belongs to the end of the VIth century and the first half of the Vth.

Parmenides' only work, a poem in hexameters, the title (at least, the present title) of which is *On Nature*, began with a grandiose introduction. Borne on a chariot, the poet is led by the Daughters of the Sun to the place where the roads of Night and Day part and there is the gate which gives access to the Goddess who leads the man endowed with knowledge through all things. This gate is guarded by Justice (*Dike*). She allows the poet to enter. " Thou must learn all things," she says to him, " both the unshaken heart of well-rounded Truth and the Opinions of mortals. In their opinions there is no true belief ; but thou must know them too, that thou mayest know, making an inquiry which reaches over all and into all, what judgment to make on the reality of the objects of these opinions." But let him turn away from " that way of inquiry," where the constraint of " habit with its manifold experiences " renders him subject to all the illusions of his senses ! It is the other road which he must follow, when he has received from the Goddess " the abundant proof in argument," which is known only " by thought " (Frag. 1, especially ll. 28-end). Thus there are two roads or methods ; one is that of unchangeable, perfect truth, to which logical thought is suited, and the other is that of opinion and its diverse and changing appearances, ruled by habit and the confused experience of the senses. It is indispensable to know the latter road and its dangers, but only after first taking the former, and forearming oneself with a good instrument with which to conduct a war without mercy against error. The whole spirit of Parmenides' philosophy is in this fragment. It also clearly marks the order of the two big divisions of the poem—*On Truth* and *On Opinion*.

But the opposition is not only between logical thought and empirical thought. It is also between two essences, one of which is imposed with an immediate and absolute necessity, so that the other, being the complete negation of the former, is immediately excluded. For one of the " roads " is " that Being is, and it is not possible for it not to be ; that is the road of certainty, for it accompanies Truth. The other is, that Being is not, and, necessarily, Not-being is—a narrow path, on which," the Goddess says, " nothing will light your footsteps " (Frag. 4. 1–6). If Being has relation only with itself, it is all the real ; that which, denying it, has no relation with it cannot have any reality. Hence the decisive axiom, which cuts all the pretensions of false knowledge to the root : " No ! Let there never be victory for this, ' Not-being is ' ! " (Frag. 7). Of this impossibility there can be neither knowledge, for Not-being is " never realized," nor expression (Frag. 4. 7 ff.).

So it is ontological reality, that of the object, that governs the truth of knowledge. That is the meaning of the famous phrase, often misunderstood, " Thinking and being are the same thing " (Frag. 5). The essence of being, the only possible object of thought, is what founds thought ; " Thinking and that for the sake of which thought takes place are the same thing, for, without the Being regarding which the utterance is made, you will not find thinking, seeing that there is nothing that is or should be, other than Being and outside it " (Frag. 8. 24–37). So the ontological law determines the " road " for thought, that is, its rule. " It must be absolutely or not at all. No power can compel it to be said that from Not-being something can arise by its side. . . . Our decision upon that depends on this : it is or it is not. Therefore, of necessity, we must abandon the unthinkable and unnameable road, for it is not the true road ; " therefore the other is the true road (Frag. 8. 10–13, 15–18). The principle of contradiction being the necessity in which thought is placed of choosing between a Yes and a No which are equally absolute, is thus brought out for the first time, and based on the ontological impossibility of a thing which, being distinct from being, should claim not to be not-being. This is a fact of capital importance in the history of thought, for the problem of judgment is thus raised. For how can the existing subject receive an attribute which is not the subject itself, or something of the subject which can be obtained from it by analysis ? Being is the only attribute which suits being as a subject. Therewith the requirements of analytical philosophy, the impossibility of empirical thought, are laid down in all their rigour. To evade these destructive requirements will be the aim of the greatest endeavour of the philosophy of Plato and Aristotle.[1]

This kind of thinning-out of the real, thus reduced to the most abstract and least comprehensive of notions, and, still more certainly, the méthod of deducing from the essence the attributes which it contains, seem, at least in part, to bear witness to the influence of the mathematical formalism of the Pythagoreans. Since Being is, it is necessarily not generated, for it does not need to arise from what is already, and, if it arose from Not-being, one would have to think, contradictorily, that Being is not ; " besides, what necessity would make it arise later or sooner ? " From a Not-being, only a Not-being can arise. For Being there is neither past nor future ; it is in an eternal present. " Thus generation is abolished, and destruction is inconceivable " ; there is no becoming. So, too, it would be contradictory for Being not to be " of one single nature," not to have a perfectly homogeneous unity, wholly " filled with being," without anything which was more being or less being than itself, and, therefore, without discontinuity or vacuum. It follows from that that it is also immovable " in the limits of the great bonds " in which " mighty Necessity " holds it fast. Therefore it is unchangeable, as " residing " wholly " in itself " ; and it is perfect and finite, for " it lacks nothing, whereas, if it were infinite, it would lack everything." So, after becoming, change in quality and motion are distinctly excluded from the real. Lastly, Being, since it is perfectly finite, must be so in every direction, resembling, like Truth, the mass of a well-rounded sphere, balancing itself on all sides (Frag. 8. 1-49). In short, Being has no determinations except those which it would be contradictory to deny it, because they are Being itself.

As an object of logical thought, the single Being of Parmenides is, in this sense, something intelligible ; and that is why Aristotle says that it is " formal " ($\kappa a\tau\grave{a}\ \tau\grave{o}\nu\ \lambda\acute{o}\gamma o\nu$). But moreover, being indivisible, continuous, finite, and spherical, it is, again in Aristotle's words, a physical reality. Parmenides conceived of Being in the spirit of a physicist, and then transferred the conception to the plane of logical thought, so that he may for this be regarded as an early professor of the

---

[1] See below, Bk. iii, ch. iii, the paradoxes of the Megarics and Cynics on predication, and the refutation in the *Sophist* in particular.

existence of motionless essences, Ideas or substantial forms.[1] Therefore the only way to understand the strange nature of this logical body seems to be to conceive of it as extent whose indivisibility and continuity are wholly intellectual, an intelligible extent without parts, like the Cartesian extent later. Whether we imagine it as scattered about, or as collected and arranged in a universe, " thought will never cut Being off from its continuity with Being " (Frag. 2). We must not forget that the Pythagoreans were incapable of thinking of the concept of number except in extension, and that the incorporeal and corporeal were not yet distinguished. There does not, therefore, seem to be any anachronism in this interpretation of the thought of Parmenides.

Next, passing from " trustworthy speech and thought of the True " to the Opinions of mortals (Frag. 8. 50 ff.), we leave a physical science of the intelligence for one of the senses, that is, one which does not allow of rational determinations. Although one must turn away from this deceptive road, one must also, as we have seen, know it as a precautionary measure. It runs in two directions, which seem to correspond to two degrees of irrationality (Frag. 6). One direction, the worse, seems to be that of the philosophy of Heracleitos, for those who take it " wander this way and that," they are " two-faced men," who " let themselves be carried away," for whom " to be and not to be are and are not the same thing," who hold that " in everything there is a road which runs opposite to itself."

The other direction, corresponding to the physics of Opinion set forth in the second part of the poem, seems to be that followed by men who, while recognizing that Being is, at the same time hold that it is unreal ; that is, they confound Being and Not-being, but without any intention of identifying them on principle. The corresponding physical theory is presented in a form too elaborate to be regarded [2] as a kind of dramatic fiction by which Parmenides, without expressing his personal ideas, explains how, by hypothesis, Not-being might be conceived, namely, as false appearance. It is, perhaps, more likely that he set forth definite opinions fo others, either those of the Pythagoreans themselves,[3] in

---

[1] *Metaph.*, A. 5, 986 b 18, 32 ; *De Caelo*, iii. 1, 298 b 14–24.
[2] As does **II**, 723 ff. (French trans., 66).   [3] **LXX**, 225 ff ; **LXXI**, § 90.

which case we thus have information about their physics, of which we know so little, or a kind of doxography, preparatory or ancillary to the teaching of his own doctrine ; [1] this would explain certain characteristic traces of the theories of Anaximandros and Anaximenes and, inversely, the absence of certain specifically Pythagorean dogmas.

Whatever may be the truth in this much debated question,[2] we note, first of all, that the first error of mortals to which Parmenides refers is that they have admitted two " forms," one of which, he says (Frag. 8. 53 ff.), " is not necessary." These are two bodies of absolutely opposite nature—the ethereal Fire, " devoid of violence, in all things like to itself," and Night, dark, thick, and heavy, the only designations, among many, which are perfectly authentic. Now, if Parmenides had only meant to rationalize physics in general, it is clear that Ionian monism, in his monistic eyes, would have answered the purpose much better. It is, therefore, probable that, in mentioning two physical principles, he had a special doctrine in view, and it is not impossible that it was the Pythagorean, if one remembers the importance which it attached to oppositions. Moreover, Parmenides is said to have arranged the two principles on the side of Being and on that of Not-being respectively.[3] Now, since the physicists whose theory he is describing place Not-being in Being, without being especially aware of it, he might regard these false principles as external denominations or symbols, only one of which corresponds to the real, and yet he might condemn the error which consists in admitting collaboration between Not-being and Being.

The generation of things from these two principles downwards was probably presented in a sexual aspect, as a succession of unions and births or separations, which were referred to the action of mythical forces—a Goddess who governs all and apportions lots, rather vaguely designated by the name of Necessity or Justice, who seems to have her seat in the heart of the universe, like the central fire of the Pythagoreans ; Love, " the first of the gods whom she bore " ; and lastly, perhaps, Discord.[4] His system of the universe, so far as we

---

[1] **LXXXIII**, 63.
[2] Cf. the review of interpretations by W. Nestle in **II**, 729–32.
[3] Arist., *Metaph.*, A. 5, 985 b 34 ff. ; *De Gen. et Corr.*, i. 3, 318 b 6.
[4] Frag. 12, 10, end. Cf. **LXVIII**, ch. 18, A. 37.

can gather, recalls both the last two Milesians and the Pythagoreans, but there is no " Counter-earth." It is a system of
" crowns." Some are unmixed—that is, made entirely of
fire, or of night, juxtaposed in pairs. Thus, on the circumference is " outermost Olympos," composed of the solid
envelope of the sky and of the ethereal fire, which, in its turn,
envelops all the rest ; in the middle is the earth, with its
solid crown and its central fire. The others are mixtures of
fire and night ; the Milky Way, planets, sun, and moon are
alternate aspirations by Night of the ethereal fire and of the
igneous element of the immediately surrounding crown, so
that all the stars are " compressions " of fire. If Parmenides
really maintained that the earth was spherical, it is possible
that he regarded the crowns as the " rinds " of spheres.[1] But
the question is as difficult in his case as in that of the Pythagoreans.

In what the physics of Opinion said of the phenomena of
life and thought, we recognize the same inspirations, and, in
addition, that of Alcmaeon—inquiries about the origins of
life, the determination of sex in relation to heat and cold, the
production of monsters, etc.[2] Knowledge, either in the
fundamental form of sensation or in that of memory or
thought (which is just the same), requires, in order to be true,
that there should be, in the sentient body, a well-proportioned
mixture of hot and cold, and, in order to be pure, that fire
should predominate in it. A predominance of cold allows
sensation to survive, for the dead body perceives cold, silence,
and, no doubt, darkness. The diversity of sensations, present
or reviving, was explained by the effluences which bring a
resemblance of the object fitting into the pores of the sentient
subject, while the subject itself exerts an action of its own,
for the eye has rays which touch outside things, as with hands.[3]
Lastly, the destiny of souls was perhaps set forth in the spirit
of the Pythagorean doctrine.[4]

This physical theory of illusion already enables us to
define the position of Parmenides in the history of thought.
It does more. If he was not an idealist, at least, by his
conception of the real of the physicists, he opened the path to

---

[1] Cf. especially Frag. 10 ff., and op. cit., A. 37, beginning, and 44.
[2] Frag. 17 ff. and A. 51–4.   [3] Frag. 16 and A. 46–8.
[4] Frag. 13 with its context.

the philosophy of Ideas. Secondly, in laying down as a rule of thought the principle of contradiction, itself based on the law of being, he founded speculative ontology, and, more generally, all rationalistic philosophy. Lastly, by the logical intoxication and the passion of the dialectical audacities with which he surrounded this discovery, he straightaway gave the problem of the relationship of being to its determinations the striking form which was most likely to stimulate reflection.

III

ZENON OF ELEA

The uncertainties of the dating of Parmenides affect that of Zenon, his favourite pupil and probably his successor in the direction of the School of Elea. But, although the purpose of the *Parmenides* makes us suspicious of Plato with regard to the date, if not the fact, of Zenon's visit to Athens, there is no good reason for suspecting his evidence with regard to the significance and subject of Zenon's book, which was doubtless in his hands. First of all, it was a book of the writer's youth, and he wanted it to be " a reinforcement for the theory of Parmenides against those who try to make fun of it on the ground that, if one admits oneness, the theory is involved in a mass of absurd consequences which contradict it." Against the champions of the Many " he turns their own arguments, and others to boot," showing that the assumption of multiplicity " has consequences even more absurd than that of unity, if one works them out far enough." It is an unpretending work, which sets out to say no more than what Parmenides has said, but does so with the ardour of a young man who wants to get the better of his opponent.[1] It was, then, a book against the theory of the Many, doubtless the work of which Simplicius has preserved three fragments. The famous arguments against motion do not appear in it, and it is remarkable that Simplicius knows them only from Aristotle's account. Perhaps we should infer from this that, regarding these arguments, Aristotle merely echoes the tradition of the school, and that Zenon published no book except that

[1] *Parm.*, 128 c-e.

mentioned by Plato. To what do the other titles preserved refer—the *Disputations, Against the Philosophers?* We do not know, nor do we know whether Zenon really wrote a book *On Nature* and an *Explanation of Empedocles*, containing a physical theory of appearance similar to that of Parmenides.[1]

Zenon's method, defined with such exact precision, is what, since Aristotle, has been called the " dialectical." With reference to a given question, from a " probable " answer—that is, one approved by an imaginary interlocutor, or by some philosopher, or by common opinion—you deduce the consequences which it entails, and you show that these consequences contradict each other and the initial thesis and lead to an opposite thesis, no less " probable " than the first ; with the result that your opponent, having to choose between two alternatives, will have admitted " Yes " and " No " in turn on the same subject. So the method is based on the principle of contradiction, in the strict form given to it by Parmenides. Its effect is to confound the opponent and raise a laugh at his expense, but it is also to close two opposite ways, in order that only one of them may be left on which it is possible to go. The method is, therefore, disputatious or " eristic " ; but it has a positive end, namely, to clear the ground for the dogmatic thesis of Parmenides, to " reinforce him." So we should only be justified in rejecting Zenon's arguments as sophisms if he had adopted the consequences deduced as truths ; but to him they are only as " probable " as the opposite, and the truth lies elsewhere. In giving a technical form to a process of discussion which, before his time, had been conducted haphazard and unconsciously, Zenon appeared to the ancients, and not without reason, to have made a very important discovery. Plato calls him the " Palamedes of Elea."[2] To his method we owe, if not the application of dialogue to philosophical inquiry, at least a certain way of disentangling and debating questions, which is equally found in the rhetoric of the Sophists and in Socratic philosophy.

The notion of plurality, first of all, provoked four arguments.

---

[1] H. Diels holds that the former title is that of the book on the Many.
[2] *Phaedros*, 261 d. Cf. Aristotle, Frag. 65 (saying that Zenon "invented" dialectic).

(i) The first envisaged it under the aspect of size. Now, size is either composed of indivisibles which are distinct unities, or is a continuum, the parts of which are not distinct. If size is a sum of parts (the first case), one must admit that, being made of things which are nothing in size, it will itself be nothing in size, and no addition or subtraction will increase or diminish it, so that things will disappear in infinite smallness. In the second case, a real finite thing will contain an infinite number of real parts, and so will be infinitely great (Frags. 1 and 2).

(ii) The second argument envisaged plurality as number. Since it is real, things, being really distinct, will be finite in number ; but they will also be infinite in number, for if they are to be distinct there must be things between them, which, if they are to be distinct in their turn, require further things between them, and so *ad infinitum* (Frag. 3).

(iii) If plurality is real, said the third argument, things are outside one another and each occupies a real place. But that real place must in its turn be in a place, and so *ad infinitum*. Therefore plurality is not real.[1]

(iv) The fourth argument, which was later set in the form of a dialogue between Zenon and Protagoras, was as follows. If plurality were real, the numerical ratio between a bushel of millet, one millet-seed, and a ten-thousandth part of a grain would be equal to the ratio between the noises which they make when they fall on the ground ; and that is not the case.[2]

The notion of movement likewise gave occasion for four arguments. The first two, generally known as the " Dichotomy " and " Achilles and the tortoise," differ only in that the second presents in a dramatic form, with reference to a particular ratio of division, the reasoning set forth in the first. A moving thing will never reach the end of its trajectory until it has gone half of it, and half of half, and, in short, has numbered an infinite number. Consequently, when the swiftest runner, the light-footed Achilles, chases a tortoise, the slowest of creatures, he will never catch it ; for if the amounts of their speeds are real, they will always be in the same ratio, and the division will go on to infinity. So

---

[1] **LXVIII**, ch. 19, A. 24. [2] *Ibid.*, A. 29.

the unintelligibility of movement was proved by the impossibility of infinite composition.[1]

The other two arguments, the " Arrow " and the " Race-
course," are also parallel. Both presuppose the composition
of indivisibles, but the first supposes that of moments of
time only, and the second that of moments of time and points
of space. Also, the first considers only one moving thing,
the second several. A thing is always in a place equal to
itself ; an arrow in flight cannot, in an indivisible moment,
go out of the place which it occupies ; therefore, since it does
not change its place, it is motionless,[2] and it will always be
so, if time is, by hypothesis, a sum of moments. Now let
us imagine, on a race-course, three parallel groups, each of
four indivisible " masses " or points. Two of these groups,
which take up half the course, each from
a different end as far as the middle, are
moving in opposite directions with equal
speed. The third remains stationary in
the middle of the course, occupying the same length as the
others. When the other two move, they cover the whole length
of each other, but only half the length of the third ; therefore
they do it in a time which is at once double and single, since,
if the speed is equal, the time is proportionate to the distance.[3]
In other words, if movement is real, the mutual passing of
moving masses, in relation to one another and in relation to
stationary masses, cuts or divides pieces of space and of
time which, by hypothesis, were points and moments, that
is, indivisible. Therefore, either all is equal to the half, or
real motion, as conceived by the initial hypothesis, is unintelligible.

So it was by *reductio ad absurdum* that Zenon cleared the
ground for the demonstration of the thesis of Parmenides.
In form, his arguments are " serious games," [4] and have the
fancifulness with which the Greeks often liked to enliven the
dryest subjects. Fundamentally, they are not a criticism of
the continuous itself, for that is one of the predicates which,
according to Parmenides (Frag. 8, ll. 6, 25), are part of the
essence of Being, but a criticism of the composition of the

---

[1] *Ibid.*, A. 25 and 26.   [2] *Ibid.*, A. 27, and Frag. 4.
[3] *Ibid.*, A. 28. Bayle represents the argument ingeniously by means of two
pieces sliding in a groove (*Dic. Hist.*, art. "Zénon" F. ; cf. **VII**, i. 160).
[4] Plato, *Parm.*, 137 b.

continuous, whether by indivisibles or by infinitely divisible parts.[1] Lastly, what vitiates them is their very principle, the vice of Eleaticism—the absolute conception of the principle of contradiction and the abstract realism which makes relations into things in themselves. Such as they are, however, it is undeniable that, by the effort of reflection and discussion which they provoked, they greatly benefited the philosophical analysis of the notions of infinite and continuous, number, space or time, and movement.

IV

MELISSOS OF SAMOS

That the last representative of Eleaticism should have been an Ionian shows how that philosophy had spread. The fact that Melissos was the admiral of Samos when it revolted against Athens is another proof, and no doubtful one, of the frequent union at this time of philosophical speculation with active participation in public life. But the date of his brilliant naval victory, 442 B.C., does not authorize any probable inference regarding his chronology. His book *On Nature or Being* seems to have been read by Simplicius, who has preserved ten fragments of it, some fairly long, tells us the plan, and gives a paraphrase. This last is not a citation, as was first thought, but it may possibly contain some extracts from the original.[2]

What first strikes one is the novelty of his method. Instead of reasoning in the abstract, like Parmenides and Zenon, he places himself on the same ground as the physicists, and makes use of their speculations on manifold, changing experience to prove the unity and immobility of Being.[3] Moreover, he places the Eleatic problem on a new ground, that of knowledge, and, in conformity with his method, he criticizes empirical knowledge. If, he says, all the things and all the qualities determined by our experience—earth, water, fire, gold, iron, white, black, living, dead, etc.—are real and " true

---

[1] **LII**, especially the second study

[2] **LXXI**, 370, n. 4 ; 371, n. 2. The pseudo-Aristotelian treatise *On Melissos, etc.*, the first two chapters of which deal with our philosopher, may be utilized, but with caution.

[3] **LXVIII**, ch. 20, A. 14. Cf. below, Chap. VI, on Leucippos.

things," and if there is no failing in our senses and mind, " then each of these things must always be what it is." But experience shows that they change incessantly, disappearing and being transformed. Therefore there is no truth in our knowledge of this multiplicity ; its object is not real. For " there is nothing stronger than the truth of real Being. Now, if it changed, it would mean that Being perished, while Not-being came into existence. So, therefore, if there were multiplicity, it would have to be exactly what the One is " (Frag. 8)—which is contradictory. It seems, lastly, that in the starting-point of his demonstration that Being cannot be generated or perish (a less abstract and more rapid argument than that of Parmenides), Melissos intends to prove to the pluralistic physicists that their axiom, " Nothing arises from nothing or returns to nothing " turns against themselves.[1]

The impossibility that Being should ever begin to exist then leads Melissos to a proposition which, at first sight, seems serious treason to Parmenides. Parmenides had said that Being is finite. Melissos declares that it is infinite. It is infinite because, unlike what is generated, it has neither beginning nor end, and it is infinite just as it is eternal (Frags. 2, 3). Aristotle, who conceives of no infinity but infinity of composition, and denies to space an infinity which he allows to time, is particularly hard on this innovation.[2] But that is perhaps because he fails to understand that, since the Being of the Eleatics was something really incomposite, and not something always unfinished and potential, Melissos wanted it to be truly absolute. Now, if it is absolute in time, in that it is eternal, it must, by analogy, also be absolute in space, that is, infinite. Far from thinking that he was preaching heresy in this, Melissos may have said that he was most truly satisfying the demands of Eleaticism.

The unity of Being follows from its infinity. For, if infinite Being is not one, either one part of itself limits another, or another being limits it (Frags. 5, 6). To this original argument, which reminds one of Spinoza, Melissos adds another based on physical considerations. If the continuous is not simple and one, its parts must be separated by vacuum.

---

[1] Frag. 1 and § 1 (bottom of the page) of Simplicius's paraphrase.
[2] *Phys.*, i. 2, 185 a 32 ; 3, beginning ; *Metaph.*, A. 5, 986 b 19 ; *Soph El.*, 5, 167 b 1–20 ; 6, 168 b 35 ff.

But if there were vacuum, it would insinuate itself everywhere, and so would end by dissolving Being into nothing, which we already know to be impossible. Therefore Being has no parts and is one.[1]

The negation of vacuum proves the immobility of Being in two ways. First, Being has nothing into which it could withdraw if it left its place, and secondly, without vacuum, it cannot contract or dilate in itself (Frags. 7, §§ 7-10, and 10). Furthermore, it is unchangeable, in virtue of its very unity ; for if it could grow greater or less or suffer any pain or alteration, it would become unlike itself, and would in a way double itself. Besides, if Being changed by as much as the thickness of a hair in ten thousand years, it must be completely annihilated in the whole of time (Frag. 7, §§ 1-6). Is this unchangeable being God, and has it blessedness ? [2] Such ideas seem very foreign to the spirit of Melissos. In any case, that blessedness would be without consciousness, for one cannot see what a consciousness would be, without alteration or change.

Lastly, since Being is one, it cannot have body. For, if it had " thickness," that is, volume, it would have parts and would no longer be one (Frag. 9). Parmenides, on the contrary, had defined Being as a sphere. But on this point, too, Melissos seems to have wished only to formulate his master's thought more precisely, not to break with it. He is afraid lest that spherical Being should be taken, with its centre and its circumference, for a limited portion of space. He wants to show that space, which is full, and in his eyes is infinitely large, is also, without possible equivocation, truly indivisible and one. He does what Spinoza did later, in attributing extension to God while denying him a body.

Melissos was an original, vigorous thinker, remarkably firm and lucid, and is more fairly appreciated by Plato, who places him almost on a level with Parmenides, than by Aristotle, who heaps insults on him.[3] Eleaticism survived him, its critical and negative elements in the Sophists, and its deeper and more philosophic elements in an interpretation of the Socratic doctrine of the concept which holds an important place in the history of Greek thought—the Megaric interpretation.

[1] Frag. 7, § 7, and the passages of Aristotle, **LXVIII**, ch. 20, A. 8.
[2] Cf. **XI**, i. 199
[3] Plato, *Theaet.*, 180 e, 183 a. Aristotle calls him " disputatious," " loutly," " far too coarse " a spirit ; cf. Bonitz, *Ind. Ar.*, 452 a 52.

CHAPTER V

ALTERNATION OF THE ONE AND THE MANY. EMPEDOCLES OF ACRAGAS

THE doctrines of Empedocles seem to derive from the mixture of three influences, however they may have come to him— Pythagoreanism (in the religious beliefs which make it akin to Orphicism and also in its scientific spirit), Eleaticism, and the philosophy of Heracleitos. It is doubtful whether he owes anything to Leucippos the Atomist or to Anaxagoras ; though he was younger than the latter, his writings are earlier, according to Aristotle.[1] He belonged to an aristocratic family of Acragas, one of the liveliest and most prosperous cities in Sicily. His life, which seems to fall between the ten first years of the Vth century and about 430, is less known to us than his character, about which tradition and his own utterances give us information. He believed himself invested with a supernatural power. " Friends," he says solemnly at the beginning of his poem, the *Purifications* (καθαρμοί), " I am come to you as an immortal god, honoured among all as is fitting to my nature, my brow bound with fillets and flowery wreaths. When I go into the thriving cities with this train of men and women, I am venerated. Thousands hasten to follow me. They ask me the road which shall lead them to advantage ; some ask for oracles, others, who suffer from a thousand maladies, would hear the word which heals " (Frag. 112). He knows that he brings truth, but " the assault of belief on the heart " is jealously combated by incredulous distrust (Frag. 114). Moreover, the end of his poem *On Nature* hardly leaves any doubt that the object of the study of nature is, in his eyes, to enable us to exert arbitrary, absolute influence on things by magical means. " All the remedies which are a succour against ills and old age," he says to his disciple

[1] *Metaph.*, A. 3, 984 a 10 ; **LXVIII**, ch. 21, A. 7.

Pausanias, "you shall learn them. . . . You shall calm the rage of the unwearying winds . . . and you shall bring back repairing breaths when you wish. For the good of men, you shall make drought follow rain, and rain follow drought. . . . And you shall make the soul of a dead man come out of Hades " (Frag. 111). Tradition, too, speaks of the sombre gravity of his pose, the royal pomp with which he surrounded himself, and the various miracles which he performed. In short, it seems that, like Pythagoras, Empedocles was at an early date recognized by enthusiastic admirers as the supernatural man he believed himself to be.

This conviction, instead of strengthening his ties with aristocracy, threw him on the side of the people. He was a fierce, jealous champion of equality, mercilessly unmasking and denouncing the smallest threat to democracy. He sacrificed his fortune to the good of his fellow-countrymen. He was a kind of Savonarola, or, as he has been called, a mystical Jacobin. Then, probably about 440, the friend of the people of Acragas felt himself called to bring about the happiness of all the Greeks. He roamed about Sicily and Great Greece, crossed over to the Peloponnese, read his *Purifications* at the great gathering at Olympia, and perhaps went to Athens, unless the trial of Anaxagoras (432) deterred him. The very fact of this apostolic tour and the ascendancy which he obtained over his hearers allow one to assume that he had oratorical gifts which could arouse the enthusiasm of crowds. Timon called him a " rattle of the market-place." [1] Perhaps this is the origin of the tradition that Empedocles was the inventor of rhetoric and the master of the other Sicilians who are credited with such an important part in the creation of that art—Corax, Tisias, and, lastly, Gorgias, who was certainly influenced by Empedocles. [2] He was trained in the dialectic of the Eleatics, and to develop a technique of speaking from it he had only to adapt it to wider purposes, with other methods. However that may be, it seems that during his Panhellenic mission, by not keeping the people of Acragas under the influence of his tongue, he lost his credit with them, and was sentenced to banishment. The story of his death is that of an apotheosis, and was gradually embellished with all

---

[1] Frag. 42. 1. [2] **LXVIII**, ch. 21, A. 19 ; **XCIII.**

the usual features of such myths. One night, after banqueting with his followers, he vanished at the summons of a voice ; a light shone in the sky ; he was seen no more ; Etna received his body and gave up the bronze of his shoes. Henceforth he was a god again, and sacrifices must be paid to him. For the character that he wished to be, it was certainly, in the words ascribed to his disciple Pausanias, the end " which one should wish."

The literary magnificence of the two poems mentioned above, the only ones which can be attributed to Empedocles with certainty, earned them such general admiration [1] that about a thousand lines, roughly a fifth of the whole, have been preserved. The poem *On Nature* is probably earlier than the *Purifications*, although this has lately been contested by arguments which are sometimes plausible.[2] In any case, if it is true, as we have seen, that the two poems bear witness to the same spirit and to the alliance of religious sentiment with science already encountered in the Pythagoreans, the question is of no great importance to the study of the author's thought.

The most immediately obvious feature of Empedocles' physics is his abandonment of the single matter which, for the Ionian naturalists, was the permanent foundation of becoming, in favour of several elemental determinations of things. As a fact, he does not know them under the name of " elements," which was not used in this sense before Plato ; [3] he calls them " the roots of all things " (Frag. 6. 1). Then, when he sets out to prove that, like the single matter of the Ionians, they are the eternal substance of things, he uses Parmenides' demonstration of the eternity of Being, translating it into majestic language (Frags. 11-14). In the All there is no vacuum, in which something, no one knows how, could come into being, nor anything in excess, which could be destroyed. Everywhere are the roots of Being. " Identical with themselves " (Frag. 17. 32 ff.), they are what they have always been, and will always be what they are.

There are four such roots—fire, water, ether (more rarely called air), and earth. Often he seems to deify them, when he calls them " shining Zeus, nourishing Hera, Ædoneus

---

[1] See the enthusiastic eulogy of Lucretius, i. 714-34.
[2] Cf. **LXXXIV,** 159-74.   [3] **XL,** 15, 3.

(Hades), and Nestis, who with her waves feeds mortal springs "
(Frag. 6). The mythical names, about the application of
which it is not always easy to agree, do not at all take away
from the phenomenal reality of these foundations of Being.
They have their reality in extension ; they are bodies which,
without having weight, have each an essential qualitative
" form." These " forms " are single, for their number can
neither be increased nor lessened. For experience reveals
neither more nor less to us—" the sun, which we see everywhere, hot and bright, the immortal bodies (the stars), bathed
in vapour and white light, the rain, which everywhere brings
darkness and cold, and the earth, from which all stable, solid
foundation derives " (Frag. 21. 1–6). They are, then, the
great masses among which things are distributed, and one
need not look beyond them for elements of elements.[1] They
are not generated, and do not perish. " All are equal and of
the same age. But each takes care of its dignity and each
has its character, although they are in turn uppermost in the
revolution of time " (Frag. 17. 27–9). It follows that they
are " the seed from which comes all that has been, all that
is, and all that will be," not only mortal things, but also
" the long-lived gods, high in honour " (Frag. 21. 9–12). So,
placing himself at the point of view of the most manifest
sensuous experience, which most affects us practically,
Empedocles thought that one should take as they are the big
differences which it imposes on the attention, and that the
older philosophers were wrong in trying to choose between
them. It is not impossible, too, that this belief was reinforced by the influence of the Pythagorean Tetractys, which
thus helped to found a division which was to reign unchallenged
for centuries.

So, having said that at the origin there were a number
of qualities, already specified and unchangeably specified,
Empedocles now had to explain how things came into being.
But, like Parmenides, he denied all qualitative becoming and
even all generation of substance, in a word, *physis* itself, in
the sense of the ancient physics. " There are," he said, " only
mingling, and then exchange between the things which have
been mingled. Generation is but a name, accredited by men "

---

[1] The contrary evidence (**LXVIII**, A. 43) is the result of a confusion. Cf. **LXII**,
223 ; **LXXI**, 265, n. 3.

(Frag. 8). So, starting from quality, he defines change by mechanical processes—mixture and exchange. " By running after one another," the elements, which are qualitatively unchangeable, " take on different aspects " (Frag. 21, end). Here no combination takes place which transforms them. But everything happens as when a painter, taking paints, each with its own colour, and mixing them in various proportions, makes of these mixtures paintings which resemble the infinity of real things of which Empedocles has been speaking (Frag. 23). That, then, is the exact sense in which we must understand that the elements are the " seed " or " source " (Frag. 23. 10) of all things. Moreover, the particles thus set side by side are mixed, as in the example of the painter, in definite proportions. " Of the eight parts, the earth received in its wide funnels two parts of the brightness of Nestis (water) and four of Hephaestos (fire) ; so white bones were produced " (Frag. 96. 1–3), or, as he says elsewhere, the flesh, tendons, and blood.[1] The general law governing these mixtures is a law of mutual " adjustment," or, as we should say, affinity ; " the things most favourable to mixing with one another cherish one another " (Frags. 22. 1–5 ; 90). How does this movement of like to like take place ? " Effluences " (ἀπορροαί) constantly emanate from the compounds or from the elemental masses, enter the " pores," or minute, invisible passages of other bodies (those of a looser texture having more pores), and flow through these passages.[2] There is affinity between bodies where there is a " common measure " (συμμετρία) between the emanations of one and the pores of the other ; otherwise, like oil and water, they cannot mix.[3] But does not this imply that if effluences are too big to go into small pores they cannot be divided ? So Empedocles was on the road to atomism.[4] Yet, since he also denied vacuum (Frag. 13), he should not have failed to say how the circulation of indivisible effluences agrees with the hypothesis of the plenum.

But the echanical process by which these mixtures and exchanges take place, so as to produce and govern an apparent

---

[1] Frag. 98 ; LXVIII, A. 78, beginning. Cf. the context of Frag. 96.
[2] Cf. Alcmaeon, p. 79.
[3] Frag. 89 ; Plato, *Menon*, 76 d ; Arist., *Gen. et Corr.*, i. 8, beginning ; Theophr., *De Sensu*, 12 (LXVIII, a. 86).
[4] Arist., loc. cit., 325 b 5–7.

becoming, also requires, according to Empedocles, two other
principles, one " outside " the elements and " weighing on
them equally in every direction," namely Discord (νεῖκος) or
Hatred, and the other " inside " the elements and " equal to
them in length and breadth," namely Friendship (φιλότης),
Aphrodite, Cypris, or, again, Harmony, Tenderness, Joy
(Frag. 17). These seem to be a sort of material environments,
but perceptible only to the mind (Frag. 17. 21), and, being
conceived on the type of the spontaneous forces which are
living beings or act in living beings, they are represented
anthropomorphically. In doing this, Empedocles added on
to his mechanical theory a dynamic theory by which, in his
own way, he separates the vital principle which the Ionians
placed in their single substance from matter, without, however,
ceasing to regard that principle as material. If the two
tendencies had been explicitly distinguished before, we might
suppose that Empedocles deliberately tried to reconcile them,
as an eclectic. The truth is rather that he tried them both
in turn. But this very vacillation of his thought helped to
make philosophic reflection more clearly aware of their
opposition.

By the action of Friendship the many tends to form a
unity ; by that of Discord, unity breaks up and gives place
to plurality (Frag. 17. 16 ff.). The two motive forces are
perpetual antagonists, but one or the other in turn tends to
get the upper hand, without absolutely excluding the other ;
otherwise there would be either absolute unity and immobility,
or absolute multiplicity and ungoverned chaotic movement
(Frag. 17. 4-8). So the reign of Friendship, traversed by the
dissensions of Hatred, is followed by a reign of Discord, which
Friendship labours to bring to an end. Then the cycle recommences, identical with itself. Thus Empedocles can say
that, " in one sense, things begin to exist " and " theirs is not
a perpetually unchangeable existence," for the sceptre changes
hands ; but that, " in that perpetual exchange never ceases,
there is always immobility in the circular movement," that
is, in the alternation of the two reigns (Frag. 17. 1-13). The
state of things in which Friendship reaches the height of its
reign is what Empedocles, doubtless in memory of the spherical
Being of Parmenides, calls the Sphaeros (sphere). " So
securely," he says, " was the well-rounded Sphaeros held in

the deep fastness of Harmony, joyous and proud of his independence " (Frag. 27. 3 ff.). This chaos in which all the elemental particles, however much intermingled, retain their unchangeable specification, but without it being possible to distinguish it, is more like the *Migma* of Anaxagoras than the wholly indeterminate chaos which was Anaximandros's Infinite.[1] Empedocles speaks of it as a god (Frag. 31). But, apart from the fact that the elements, too, are gods, and yet other gods are formed from them, one may doubt that the blessedness bestowed on him in the quotation above was more than a moral symbol of the victory of Love in nature.

In the " limbs " of the Sphaeros there is no " dissension " (Frag. 27 a). But from outside, or rather " from the outermost bounds of the circle," Discord " sprang forth towards the honours, when the time was accomplished which brings their return in virtue of the great pact," [2] and this assault " shook the limbs " of the Sphaeros (Frag. 31). Friendship resists. This struggle seems to give rise to an eddying movement (δίνη), and Discord comes almost " to the centre of the vortex." But there Friendship holds its ground. So when the time comes round for " the immortal onrush of victorious Friendship " (Frag. 35), it drives Discord back towards the circumference, to make the Sphaeros pure once more. Thus Friendship and Discord have retreated in turn without letting go of each other, one to be confined for a time to the centre, the other to retire for a time to the boundary. Now, each of these processes is thus alike generative and destructive ; " for there are for all things one generation which is produced and destroyed by union, and another which is nourished and scattered by separation " (Frag. 17. 3-5). What Friendship has created by union, it finally destroys by confusion ; what Discord has created by dissociation, it destroys by breaking things up so small that the elements are, no doubt, as impossible to distinguish as they were in the unity of the Sphaeros [3]— there is incoherent chaos instead of compact chaos.

It is needless to dwell on the vague generality of this law of evolution. One must at least remember that the ancient critics, while pointing out its arbitrary character, condemned Empedocles for giving such an important place to chance ;

---

[1] Cf. Arist., *Phys.*, i. 4, 187 a 21.   [2] Compare Lucretius's *foedera naturae*.
[3] See **LXXXVI**, his Frag. 26 a, and App. iii. 599–611.

in more than one passage in his poem, it is said, he invoked
" the will of Fortune." [1] This is, indeed, an expedient without
which it would have been very difficult for him to construct
his twofold cosmogony. For there is hardly any doubt that
Empedocles described the formation of a world in each of
the phases of the cosmic cycle—the present phase, ruled by
Discord, which has given rise to our world, and that preceding
it, in which Friendship prevailed.[2] It was in the age of
Friendship, probably, that the organic compounds were
formed—bone, flesh, etc.—which, as we have seen, contain
the elements in definite proportions, and to it the " wondrous
sight " (Frag. 35, end) of his fantastic zoogony must belong.
" On the earth," the poet sings, " great numbers of heads
sprang up without necks, single shoulderless arms wandered
about, and eyes strayed up and down, embellished by no
forehead " (Frags. 57-8). Then these early mixtures of
previous compounds tended to unite in their turn, at haphazard, isolated limbs joining on to anything which they
happened to meet. So there appeared creatures " with their
feet turned " so that they could not walk and " innumerable
hands," creatures " with double faces and double chests,"
" cattle with men's faces and men with the faces of oxen,"
hermaphrodites, and the like (Frags. 59-61).[3]

The details of the cosmogony of Discord are better known
to us, and are rich in ingenious and acute notions. The first
effect [4] of the disintegration of the Sphaeros was the separation
first of the air, which spread everywhere in a circle, and then
of fire, which, finding no other place suitable to it, rushed
towards the circumference, hardening and vitrifying the part
of the air next to it so as to form the solid vault of the sky,
and driving the rest downwards. Thus two hemispheres were
formed, one entirely of fire, the other a mixture of air with a
little fire, whose movements round the earth and on the
heavenly dome served (not at all clearly, it is true) to explain
the succession of day and night and that of the seasons.
The revolution of the heavenly dome itself was the result of

---

[1] Frag. 103 and the passages from Arist., **II**, 776, 2 (French trans., ii. 222, 1).
[2] Arist., *De Caelo*, iii. 2, 300 b 26–31. It is only with reference to the sky that
Aristotle blames Empedocles for paying too little attention to generation in
Friendship (301 a 14–19).
[3] Cf. **LXVIII**, A. 72, beginning.
[4] On what follows, cf. op. cit., A. 30, 50, 67, 75, etc., and Frag. 42.

equilibrium being broken by the pressure of the mass of fire on the hard wall of the surrounding air. The advance of Discord caused a gradual acceleration of this revolution, and so a decrease in the length of the day, which was equal to ten months when the first men appeared on earth, and then became equal to seven. The speed of this movement of the sky is what fixed the earth in the centre of the universe and keeps it motionless, just as water remains in a vessel if you whirl it very fast. The whole universe is shaped like an egg, with the major axis horizontal. Lastly, Empedocles is the first thinker in whom we find with certainty the idea that the moon borrows its light from the sun and a correct explanation of solar eclipses.

His account of the nature of the earth seems also to have ascribed all kinds of dissociations to Discord.[1] The sea is like a sweat, separated from the earth under the pressure of what surrounds it and the heat of the sun. The salt of the sea was separated from it by coagulation, and patches of fresh water can be distinguished in the sea. So, too, rocks, stones, and mountains were separated from the mass of the earth by the action of subterranean fires. Light is an emission of effluences, which only reach us some time after breaking off from the luminous body. Magnetic force is explained in the same way : the compression of the mixture which constitutes iron violently expels effluences which all go towards the pores of the magnet, to which they are proportionate.

His applications of the same principle to the phenomena of life are often very original. He supposes an analogy of organs and functions between animals and vegetables, and between different species of animals. Feathers and scales are analogous, and so are leaves and hairs ; grains and fruits are the eggs and excretions of plants ; plants break loose from the earth as the embryo from the womb, and have a psychological life like animals. On both sides, the spontaneous movement of like towards like served to explain, by analogy with what happens in the universe, the differentiation of organs, their position in the body, and the place of living beings on the earth.

This is how Empedocles imagined the appearance of the first animal forms in the age of Discord. In a first phase,

---

[1] Frags. 55 ff. ; op. cit., A. 68 ff., 57, 89.

when, after air, fire and water were trying to separate themselves from the general mixture, the attempt of fire to join
its like at the circumference caused to " rise " to the surface
of the earth " forms all of one piece " (οὐλοφυεῖς τύποι),
sharing equally in heat and moisture, hardly different from
the plants, which seem to have been earlier than they, very
poor in organic specifications, and in any case, like the first
vegetables, completely devoid of sexual differences, and therefore capable of being generated by the earth only. In the
second phase, the sexual organs had somehow or other been
constituted, and living creatures could co-operate to reproduce
themselves. The factor which determined this change in
animal life seems to have been the separation of the moist,
which had hitherto been combined in it with the hot.

The immediate result was a new function—respiration—
and, no doubt, a transformation of the manner of nutrition.
When the moisture left the vessels, the outside air came in
and filled the place left empty. But at once, doubtless
because it finds less resistance in front of it, the internal
heat tends to escape outside, and draws with it a wave of
blood which drives the air before it. But, while the air
escapes easily through the " tubes of flesh " (pores of the
mucous membranes ?), the blood cannot pass through them.
It therefore stops, checked in its rush, and the outer air,
driving it back, comes back into the vessels. To illustrate
this mechanism of inspiration and expiration, Empedocles
resorted to the experiment of the water-clock. When you
dip that vessel in water, stopping the mouth, the pressure
of the air inside prevents the water from entering through
the small holes in the bottom ; but if you unstop the mouth,
the pressure of the water forces the air to come out and
make room for it (Frag. 100). So, too, in this second phase,
the nourishing moisture seems to dissolve, producing various
fermentations or putrefactions ; the blood, in its turn, produces
others, such as milk and sweat.[1]

There is no place in this biology for finality. Everything
is explained by the action of mechanical causes and change
in the conditions of existence ; that is what Aristotle,[2] who
believes in finality, calls the production by " chance " of

---

[1] Cf. especially Frags. 62, 68, 77–82, 90, 100, and op. cit., A. 70, 72, 74, 78.
[2] *Phys.*, ii. 8, esp. 198 b 19–32.

organs capable of certain functions and like what they would have been if they had been produced with a view to those functions. What Empedocles means, is that the physical conditions of life have compelled the living creature to adapt itself to them by appropriate organs ; if the conditions alter, the creature must alter its organs or get new ones. If, for example, some external cause forces an invertebrate to twist itself, behold, the vertebral column appears ; if the air hardens tendinous parts, you get nails and claws. In the same way, the acceleration of the movement of the heavens has caused the degeneration of the present species ; a human gestation now takes a time which was once equal to one day, and the men of to-day are like children in comparison with their remote ancestors. Only those beings which could adapt themselves to the conditions of their life have survived ; the rest have perished.[1] Such are the remarkable views, which may have been influenced by his researches in embryology,[2] by which Empedocles gave a new development to the previous transformism.

Empedocles' psychology, probably derived from Alcmaeon, is essentially mechanistic. We have enough information to study it in detail, and it is often interesting. We must, however, confine ourselves to noting its principal features. Every sensation is a contact of likes, and that is perhaps why Empedocles considered it unnecessary to lay stress on touch as a distinct kind of sensation. What he wanted was to explain the various kinds of sensation by a special correspondence between effluences and pores. When the pores are too large or too small for certain effluences, they are traversed without contact taking place, or they close the way to them, as the case may be. It follows that no one of our senses can perceive what is proper to another, and also that the varieties and the very existence of every object of sense depend on the existence and properties of an organ of sense. The effluences of fire, for example, would not be sensible and there would be no colours, if there were not an eye in which fire " lies in wait," and if that eye were not made up of membranes variously composed, and therefore containing various kinds of pores. There is also water in the eye, and a greater amount of water explains why some animals see

[1] Frag. 97 ; **LXVIII,** A. 75, 77 ff   [2] *Ibid.,* A. 81–4.

better at night than by day. So, too, the conformation of the ear is what causes sounds to exist. A bell, the "sprout of flesh," hanging inside the ear, is set swinging by the movements of the air outside, and that is what, by driving the inside air against solid walls, produces a sound.[1]

Neither the distrust which Empedocles shows for sensuous knowledge (Frag. 4. 9–13) nor even the existence of a supernatural truth as against that which is allowed to the mortal intelligence (Frag. 2) prevents him from regarding thought as the same thing as sensation, but subject to a twofold operation of criticism and synthesis. Thought, too, consists in an agreement of like with like, while ignorance comes from a disagreement or unlikeness. Thought has also an organic condition, which is the blood (and especially the blood surrounding the heart), since it is the most perfect mixture in us of the elements, and the elements constitute the objects of knowledge. So, in agreement with the teaching of the medical school of Sicily, Empedocles places the seat of thought in the heart, and not, like Alcmaeon, in the brain. The synthetic character of knowledge bears witness to the resistance of Love to the increasing dominion of Discord. Lastly, the intellectual differences of men and their special aptitudes are to be explained by the size of the particles composing their blood, by their distribution, and by the various ways in which they are mixed.[2]

We still have to consider the ideas of Empedocles regarding the gods and the destiny of man. We have already seen that, apart from the "long-lived" gods who are formed in the same way as mortal things, he ascribes divine nature to the elements, to Love and Discord, and, lastly, to the Sphaeros.

In general, he seems to exclude all anthropomorphic features from his notion of the divine, and to conceive of it by analogy with the perfect mixture which constitutes thought. In godhead "there is nothing but the movement of an inexpressibly holy mind which flies through the whole world with its swift thoughts" (Frag. 134, end).[3] But in a world

---

[1] See especially the important fragment of the *De Sensu* of Theophrastos, §§ 7 ff. (op. cit., A. 86), and the evidence in A. 91–4.

[2] Frags. 105 ff. ; op. cit., A. 86, §§ 9–11.

[3] Frags. 131–4, on godhead, are from the *Purifications*, according to Diels. This view is contested in **LXXXVI**, App. v, where they are ascribed to the third book of *On Nature*.

which is formed mechanically, starting from divine elements, and is governed in its evolution by the alternate rhythm of two forces, likewise divine, what is there for other gods to do ? Are they the spirits which concluded the " great pacts " which are a sort of oath of collective loyalty to the universal order ? These are questions without answers, questions which Empedocles, perhaps, never asked himself, and yet they have their place in his system.

In his doctrine of the soul there is an evident adaptation of Orphico-Pythagorean ideas to the principles of physics, but it is one which again raises all the problems of theology. The souls of mortals are long-lived gods, but gods who have " failed, staining their hands with murder," and, " breaking their oath, have followed Discord." Therefore, " in virtue of the oracle of Necessity, of the ancient, eternal ordinance of the gods," they are compelled, " for thrice ten thousand years, to wander up and down, far from the blest," and to assume every mortal form in turn, tossed about from one of the four great elemental regions of the universe to another. Such an outcast, " one region takes him from another, and all view him with horror. One of those am I now, banished from the divine abode, a vagrant who has put his faith in raging Discord " (Frag. 115). Moreover, he has not lost all memory of his transmigrations (Frag. 117), and he knows that, on the way of expiation, his activity as a prophet, healer, and poet marks the last stage before he reaches his former abode, outside the " cave," far from misfortune and suffering. For, if mortals ever knew the Golden Age, it can only have been under the guardianship of Cypris ; so it must have been an episode in the age of Love. In the present age, we can only reach salvation by purifications and abstinences like those prescribed by the Pythagoreans.[1]

To end with a definition of the properly philosophical thought of Empedocles, we may say that, into the Eleatic unity of Being, having extension but no qualities, he began by introducing the limited plurality of the elemental qualities, and then arrived at the unlimited plurality of experience by introducing movement into quality, so giving partial satisfaction to the Heracleiteans ; that, under the influence of the Pythagorean mathematical explanation, he gave to the

[1] Cf. Frags. 120, 126–8, 137, 140 ff., 146 ff. ; LXVIII, A. 62.

composition of quality according to numerical proportions the form of quantity ; and, lastly, that he made mechanism depend on a dynamism—that of motive forces. It is a hesitating, confused synthesis. Interesting views about details emerge here and there, but it is dominated by no higher point of view, and it is much too emotional to be sufficiently systematic.

CHAPTER VI

ATOMISTIC MECHANISM.   THE SCHOOL OF ABDERA.
LEUCIPPOS AND DEMOCRITOS

LEUCIPPOS came from Miletos or Elea, studied in the school of Parmenides, and founded a school at Abdera ; he is another example, almost in the time of Melissos, of the intellectual exchanges which went on between Great Greece and Ionia. He seems to have been a contemporary of Empedocles and Anaxagoras, but wrote earlier than Anaxagoras, if it is true that the latter plagiarized from him, as Democritos says (Frag. 5).   The development given to the school by Democritos of Abdera, the scientific activity of that thinker, and the formation of a school library (whose catalogue, compiled in tetralogies by Thrasyllos at the beginning of our era, proves that Leucippos's works, the *Great System of the World* and the treatise *On the Mind*, were not distinguished from those of his successor), all helped to efface the personality of the master. No doubt, we can presume that all that bears on the interests of a later period, the theory of conduct and the theory of knowledge, belongs rather to Democritos.   But there are so few instances in which we can say what is Leucippos's share that it is, perhaps, wisest [1] to follow Aristotle's example, and not to separate the two.   But if we do this we must not forget that Democritos, who was probably at least ten years younger than Protagoras, was a contemporary of the Sophists and Socrates ; that he died at an advanced age, surviving Socrates twenty years, if not more ; and that Anaxagoras was not yet dead when Democritos, still a young man, published his *Little System of the World*.   The encyclopaedic and didactic character of his work, in which medicine, agriculture, and other arts have their place, makes it like that of Aristotle, and is typical

[1] In **XII** Democritos is discussed after Socrates, and in **X** he is taken with Plato.

of the times in which he lived. It is strange that, of all that vast work, so little, in proportion, has survived. It seems to have been lost after the IInd century of our era, though the name of Democritos continued to enjoy an extraordinary prestige, earned by his alleged journeys in the East and all the romantic tales of his magical exploits.

The School of Abdera was probably connected with the Eleatics historically ; that its doctrines were derived from theirs is asserted by Aristotle no less definitely than forcibly. The Eleatics, he says in substance, had, in contempt of facts, and " at the risk of verging on madness," proclaimed the absolute unity and immobility of Being. Leucippos keeps clear of their logical intoxication, he makes concessions to sensuous experience, he wants to save plurality and movement, generation and becoming. But, on the other hand, he concedes to the Eleatics that true Being allows of no vacuum and that without vacuum there is no movement. Therefore, since the reality of movement is admitted, vacuum must constitute, in the face of Being, a Not-being which is equally real ; and, since plurality is admitted, it must exist in the Not-being of the vacuum, and not in Being, from which it could not proceed. So Being is in his eyes an infinite multiplicity of masses, which are invisible because they are so small. They move in vacuum. When they come into contact, they do not make a unity, but by these meetings, uniting, they produce generation, and by separating they produce corruption.[1] Consequently, Leucippos, and Democritos with him, " coined " the Eleatic Being, which was a homogeneous body, into an infinite number of pieces, full and " solid, indivisible bodies, atom-masses " (ἄτομα σώματα, ἄτομοι ὄγκοι). Correlatively, the continuity of homogeneous extension is still a reality, but without body, and therefore without being, the not-being of the vacuum, the infinite receptacle of the movement of an infinite number of atoms, the necessary condition of condensation and of mixtures without increase of volume. So reality is broken up into what Democritos called the " something " (δέν), the atoms, and the " not-something " (μηδέν), the vacuum. It is " in truth," he said again, that the atoms and the vacuum exist, the only objects of " true-born "

---

[1] *Gen. et Corr.*, i. 8, 325 a 2–36. Cf. **LXVIII**, ch. 54, A. 8 (Theophrastos).

knowledge, whereas it is " by convention " ($\nu\acute{o}\mu\varphi$) that sweet, bitter, colours, etc., exist, the objects of an " obscure " knowledge. This is a new adaptation, a translation into the language of another time, of the Eleatic distinction between Truth and Opinion.[1] Lastly, if it were well established that Melissos was later than Leucippos, we could regard the former's teaching about the infinity and incorporeality of Being and his refutation of the physicists as both a protest of Eleaticism against the heresy of Leucippos and an attempt to rescue the philosophy of Parmenides from the difficulties raised by that heresy.[2] Now, the existence of a heresy would be a further evidence of direct descent.

Since the atoms are full extension repeated in an infinite number of specimens, every property which is not contained in that fundamental essence of Being will, in virtue of the Eleatic method, be excluded from the atoms. They therefore all have the same nature, without any variety of quality, just like the Being of the Eleatics ; they can no more be changed in quality than they can be divided, so that they are doubly impassible ; since Not-being cannot produce Being, they are not generated, and therefore cannot perish. On the other hand, they have positive determinations, namely, those which are implied by extension. First, they differ in *shape* ($\rho\upsilon\sigma\mu\acute{o}\varsigma$), like A or N, and are therefore called " forms " ($\iota\delta\acute{\epsilon}\alpha\iota$), some angular, others round, others concave or convex, smooth or covered with more or less regular roughnesses, and sometimes armed with hooks. This diversity is infinite, for there is no more reason in favour of this than of that, and, besides, there is no other way of explaining the infinite diversity of phenomena. Secondly, there is the *order* ($\delta\iota\alpha\theta\iota\gamma\acute{\eta}$ or $\delta\iota\alpha\theta\acute{\eta}\kappa\eta$) in which atoms having the same shape are arranged, as AN and NA. Thirdly, two atoms of the same shape may be set in different *positions* ($\tau\rho\sigma\pi\acute{\eta}$), as ⊏ and H, Z and N. Lastly, every atom must have its *size ;* although in fact this size is always smaller than the smallest thing which the senses can perceive (so that the atoms are a kind of intelligibles, which only thought can apprehend), it is logically something, as soon as you do away with its relationship to our sensuous knowledge,

[1] Cf. *ibid.*, ch. 55, Frags. 156, 9, 11, 125 ; A. 39, 47 ; ch. 54, A. 16, 19.
[2] Cf. above, pp. 85 ff. ; **II**, 776 ff. (6), 953 ff. (5) (French trans., ii. 91, 368 ff.).

and there would be no absurdity in an atom being as large as a world.[1]

All these differences are properly geometrical, and analytically connected with extension. It therefore seems difficult, in spite of all that has been said, to add weight, in proportion to the size of the atoms. No doubt, when we consider the atoms in their sensible compounds, one can envisage the proportion of weight to size. But that is not an essential, primary relation. Otherwise, would Aristotle have reproached the Atomists with failing to seek in the very nature of the atoms for a cause of their motion ? On the contrary, this was the charge of which Epicuros thought he was clearing the Atomists when he gave atoms an essential weight, and it is doubtless by confusion with him that the same doctrine has been ascribed to Democritos.[2] But, since Leucippos and Democritos, by the side of the extended body of the atom, supposed extension without body, or vacuum, they wanted to prove that the former has a physical, and therefore not purely geometrical, quality which excludes the latter. This quality of the atom, its only quality, is its absolute " fullness " ($\nu\alpha\sigma\tau\acute{o}\tau\eta s$), its indissoluble " solidity " ($\sigma\tau\epsilon\rho\rho\acute{o}\tau\eta s$), in short, its impenetrability and impassibility, based on a positive character which wholly excludes vacuum. This property is not affected by the extreme smallness of the atom, and that is doubtless why the possibility of very large atoms was admitted without difficulty. The early Atomists laid such weight on this property that one cannot suppose that Epicuros was the first to maintain the physical indivisibility of the atom. Lastly, it is remarkable that, according to Aristotle, there was at the bottom of Democritos's system a qualitative opposition, between vacuum, or the rare, and the solid.[3] So, then, there are two extensions, that which does not resist, or vacuum, and that which resists, or the atom. Consequently, the School of Abdera did not follow its quantitative and geometrical conception of nature to the end.

---

[1] On all this, cf. **LXVIII**, ch. 54, A. 6, 8 ff., 11, 13 ff. ; ch. 55, A. 5, i. 37 ff., 41, 43 ff., 49, 57, 135, §§ 65–7, etc., and Frag. 141. Aristotle calls the three principal differences of atoms $\sigma\chi\hat{\eta}\mu\alpha$, $\tau\acute{\alpha}\xi\iota s$, $\theta\acute{\epsilon}\sigma\iota s$.

[2] *Ibid.*, ch. 54, A. 6, end, and 16 ; ch. 55, A. 47, 58, 61. In favour of this interpretation, cf. **LXXXVII, LXXI**, § 179, etc. Against it, **II**, 859 ff. (French trans., ii. 307 ff.) and *ad* **LXVIII**, A. 47, etc.

[3] Cf. Arist., *Gen. et Corr.*, i. 8, 326 a 1 ff. ; *Phys.*, i. 5, 188 a 22 ; *Metaph.*, A. 4, 985 b 7, 10–13 ; Diog. Laërt., ix. 44, end ; **LXVIII**, ch. 55, A. 43, end, and 56. On the other side, **LXVIII**, ch. 54, A. 13 ff. ; cf. ch. 55, A. 49, end.

However, this surreptitious introduction of quality into the principles of the doctrine must not lead us to misjudge the reflective, decided attempt of the Atomists to give strictly mechanical explanations. Qualities, qualitative changes, substances as " fixed " (συμμένειν) totals of qualities collected together, all that is explained by the assembling of atoms, their shapes, their arrangement, and their position. The changes and annihilation of a thing are a shifting of the parts of the assemblage or its break-up, due to the incidental action of some small outside cause of movement. Nature is the universal store of the " seeds " (πανσπερμία), impassible, indestructible, unchangeable, infinite in number, which, by the various modes of their movement and aggregation, produce all things and all becoming. But movement cannot take place without the Not-being of vacuum, correlative with vacuumless Being. Thus movement and diversity, banned by the Eleatics, are re-established by a synthesis of Being and Not-being.

The first cause of the movement of atoms—to the horror of Aristotle, who can conceive of none but an internal tendency, such as an absolute weight or lightness—is, in their view, the vacuum.[1] Like multiplicity, movement appears with that which contradicts the plenum. As with the infinite number of the shapes of atoms, there is no reason why it should not happen, since the resisting atom has before it on every side nothing but a vacuum which offers it no resistance. If, then, the resisting and the unresisting, Being and its correlative, are eternal, movement has always existed, and a present movement is always determined by a previous movement. This was an original and powerful attempt to conceive of the motive cause as a purely mechanical cause, and not (as Aristotle did later) as a formal and final cause. Throughout all time, therefore, the atoms have been hurtling at infinite speed from the depths of the infinite in which they are like an infinity of separate islets. What thinkers imbued with dynamism call generative and creative nature, *physis*, is this " spattering all round " (περιπάλαξις). Now, their " trajectories " cannot fail to " intersect " (*concursus*, συγκατατρέχειν), so that there are " brushings " (ἐπίψαυσις) or " shakings " (παλμός), with " rebounds " (ἀποπάλλεσθαι), mutual " blows "

_____
[1] Arist., *Phys.*, viii. 9, 265 b 23 ff.; cf. iv. 8, 214 b 32 ff.

and " collisions " (πληγή, συγκρούεσθαι), and also " inter-
weavings " and " accumulations " (συμπλοκή, ἀθροίζεσθαι). So
entirely free movement is replaced by reciprocal, communicated movement.[1]

Accumulations of various sizes having thus formed, certain
atoms, perhaps by a sort of lateral rubbing of the accumulations, take on a circular motion and form a " vortex " (δῖνος).
The original " equilibrium " (ἰσορροπία) is succeeded by a
kind of " sorting out " (διάκρισις), which mechanically
combines atoms which are alike in size and shape, " expels "
(ἔκθλιψις) those which are not, and fixes certain assemblages.
In the same way, the waves breaking on the beach sort out
the pebbles, and under the winnowing-fan grains of wheat,
barley-corns, and lentils separate from one another and join
those like themselves. With composition, there now appears
the distinction between light and heavy. The heavier is that
which is more massive or more capable of hooking on, and
therefore that which becomes more stable and changes its,
place less ; the lighter is that which scatters more easily and,
while the heavier settles in the centre, flies further towards
the circumference. That is how things first come together ;
these elemental physical relations are the starting-point of
generation.[2] In the centre of the spherical assemblage which
constitutes a vortex, a resisting core is formed, against which
the atoms or accumulations of atoms at the circumference
" thrust " (ἀντέρεισις). Consequently, the surrounding
membrane will grow thinner and thinner, according as the
atoms composing it are absorbed or slowed down by the core.
Thus a world commences to form. But an infinity of other
vortices can equally give birth to worlds. Therefore the
number of these worlds is infinite, whether they are very
different from one another or quite alike.[3]

In a conception of this kind, finality can have no place, and
chance is equally excluded. When Leucippos, in what is
really our only fragment of him, a quotation from his book
On the Mind, tells us that " nothing is produced in vain," we
must understand the expression in the light of what follows—
" but all things are produced starting from a reason and in

[1] Diog. Laërt., ix. 31 ; **LXVIII,** ch. 54, A. 14, end, 15 middle, 24 (1) ; ch. 55,
A. 58, 37 mid., 47 ; Frag. 168.
[2] *Ibid.*, ch. 54, A. 24 (2 ff.) ; ch 55, A. 106, 128, and Frags. 164, 167.
[3] *Ibid.*, ch. 54, A. 21 ; ch. 55, A. 40 (2), 81 ff. ; Diog. Laërt., 31 ff., 44.

virtue of a necessity " (Frag. 2). So, too, if, in respect of the
origin of movement, the Peripatetics can say that in Democritos chance is in one sense a principle, on the other hand
they admit that according to his theory nothing happens by
chance, and the explanation by the immediate mechanical
cause suffices in all cases. For, in his eyes, necessity is " resistance, change of place, and collision," or, if you will, the vortex.[1]
This purely mechanical conception of necessity was, in the
time of Empedocles and Anaxagoras, a great novelty, while
agreeing with the prevailing tendency of the doctrine to
explanations of a quantitative kind. According to Aristotle,[2]
the Atomists' intention, not always explicit, was to show that
everything is number or the result of numbers, and we are
assured that Democritos specially studied the Pythagoreans.
Perhaps it was under the influence of their spatial arithmetic
that the semi-Eleatics of Abdera managed to create a physical
theory in which there is a dim foreshadowing of the spirit of
modern science.

It is, therefore, surprising that such fertile general principles
gave birth to such a feeble physical theory. Since part of its
most remarkable features will be found, in clearer form, in
Anaxagoras, we may be content with a few indications. On
the shape of the earth, Leucippos and Democritos have not
advanced beyond the conception of Anaximenes. It is shaped
like a drum, or, as Democritos says, like an oblong disk with
hollows to hold the water. A *Geography* is said to have shown
land and sea itineraries. The *Uranography* was perhaps a
description of the heavens. The peculiar luminosity of the
Milky Way is due to the fact that it comprises a very great
number of small stars whose light extends from one to another.
Since their theory would lead one to suppose that the zones
surrounding the earth move faster the further they are away,
Democritos gave an ingenious explanation of the contrary
appearance. The moon, for example, which is nearest to us,
seems to overtake a constellation of the outer sky the more
quickly when, on the contrary, it is really passed more quickly
by the constellation ; instead of measuring its true course we
measure the relation of its course to that of the Zodiacal
circle.[3] According to this hypothesis, the relative distance of

---

[1] *Ibid.*, ch. 55, A. 68 ff., 83.   [2] *De Caelo*, iii. 4, 303 a 8–10.
[3] Lucretius, v. 621–36.

stars could be measured by their time of revolution. Lastly, it was held that every world has a period of decadence, in which, as it moves through empty space, it is liable to be broken up by collision with a stronger vortex, its debris serving to form a new world.

One can easily guess what place the theory of effluences and pores must have had in atomistic physics. All action and affection are explained by a stream of atoms entering appropriate pores. Acidity, for instance, is due to the presence of subtle, angular atoms which slip in easily, while the similar atoms which constitute astringency block the pores which they enter.[1] It follows that these properties do not exist in themselves, and are the consequence of a contingent relation, or, as Democritos says, a conventional relation between the shapes, sizes, and arrangements of the atoms on the one side and the constitution of the pores of the perceiving subject on the other.[2] For this reason Democritos has been credited with distinguishing between primary and secondary qualities. But really his view is that what is primary is not properly qualitative. In the application of this theory to sensations, we must note the appearance of the theory of "simulacra" (δείκελα). These emanations, which preserve the specific characteristics of the objects from which they proceed, act like stamps on the air between the object and the eye ; then the impressions thus left on the air are reflected by the eye as by a mirror (ἔμφασις). Lastly, thought is simply a wholly internal movement of these same images, in consequence of the sensations. Yet, according to Democritos, there is a relationship between truth or error and the quality both of the mixture constituting the body and of that which constitutes the soul and gives it its temperature.[3]

The soul is, of course, material, and is composed of very subtle, very mobile atoms. Since these atoms are those of which fire is made, the soul must be a fiery body, comparable to the quicksilver which communicated its own mobility to the wooden Aphrodite of Daedalos into which it was poured. Such souls float in the air, whose pressure drives them into bodies. That explains why respiration maintains life and

---

[1] **LXVIII**, ch. 55, A. 135 (Theophr., *De Sensu*), 128–30.
[2] *Ibid.*, A. 135 (64) ; Arist., *Gen. et Corr.*, i. 2, 316 a 1 ff.   Cf. above, p. 114.
[3] **LXVIII**, A. 135 (68).

ceases with it, why the embryo in the womb develops by suction the miniature organs which the semen has introduced already formed, and so on. The soul is the principle of life, and also of thought, since thought is derived from sensation, which is a state of the living body. What is still obscure, is the process by which thought can rise above sensation to those intelligible realities, the atoms and the vacuum. Perhaps the Atomists said that the motes of dust which float about in a sunbeam are a sign to us of the incessant movement of the atoms and also of the existence of souls in the air.[1] It should still be explained by what imagery thought, in this case or in any other, goes beyond the given sensation, and even beyond all sensation.

Although Democritos's moral philosophy is the part of his work of which most fragments survive, it does not seem necessary to linger over it. The fragments hardly give a complete conspectus, whose connexion with the general principles of the system can be seen. Moreover, they contain nothing which we shall not find again, in a less scrappy form, in the first Socratics or in their successors—for example, the notion that the good is the object of universal knowledge (Frag. 69), that ignorance of that good is the principle of our faults (Frag. 83), that it is better to call down punishment on the faults which you have committed than on those of which you are the victim (Frag. 60), that happiness does not lie in the pleasures of sense (Frags. 37, 189) but in measure and suitability, in imperturbable serenity ($\dot{\alpha}\theta\alpha\mu\beta\dot{\iota}\alpha$), in tranquil peace of the heart ($\epsilon\dot{\upsilon}\theta\upsilon\mu\dot{\iota}\alpha$, $\epsilon\dot{\upsilon}\epsilon\sigma\tau\dot{\omega}$) (Frag. 4). These are beautiful maxims, but nothing more, to us who do not know their connexion.

When we come to Scepticism and Epicureanism we shall have occasion to see the actual development and action of true Democritean thought, a thought which combines the old naturalism with the kind of humanism which was characteristic of a new age. The problem which Leucippos had attacked, before which Empedocles had failed, was how to escape both the immobilistic monism of the Eleatics and from the mobilistic pluralism of Heracleitos. In extension, with all the quantitative determinations which it involves, he con-

---

[1] Arist., De An., i. 2, 404 a 1 ff. The passage is obscure, and there may be some confusion with the Pythagorean opinion mentioned above, p. 67.

ceived of the one and the many, the possibility of movement and real movement, as two correlative opposites which call one another and cannot be separated. This original and self-consistent solution, in which the elements of the problem raised by Ionian naturalism were reconciled, might, if the philosophy of Ideas and its finalism had not prevailed, have given the science of nature, in mechanism, a methodological hypothesis which would limit and organize its inquiries, without subordinating it to one philosophy or another and also without isolating it in technical specialities. But the attempt of Straton, in the school of Aristotle, to avoid both that divorce and that subordination was to remain an episode without consequences, and mechanism was to serve only as an instrument for the moral empiricism of Epicuros.

Chapter VII

THE MECHANISM OF QUALITY AND MIND. ANAXAGORAS OF CLAZOMENAE

With Anaxagoras of Clazomenae, for the first time in the history of Greek thought, philosophy took up its abode permanently in Athens. The date and circumstances of the arrival of that Ionian Metic, coming from the school of Anaximenes, are very obscure. He is said to have lived in Athens for thirty years, until the day when his notoriety and his friendship with Pericles exposed him, like Pheidias, to attacks which were chiefly aimed at his protector. By taking flight he escaped the dangerous consequences of a trial for impiety—a menace which was henceforward to hang over the heads of all philosophers in Athens. Retiring to Lampsacos in Asia, he is said to have died aged over seventy, about the beginning of the last third of the Vth century, amidst the unanimous veneration earned by the loftiness of his character and his indifference to personal gain. He probably started a school in Lampsacos, and was perhaps succeeded in it by Archelaos of Athens, before Metrodoros of Lampsacos, famed for his allegorical interpretations of Homer. His *Physics*, the only work which we can attribute to him with certainty, dealt, in its first book, with the principles, in a prose style which, as we shall see, was full of majesty. Yet absolute precision of detail was not sacrificed to style, and we are told that the work was illustrated with figures—for example, to describe the phases of the moon.

Like Empedocles before him, and Leucippos about the same time, Anaxagoras started from Eleaticism. " The totality of things," he says, " is eternally equal to itself " (Frag. 5). He therefore denies becoming—" coming into being " and " perishing " (Frag. 17). So he only takes up the old physics in the form given it by the philosophy of the Eleatics ; but he, too, does so with the object of reconciling that philosophy with the empirical reality of plurality and movement. Now, in doing this, he opposes both Empedocles and Leucippos, denying the former the right to obtain the infinite diversity of qualities from his four irreducible " roots," and denying the latter the finite divisibility of space without qualities and the reality of vacuum. If the alleged simple bodies seem to be that from which everything comes, it is just because they are the most thorough mixtures given to our experience,[1] and, in general, no generation of a composite thing can be understood unless all the qualitative variety which it has when it comes into being already exists in the principle. That is the meaning of the famous proposition with which his book began : " All things were together, infinite both in number and in smallness," but " none appeared distinctly because of that smallness." It was " a confused mixture of seeds ($\sigma\pi\acute{\epsilon}\rho\mu\alpha\tau\alpha$) . . . in no way like one another " (Frags. 1 and 4, § 2). These seeds, really side by side, and not potentially contained in a real mixture, are not merely common, superficial qualities, such as hot and cold, bright and dark, dry and wet ; they are, above all, the most determinate and richest qualifications, those which have the names of things and in which the common qualities are contained. " How could hair come from not-hair, or flesh from not-flesh ? " (Frag. 10). For an animal to have flesh and bones, there must be flesh and bones in the food on which it nourishes itself. Otherwise, Being would not be the All, and the mixture would not be a mixture of all things. Therefore qualitative differences are so infinite in number as to be quite indistinguishable. But, on the other hand, that infinite distinction is real, and the actually infinite division of quality is accompanied by a no less actually infinite division of space ; otherwise, new " seeds " would have to appear, to correspond to a dynamic development of such-and-such a quality in various degrees.[2] Every qualitative difference therefore, is a " portion " ($\mu o\hat{\iota}\rho\alpha$), and these portions, contrary to the view of the Atomists, are divided *ad infinitum* into identical portions ; for " there is something smaller, to all infinity, since Being cannot cease to be," just as it is impossible that the original mixture should lack something and not be infinitely large (Frag. 3).

[1] Cf. Frag. 1, end, and Arist., *De Caelo*, iii. 3, 302 a 28–35.
[2] Contrary view in **LXX**, 283–8 ; cf. **LXXI**, 305, n. 1.

These " portions " are objects for the intelligence only, and, indeed (a memory of the arguments of Zenon), even the intelligence cannot imagine their infinite division, which cannot be effected in fact.[1] Since, in one qualitative " seed," all portions are like one another and like that seed, they are what are called, in the language of Aristotle, " homoeomerous " things, things of like parts, and consequently the word " homoeomeries " (ὁμοιομέρειαι) became the technical name of the qualified portions of Anaxagoras.[2] Thus, it seems, extension, being never separated from quality, ceases to be something altogether abstract, while, on the other hand, quality, being always bound to extension, becomes something intelligible. So we go beyond sensible appearances, as the truth of science commands us to do, since they are " a vision of hidden things " (Frag. 21 a ; cf. 21). So sensible becoming, which is unintelligible in respect of quality, becomes intelligible as soon as it is transferred to extension and, the being of quality remaining unchangeable, brought down to movement in place. The Greeks would speak properly if they called coming into being " being mixed " and perishing " being separated " (Frag. 17). Every sensible thing is a mixture of qualified portions, like the original mixture itself. It has " a portion of everything " (Frag. 11) ; " all things are in each thing " ; none exists " in isolation, but, as it was at the beginning, so now, too, all things are together " (Frag. 6) ; they are not " isolated from one another, nor cut off as with a hatchet, nor hot separated from cold, nor cold from hot " (Frag. 8), any more, no doubt, than the quality of hair is isolated from the quality of grass. Only, whereas the original mixture was so perfectly equal that nothing in it was distinct from anything else, in the secondary, empirical mixtures, on the contrary, certain assemblages of qualitatively identical portions predominate in volume in the whole mixture. Now, " that of which there is the most, appearing most distinctly, gives and gave each thing its individuality," and causes " each thing to be unlike anything else " (Frag. 12, end). So every sensible thing is a universe, but a universe in its own way, only differing from all others or changing its own previous manner of being by a wholly extrinsic character, namely, the mode

---

[1] **LXVIII**, ch. 46, A. 46, middle, and Frag. 7.
[2] Cf., e.g., Lucret., i. 830.

of distribution or the quantity of its qualities. Thus, as with the alchemists later, everything can become everything and change into everything by a mere mechanism of quality.

Anaxagoras shows equal originality in his conception of the motive cause. He boldly accepts the Eleatic doctrine of essential immobility, for infinite time, of the infinitely qualified Being which he supposes. The whole primitive mixture would never come out of its inertia,[1] if a movement of " separation " had not been set up in it by what Anaxagoras calls " Mind " (*nous*). This movement at once takes the form of a " rotation," which, after starting in a small part, " spread further," and " will spread yet further " (Frags. 13, 12). So Mind gives a sort of fillip to the balanced, motionless confusion of the primitive *migma*, and the mechanical effect increases continually by more and more break-downs of equilibrium, each of which constitutes one of the unequal redistributions of the whole mixture which, as we have seen, make specifically and individually distinct things. Of course, Mind is not in the mixture ; for, if it were, it would be combined confusedly with all the rest and would exert no separating action. Apart from all the rest, which is not apart from anything, it is " a thing infinite and all-dominant (αὐτοκρατές) ; alone it is in itself and for itself " (Frag. 12 ; cf. 11).[2] It is, therefore, something quite different from the *logos* of Heracleitos, which is immanent in the becoming in which it goes about.

When we try to say what Mind is, we come to difficulties. We see that it is not only a motive cause, but an intelligence, for " it knows " both the mixture and what is distinct and separate in it ; and it is an arranging intelligence, for " how everything must be, and how everything has been and is no longer, and how everything is, Mind arranged it " (Frag. 12). Correlatively, we are told that, in the eyes of Anaxagoras, chance is merely our inability to discover the cause, and fate is an empty word.[3] Yet, on the other hand, Mind does not seem to be an intelligence which reflects and calculates ; it is, rather, similar to the soul of living beings.[4] And, indeed, after saying that Mind is the only thing of which there is not a part in everything, Anaxagoras adds that " there are, however,

[1] Arist., *Phys.*, viii. 1, 250 b 24 ff. ; **LXVIII**, ch. 46, A. 59, 48 beg., etc.
[2] Cf. the passages of Plato and Aristotle, *ibid.*, A. 55–6.
[3] *Ibid.*, A. 66.　　　　　　　　　　[4] *Ibid.*, A. 58, 100 (Aristotle(.

things in which there is Mind," and which have " Mind for a master " ; they are " all those which have breath." But, he goes on, " Mind is always alike, both the greater and the smaller " (Frags. 11, 12). That means, no doubt, that it is always outside the mixture, whether that be the original mixture or the mixture constituted by a living creature. So, too, it is not by a higher *mind* that the beasts are superior to the plants, and men to the beasts, but, respectively, because they are not attached to the earth, and because they have hands.[1] Mind must, therefore, be like an independent soul, from which other souls, equally independent, emanate.[2] Lastly, what definitely forbids us to suppose that this Mind, for all its arranging activity, has ends in view, is the statement that it owes its " whole knowledge of everything " and its " greatest strength of all things " to merely being " the thinnest and purest of all things " (Frag. 12), in short, that most able to slip between them, first dividing them and then animating them, yet without risk of becoming mingled with them. We can, therefore, understand the disappointment, so strongly expressed by Plato and Aristotle,[3] of those who, with Socrates, reproached the old physicists with asserting only mechanical causes, and found nothing in the philosophy of Mind but a " theatrical apparatus, dragged on to the stage " when the author found himself in difficulties, having to explain the origin of movement, or life.

The first distinction to appear is that of the fiery ether and the air. Two masses are formed, one composed of all the seeds which have the common quality of being tenuous, hot, bright, and dry, and the other of all which are dense, cold, dark, and wet. Each mass can, in a sense, be called infinite, for it contains an infinite number of different seeds, collected together (Frags. 1, end, and 2). At the same time, the two masses take their relative places, the air in the centre, where it forms the earth, and the ether, in which the stars will gradually become distinct, at the circumference. In the theory of the constitution of the stars there may, perhaps, be an anticipation of the hypotheses of Kant and Laplace, whether the coagulated, petrified parts of the earth tend, by the acceleration of the

---

[1] *Ibid.*, A. 102, 113, 115 ff.
[2] For the story of Hermotimos of Clazomenae, who from time to time lost his soul, see Diels' note, *ibid.*, A. 58.
    Phaedon, 97 b ff. ; *Metaph.*, A. 3, 984 b 17 ff. ; 4, 985 a 18 ff.

revolving movement, to " fly outwards," or the circular vortex by its force attracts to itself stony masses torn from the surface of the earth, communicates its fire to them, and holds them by its extreme velocity.[1] In any case, the stars are " incandescent masses," whose nature is in no way different from that of terrestrial bodies, as we can see if we note the similarity between our rocks and the stones which, by some accident, fall on to the surface of the earth, being extinguished as they do so. This theory is said to have been suggested to Anaxagoras, or it may have been confirmed, by observation of the fall of a meteor at Aegospotami about 468–6. Why did it give such offence ? Hitherto, scientific thought had given many signs of its freedom, but it had been in the seclusion of a school, far from contact with the popular conscience. Besides, we have seen that the scandal must have been fomented by political rivalries. One must add, too, that his desire to bring the heavenly bodies down to the terms of experience led Anaxagoras to declare that the moon was no larger than the Peloponnese, and that the sun was only a good deal larger. Lastly, the reputation which he enjoys of having been the first to understand the true reason of eclipses may be undeserved, especially in respect of eclipses of the moon. It is, at least, remarkable that he retains, as a complementary cause of the phenomenon, the invisible bodies of which Anaximenes spoke. The question whether he believed in the existence of several universes, simultaneously or in succession, appears to be insoluble.

Of the biological or psychological opinions of Anaxagoras, perhaps that most worth mentioning is the theory that, contrary to what Empedocles taught, opposites are known by opposites : cold is felt only in contrast to heat. Every sensation, therefore, is a change ; from which it follows that it is a pain, which becomes dulled by habit, but is keen if the excitement is too intense.

Historically, and with reference to the periods of Greek philosophy and science, Anaxagoras marks a decisive transition. Of the heritage of earlier philosophies he has sacrificed nothing —not the qualitativism of the Milesians, Heracleitos, or Empedocles, nor the Eleatics' negation of becoming, nor that combination of their extension with the Pythagorean number

[1] Frag. 16 (cf. Frag. 9) and A. 71, 72, 42 (6).

which was the quantitativism of the Atomists, nor their mechanism. But, on the other hand, he opens the path for a new philosophy. By placing being in quality, as he did, by striving to raise it from sensation to intelligibility, he was preparing thinkers to construct the real with specifically distinct forms or ideals. What is more, by attributing efficient causality to Mind, even incompletely, he suggested the replacement of mechanical, material causality by an ideal causality of the end and of the good. Not without reason, therefore, did the last of the natural physicists appear to Plato and Aristotle as a forerunner of the Socratic revolution.

BOOK THREE

HUMAN CULTURE

Chapter I

ECLECTICS AND SOPHISTS

I

Eclectic Physicists

After the Eleatics, the endeavour of philosophers had been to modify the terms of the problem which the Ionians had attacked. Instead of inquiring what is the one thing which becomes all other things, they asked what essential plurality can be reconciled with the true unity of Being and, by unions and separations, account for the appearance of becoming. On the other hand, the physicists whom we shall now discuss behaved as if the Eleatic criticism had never existed. For them, the problem of becoming took the form which it had had for the philosophers whom the Eleatics had combated ; their monism was that of the old Milesians. Herein they were reactionaries. But, in order to invest their erudite resuscitations of a vanished past with a semblance of youth, they gave them a colouring borrowed from later doctrines. So they were, at the same time, " eclectics."

The doctrine of Thales was revived, about the middle of the Vth century, by the Samian Hippon, who is said to have been born in Great Greece. Some of his opinions recall, with differences, the medical theories of the Pythagoreans. He appears to have been chiefly interested in physiological or embryological questions. There are, however, traces of his cosmology, and the only fragment of him which we possess, on the marine origin of springs, seems to indicate that, like

Thales, he made the earth float on water. What innovations he made, it is hard to say in the present state of our knowledge.

Diogenes of Apollonia, a product of the school of Anaximenes and a young contemporary of Leucippos and Anaxagoras, seems to have cut more of a figure as a philosopher and as a scientist. It is not impossible that he taught in Athens. In addition to his treatise *On Nature*, which contained a *Meteorology* and an *Anthropology*, he probably wrote a book *Against the Sophists*, that is, doubtless, against the physicists who had abandoned the old tradition. While showing an interest in matters of method and form characteristic of a Sophist in the strict sense of the word (Frag. 1), he tries to prove that change cannot be explained without transformations of a single, unchangeable foundation of all things, which must be such that it can account for the stability of their organization (Frags. 2, 3). Now, what best fulfils this twofold condition is the principle of Anaximenes, air, provided only that it is given thought and some of the attributes of the Mind of Anaxagoras and, in fact, a divine nature, without, however, being separated from the matter which it organizes (Frag. 5). Air produces all the diversity of things and worlds, infinite in number, by a process of rarefaction and condensation, the details of which are rather obscure. It is the principle of movement, because it is eternal and universal mobility ; it is the common principle of all life, as is shown by the fact that all living things, including fish, have to breathe, in different ways (cf. Frag. 5) ; and it is the principle of intelligence, because it is itself " that which knows many things " (Frag. 8). By the union of air with the blood in the vascular system, their reciprocal movements towards the brain or towards the thoracic region, and the entry of air and its fixation at one point in the brain, he explained sensation and sleep, distraction, forgetfulness and memory, and the variety of intelligence among living creatures and among men. As the air circulates all through the body, every organ, in normal conditions, will perform its special function, and the purer this air-intelligence is, the subtler will thought be. We see how important the study of the circulation is in Diogenes' biology, and his description of the veins, quoted at length by Aristotle, is a remarkable evidence of his anatomical investigations (Frag. 6).

The eclectical tendency is still more manifest in a pupil of Anaxagoras, Archelaos of Athens, whom one tradition makes the master of Socrates. He follows Anaxagoras in almost everything, but distorts his doctrine on essential points. Thus, he makes Mind a mixture, and for the mechanical process of separation and rotation which distinguishes things he substitutes a process of condensation and rarefaction. So he touched up Anaxagoras with the help of Anaximenes and Diogenes of Apollonia, declaring, moreover, that the latter's air-intelligence was the very mixture of which Mind is made. Consequently, the two first things to become distinct cannot be the same as in the theory of Anaxagoras ; they are, in his view, heat, or fire, which is mobile and active, and cold, or water, which is at rest and passive.

Idaeos of Himera is usually mentioned in this group. By a wholly gratuitous conjecture he is credited with an opinion recorded by Aristotle, to the effect that certain physicists maintained a first principle of a nature intermediate either between fire and air or between air and water. To tell the truth, we know nothing about him or the physicists in question.

II

THE SOPHISTS OF THE FIFTH CENTURY

Down to the middle of the Vth century, the object of philosophic thought had been to say what is the underlying reality, or what is the true being, of the visible universe. Reflection on conduct had been left to poets and lawgivers, and philosophy had not regarded it as one of its proper objects. Philosophy had confined itself to the problem of becoming, considering all its aspects and attempting every solution. To continue to be able to move in the blind alley in which it found itself, it returned upon its first footsteps, rejuvenating its gait, and gave itself up to the fruitless game of eclectical constructions. If it was to escape from this, there must be a complete revolution.

This revolution was partly due to social and political factors. After the Persian Wars, Athens, brought into the front rank of the Greek states by the part which she had taken in the struggle, organized the Ionian Confederation under her protection. Along with her imperialist policy there went, inside the city, which contained more Metics and slaves than free citizens, a break-down of the old unity and a complete collapse of equilibrium. The constitution became more and more democratic, and the line taken by statesmen was to increase the sovereignty of the people without ceasing, and to pay them, in order to divert the greed of the poor citizens from ancient or newly acquired fortunes. The instability of such a state of things was disguised for a time by the personal ascendancy of Pericles, but became evident when the Peloponnesian War broke out. But reverses did not rob Athens, for a long time yet, of her power of radiation and attraction. To Athens men came from everywhere, to test the virtue of new ideas or beliefs. As the collective bond weakened, the individual personality had more play. Every man wanted liberty for himself, and sought it the more eagerly as he felt the State growing more helpless. He sought, by the possession of political credit and wealth, to give rein to his personal power of enjoyment. In Athens, and in the cities which came under her influence, a fierce, unruly individualism reigned.

Another factor of the transformation then taking place in thought was of an intellectual order—the advance of specialization in the sciences and crafts, going with the division of labour in industry and trade. Hitherto philosophy had not by any means neglected the practical requirements which had provoked its earliest speculations. Indeed, its most striking characteristic was that it was mingled with scientific inquiry. But practical applications, by the very fact that they had so increased, finally broke off from the tree of which they were the fruit, and it was felt to be dangerous to keep special investigation too closely bound to a general doctrine. The divorce was not always equally complete, but, at any rate, specialists did exist—mathematicians, like Œnopides and Hippocrates of Chios, astronomers, like Meton, who reformed the Attic calendar, theorists of music and gymnastics, writers on agriculture, tactics, stage-perspective, the rules of sculpture, and even cooking. Medicine, which had long been taught as a lay science in the schools of Croton, Cyrene, Cnidos, and Cos, definitely became an independent study. Hippocrates of Cos flourished about 420, and most of the writings in the

Hippocratic Collection, among which the personal work of that great man is hard to distinguish, doubtless belong to the second half of the Vth century. It was at this time, too, that history had its birth. Herodotos finished his work about 430, and Thucydides was a pupil of the Sophists. In short, without dwelling on the matter further, one may say that all personal ability and every secret prescription of a school was brought out into public and became something which could be communicated by a special branch of teaching.

Now, this development of special technical branches brought questions of method and the formal aspect of knowledge to the forefront. As soon as technical skill ceases to be regarded as an innate talent or a privileged tradition, men reflect on the technique of technique, and this makes them ready to reflect on the method of thought and philosophy. In addition, in the eyes of the individual who is tending to break loose from the leading-strings of the State and religion, it will seem that this general technique must furnish the principles on which to organize his existence and that of the State, with a view to happiness. So the problems of the essence of individual happiness and its conditions, or of the constitution of society, become objects of philosophical discussion. A last consequence of the same movement is a more marked tendency of the mind to question itself about its power and the rôle which it can claim in the representation of the real and in the determination of conduct. Thus critical, reasoning thought grows up, subjecting collective opinion to examination and rejecting it in favour either of individual, contingent theories, or of a combination of concepts which is supposed to have necessity and universality. So, for many reasons, man takes the place of nature as the centre of speculation. In various aspects, " humanism," in the widest sense which the word can have, succeeds the " naturalism " of previous philosophers.

It is possible that this revolution, which meant the advent of a philosophy which was dialectical or abstract and wholly logical, was injurious to the development of the experimental sciences, which had been encouraged by naturalism. But we must remember that the attempts of naturalism at positive investigation were taken up by the specialist scientists, and the real question is rather whether specialization, the independence of the sciences, is a good or a bad thing. Moreover, it is not to be denied that the earlier philosophy contained the germs of that which followed it. The Pythagoreans, Anaxagoras, even the Atomists in a sense, were on the way to a formal representation of things ; dialectic came from the Eleatics ; Pythagoreanism had already made man think of his destiny and personal salvation. Lastly, the special tendencies of the old physics did not disappear altogether. But, where they survived, physical science was no longer the main stem of philosophy, but only one of its branches.

The revolution which took place in the orientation of thought about the middle of the Vth century was mainly the work of the Sophists and Socrates. Although the tradition of their mutual antagonism is in a sense true, there is no paradox in regarding them as fellow-workers in the same achievement.

It will be noticed, first of all, that when we regard the Sophists as false philosophers, in contrast to the true philosopher, we are relying on a tradition of doubtful historical value. The " Sophists," in the language of the Vth and early IVth centuries, were the men whom Descartes would one day call *les doctes*, the " learned "—men who, like Homer, Hesiod, Solon, the Seven Sages, or Pythagoras, were held to be store-houses of wisdom, or else specialists (masters of palestras, musicians, rhapsodes, mathematicians, physicians), who, having elevated some special skill into a science, flattered themselves that they could teach it to others.[1] Incidentally, the term may be used disparagingly, but in this sense it is applied to Socrates and the Socratics themselves. When, therefore, we give the word an abusive sense, using it as a definition of certain persons, we are adopting a particular use which only became general later, and comes from Plato and Aristotle. Now, in the former it is not constant, and in the latter it implies an important distinction, between the Sophist, who sets out to win glory and riches, and the " eristic " or argumentative man, who only wants to get the better in a discussion, both of whom may, of course, be the same man at bottom.[2] Correlatively, we may ask whether the Sophists who

---

[1] Cf. **II**, 1075 ff. (French trans., ii. 480–2) ; passage from Aristotle, in **LXVIII**, ch. 73 b, 1.

[2] *Top.*, viii. 11, 162 a 16 ; *Soph. El.*, 11, 171 b 25–31.

appear in Plato's dialogues as contemporaries of Socrates are not sometimes disguised portraits of certain of Plato's own opponents. Furthermore, his testimony, like Aristotle's, is that of an enemy of the Sophists. The rest of our evidence is not usually independent of these two ; it is derived from them and does not enable us to check them. The surviving summaries or fragments of books of those whom we call the Sophists are often suspect, when their attribution is not wholly fanciful, of being remodelled versions, or, especially in Plato, imitations and parodies. At all events, they throw very little light on the personality of their authors.

Whatever the truth of these difficult problems may be, we have a traditional catalogue of our Sophists. According to Plato, the first man to think of calling himself a " Sophist," meaning that he was a teacher of wisdom, that wisdom was his " art " or speciality, was Protagoras of Abdera. He was about twenty years older than Socrates, and was certainly dead when Socrates was tried. Was his long career an unbroken succession of triumphs, as Plato declares ? Or should we believe a tradition, probably coming from Aristotle, to the effect that, towards the end of his life, he was accused of impiety in Athens, and only saved himself by flight?

Between Protagoras and Gorgias of Leontion in Sicily we know of no connecting link. In 427 Gorgias came to Athens as ambassador of his fellow-townsmen, to ask the city for help against the Syracusans. He already had a great reputation as a rhetor in Sicily, and in Athens, it is said, it received brilliant and profitable confirmation. No doubt, he returned to Athens more than once, and among his pupils he numbered Isocrates, Thucydides, Æschines (the rival of Demosthenes), Critias, and the poet Agathon. When he died, aged almost a hundred (between 380 and 370), in Thessaly, perhaps at the court of Jason of Pheræ, the glory and wealth which he had earned by his profession were very great.

The reputation of Prodicos of Ceos seems to have been no less than that of the two others. Since Ceos was not far from Athens, he was able to stay in the latter city frequently, and, from the way in which Aristophanes speaks of him in the *Clouds* and the *Birds*, he must have been a well-known figure there. He was perhaps a little older than Socrates, and was alive at the time of the latter's trial.

The same is true of Hippias of Elis, who seems to have been rather younger than the Sophists mentioned above. He was an encyclopaedic virtuoso of the picturesque type produced by the Italian Renaissance, and Plato may not be painting an utter caricature when he describes Hippias parading himself before the money-changers' tables and telling the gaping onlookers that when he went to Olympia everything which he wore had been made by himself—cloak, tunic, rich embroidered belt, shoes, ring, seal, oil-flask, and scraper (*Hipp. Min.*, 368 b-d).

The identity of some others is harder to determine. Even in ancient times there were doubts whether Antiphon the Sophist was the same as Antiphon of Rhamnus, " logographer " or writer of forensic orations, rhetor, and politician, who took an active part in the constitution of the aristocratic government of the Four Hundred (412–411). No decisive reason seems to have been adduced for distinguishing them, and there is nothing surprising, as we shall see, in the notion that a man like Antiphon of Rhamnus should also have specialized in divination and the interpretation of dreams, taught physics and geometry, and written on morals and politics.[1] So, too, there is some uncertainty about Thrasymachos of Chalcedon, who appears in Book I of the *Republic* as a violent, brutal debater, whereas elsewhere, in Plato's own *Phaedros* and in Aristotle, he is a master who can handle all the " resources " of oratory with a sure touch, having analysed, collected, and classified them in the most exact and complete " Summa " yet composed, and is a sober writer with a beautiful style. The care with which he avoids the hiatus seems to show that he belongs to the second generation of Sophists, and that he is nearer to Isocrates or Plato than to Socrates.

The question of the Platonic pseudonyms has been raised in connexion with the two chief speakers in the *Euthydemos*. These Sophists, Euthydemos and Dionysodoros, are brothers, natives, " it is believed," of Chios, who had emigrated to Thurii. They are men who know everything and can teach everything, theory and practice alike, logographers and rhetors, subtle inventors of the art of fighting without an object, always refuting everything, whether it be false or true.

---

[1] This is the opinion of Alfred Croiset, in *Revue des Études grecques*, xxx (1917). H. Diels (**LXVIII,** ch. 80) distinguishes between the two.

Formerly they taught tactics and the use of all kinds of weapons in Athens ; now they teach a manner of " exhorting " men to philosophy and virtue (273 d-275 a, 278 c-d). In addition, they have an infallible method of shutting any adversary's mouth—by saying that nothing is anything, since nothing can be " other " than it is (303 d-e). Was it not Plato's intention to combine here, in a single caricature, as a picturesque pendant to the analysis in the *Sophist*, all the characteristics scattered about elsewhere ? What is more, certain features in the portrait of the two brothers seem to be allusions to the polemic which went on between Antisthenes and Plato. If so, the pair in the *Euthydemos* symbolize the kinship of sophistry and eristic, which Aristotle also points out. If there are often coincidences between Aristotle's *Refutation of Sophistic Arguments* and the *Euthydemos*, it is because both writers consider their Socratic opponents as standing in the same relation to the Academy and Lyceum as the Sophists did to Socrates. That there is some truth in this, is possible. But, while it is probable that Plato is the source of the sole mention which we have of Dionysodoros (Xen., *Mem.*, iii. 1. 1), the real existence of Euthydemos as an author of captious arguments is attested beyond dispute by Aristotle.[1]

In the second rank in this survey we might mention Euenos of Paros, Xeniades of Corinth, who seems to be connected with Gorgias as much as with Protagoras, Polos of Acragas, a pupil of Gorgias, and Lycophron, who is usually said to have raised certain objections against the decomposition of the verb into predicate and copula.[2] Polyxenos, who is said to have invented the argument of the " third man," Protarchos, who speaks in the *Philebos*, and the rhetors Theodoros of Byzantion and Alcidamas, the rival of Isocrates, are, even more certainly than Lycophron, Sophists of the second generation.

Lastly, if being a Sophist is a profession, one cannot properly include in the list men who were not masters of the art, but politicians trained in the school. Such was Critias, Plato's kinsman, who was one of the Thirty Tyrants, a

---

[1] *Soph. El.*, 20, 177 b 12 ; *Rhet.*, ii. 24, 1401 a 26. Cf. Plato, *Crat.*, 386 d.

[2] Arist., *Phys.*, i. 2, 185 b 25–32. But it should be noted that (i) Simplicius (*Phys.*, 91/29, 92/33) and Philoponos (*Phys.*, 49/19) ascribe this idea to Menedemos and the School of Eretria, and (ii) Diog. Laërt. (ii. 140) mentions a book by one Lycophron on Menedemos.

literary nobleman given to audacities of a purely verbal kind, who is represented by extensive fragments in verse and prose. Such, too, was the mysterious Callicles of the *Gorgias*, in whom Plato the aristocrat wished to expose the reverse side of the demagogue ; it cannot be proved that he is a fictitious character.

The time has come to determine certain collective features, by which one may justify the classification under one name of individuals who are not connected with one another by any school tradition.

In the first place, the Sophistic movement of the Vth century represents a sum of independent attempts to satisfy the same needs by similar methods. The needs are those of a time and a country in which every citizen can have a share in the management of the business of his city, and can obtain personal predominance by words alone ; where the competition of individual activities gives rise to numerous conflicts before the popular law-courts ; where every man wants to assert, in the eyes of all, the superiority of his " virtue " ($\dot{a}\rho\epsilon\tau\dot{\eta}$)—that is, of his talents and his ability to rule his own life and that of others. Eagerness of thought and greed for enjoyment, the ambition to dominate and to emancipate one's own activity, exuberant, superficial curiosity, combined with a supple strength and penetrating subtlety, enthusiasm and versatility —these are the characteristics of the social environment, and above all of the younger generation which aspires to make the best use of its advantages of wealth and birth. It therefore needs masters, to teach it the art of individual success in social life, while sparing it the delays and disappointments of experience. This is the art, on principle, which the Sophists taught. They taught the science of " good counsel " in private or public affairs, that is, " virtue," in the precise sense defined above, and the means to " become superior " to one's rivals.

Since the need which their teaching met was a need of all democratic cities, they went from town to town to the pupils who awaited them. That is why there was no Sophistic school, for a school implies that pupils go to a master, who has a fixed abode somewhere. Moreover, whereas the fee paid by the pupil served solely for the upkeep and prosperity of the school, the Sophist profited by it personally. His charge varied according as a complete course or a single lesson was taken, and as it was private or public. Like any tradesman, to the great indignation of Plato and Aristotle, he measured the extent of his spiritual influence by his takings.

In exchange, what did the Sophists give their pupils ? They uttered before them " show-speeches " (ἐπιδεικτικοὶ λογοί) as samples of what they could do and what they hoped to teach. With a view to advertisement, on the days of the great Panhellenic gatherings they doubtless gave performances for nothing, and in many cases their published writings may have been intended only to further this publicity. The theme of such speeches might be a political or philosophical question of a very general nature, a panegyric on a city, a funeral oration, or a dissertation on the moral worth of some person sung by the poets, such as Helen or Palamedes. Sometimes they displayed their art in an amusing fancy about some trivial subject—the praise of peacocks, mice, silk-worms, salt, pots, and the like. The Sophist was a rhetor, and also a teacher of rhetoric. After giving examples of the art of speaking or writing in an ordered, correct, elegant manner about every possible subject, he taught that art. But, since the practice of such an art necessitated a prodigious variety of information, he used to reduce his subjects to general themes, or, as they were called later, " common-places "—moral or psychological themes furnished by the reading of the poets, political themes, or legal themes, of which Antiphon has left remarkable analyses. To succeed, therefore, he had to have encyclopaedic knowledge himself, and to pay heed to the taste of the public and to the fashionable questions of the day. In philosophy he would aim at paradox ; in mathematics, he would attempt to square the circle (Hippias and Antiphon) ; in physics he would simplify by combining, and would be an eclectic. Moreover, to control all this mass of knowledge, formal as it was, he sought for a method, equally formal. So, with reference to the object of Sophistic teaching, Hippias's system of mnemonics was a discovery of great importance. In short, the Sophists tried to superimpose on the old traditional and purely civic education—thereby endangering that education— a wider teaching, even aiming on principle at universality, emancipated from tradition and valid for all men. They wanted to be, not " pedagogues " (in the Greek sense), nor philosophers of a school, but professors. They mark a stage in the history of education.

What, exactly, were the spirit and method of their teaching ? Since their object was to prepare the pupil for every conflict in thought or action to which social life might give rise, their method was essentially " antilogy " or controversy, the opposition of the theses possible with regard to certain themes, or " hypotheses," suitably defined and classified. The pupil had to learn to criticize and to argue, to organize a " joust " of reasons against reasons. The Sophist may not have been an " arguer," but he taught his pupil to become one. It does not matter whether the opposition was between two long speeches or between the questions and answers of a conversation. This method is the practical application of the Heracleitean conception of a dynamic contrast between successive judgments, and also of the process of argument by which Zenon brought out the static opposition of simultaneous judgments about the fundamental notions of experience. Now, it was Heracleiteanism which gave Protagoras his theoretical basis, and Eleaticism which provided that of Gorgias.[1] The fact that the works of Protagoras included *Controversies* and an *Art of Argument* shows that he was the originator of this method of forming the intellect.

A significant example has been preserved in a small anonymous work of the end of the Vth century, a short and incomplete school-exercise entitled *Double Reasons* (δισσοὶ λόγοι, formerly called διαλέξεις).[2] The author considers in succession nine themes on which philosophers do not agree, some of them, be it noted, being themes with which the Socratic conversations deal—good and evil ; the beautiful and the ugly ; the just and the unjust ; the true and the false ; folly and wisdom, ignorance and knowledge ; whether knowledge and virtue can be taught ; whether magistracies should go by lot or by capacity ; that the man who can best make and apply laws is the dialectician, for he knows all oppositions ; that the mnemonic system is the best of all inventions. These themes give occasion for arguments for and against ; they are the subject-matter of an exercise. Thus, for example, on good

---

[1] This seems to be indicated by Plato, *Phaedon*, 90 a-b, and *Phaedros*, 261 d-e. Cf. *Soph.*, 232 d-233 a, 225 b-c ; *Protag.*, 329 b, etc. ; *Theaet.*, 167 d ; *Rep.*, vii. 539 b-c.
[2] **LXVIII**, ch. 83

and evil, you can say that their opposition is essential, or that it is merely relative to the various characters of individuals and to the circumstances in which each in his turn may find himself. The pupil declares for the second thesis, and proves it by examples—it is evil for one who is not physically strong to be unable to resist his passions, but is good for a man whose trade is to encourage the intemperance of others ; illness is good for the physician, death is good for the tomb-seller, and so on. The other thesis remains, however, and, without inquiring what is in itself the " essence " ($\tau\iota$ $\dot{\epsilon}\sigma\tau\iota$) of good and evil, the pupil now sets out to prove that they are distinct. He asks an imaginary supporter of the other thesis questions which make him contradict himself : " Are you good to your parents ? " " Yes." " Then, since you say that good and bad are not distinct, you are bad to them," . . . and so on.

By this example we see that the Sophists used the method of antilogy to teach their pupils to invent mechanically, on any question, the ideas which should feed the spoken or written discourse, and the mainspring of the method was the opposition of judgements. So, whether he called himself one or not, the Sophist was always a professor of the art of speaking or writing, a master of rhetoric.

This technique of " persuasion " which he taught was special in appearance only. In reality it was universal in application ; without it, the really special arts—politics, medicine, etc.—had no value or efficacity. Now, if rhetoric has this supremacy, it is just because it teaches you to put the processes of antilogy into practice. Antilogy supplies a uniform scheme of the construction of discourses. You can fill up this scheme, according to the occasion and the time at your disposal, with few words or many. In any case, since the pupil always has it ready to use, he is in a position to improvise without having worked up the subject. This decisive test of their art Gorgias and Hippias sought to obtain from the public. The mechanism which they set working appears clearly in the *Funeral Oration* spoken by Gorgias in honour of those killed in war, or in Agathon's speech in Plato's *Symposium*. " What was absent in these men," said Gorgias, " which should not be present in men ? And what was present in them which should not have been present ? " and so on. This balancing of antithetical words and sentences is the process by which the speaker breaks up his thought and develops it, in the air, as it were, on a purely formal plane. Lastly, verbal oppositions presuppose an exact distinction of terms, so that it is natural that the Sophists, particularly Protagoras and Prodicos, should have insisted on the necessity of defining words precisely and using them properly. Here, too, there is another method of setting forth ideas and feeding discourse. The reading of the poets, with a commentary, not only supplies themes for discussion ; it gives practice in the analytical study of expression.

The Sophists devoted all their energies to perfecting this verbal formalism, and remained indifferent to ideas. For the spirit of their teaching required that they should have no doctrine of their own, but should show how all doctrines could be defended, the most paradoxical and outrageous no less than those most commonly accepted, doubtless keeping the former for limited, discreet audiences, while, with sound commercial instinct, they gave the latter every publicity. For it is not solely by differences in the conscience of individual Sophists that we must explain the remarkable differences of attitude towards morality revealed by the expressions, more or less direct, of their teaching. In great part, these differences are perhaps due to the fact that we are considering sometimes one and sometimes the other of the terms of an antilogy— sometimes that which a master deliberately published in order to protect himself against his enemies, sometimes that which, though not publicly expressed by the master, was put into his mouth or his pupils' mouths by opponents who wished to discredit him. The bravado of Thrasymachos in Book I of the *Republic* or of Callicles in the *Gorgias* bears little resemblance to the anonymous Sophistic fragment found in the *Protreptics* of Iamblichos, of which Callicles' speech is the exact opposite, or to the fragments of Antiphon's edifying sermon on *Concord,* or even to the little moral discourse of Hippias in the *Protagoras.*[1] When, too, in the *Clouds,* Aristophanes speaks of the new education as of two arguments pitted against each other like a couple of fighting-cocks, and of its art of making the " stronger appear the weaker," in other words, of making the Unjust get the better of the Just, he is wrong in making Socrates responsible for the method ;

[1] *Ibid.,* ch. 82 ; ch. 80, esp. frags. 58 ff., 61 ; Plato, *Protag.,* 337 c-e.

the method which he describes to the life is that inaugurated, years before Socrates, by Protagoras.

One of the chief methods used by the Sophists to make an antilogy appear automatically was the old distinction of the point of view of " nature " and that of " convention " or " law," and it was eminently favourable to the professional tactics of the masters. The former enabled them, now to present the most dangerous audacities in a mythical guise, and now to justify the principles of social conservativism. One may doubt whether their efforts to ascertain unwritten law and natural rights were dictated by any but a formal, dialectical interest.

The same may be said of their contribution to the study of the arts and sciences. Their object was to enable their pupil to assume an air of technical mastery in any subject, in order to contest or defend that of others and to talk to craftsmen like a connoisseur. This, according to Plato (*Sophist*, 232 d-233 a), seems to have been the object of Protagoras's treatise *On the Palaestra*. This, too, must have been the object (here defensive) of the little treatise *On the Art* (of medicine) in the Hippocratic Collection, an essay full of interesting views, but quite in the spirit of the Sophists in its general character and methodology. The " polymathy " of a Hippias was an erudition for show purposes only ; its foundation, mnemonics, gave it its real significance, and its object was to preserve the pupil from ever being found at a loss. So, too, the physical propositions ascribed to Gorgias, in which the influence of Empedocles is obvious, or to that wide eclectic Antiphon, and the mathematical speculations of Antiphon or Hippias, all bear witness, not, as has often been said, to positive application to science, but to the fact that an educational enterprise which was to succeed could not neglect the subjects which enjoyed even the passing favour of the public. Protagoras, ever anxious to keep education on the more general ground of antilogy, questioned even the principle of geometrical abstraction and exactness ; a tangent, he said, does not touch a circumference at a point, but along a length, or even a plane.[1] So, lastly, when Prodicos is said to have discussed the exactness of the medical vocabulary,[2]

---

[1] Arist., *Metaph.*, B. 2, 997 b 35 ff.
[2] **LXVIII**, ch. 77, B. 4.

it may only mean that he applied his famous method of semantics to criticizing the competence of physicians.

Nor is there, probably, any real originality of thought in what we know of the moral, political, and theological speculations of the Sophists. When, for instance, Menon, the pupil of Gorgias, defines virtue, no doubt according to his master's teaching, by enumerating all its varieties,[1] he is merely laying the groundwork for an oratorical picture. What is the myth of Protagoras on the origin of human societies,[2] but a defence of the Athenian democracy, and of the Sophistic method at the same time ? If Hermes distributed honour and justice to all men equally, all must be equally capable of using these advantages, if they learn the art of managing their own affairs and those of the State properly. Can Prodicos's nominalistic interpretation of belief in the gods be regarded as a serious essay in religious criticism ? The gods, he said, are merely names given by men to the natural objects which are most useful or familiar to them ; religion is derived from rites and festivals connected with the work of the fields.[3] It is an interesting idea, but to its author it was doubtless interesting only as a thesis, to which the myth of Heracles at the Crossroads would have furnished the necessary contrast. These are, perhaps, only the remains of an antilogy. It is true that Protagoras wrote : " Of the gods it is impossible to know whether they exist or do not exist " (Frag. 4). But it is hard to believe that that old warrior of antilogy stopped at this agnosticism, in his long career. In general, there does not seem to have been any definite opposition to religion among the Sophists, as there was in their contemporary Diagoras of Melos.

Their really positive work lay in all that concerns the study of the forms of thought and discourse. This was the value of their works on rhetoric, especially those of Antiphon (who was also a " logographer ") and Thrasymachos on forensic rhetoric and on the character-study, situations, and mimic methods of expression which it entails. They made a useful contribution to precision of language and to grammar in general ; Protagoras is said to have especially studied the distinctions of gender and of the tenses and moods of verbs, and the various kinds of proposition.

---

[1] Plato, *Menon*, 71 d-e.   [2] *Protag.*, 320 c-323 a.   [3] **LXVIII**, ch. 77, B. 5.

There remains properly philosophic speculation. We only find it, and with a different character, in Protagoras and Gorgias. Of the former's book, *Truth*, or *Overthrowing Discourses* (καταβάλλοντες), only one phrase survives, but it is very significant in itself, and the development, summarized by Sextus, agrees on the whole with all that Plato and Aristotle say about him. It is the formula of a theory of knowledge : " Man is the measure of all things, of the being of those which are and of the not-being of those which are not." The clearest and most consistent interpretation of this is as follows. Sensation is individual and contingent ; it is, as we should say, a wholly subjective phenomenon. Wind is cold only for me, and at the moment when I feel cold. The object of sensation *is*, properly speaking, only in that measure ; really it *becomes* incessantly. For everything is incessant movement and change. A man, whom you call the same, is always another ; he knows and he does not know ; his memories are so many new states ; he is not one, but infinitely many. It does not matter whether you consider a single consciousness or several in agreement ; the sole measure of the real is the transitory individuality of the state of knowledge. It does not matter whether you consider a man, or a pig or baboon ; what you must do is to break up the unity and identity of the individual and adapt it to the infinite multiplicity and mobility of becoming. Does this mean that there is no wisdom, and no wise man ? Not at all. No doubt, there is no error, for you cannot imagine anything but what you imagine at a given moment. But there are representations which " are better " than others. The physician is wise who, by his drugs, substitutes better representations, those of the healthy man, for worse representations, those of the sick man. Even more is the Sophist, or the orator whom he has trained, wise, who, by individual and political education or by persuasion, effects a similar but more important change. What is improperly called " true " is that which, at a given moment and in given conditions, is profitable and salutary.[1]

Thus, on Heracleiteanism, as against Eleaticism,[2] and perhaps even that of Melissos, quite in harmony with his

[1] According to the curious "apology" of Protagoras in *Theaet.* (166 a-168 c ; cf. 152 a-b), the accuracy and impartiality of which are emphasized by Plato. Cf. **LXVIII**, ch. 77, A. 19 and 17, end (Aristotle).

[2] *Ibid.*, B. 2.

146   HUMAN CULTURE

known opposition to geometrical rationalism, Protagoras seems to have based a decidedly empiricistic and relativistic theory of knowledge, capable of justifying the Sophistic method of the practical organization of experience. If this was so, it was an incomplete first sketch of a pragmatistic, humanistic doctrine; for judgements of existence it substituted judgements of worth, and conceived of truth only in an instrumental form.

But, it is said, this phenomenalistic, subjectivistic relativism would be an anachronism, and contrary to the ancient tradition of an objectivistic, realistic relativism. This second interpretation of the theory of Protagoras is based on another thesis attributed to him ; namely, that becoming is universal and incessant, and nothing *exists* or *is* what it is permanently, but everything results from the meeting of two kinds of movement, infinitely varied and of every degree of velocity, one of which comes from the object and produces the sensible quality at the same moment as the other, which comes from the organ, produces sensation ; action exists only in relation to affection (πάθος), and there is nothing determinate except in and by relation.[1] But, for reasons which we shall see later, it does not seem that the thesis on which this interpretation is based, a thesis which Plato very vaguely ascribes to Protagoras, can be attributed to him historically. Therefore Protagoras must have held that there is no analytical connexion between what appears and what is, even if the latter be unknowable.

In Gorgias philosophical speculation seems to have been merely the occasion for a master of rhetoric to make a dazzling display of his virtuosity and the power of his art. His treatise *On Not-being* tends to show how the dialectic of the Eleatics can, by subtle, plausible arguments, be turned against themselves.[2] Nothing exists, says Gorgias, neither the Not-being of experience, for it is the negation of being, nor single, eternal, absolute Being, for it excludes all the conditions of experience, nor yet a relation of one to the other as of an attribute to a subject, for that would be a reciprocal negation which, either absolutely isolating the two terms or confounding them together, would in any case condemn judgement and predication.

[1] According to Sextus, *Pyrrh.*, i. 216–19, and Plato, *Theaet.*, 152 c ff., and esp. 156 a–157 c. Interpretation of LII, 23–9. Cf. below, pp. 170-1.
[2] According to the *Melissos, Xenophanes, and Gorgias*, 5–6, and Sextus, *Math.*, vii. 65–87. Cf. Gorgias, *Helen*, 13, end.

But let us suppose that something exists ; it will not be knowable, for the reality of sensible things is not intelligible, and inversely the conceivable is often shown to be non-existent. Furthermore, even if we allow that what exists could be known, the knowledge of it could not be communicated to others, for language does no more than symbolize by arbitrary signs the things which it pretends to express, and, moreover, words have not exactly the same meaning for the thought of the speaker and for that of the hearer, and so duplicate things. There are, therefore, no general ideas, nor even common names ; Gorgias follows the dictates of nominalism to the very end. In sum, his theory is an essay in thorough-going nihilism, which at bottom is just a learned game, an exhibition of dialectical acrobatics.

For all its weaknesses and serious blemishes, the work done by the Sophists of the Vth century must not be under-rated. No doubt, their method is formal, generally empty of personal thought and sincerity. Yet the very effort of thought required to construct paradoxes, against one's own theory, if need be, cannot be altogether sterile ; and, as a fact, the Sophists were, by accident, pioneers. Moreover, there is no doubt that they laboured to make general culture universal, by dragging it outside the walls of the old schools, for whose transformation they thus prepared. By their criticism of competence in the various sciences, confining themselves to considering them from outside, they were led to study their methods, and so were the promoters of epistemology. Lastly, they were themselves the creators of a method of expressing thought, and with rhetoric and grammar they made a real contribution, even if it was on the field of pure empiricism, to the work which was carried on by Plato and Aristotle—the constitution of a logic.

Chapter II

SOCRATES

THE activity of Socrates, in competition with the Sophists, began at a time when the success of the latter was already great. It was exercised in the same social environment, in answer to the same intellectual and moral needs. His methods were, at least outwardly, so like those of the Sophists that he seemed to Aristophanes, and doubtless to many other contemporaries, to embody the Sophistic spirit as well as anyone. Plato himself, when he tries to define the Sophist, notes an air of kinship between his manner of being and that of the true philosopher (*Soph.*, 230 d ff.). Lastly, it was a school of Socratics, namely, the Megarics, who gave Aristotle some of his best specimens of sophisms.

Unfortunately, if we know little about the Sophists, we know still less about Socrates. He is the greatest figure in the history of Greek thought; from him, directly or through intermediaries, all the later currents of philosophy are derived. Yet he is almost a figure of legend. About his personality, his acts, his talk we have an abundant harvest of testimonies, immediate or very nearly so. Most agree in giving us a high idea of his importance as a man. But they contradict each other flagrantly, or at least are hard to reconcile. We do not even know exactly why his fellow-countrymen made him pay for his work among them with his life. The existence of several Socratic schools, distinct and sometimes hostile, makes it all the harder to say what his philosophy was. Nor can we hope to form a personal opinion from any writings of Socrates himself, for, if there is one thing certain among all our uncertainties, it is that Socrates, unlike the Sophists, wrote nothing, and taught by word of mouth only. In fact, the most difficult problem of historical criticism arises over a thinker who marked philosophy and the conscience with a stamp which time has not effaced.

Among our testimonies, some, first of all, tend to decry Socrates. We need not dwell on that of Aristoxenos of Taras, who declared that he had heard from his father Spintharos,[1] who had known Socrates, all the ill which he spoke of him— it is not clear for what reason. Even if Socrates was a bad lot in his youth, how can one believe that, if he was as destitute of culture as of dignity and scruples, openly abusive, violent, licentious, and a bigamist into the bargain, he was able in his riper years, not only to arouse such passionate admiration, but to take that foremost place in Athens which is proved by the equally adverse testimony of Aristophanes ?

In the *Clouds* (423 B.C.), and incidentally in the *Birds* (414) and the *Frogs* (405), we find, not obscure, disconnected gossip, but a vigorous portrait, the concrete and very living character of a philosopher whose notoriety and ascendancy are considerable.[2] It does not matter that the malice of the portrait is due to political motives and betrays an aggravating lack of perception in the painter. What is interesting, is to note, shorn of their comic exaggeration, the features in which Aristophanes saw Socrates in the maturity of his forty-seven years, and represented him for a public which was the eye-witness of his daily activity. He is a master, who has a school, a " thinking-shop " ($\phi\rho o\nu\tau\iota\sigma\tau\eta\rho\iota o\nu$), and disciples who work under his direction and follow a common rule of life. To be admitted to his teaching, they have to pay a fee. The discipline of the school is ascetic ; the disciples have pale faces, they are pure " spirits," already " half-dead," they are dirty, ragged, and barefooted, and have nothing to eat. Before they enter the school they must undergo initiation. They study geometry, physics, astronomy, meteorology, geography and the abysses of the earth, and living creatures. Air is the principle of things and of thought ; from the " vortex of the ether " all phenomena naturally result. Socrates is an atheist, since he does not believe in the gods of the city ; the burning of his school and the death of himself and his pupils will be a just chastisement of their impiety.

---

[1] The identity of Aristoxenos the musician with the son of Spintharos seems to be fairly certain from a comparison of Diog. Laërt., ii. 20, with Sextus, *Math.*, vi. 1.

[2] Attested also by the attacks of other comic writers, Eupolis, Ameipsias, etc.

But Socrates is not only a physicist ; he is also a master of rhetoric. Speech is one of his gods. He teaches a method of inventing ideas, which is " antilogy." As a professor of fine speaking, of forensic and political eloquence, he is a master of chicanery, who teaches you to make the " weak " argument, or the Unjust, triumph over the " strong " argument, or the Just. To law, arbitrary convention, he opposes the rights of nature. Lastly, his lessons treat of grammar, metre, and rhythm. So the Socrates of Aristophanes is an upholder of the doctrine of Diogenes of Apollonia, and is of the same family as the eclectic physicists who are themselves related to the Sophists. In other things he is a Sophist like the rest of them, like Prodicos, for example, and Aristophanes' charges against him are almost the same as Plato's against the Sophists.

Against these attacks of Aristophanes, Plato made a direct and detailed protest in the speech which he makes his master utter before the judges, and he even makes Aristophanes chiefly responsible for Socrates' death (*Apol.*, 18 a-20 e). What made him think of reconciling them in the *Symposium* ? This is a problem on which it is easy to make suppositions, but it does not concern the personality of Socrates. It is more important to observe that, whereas Aristophanes knew him in his maturity, Plato only knew him in his old age, about fifteen years after the *Clouds* was produced. But from older disciples, from various members of his family, Critias the oligarch, his mother's cousin, and Charmides, her brother, or his own brothers Adeimantos and Glaucon, Plato was able to get information about his master's life. After the death of Socrates, Plato seems to have continued to collect information, and the introductions of the *Symposium* and the *Theaetetos* may give a reflection of his inquiries.

In any case, we can extract the elements of a biography and a character-study from Plato's dialogues.[1] Socrates belongs to the Fox Deme (Alopece) of the Tribe of Antiochis. His father Sophroniscos, perhaps a sculptor, is of good family, and is an old friend of Lysimachos, the son of the great Aristeides ; his mother Phaenarete is a capable midwife. After the traditional education, he must have gone on to

---

[1] Cf. A. E. Taylor, *Plato's Biography of Socrates* (*Proceedings of the British Academy*, viii. 1917).

study mathematics and physics, showing great eagerness to learn. But the study of the teachings of the physicists, according to the famous account in the *Phaedon* (96 a-99 d), about which there has been so much argument, revealed their divergences to him, and these were further emphasized by the eclecticism of the day, which restored abandoned systems. If that of Anaxagoras did not satisfy him, the theory of Mind at least, for the first time, suggested to him a way of putting an end to his doubts. Critical reflection, a suggestion, and then internal, original meditation—in the end he arrived at an explanation of becoming by essences or intelligible forms. If we are to believe the *Parmenides* (127 c, 130 b-e, 135 d), Socrates was still young when this revolution in his thinking took place. According to Plato, and contrary to what Aristophanes says, he never taught physics as a physicist ; on the contrary, he devoted the first manifestations of his philosophic activity to spreading his discovery abroad.

No doubt Socrates had already acquired the authority of a master when one of his " familiars," Chaerephon, was led by his enthusiasm to ask the Pythia at Delphi whether there was anyone wiser. The answer of the god was in the negative. From then onwards, Socrates regarded himself as being in the service of Apollo, invested by him with a " mission," which was to seek the reason for that reply. In himself he saw no kind of wisdom ; he would therefore " examine " those who believed themselves wise in one domain or another. Now, he soon perceived that he was superior to them in one respect—that he was not duped by his ignorance, that he was aware of his lack of knowledge. He laboured to awaken in others the same critical reflection, which delivered the mind from opinions accepted without examination ; " to know oneself," in order to reform oneself was what he called " taking care of one's soul " (*Apol.*, 20 e-22 e, 29 e). This new education, therefore, allowed of no dogmatism ; it was based on a method of " search in common," by dialogue. There was nothing to which Socrates was more passionately attached than to his influence on the young, in whom the stamp of another education is still fresh, and who bear in themselves, with their own future, the future of the city. Did he explicitly make love, which makes souls fruitful, the driving-power of his method ? Did he say that love was the only thing which he knew? At least, it seems quite certain that he loved young people and wanted to be loved by them.

He had no school in the strict sense. The gymnasium of the Lyceum was, however, the place where he preferred to go, when he did not visit the palaestras where he would meet youths. He was never weary of asking questions, but his preference for conversation, which made his interlocutor take part in the inquiry, did not prevent him from also making long speeches and reading and commenting on the poets. But, although he was not and did not want to be a master, he had at least a circle of " familiars," who, if they did not constantly live with him, at least declared themselves strongly attached to himself and his principles. Most of these were present on his last day.

In addition to Athenians, there were among them foreigners who, usually living in their own cities, came to Athens from time to time to converse with Socrates. Some, such as Criton, were especially zealous for his interests. Others, like Apollodoros, were fanatical devotees, imitating his attitude with exaggeration. Others, who afterwards claimed to carry on the work of Socrates in their teaching and writings, Eucleides, Antisthenes, Aristippos, Phaedon, Plato, Æschines, seem to bear witness to the continuance of a doctrinal tendency, properly so called, by the side of the educational apostolate which ensued from the " mission." But Socrates was so little a " scholarch " that men notoriously belonging to other philosophical circles—an Eleatizer like Eucleides, Pythagoreans like Simmias, Cebes, and Phaedondes of Thebes and Echecrates of Phlius, and pupils of the Sophists, like Antisthenes or Aristippos—at the same time belonged to the circle of Socrates. If we take this original feature in conjunction with the fact that the Socratics did not all represent their master's thought from the same angle, in the practical order or in the speculative, we may infer that, round a solid core, the outlying parts of his doctrine remained plastic and could be adapted to the influence of other doctrines.

Lastly, the Socratic circle was open to yet another class of hearer. These were young men who were too much taken up with their business or pleasure to sacrifice them to the search for truth, clients of the Sophists, who enjoyed going to Socrates to hear a well-conducted debate or an ingenious idea subtly analysed. Among these were Plato's kinsmen mentioned already, Alcibiades, and, no doubt, Xenophon. The speech which Plato puts in the mouth of Alcibiades at the end of the *Symposium* is probably a fair illustration of the spontaneous respect and admiration which they felt for Socrates, and at the same time of the stubbornness with which they fought against his influence. These dilettanti were not disciples.

While Socrates thus served the god, fulfilling his mission as an educator in public and without payment, never leaving the city where his work awaited him and called for him, he did not neglect the duties of a citizen. He served in the army as a hoplite (so he must have had some property), and took part in the campaigns of Potidaea (432–429) and Amphipolis (422) and the disaster of Delion (424), always showing coolness, decision, and bravery, and indifferent to the hazards and hardships of a soldier's life. Called by lot to sit in the Council of the Five Hundred, he was a member of the commission of *prytaneis* at the time when, against the decision of the commission, the Assembly demanded the death of the generals who had commanded at Arginusae ; he alone stood up to the popular fury and refused to put the illegal proposal to the vote (406). At the risk of his life, he afterwards defied the oligarchs when they tried to make him assist their measures of vengeance.

This independence towards both the rival parties equally was bound to be fatal to him. When the democrats returned to power, they forgot how Socrates had behaved under the Thirty, and only remembered that he had been on good terms with some of the oligarchs, and that he had criticized democratic government, its principle of equality, and its system of election by lot. So political motives seem to have inspired the suit brought against Socrates by the poet Meletos, whose accusation was countersigned by the politician Anytos and the rhetor Lycon. But openly they accused him of " corrupting the young " and of being an impious man who did not believe in the gods of the city and introduced " new deities " in their place. The first charge clearly refers to the way in which the young were affected by his critical education, the anti-traditional character of which is well brought out by Plato. The second charge, according to Plato, referred particularly to Socrates' statement that he had in him a deity, a " daemon," whose voice had, from his childhood, ever turned him away, by some " sign," from what would be bad for him. These inspirations, which were always negative, might apply to acts in which there was no question of morality —which road not to follow on the retreat from Delion, a stream which he must not cross, and the like. Did he think that the privilege of this inner revelation could not belong to others ? At least by claiming it for himself, Socrates could not fail to alarm touchy democrats and to confirm himself in the belief that each one of us is, with the help of his daemon, the maker of his soul's salvation, and that all philosophy lies in that. It was, for example, to save his soul from the taint of injustice that he would not accept Criton's help to save himself by flight from a penalty pronounced in the name of the laws of the city ; a dream had foretold his coming death, and he must not evade the bidding of the god.

We know how Socrates, having been declared guilty by a small majority, angered the judges by an attitude which seemed derisive of the first sentence, so that a larger number of voices were then given in favour of his death. The moving story of his last day in the *Phaedon* is present in every memory. Here we may simply recall the portrait which Plato has given of Xanthippe, the philosopher's wife. It is very unlike the traditional picture, in which she represents one of the worst trials to which the patience of a Sage can be subjected. Plato's Xanthippe is a woman unconsolable for the death of her husband ; if Socrates makes Criton take her away, it is in order not to drive her still wilder with grief and not to disturb his own serenity. Also, the dying Socrates of the *Phaedon* is not a superman, like the Wise Man of the Cynics later ; he wants to see his children, he talks to his kinswomen, he does not repudiate any natural tie, so far as it does not conflict with higher obligations. He was then, Plato says, over seventy years of age ; it was in 399, probably in February or March, not in May.

It cannot, however, be denied that Plato's Socrates bears the marks of a symbolical idealization, constructed on the theme of a contrast between the outward form and the true nature beneath. This opposition explains the " oddity " (ἀτοπία) of which Plato so often speaks, the disconcerting impression which Socrates produced upon all who came near him. Outwardly, he performed all the actions of an ordinary man, and he lived an intense inner life, hearing the voice of a daemon, subject to ecstasies, during which he was indifferent to surrounding conditions and the demands of nature (*Symposium*, 174 d, 175 a, 220 c-d). He lived like a poor man, clad in a rough cloak (τρίβων), although he was not poor, and moved in a wealthy and fashionable circle. His sobriety was unprecedented, and there was no more stalwart drinker. His talk was coarse and full of vulgar comparisons and triviality, and by the force of his stirring eloquence he could move men's hearts as no other could. No man was more chaste, and none had more love-affairs or more exacting ones. He who professed to know nothing compelled those who professed knowledge to admit their ignorance. Like the numb-fish, he paralysed those whom he approached, and at the same time he awakened them to the truth (*Menon*, 80 a). His flat face, snub nose, and thick lips and the bovine eyes flush with his head and looking sideways were those of a Silenos, but all this was only the cover of the box, and inside there shone the purest and most radiant beauty. Of all these features, some, no doubt, correspond to the reality. Others, however, seem to be intended to give the portrait more expressive strength. Moreover, it cannot be denied that, on the whole, this portrait of Socrates reveals Plato's conception of the Philosopher, the Soul, and Love, as intermediate beings, in which especially those opposites, the Intelligible and the Sensible, are reconciled.

There is none of this idealism in the evidence of Xenophon in his *Memoirs*, *Symposium*, *Apology* (if it is indeed his), and *Œconomicus*. Is it therefore, as has often been said, historically truer ? Perhaps the Socrates whom he gives us is more human. But his humanity is so dull and commonplace that his profound influence and the wild enthusiasm and hostility which he aroused become quite inexplicable. Besides, far from being the scrupulous observations of a historian who witnessed the facts, the *Memoirs* are manifestly a composition of a romantic kind, strongly marked with the personality, tastes, and memories of the author, bigoted, canny, meanly utilitarian, swollen with military and political pretensions which he can only display on paper, a country squire fond of dogs and horses. The book is a pendant to the *Cyropaedeia*, in which one might as well look for the real Cyrus as in the *Memoirs* for the real Socrates. Moreover, Xenophon left Athens two years before the trial of Socrates, to take part in the expedition of Cyrus the Younger. He does not seem to have returned there after the retreat of the Ten Thousand, and he was certainly kept out of the city by a sentence of banishment for thirty years, until 369. Down to 387 he had always lived at Sparta or in Asia, and had taken part in the campaigns of Agesilaos. In every respect, therefore, he was not in nearly such a good position as Plato to check his recollections and to complete his information, which can hardly have been very full, since it is unlikely that he ever belonged to the Socratic circle properly so called. Lastly, without laying too much weight on the accusations of the rhetor Polycrates (about 388), who declared that Socrates was the evil genius of Alcibiades (i. 2. 24) or on the signs of still later composition in the two last books, it seems that we must recognize in the *Memoirs* the marks of a compilation of several dialogues of Plato and, no doubt, of Antisthenes ; by using these, Xenophon would have at last succeeded in giving his chief character some philosophy to talk. Even for biographical information, Xenophon's evidence is less valuable than Plato's. He does not, therefore, seem to deserve the special confidence which has often been placed in him.[1]

The evidence of Aristotle, on the contrary, whatever may have been said of it lately,[2] is of capital importance. No doubt, it is not immediate, for when Aristotle arrived in Athens Socrates had been dead thirty-two years. But this was not such a long time but that a pupil of Plato could, by questioning witnesses and reading, find many means of satisfying his critical curiosity on the spot. The fact that he often speaks of Socrates meaning, explicitly or not, the Socrates of Plato, does not prove that he knows no other. On the contrary, he knows quite well that a " Socratic work " (λόγος Σωκρατικός), is a dramatic work, a philosophic " mime," in which fiction is mixed with fact. Moreover, he is at the greatest pains to distinguish the real Socrates from Plato's Socrates, or from Plato himself. Socrates, he says, speculated

---

[1] For further details, see my essay in *Année philosophique*, xxi (1910), pp. 1–47.
[2] **XCVI, XII.** Cf. my article, *Rev. Études grecques*, xxix (1916), esp. 148–63.

not on nature, but on moral matters, and with reference to these he was the first to seek, consecutively and methodically, " universal definitions " ; for he sought the " essence " (τὸ τί ἐστιν) as being the starting-point of reasoning, and consequently of knowledge. Knowledge is based on " universal definition " and on " inductive arguments " (ἐπακτικοὶ λόγοι). Now, these are the two things " the credit of which one can fairly give to Socrates." [1] But Socrates did not make the universal definitions " separate " things, whereas Plato set them " apart from " sensible things, under the name of " Ideas." The second doctrine proceeds from the first : it was " by the method of logical search " for concepts, that is, the method of properly Socratic speculation, that the philosophy of Ideas was " brought on to the stage " ; if it was brought forth, it was " because Socrates set it in motion." [2] It is true that Aristotle is inclined to present other doctrines in the terms of his own, but it is none the less true that, when he connected Plato with Socrates as he did, he clearly distinguished them from each other, and that, in his view, Socrates' own philosophy, although specially moral, contained a general method of inquiry.

There remains a whole class of evidence—that obtained from Socratics other than Plato and Xenophon. But this evidence does not deal with definite facts so much as the spirit of Socrates' teaching ; moreover, it requires peculiarly delicate interpretation, and must be the object of a special study. We must now, therefore, construct a first portrait of Socrates from our other sources of information, with a view to comparing it with that evidence later.

First of all, he was not a kind of genius standing outside time. He was very much a man of his day, who had received the culture of his day. In this Aristotle's evidence agrees with Plato's, in respect of physics, and there is no reason to reject the tradition which makes Socrates a disciple of Archelaos.[3] What is doubtful is that Socrates ever taught physics. He also came under the influence of the dialectic and methods of the earlier Sophists, and perhaps Plato is not altogether ironical when he makes Prodicos, who of all the

[1] *Metaph.*, M. 4, 1078 b 17 ff. ; A. 6, beginning.
[2] *Ibid.*, A. 6, 987 b 31 ff. ; M. 9, 1086 b 2 ff.
[3] **LXVIII**, ch. 47, A. 1, 3, 7.

Sophists was most mixed up with Athenian life, one of his masters.[1] It is not even impossible that Socrates gave a kind of teaching in rhetoric, though doubtless not in the spirit presented in the *Clouds* ; his search for and analysis of essence would have made the method of his teaching different from that of the Sophists.[2] That, no doubt, was what more than one man came to Socrates to learn, and Xenophon may be referring to this when he says that the Thirty forbade Socrates to teach the art of " reasons " (*Mem.*, i. 2. 31 ff.).

Thus placed in his true environment, Socrates takes—not so soon as the *Parmenides* makes out, but soon enough—an original position. What he rejects of the doctrine of Anaxagoras is the points in which it resembles the other physical doctrines ; but it satisfies him by its qualitativism and by the theory of Mind. Yet quality cannot be separated from Mind ; it will be that which is intelligible in things, their universal *raison d'être* or essence, the perfection of nature, the end or good towards which each of them tends. On another side, although Plato indicates no other determining influence than meditation on the philosophy of Anaxagoras, it is hard to believe that Socrates did not know other doctrines, and that his relations with the Pythagorean circles of Thebes and Phlius or with the Eleatic circle of Megara did not incline his thinking in the same direction. Among the forerunners of the Socratic search for the universal definition, Aristotle even adds Democritos to the Pythagoreans. However that may be, by making that search the condition of all knowledge of nature, Socrates completely changed the spirit of physics, that is, of philosophy.

In conceiving of physics as a logical analysis and a construction of concepts, he asserted the pre-eminent excellence of a formal method and of a general discipline of the intelligence. Once again, he seems very close to the Sophists, and with them he is linked to the dialectic of Zenon. The antilogy of the Sophists and the Socratic examination are varieties of the method of refutation, by which the opponent was involved in contradictions and so made to abandon his original thesis for the antithesis, then led, by further contradictions, to admit that the antithesis was likewise untenable, and finally

---

[1] Passages collected in **II**, 1062. 3 (French trans., ii. 471, 1).
Cf. above, pp. 140-1.

left quite helpless. But, although the two processes are very much alike, as one sees in the *Protagoras*, for example, the resemblance is only external. Here, too, a revolution has taken place, for Socrates conceived this formal method quite differently from the Sophists, from whom he took the original idea of it.

First of all, the method of the Sophists is erudite. To destroy tradition, it sets one tradition against another ; while formal, it is encyclopaedic, but has acquired this quality cheaply thanks to mnemonics ; whether semantic, grammatical, or rhetorical, it is always verbal, never reflective. But Socrates' method is above all things reflective, it condemns erudition by the very assertion of " lack of knowledge," and it liberates the conscience from all traditional authority—the chief charge which Aristophanes brings against Socrates. Secondly, whereas the formalism of the Sophists receives a content which varies with external circumstances, the method of Socrates, formal though it is, has a permanent content, which is the content of the consciousness itself, to which his method is a perpetual return—" Know thyself." This difference brings with it another. Whereas the method of the Sophists aims at individual adaptation, by the tricks of antilogy, to contingent circumstances, Socrates, in analysing the content of the individual consciousness, clears it of everything individual and everything contingent ; he seeks to extract from it what is universal and permanent, that on which there can be " homology " or agreement of minds— in short, the intelligible. This is the object defined by his meditation on the old physics, the essence of things or their good ; for to reflect on oneself in order to know oneself is to try to discover in oneself the essence of man or his good.

That was how the necessary object of his method came, as Aristotle says, to be confined to moral matters ; but in itself that object was really the essence, the τί ἐστι. Having said this, we need not dwell further on the details of the Socratic method. Inquiry in common, dialogue, and love are, as we have seen, the conditions of it. To the processes of " examination " and of " induction," which extracts the universal notion from particular experiences, we must add others— the exact determination of the theme under examination, of the " hypothesis " from which the induction starts ; " irony," not what we call irony, but a sly kind of "dissimulation" (εἰρωνεία), which consists in asking questions under pretence of ignorance, in fact a simple application of "lack of knowledge"; and lastly, perhaps, the "midwifery" (μαιευτική) by which souls are brought to birth, if this is not an invention of Plato (*Theaetetos*), a symbol taken from the profession of Phaenarete.

If the good of man is his essence, we see wherein the intellectualistic utilitarianism and eudaemonism of Socrates will consist. How could a man, knowing the good which is his good, wish, under the empire of his passions, for what is contrary to his good? The passionate man and the vicious man are men who do not know their good, who have not perceived the essence of man in themselves; "nobody is wicked willingly." Reciprocally, "the virtues are branches of knowledge"; to know is to do. This basing of morals on logic has practical effects. If the object of moral reflection is to bring out the essential man, everything that belongs to his sensible, contingent environment must be removed, or at least placed on a subordinate plane, and one must be ready to sacrifice it when a higher end requires it. So we have the asceticism of Socrates, which recalls that of the Pythagoreans. Both Aristophanes and Plato depict it, but in the latter's account it has a remarkably complex form. Now, the essential man is the Sage, the Wise Man, and it will be the aim of the post-Aristotelian schools, following the Socratic schools, to determine the nature of that ideal of humanity and the conditions of its realization.

To sum up, we may fairly speak of a Socratic revolution, and in the sense in which we speak of a Cartesian revolution. In neither case was there a breach of continuity, a complete rupture and a spontaneous creation. Each thinker rebelled violently against the conditions amid which his mind had been formed, but each appropriated the existing forms of thought. Socrates made use of the Sophistic method to destroy the old physics and the Sophists' own principles. It is none the less true that, even when understood thus, his work meant a complete reformation and the creation of a new world of thought.

CHAPTER III

THE SPREAD OF THE SOCRATIC SPIRIT

To some men Socrates seemed to offer an example of a new life, and of a new orientation of philosophical reflection. All these, except Æschines, in the master's lifetime or after his death, in schools which they already directed or in new schools, taught a rule of life and a doctrine which claimed to be based on the inspiration of Socrates. All, without exception, wrote free " Socratic works," in which they put in their master's mouth their personal interpretation of his thought. Tradition has established a curious order of rank among them, with Plato at their head, and all the others as " the lesser Socratics." Is this just ? A school owed its name to its site, the variety of subjects which it could teach, its material resources, and political circumstances as well as to the personal worth of its founder. Moreover, we have the whole of Plato's works, while we know the others only by rare and small fragments, conjectural traces, partial contemporary evidence which can never be identified with certainty, or later evidence in which their ideas may have been modified by their successors. Between them and Plato there is no common measure offered to the judgement of the historian. We should note in particular that, if we are to obtain a rough notion of their tendencies, we must follow the refraction of those tendencies in their successors and therefore widen the historical limits of our study, down to the middle of the IIIrd century and even beyond, until their schools are absorbed by more powerful schools. Nor can we, without engaging in a vicious circle, call these men " semi-Socratics," for the question is, what the thought of Socrates really was, and we cannot presuppose that Plato alone represents it, pure and complete.

I

THE SCHOOLS OF ELIS AND ERETRIA

Phaedon of Elis was probably not quite a young man at the death of Socrates.[1] When the Socratic circle broke up, he returned to his city and gathered some disciples about him. His interpretation of the master's doctrine may be guessed—no more—from a fragment of Timon the Sillographer, in which he is connected with Eucleides and the Megarics (Frag. 28), and from the connection of his school with that of Eretria, whose doctrinal kinship with the Megarics is more certain. Menedemos of Eretria, who died about 270, and his friend Asclepiades studied first under Stilpon of Megara and then under the successors of Phaedon at Elis. Menedemos seems to have used a formidable power of dialectic and an extreme logical subtlety as a means of moral cultivation. At least, the noble independence of his character and the dignity of his life, which earned him great personal authority in his time, made him an excellent example of the Wise Man, without the brutal features of the Cynics. Now, he certainly seems to have aimed at being a copy of Socrates. His example and words were his only methods and he taught in an unpedantic, free-and-easy way ; anyone who wished might hear him, and whenever he wished.

II

THE SCHOOL OF MEGARA

It is very hard to say exactly what the doctrine of Eucleides, the head of the School of Megara, was. That he was at first attached to the principles of Eleaticism is certain, but it is also certain that his ideas came under the influence of Socrates. The evidence of Plato, at the beginning of the *Theaetetos*, allows no doubt of it. If, too, Eucleides had not belonged to the Socratic group, would the Athenian disciples

[1] L. Parmentier, " L'Âge de Phédon d'Élis," in *Bull. de l'Association Budé*, Jan., 1926, and my ed. of the *Phaedon* (Coll. Budé), pp. ix-xi.

have taken refuge with him when they fled the city after their master's death ? This fact at least proves that he already had a school. The Good, he is alleged to have said, is one, as virtue is one ; but it is called by different names, sometimes " prudence " (φρόνησις), sometimes " thought " (νοῦς), sometimes God, or other such names, yet it is really one and unchangeable ; outside it there is nothing real.[1] Does this mean that there is only one essence, that of the Good ? If so, Eucleides is a pure Eleatic, as, indeed, has been said of the Megarics in general,[2] and is a Socratic only in that Being for him is the Good, a reality of a moral nature. But, if we consider the further doctrines of the school, another interpretation is possible : that the single Good is the being of every essence, so that each essence is in itself one and unchangeable, independent and excluding all the " other " as a not-being, and capable of being known by thought alone. The oneness of the Good is no more incompatible with plurality of essences than the oneness of Being with plurality of atoms ; we have a logical atomism forming an antithesis and pendant to the material atomism into which the Being of the Eleatics was broken up. In spite of what critics have recently said, it must be against the dialectical method of splitting-up practised by these Eleatizing Socratics, the " friends of Ideas " who are at war with materialism, that Plato, compromising as a friend should, defends the legitimacy of the relation of essences in judgement, as well as the reality of the Other and Not-being (Sophist, 246 b, 248 a ; cf. 252 a). It was an answer to the objections of Parmenides (that is, of Eucleides) to the Platonic Ideas in the Parmenides.

Eucleides, it is said,[3] abandoned the inductive dialectic of Socrates, based on examples ; one should attack, not the opponent's premisses, but his conclusions. So he probably argued, like Zenon, by reductio ad absurdum. And he probably practised this dialectical method, which earned his school an inconvenient popularity, although it is chiefly ascribed to his second successor Eubulides, the stubborn opponent of Aristotle, and to Alexinos, who combated Zenon the Stoic. Yet the supposed sophisms of the Megarics seem to have been only comic ways of proving by absurdity the two parts of their

---

[1] Diog. Laërt., ii. 106 ; Cic., Acad., ii. 42. 129.   [2] Aristocles, **XIV**, 290.
[3] Diog. Laërt., ii. 107.

thesis. Some, such as the " Man in Disguise," the " Liar," the " Electra," and the " Horned Man," aim at showing that common knowledge confounds in a false universality notions which are distinct, that is, essences each of which has its individuality and none of which is ambiguous. If, for example, you say, truly, that you lie, you must lie when you speak the truth. The other sophisms, of which the " Heap " (*soros*) is the type, consist in showing, inversely, that common knowledge distinguishes between terms arbitrarily, for instance, between " much " and " little," which are seen to be indistinguishable when they are replaced in the continuity of becoming, with the infinite number of intermediaries which may be inserted between them. A grain of corn, you say, is the contrary of a heap of corn, and two grains, or three grains, do not make a heap. Then, when do they begin to be a heap ? And, whatever the number chosen may be, how can you start the heap by adding one grain ? Take the argument the other way round, and subtract instead of adding ; then you have the " Bald Man." That, in general, is the essential form of an argument of which the Neo-Academicians made great use in their war on Stoic dogmatism ; from the first example cited, it is called the " sorites."

In the eyes of the ancients, the prince of dialectic was a young contemporary of Aristotle, the famous Diodoros, whose enigmatic surname, Cronos, had already been borne by his master Apollonios of Cyrene, a disciple of Eubulides. All his arguments, the substance of which, often attacked by Aristotle, doubtless belonged to the school before him, aimed at proving the unintelligibility of empirical knowledge. There is no movement as such ; there are only limits of movement, marked by the positions of the moving thing. There is no becoming ; there are only present states. There is no possibility, but only that which has already come about, or which must of necessity do so. The famous instance of the Master (ὁ κυριεύων) showed the absurdities to which the common notion of possibility led. Every essence contains in the necessity of its being its whole future, which is really only its eternal present. That future is neither contingent nor subject to outside conditions, for that which conditions and that which is conditioned are merely two aspects of one same necessity. Philon, a disciple of Diodoros, afterwards softened down this doctrine. But for the uncompromising necessitarianism of a thinker like Diodoros there is no " perhaps " and there is no " if." This is the point of the example of the " Reaper." It is inevitable that you will reap or that you will not reap ; it cannot be one or the other ; therefore you will of absolute necessity do either one or the other, whatever happens.[1] The " inactive argument " (ἀργὸς λόγος), which was to enjoy such success later, is already there, all complete. In short, the real is governed by the logical necessity of the principle of contradiction ; empirical individuality, with its undetermined potentialities and its development, gives place to a plurality of essences each of which is a complete, water-tight universe, which from all eternity has been all that it ever will be.

These essences of the Megarics are not kinds, like the Ideas of Plato. This fact enables one to understand the out-and-out nominalism of another equally famous dialectician, Stilpon of Megara, among whose pupils were Menedemos, Zenon (the founder of the Porch), and Timon the Sceptic. In his view there are no common names, but every indivisible intuition of an essence should receive one denominative sign of some kind. Also, if every logical moment of an essence is, with the essence, independent, the liberty of the Wise Man, his " imperturbability," his " impassibility," are assured. All that is outside his essence as a Wise Man is pure not-being, which cannot in any circumstances act on his essence.

III

The Cynic School

The use of logical speculation for moral ends, so apparent in Stilpon, is also characteristic of the Cynics, whose resemblance to the Megarics is more complete than is often allowed. But what this new school shows more obviously is an adaptation of the methods of the Sophists to the spirit of Socraticism. Its founder Antisthenes, the son of an Athenian and a Thracian slave-woman, probably rather older than

[1] It is quoted by Lucian (*Auction of Sects*, 22) together with the " Master " and other Megaric arguments, so it probably belongs to the school. Cf. Diog. Laërt., vii. 25

Plato, belonged to Sophist circles and is said to have been a pupil of Gorgias before he entered the circle of Socrates. After Socrates' death, he opened a school in a gymnasium at the Cynosarges (the Swift Dog). This was the origin of the name " Dogs," or Cynics, by which the followers of the school recalled its first site, and at the same time symbolized their cantankerous moral vigilance, always on the bark, and, in some measure, the very nature of their life. Of the very copious literary output of Antisthenes—discourses in the manner of the Sophists on themes taken from the poets and Socratic dialogues, all much admired by the ancients—hardly anything has been saved which is certainly authentic. Apart from tradition and some statements of Aristotle, almost all that one can say about early Cynicism is based on inductions—on the interpretation of certain passages in Plato, which are supposed to contain allusions to Antisthenes and indications of their rivalry, or of Xenophon, who makes him one of the characters in his *Symposium* and is alleged to show signs of his influence.

The successor of Antisthenes was Diogenes of Sinope, who was celebrated for his eccentricities and his witty sayings. Crates of Thebes, a contemporary of Stilpon and Menedemos and one of the teachers of Zenon, wrote verse parodies, fragments of which survive, in which he defended the Cynic's life. With his wife Hipparchia and her brother Metrocles, he affords a characteristic example of the way in which the school conducted its propaganda. It sought to make converts, and conversion meant renouncing worldly goods and social position. The austerity of the Cynic life must also, as we see in Diodoros of Aspendos (end of the IVth century), have been easily reconciled with the Pythagorean rule. In the IIIrd century the school, now very flourishing, shows its Sophistic tendency more and more markedly. Bion of the Borysthenes, Menippos, who had such influence, Cercidas, whom we know from a papyrus, and Teles wandered from town to town in their short cloaks ($\tau\rho\iota\beta\omega\nu$), carrying the staff and wallet of the beggar. They uttered speeches, ingenious in construction and popular in language, which permanently established a new form of composition, which enjoyed its greatest success in the time of the Roman Empire—the " diatribe," or lecture in dialogue form, based on the fiction of constant intervention by the hearer. These speeches seem to have been full of colour and packed with edifying anecdotes (χρεῖαι), parallels, and moral fables, at the same time preaching morality and popularizing philosophical themes in brilliant fashion. The old show-speech became a sermon, and these Cynics, whom one may fairly call, with Zeller, " the Capuchins of antiquity," at the same time effected a particular specialization of the Sophistic method. This Sophistic stylization of Cynicism is revealed to us in the very varied work of the man who, shortly after the revival of Pythagoreanism, 'about the end of the Ist century after Christ, took up the Cynic tradition once more—the rhetor of Prusa, Dion " Gold-mouth " (Chrysostom). If the personality and ideas of the Cynics of this later time— Demetrios, the friend of Seneca, Œnomaos, Demonax, Peregrinus—so interest the lively intelligence of Lucian of Samosata, does that not show that they attracted much attention among the cultivated public ? Indeed, their sermons and their rather charlatanish asceticism may have had some influence on Christian thought and life in the first centuries. There were representatives of their spirit even in the IVth century, and the Emperor Julian wrote against the Cynics of his day.

To return to early Cynicism, it seems that the logical doctrine of Antisthenes [1] was before all a search for the proper essence of each thing. But that essence is not something universal, and Antisthenes' hostility to the notion of Plato, whom he ridiculed in his *Sathon* (the title is a pun), has remained famous. " I see a horse, all right," he said, " but I don't see horsiness." For him as for the Megarics, an essence is an indivisible and therefore individual reality, and is wholly expressed by a singular noun, by its proper name ; so " the beginning of all instruction is the study of names." In consequence of this strict, and therefore immoderate, nominalism, definition, in its ordinary sense of general definition, is nothing but " stammering " and " drivelling " ; all that one can do, is to give an image of the thing by comparing it with another thing. Of course, the indivisible intuition which apprehends the essence of a thing cannot be empirical intuition,[2]

---

[1] The chief evidence will be found assembled in **XIV**, 286 ff.

[2] Our least uncertain data are hard to reconcile with the materialism which some would ascribe to Antisthenes in virtue of *Soph.*, 246 a-247 e and *Theaet.*, 155 e (cf **III**, 296-301), and which is supposed to be the source of that of the Stoics.

which is merely an opinion which distinguishes parts in the thing for convenience, a vain " smoke," in the words of Monimos, a disciple of Diogenes. That being so, attribution and judgement are impossible, in so far as they would consist in putting into one essence, the subject " man," for example, a totally distinct essence, such as the attribute " white " ; man is man and white is white—that is the truth. In expressing a thing which is, a notion also expresses the absolute truth. Hence it follows that when one confines oneself to naming an essence there is no possibility of contradiction or error. This complete negation of relation leads straight to utter contempt for knowledge, in so far as it claims to express the true in a system of relations. We need know only so much as we must know in order to live. One can understand that pragmatism like this, which used the logical consideration of the essence to deny knowledge, reflecting Socrates through the nihilistic Eleaticism of Gorgias, was regarded by Plato and Aristotle as a monstrous distortion of the philosophy of the concept.

This paradoxical logic is none the less the foundation of ethics. From the indivisibility and unchangeableness of essence the Cynics deduce that virtue is one, to be possessed wholly or not at all, and unfailing, so that a Wise Man never sins. It resides in intelligence, which is our surest rampart, and, if it can be taught, it is not done by a " protreptic " of discussion, a dialectical exhortation without efficacity, like Plato's, but by practice, which gives us the intuitive vision of the good. For the good of man is that which is proper to his essence, and evil is what is foreign to it. That is the secret of the happiness of the " Sage " or " Wise Man " and his independence, and the secret of the misery of the " fool " and his servitude. Only the former has seen what is his and what is not ; " to live in company with yourself," that is philosophy (Diog. Laërt., vi. 6). Outside the good of virtue and the evil of vice, everything else—honours, good repute, wealth, life, and their opposites—is distinguishable only in the eyes of the fool, the dupe of opinion. Really all this is " indifferent," vain " smoke " ($\tau\hat{v}\phi o\varsigma$), which does not get into the head of the Wise Man ($\dot{a}\tau v\phi\acute{\iota}a$). The worst folly is to seek the pleasures of sense, and, above all, love. The cure for love is fasting and time, and then, if they do no good, a cord to strangle yourself. " If I met Aphrodite," said Antisthenes, " I should throttle her with my own hands." True joy lies in effort (πόνος) and exercise (ἄσκησις), the physical and moral training by which one " delivers oneself " from the bondage of passion and external circumstances. So the Cynics took Heracles as their patron. Their life was an application of these principles. What they wanted to realize by their " asceticism " was the man of nature, that is, the real man, and for him Diogenes went seeking everywhere. So they adopted for their own purposes the distinction between " nature " and " convention." Family, city, political rights are merely artificial ; the Wise Man is a " citizen of the world " (κοσμοπολίτης). So, too, the gods are creations of law, whereas, by nature, godhead is one. In the myths one should look only for moral symbols.[1]

IV

THE SCHOOL OF CYRENE

The relationship of this last group to Socratic thought is a difficult and interesting question. The founder, Aristippos of Cyrene, seems to have practised the profession of Sophist before he joined the Socratic circle. There can be no doubt that he belonged to it ; he is, for example, one of those whose absence on Socrates' last day surprises the interlocutor of Phaedon. His absence seems to have been as justifiable as that of Plato himself, and we need not consider the adverse explanations which were afterwards invented, in view of the moral doctrine of Aristippos. So, too, all that has been told of his servility to the two Dionysioses, the Sicilian tyrants, is probably only a fable intended to contrast his attitude with Plato's. It seems that his daughter Arete succeeded him in the direction of the school, and that her son, Aristippos *Metrodidaktos* (Taught-by-his-Mother) was the first to teach the doctrine of pleasure which tradition ascribes to his grandfather. Certainly we have, against the tradition, the fact that when Aristotle is discussing a doctrine of the kind, in the *Nicomachean Ethics* (x. 2), he refers to Eudoxos of Cnidos,

[1] Chief texts in **XIV**, nn. 279–85.

and does not even mention the elder Aristippos. The later history of the school is equally obscure. It seems to have split up. Hegesias, who by his sermon on the evils of life earned the surname of "Recommender of Death" (Πεισιθάνατος), and Anniceris seem to have attached themselves to a disciple of the elder Aristippos, named Antipatros, while Theodoros of Cyrene, the Atheist, succeeded Aristippos the younger. Diogenes Laërtios speaks of Theodoreans, Hegesiacs, and Annicereans. Theodoros, driven from Cyrene by a democratic revolution, lived first at the court of Ptolemy Soter and then with Demetrios of Phaleron in Athens, before returning to his country. These three philosophers belong to the end of the IVth century and the beginning of the next.

Like the Cynics, the Cyrenaics disdained purely speculative knowledge, as being far inferior to the manual crafts, in that it teaches us nothing of what is better or worse. Aristippos, says Aristotle,[1] is one of the " Sophists " who think thus. Nor could anything be more in accordance with the spirit of Protagoras than this opposition of a knowledge of " values " to that which speculates abstractly or tries to reach the real. Logic and physics are valuable only as means with a view to ethics, by which we are taught what is good or bad for us (for example, to fear or not to fear the gods and death), and, by means of a study of our " affections " and " actions," that is, of our impressions and reactions, can distinguish what is " to be sought and what to be avoided."[2] Do these ideas, which will be found again in Epicuros, belong only to later Cyrenaicism ? It was in this later time, towards the end of the IVth century, that Epicuros began to teach in Athens ; but in any case the question of priority is insoluble. But the fact remains that, in relation with these ideas, under the influence of the relativism of Protagoras and Democritos or their pupils, the Cyrenaics taught that there is nothing true but the inward feeling of pleasure and pain. That is all that we can know—namely, what things *appear* to us to be, not what they *are*. We are " shut off from the outside, as in a besieged city." What I perceive, I *become ;* I become the sweetness of honey, but I do not apprehend it in itself outside me. Every judgement about the external reality of a thing is

---

[1] *Metaph.*, B. 2, 996 a 32 ff.; cf. M. 3, 1078 a 33.
[2] Seneca, *Epist.*, lxxxix. 12 ; Sextus, *Math.*, vii. 11 ; Diog. Laërt., ii. 92.

necessarily disputable, whereas the *phenomenon*, the subjective appearance, is indisputable. Moreover, do we even know that it results from some external cause ? The only thing underlying our personal, contingent affections is the common name by which, among men, we designate them.[1] This is a sensualistic nominalism, very different from that of the Megarics and Cynics. At least the foundation of this sub-jectivistic theory seems to belong to early or middle Cyrenai-cism. Indeed, it may be to those Cyrenaics, who, as we shall see, gave a large place to movement in their theory, that we should refer the much discussed passage in the *Theaetetos* mentioned above, which does not seem applicable to Protagoras himself.[2]

On this foundation their moral theory is based ;[3] the personal subjective impression is the criterion of the value of our ends and the rule of our action. Now, this " affection " ($\pi \acute{a} \theta o_S$) is a movement ; if it is gentle, the impression is agreeable, if rough or violent, disagreeable, if too weak, nil. Movement is, therefore, the under side of a phenomenon, as is set forth in the *Theaetetos*, while sensation is the upper side. At least, the sovereign good can only reside in pleasure ; pleasure is the measure of all other values. Therefore, what does not give me pleasure is neither good nor bad ; it is an " indifferent " thing, with regard to which I am as if asleep or dead. Consequently, too, since the object of pleasure, such as wealth or good cheer, is only the external occasion of pleasure, that object is in itself an indifferent thing. " Convention " and prejudice make distinctions between these objects and impose limits on them, none of which is acknowledged by nature. " Wealth," said Aristippos, " is not like a shoe, which you cannot use because it is too big." Everything agreeable is equally good, and made to be enjoyed, as much and as long as you do enjoy it ; let us have no false shame about it ! It was doubtless from particularly free expressions of this anarchic individualism that Theodoros earned his reputation for shameless audacity. Of course this pleasure cannot be anything general ; it is personal and " confined to the single instant " during which it is experienced.

---

[1] Cic., *Acad.*, ii. 7. 20, 24. 76, 46. 142 ; Plut., *Against Colotes*, 24 ; Aristocles, in Eus., *Praep. Ev.*, xiv. 19. 1 ; Sextus, *Math.*, vii. 191–200 (cf. *Pyrrh.*, i. 215) ; Diog. Laërt., ii. 93.

[2] 155 e-157 c. Cf. above, p. 146.   [3] Cf. **XIV**, nn. 266–71.

A past or future pleasure is nothing real ; it is a movement which is no longer or is not yet. Concentrated on his present, the Wise Man gathers enjoyment whenever and however it comes ; that is always in his power. The objective conditions of enjoyment are outside him and have no relation to him, and it is his independence with regard to them which makes his liberty. " I possess," Aristippos said with reference to his relations with the lovely Laïs, " I am not possessed." Why grow passionate ? You only change a gentle movement into a violent movement, and therefore a painful one. Always equal to circumstances, the Wise Man endeavours to rule them, instead of letting them rule him.[1] He is as much at ease in rags as in purple ; sometimes he flatters the powerful, but he can also defy them on occasion, as we are told of Theodoros. Seen from outside, and with reference to social prejudices or imaginary distinctions, his conduct may appear scandalous or contradictory ; inside, he is always consistent with himself and in accordance with nature. In fact, his paraded hedonism is often very close to the asceticism of the Cynic, but is based on other principles.[2]

We must make no mistake : what Cyrenaic hedonism teaches is not mere complaisant obedience to instinct. On the contrary, thought is what justifies enjoyment and liberates it from the external object or circumstances. What is more, in the view of Theodoros, with regard to the tranquil " joy " of the Wise Man, defined by the reflective intelligence, pleasure is merely an indifferent thing sought by fools. If Hegesias is a pessimist, it is only because he thinks that any calculation capable of bringing about a pleasure free of all pain is foredoomed to failure. Anniceris, on the other hand, is an inconsequent eclectic, who smooths down corners and modifies paradoxes. So the path is opened to the Epicurean restoration of Cyrenaicism on new bases.

The Cyrenaic is a citizen of the world like the Cynic, and, like him, a free thinker. The surname of Theodoros, as with all the other philosophers who appear on the traditional lists as " Atheists," means nothing more than a critical attitude

---

[1] Horace, *Epist.*, i. 17. 23 ff. " *Aristippum . . . fere praesentibus aequum* " ; i. 1. 18 ff. " *Nunc in Aristippi furtim praecepta relabor et mihi res, non me rebus, subjungere conor.*"

[2] Bion of the Borysthenes, the Cynic, is said to have lived for a long time with Theodoros the Atheist.

towards the popular religion, not negation of the divine. There is therefore probably no very serious ground for attaching to the Cyrenaic school the famous Euhemeros (beginning of the IIIrd century), whose *Sacred History*, which was translated by Ennius and survives in some fragments, was the breviary of unbelieving pagans and later of the Christian opponents of paganism.

While the philosophers whom we have been discussing are in many respects very close to the Sophists, they all show a tendency quite foreign to the Sophists ; they would give the individual a superiority placing him above everything contingent and truly emancipating him. Moreover, the influence of the East, which had hitherto always been counterbalanced in the mind of the Greek by his rationalistic bent, appears crudely in the thought of Antisthenes, the son of the Thracian slave-woman, and Aristippos, the Greek of Africa. These forerunners of the Sceptics, the Stoics, and the Epicureans are already Hellenistic. All, too, are, in intention, prophets of Socraticism. If we compare their pictures of the master with Plato's, we do not see any contradiction. But they reflect one single aspect of a figure whose disconcerting complexity was made up of contrasts which balanced one another. They exaggerated one aspect at the expense of the rest—the Megarics, his subtlety in argument, the Cynics, his ascetic austerity, the Cyrenaics, his approval of free indulgence in pleasures provided that you can give them up if need be. But all have the same end in view—to be a man, or, what is the same thing, to depend on oneself alone. Now, this practical end, in spite of appearances to the contrary, is also, as we shall see, that of Plato.

Chapter IV

First Part—PLATO

I

His Life

Plato belonged to an aristocratic family, claiming, on his father's side, to be of the royal blood of Codros, and on his mother's being indirectly connected with Solon. Several of his near kin, Critias, Charmides, were, as we have seen, among the heads of the oligarchical party, which Sparta supported. Plato was probably born about 428–427. During his *ephebeia* he may have taken part in some military expeditions ; when it was ended he became the pupil of the Heracleitean Cratylos, and then, about his twentieth year, began to resort to Socrates. If we can believe Epistle VII [1] (324 b ff.), he had political ambitions very early. Probably, therefore, like so many other young men of his rank, like Critias and Charmides before him, or his elder brothers Adeimantos and Glaucon, he came to the apostle as a curious dilettante. But he very soon attached himself to him seriously, chiefly, perhaps, because he found in his talk the conception of a statesmanship governed by justice. Henceforward it was as a philosopher that he awaited the moment to take part in public affairs. The moment seemed to have come when, in 404, the capture of Athens by Lysander gave the power to the aristocracy. Critias was one of the thirty supreme Archons, Charmides was one of the ten Archons of the Peiræeus, and Plato himself seems to have been given duties suited to his years. But he was soon disillusioned ; it was not thus that he had imagined the government of " the best men." He doubtless broke with

[1] Its authenticity, and that of VIII, are generally admitted.

the party before the revolution which restored democracy in 401. Presently the condemnation of Socrates, an episode in a time of vengeance, destroyed all his hopes of a political regeneration of his country on the bases of its traditional social organization.

After a sojourn at Megara, which used to be wrongly regarded as a turning-point in his life, he seems, contrary to tradition, to have settled permanently in Athens and to have assumed a position there as a philosopher, perhaps even as the head of a school. A voyage, which does not seem to have lasted more than two or three years, took him first to Egypt, of which country his writings seem to show personal knowledge, then to Cyrene, not far away, where he is said to have associated with the mathematician Theodoros, one of the characters in the *Theaetetos*, then to Great Greece, doubtless with the object of learning more about the doctrines of the Pythagoreans and especially of seeing a government of philosophers at work where it still existed, for example under Archytas at Taras, and lastly, in 388 for the first time, according to Epistle VII, to Syracuse, where he may have hoped to inculcate in the reigning prince, Dionysios the Elder, ideas about the right place of philosophers in the State such as are set forth in the Vth Book of the *Republic*. The voyage had an unfortunate ending. The admiration inspired by Plato in young Dion, the tyrant's brother-in-law and son-in-law, whose energy was regarded with suspicion, the political theories of the philosopher, his protests against the dissolute life of the Court, all very soon made him intolerable to Dionysios and his friends. He was placed on a Spartan ship, which set him ashore at Ægina, an ally of Sparta against Athens. As a prisoner of war, it is said that he might have been put to death, under a recent decree of the Æginetans, but they were content to hold him to ransom. The sum was paid by a citizen of Cyrene, whom he had doubtless known in that city, and he was at last able to return to Athens.

Shortly after this, about 387, Plato founded his school or, more probably, established it at his own expense on a beautiful piece of ground, planted with trees and watered by springs, with a gymnasium standing in the middle. This was the park of the hero Academos, on the Eleusis road, not far from the Cephisos and the renowned village of Colonos. Whatever his activity as a teacher and a writer might thenceforward be, the hope of making the City of Justice a reality never seems to have left his mind.

He had kept up relations with Dion, and when, at the beginning of 367, the elder Dionysios died and was succeeded by his nephew, the second Dionysios, Plato readily allowed Dion to persuade him that the new tyrant, being still quite young, would be the willing instrument of their designs. He therefore sailed for Sicily in 367-366. But his second venture was no more successful than the first. Dionysios soon proved to Plato and Dion that they laboured under illusions. He banished Dion, whose secret policy he had discovered, and established Plato permanently in his palace, surrounding him with jealous and fussy consideration. At last, being obliged to go to war, he restored him to liberty. In Athens, Plato met Dion, in whose favour he had obtained the most binding promises from the tyrant. But Dionysios kept putting off their fulfilment, and finally made the return of Plato to Syracuse a condition. In spite of his age and the obvious risk, the philosopher decided, for the sake of his friend, to make the voyage again (361). The duplicity of Dionysios was very soon apparent ; Plato had to fear for his life, and it was only through the energetic intervention of Archytas, in the name of the Tarentines, that he escaped from the adventure without harm. The fruitlessness, so far as his political plans were concerned, of Dion's campaign against Dionysios in 357–356 and the murder of Dion after four years of difficulties and disorders, removing the man in whom he seemed to have found the perfect disciple of his philosophy and the only one capable of achieving its ultimate object, must have helped to sadden the last years of Plato. But age had not weakened his mighty spirit. His activity as a writer may perhaps have slackened, but as a teacher he did not cease, by oral teaching, to enrich his doctrine with new developments and to organize it more systematically. Nor had he completely given up writing ; he was finishing the *Laws* when death took him suddenly, in his eighty-first year (347–346).

II

HIS WRITINGS

By a rare and fortunate exception, Plato is known to us by the whole of his written works. It is very probable that the *Philosopher* and *Hermocrates*, which were to form pendants, one to the *Sophist* and *Statesman* and the other to the *Timaeos* and *Critias*, were never more than planned. The book of *Divisions*, of which Aristotle speaks several times, was doubtless not so much a work, properly so called, as a kind of school vocabulary of technical terms.[1] The problem is rather, whether all the writings in our collection are really Plato's. It is, no doubt, probable that at an early date, in the libraries and even in that of the Academy, men introduced among the writings of Plato works emanating from his circle, or works in which some fashionable subject was treated in the form of a Platonic dialogue. Thus, in the catalogues of erudite writers, such as Aristophanes of Byzantion or Thrasyllos, to the latter of whom the traditional arrangement in tetralogies is due, we find works whose authenticity was already questioned by the ancients—for instance, the *Epinomis* (or *Appendix to the Laws*), which was generally attributed to Philip of Opus, the editor of the *Laws*. The *Axiochos*, *Eyrxias*, and other works were also suspected. The *Definitions* were ascribed to Speusippos. The alleged doubts of Panaetios on the authenticity of the *Phaedon* seem to refer not to the work, but to its main thesis. On the other hand, the ancients had no doubts of the *Theages* or the *Cleitophon* or the *Minos*, which everybody to-day regards as apocryphal.[2] About others, critics are still divided —the two *Alcibiades*, *Hippias Major*, and the Letters.[3] We are a long way from the hypercritical days when Schaarschmidt (1866) managed to reject twenty-seven dialogues of the thirty-six which form our collection. The *Parmenides*, *Sophist*, *Statesman*, and *Philebos*, for example, were condemned. A dialogue would be excluded because it did not agree with the idea which the critic had already formed of Plato's system or

---

[1] **III**, 437, 3.
[2] See **CV**, 34–45. Cf. S. Reinach, "Panaitios critique," in *Rev. de Phil.*, 1916, 201–9.
[3] Cf. Ernst Howald's introduction to his edition of the *Letters*, Zurich, 1923.

of the development of his thought. By making use of objective criteria, such as the allusions of Aristotle (which, however, are not always equally explicit) or considerations of language, it has been possible to treat these fantasies as they deserve.

For long an attempt has been made to arrange the dialogues in the right order. In doing this, the ancient critics chiefly considered the form of the dialogue or the nature of the subject discussed. Modern critics have taken the problem in another way, endeavouring to find, in Plato's writings, the development of his thought, whether, like Schleiermacher (1804), they sought its logical unity, or, less arbitrarily, like K. F. Hermann (1839), saw a real historical evolution in them. Hermann shed considerable light on the path to be followed : to understand Plato in his writings, we must arrange them in order of composition. It is impossible here to follow all the complicated details of the inquiries undertaken with this object. Some critics have devoted themselves to the study of the content of the dialogues, either in order to follow the progress of a particular theory, or to discover allusions to contemporary facts or persons. But, interesting though these investigations are, it is evident that they require great caution and are exposed to great risks of subjective interpretation. For example, the same passages in the *Euthydemos* and *Phaedros* have given rise to entirely opposite views on the relations of Isocrates and Plato. The meaning of historical allusions is equally uncertain. Plato's anachronistic habit of referring to events later than the time of Socrates and his interlocutors would, no doubt, enable us to establish the earliest date at which a dialogue can have been written, if we were sure that we made no mistake about the event, which is sometimes mentioned very enigmatically. There is agreement about hardly one of these anachronisms. Moreover, our knowledge of what was happening in Athens at the time is very fragmentary ; we are always in danger of considering one single fact and neglecting many others, known or unknown.

A method calculated to give more certain results is that inaugurated by Lewis Campbell in Scotland (1867) and by Blass and Dittenberger in Germany (1874, 1881)—the stylistic method. The language of a writer never remains quite the same from one end of his literary career to the other. Now Plato's literary career covers about fifty years. It may therefore be presumed that his language developed as he grew older, in accordance with the demands of fashion and the need for establishing a philosophic vocabulary. A particle or an expression which is exclusively used in certain dialogues is constantly replaced by a synonym in others. In some cases he seems to be more especially concerned than in others with the rhythm of the sentence and the avoidance of hiatus, as was required by the new rhetoric. Simultaneously, his language is affected and his terminology becomes more technical. By the presence or absence of these characteristics we can group the dialogues. Now, there is one indisputable example of Plato's latest style, the *Laws*. Therefore the dialogues most resembling the *Laws* in style may be referred to his old age, and those lacking that resemblance to his youth. Those which combine the characteristics of both groups will form an intermediate class.[1] This method, which leaves little room for subjective interpretations and allows of many varieties of experiment, supplies the necessary check for the results obtained by the others.

So, although divergences about the historical order of Plato's dialogues are not abolished, they have been very much reduced. The beginning and end of the first group are still disputed. Did Plato write before the death of Socrates, and what dialogues?[2] Does the *Gorgias* come at the end of the first group, or does it belong to the author's maturity?[3] Nor is there agreement about the position of certain dialogues within the first two groups. But over the constitution of the group of his old age there is almost complete agreement, and this is an important fact.

The dialogues of his youth are : (i) those which defend the memory of Socrates, the *Apology*, the *Criton*, and, later, to state the Master's religious position more precisely, the *Euthyphron* ; (ii) " Socratic works " which are, in various degrees, dialogues of negative " protreptic," witty satires or burning exhortations, which show an increasing mastery of dialectic and also philosophic detachment, the *Protagoras*, *Ion*, two *Hippiases* (or

[1] **CVIII**, a very complete account of the question. But does the method allow, as the author thinks, of mathematical strictness, and can it become a " stylometry." It is very unlikely.
[2] **CXII**, i. 131, 153, regards the *Ion*, *Hippias Minor*, and *Protagoras* as prior to the death of Socrates.
[3] *Ibid.*, i. 234-7, ii. 100-5, places it before Plato's voyages and before the pamphlet of Polycrates. The opposite view is maintained by **XI**, ii. 336, 343-4.

Minor only, if *Major* is apocryphal), *Laches, Charmides*, perhaps *Lysis*, which some critics place near the *Symposium*, Book I of the *Republic*, and lastly, before his travels, the *Gorgias*.

To his maturity one may ascribe the *Menexenos*, after 386, a kind of manifesto of his return, in which Plato takes up his position against the rhetors on their own ground ; then the *Menon, Euthydemos*, and *Cratylos* and the complementary *Symposium* and *Phaedon ;* then the *Republic*, the first book of which had already appeared, as has been said, while the last book may perhaps have followed the harmonious whole formed by the three divisions II-IV, V-VII, VII-IX ; and lastly the *Phaedros*, which was long regarded as a youthful work, but is rather an episode in the polemic waged by the philosopher of the Academy against the rhetorical schools, and the *Theaetetos* and *Parmenides*.

The second journey to Sicily and the negotiations over Dion doubtless interrupted Plato's literary activity, and the first work of his old age, the *Sophist*, completed by the *States-man*, probably came some little time after the *Theaetetos*, with which it is connected. Then come the unfinished *Critias* and the *Timaeos*, and then the *Philebos*, which, if it is a criticism of the hedonism of Eudoxos, may have been written on the occasion of the latter's death, about 354. The twelve books of the *Laws*, the only work of Plato in which Socrates does not appear at all, must therefore have come fairly long afterwards.

III

TENDENCIES OF HIS YOUTH

The dialogues of Plato's youth were for a long time called " Socratic." For, to a great extent, Socrates is doubly their hero, since some are a protest against his condemnation and depict, in his likeness, the ideal figure of a philosopher, and the others are given as an illustration of his method. These latter treat of a moral quality—courage in the *Laches*, moral wisdom (σωφροσύνη) in the *Charmides*, the beautiful, in its widest acceptation, in the *Hippias Major*, the knowledge of truth in relation to action in the *Hippias Minor*, justice in Book I of the *Republic*, and obedience to the law or holiness in the

Criton and *Euthyphron*, which are, however, works of an apologetic nature.

The *Hippias Minor* may be taken as an example. Hippias has just given a public lecture on Homer. Which is more worthy, Socrates asks him, Achilles or Odysseus ? According to the poet, says Hippias, Achilles is, since he is sincere and truthful, whereas Odysseus is crafty and a liar. But surely to be crafty is to be intelligent and resourceful in respect of that which is the object of your craftiness. Therefore a crafty man or a liar is one who, knowing what he should say or do, prefers at a certain moment not to say it or not to do it. A man who is expert in the art of arithmetic is better than one who is ignorant of that art ; for, whereas the latter may, by his very ignorance, happen to tell the truth in a matter of arithmetic, the former can always, in virtue of his very knowledge, answer falsely, willingly and knowing what he is about. Therefore there is no difference between Achilles and Odysseus ; telling the truth and concealing it equally suppose the capacity to know it. Not at all, Hippias replies ; for Odysseus lies out of malice and deliberately, whereas Achilles, if he happens to do it, does it for some laudable purpose, or in spite of himself. Are we to be harder on the man who is unjust unwillingly ? Most certainly, says Socrates ; for it is better to do wrong willingly than to do it without understanding what you are doing. Is it not better (among other examples) to make faces willingly, being naturally beautiful, than to be naturally ugly ? Therefore, scandalous as it may appear, a soul capable of justice and knowing what is just would be worthier, if it could come to commit injustice willingly, than a soul which was unjust from incapacity or ignorance. The conclusion is logically necessary ; yet it leaves Socrates doubtful.

This is the common characteristic of these dialogues. They examine opinions and criticize them ; so they are " elenctic " or " refuting." They review a great number of particulars in order to extract a general notion from them ; so they are inductive. But that notion does not satisfy, and doubts subsist ; the ground is only cleared for further inquiry. Thus, in the *Hippias Minor*, it remains to be decided whether a soul capable of justice and knowing it can wish not to do it.

No, it cannot, says the *Protagoras ;* for, if virtue is the common essence of which the many virtues partake, as the gold of the ingot causes all its parts to be of gold, if it is, in general, the knowledge of what is, with reference to our being, "fairest, best, and most pleasant," it follows both that it can be taught (which would be impossible if virtue were not that very knowledge) and that such knowledge could never in any case be overcome by the attraction of sensual pleasure. So we still have to verify the condition from which these consequences ensue, that is, to determine the essence of virtue.

This object of inquiry is clearly marked in the *Euthyphron*. If one would know the " reality " or essence (οὐσία) of holiness, he must fix his eyes on the single " form " (ἰδέα, εἶδος) or the " pattern " (παράδειγμα) thanks to which holy things are always like themselves (5 d, 6 d-e, 11 a). In brief, the purely formal knowledge of the Sophists has to be given a real content. Moreover, even in these earliest dialogues a positive indication is given about the nature of that content : it is the " Idea " of the thing in question.

The *Gorgias* is in part an examination of the formal knowledge constituted by the rhetoric of the Sophists, a knowledge which serves only to furnish the ethics of instinct with arguments and maxims. This equivocal art is an instrument for the base flattery of our passions, unnecessary where there is true knowledge of the just and unjust, and dangerous where there is no such knowledge to give it a foundation. Now, what is just according to nature, Callicles says, is " to allow your personal desires to be as great as possible," and then " to be able to satisfy them by your courage and intelligence," so that " the fitter man has the advantage over the less fit " (491 e ff., 483 d). To this naturalistic conception,[1] Plato opposes another which, in great part, bears the stamp of Orphico-Pythagorean asceticism. To desire is to suffer a lack ; to increase your desires constantly with a view to satisfying them is to keep pains constantly reviving in you, as a man with the itch increases his sores by scratching himself. Such a life is a " pot with a hole in it," or, again, an incessant death ; you make your body your tomb (σῶμα, σῆμα, 492 e ff.). Now, what makes us good or bad is not pleasure or pain, but the " presence "

---

[1] It also appears in *Rep.*, i, expounded by Thrasymachos.

in us (παρουσία) of good or evil. And that good, which is the only foundation of what is agreeable, is virtue, that is, in everything, and in our souls in particular, the order and " arrangement " (κόσμος) proper to it. A wise, just, and temperate man is an image of the order of the universe. We therefore see what a power proportion and " geometrical equality " have among gods and men (497 e, 506 e, 508 a). Only justice or the expiation of the injustice which we have done can make us happy. The rhetoric capable of making men better, which the great statesmen of Athens have not known, is that which is based on the knowledge of the just. The dialogue ends with an eschatological myth. After death, our souls appear before their judges with all the deformities branded on them by an unjust life. To be straightened and purified, they will have to do expiation. Let us, then, live in justice and for justice, in order to prepare ourselves to die well.

IV

THE DOCTRINE OF HIS MATURITY

Questions have been raised, a tendency has been indicated, some flashes have given a glimpse of vast perspectives. Now they will grow definite and luminous.

1. *Menon.* First of all, the *Menon*, taking up the problem left unsettled at the end of the *Protagoras*, adds important observations to the powerful sketch of the *Gorgias*. Menon, a pupil of Gorgias, asks Socrates the question then in fashion : does our virtue come from teaching, practice, or habit ? Now, this question concerns the *qualities* of virtue. It cannot, therefore, be answered, unless one knows in what virtue consists, or what its *essence* is. An enumeration of the varieties of virtue belonging to persons of various condition brings us no further forwards ; that is a " swarm " of virtues, it is not virtue. Like the bees in a swarm, these particular virtues must have " a form, one and the same, by which they are virtues," and at which one must look if one would say what virtue is—not some part of virtue, such as justice, but virtue *itself* (αὐτή), apart from everything else and in its entirety.

An impossible quest, says the pupil of the Sophists ; you cannot seek what you do not know, because you do not know it, and therefore you cannot recognize it if you happen to meet it ; but if you knew it you would not need to seek it (80 d ff.). Plato resolves the difficulty by a novel version of the Pythagorean doctrine of " reminiscence " ($\dot{a}\nu\dot{a}\mu\nu\eta\sigma\iota\varsigma$).[1] Have we not sometimes " true opinions " about what we do not know ? Now, whenever these discoveries come to us, not from others, but from ourselves, they must be " recollections " of knowledge acquired in previous existences. The question propounded first provokes a " difficulty " ($\dot{a}\pi o\rho\dot{\iota}a$), which helps us to become " aware of our ignorance." Then true opinions awake. At first it is like " a dream " ; then, by means of well-conducted interrogation, they become knowledge, sciences (84 a-c, 85 c-d). Learning is recollecting ; not knowing is having forgotten. If we can thus extract from ourselves truths which no one has taught us, it is because, during the " eternity of time " which preceded our present life, our soul has learned them ; and that leads one to think that it is immortal. We know how Socrates tests this doctrine : by his questions he leads a young slave, who knows no geometry, to discover propositions regarding the ratio of the side of a square to its diagonal.

This doctrine of " true opinion " receives a remarkable application in the case of virtue. Men have by instinct a virtue, such as that of administering the State well ; such were the great statesmen of Athens, and Pericles among them. But they cannot either communicate their virtue or keep it undiminished. It is, therefore, based only on true and right opinions, and these opinions, if there is no reasoned reflection to attach them to their " cause " by a well-conducted reminiscence, are always ready to escape from our soul, like a runaway slave (97 e ff.). With knowledge, on the contrary, which would stop and fix them, we should always be masters of them. They must, therefore, be the effect of a " divine favour " ($\theta\epsilon\dot{\iota}a\ \mu o\hat{\iota}\rho a$), in which the intelligence has no part ; it is an inspiration. So, once again, it has not been possible to attack the question, what is the essence of virtue.

---

[1] Cf. L. Robin, in *Rev. Ét. grecques*, xxxii (1919), pp. 451–61.

2. *Cratylos, etc.* Philosophic culture and the assured knowledge which comes from it are therefore indispensable foundations of all practice. In the *Ion* Plato had already criticized the rhapsodes' formal, external conception of poetry. But the genius of poets, like that of statesmen, is based on inspiration, a precarious substitute for knowledge. They are joined to the god by a magnetic chain, of which they are the links, so long as he chooses to " possess " them and give them " enthusiasm." After the passionate condemnation of rhetoric in the *Gorgias*, the *Menexenos* showed by an example what rhetoric could give, if conceived in another spirit. In the *Euthydemos*, by the side of the parody of the ways of the Sophists, it was shown how, without scientific knowledge, there is no " protreptic " which can lead one to virtue and, in general, no fruitful use can be made of any advantage which one may have (278 d ff.).

The *Cratylos* is even more significant. It deals with the nature of language. Words are not derived from a purely artificial convention, if they were " instituted," it was, as etymology proves, by analogy with the very natures of the things which they were intended to express. So, by the letters composing them, they are an " imitation " of the actions characteristic of those things. Now, that imitation, being an imitation, is necessarily imperfect (425 d-435 c). But it would have been far less imperfect if " dialecticians," those who possess the art of " questioning and answering," that is, philosophers, had been the " lawgivers " presiding over the naming of things. For, unless one is prepared to go on from the relativism of Protagoras to total negation of the principle of contradiction, things have a fixed, stable essence (385 e-390 e). Knowledge of the " truth of things " must come before that of the words which are images of things. The system of Heracleitos is false, or rather incomplete ; the perpetual flux of things would make all cognition impossible, if it were not a flux of permanent, unchangeable realities, such as the Beautiful and the Good, which " do not at all come out of their form " or " idea." Now, one discovers these realities by a double method—by perceiving the mutual relation of those which are of the same kind, and by analysing each of these groups (438 a ff.)

So the " theory of Ideas," to give it its traditional name,

and the dialectical method both seem to be already defined in Plato's thought, although he is still content, in these works intended for the public, merely to allude to them. In dealing with the Heracleitean thesis, Plato became aware of his personal interpretation of the Socratic search for essence.[1] Essence, he thought, will be carried away in the flux of becoming, if (without denying the flux) we do not make essence independent of it.

3. *The Symposium.* While remaining in the background, this interpretation becomes clearer in the *Symposium* and *Phaedon.* The theme of the former is love ; it had long been a stock theme of mythical speculation, and Plato had already touched on it in the *Lysis.* Each of the banqueters, who are helping the poet Agathon to celebrate his victory in the theatre, pronounces an eulogy of love—Phaedros, Pausanias, the physician Eryximachos, Aristophanes, Agathon—each speech representing a point of view on the subject, or a fancy, or a literary parody. Socrates in his turn is asked to speak. His speech, the greater part of which is an account of his conversations with Diotima, a priestess of Mantineia (a round-about way of saying that it is only an *adaptation* of Socraticism) is an attempt to give love its place in a rational representation of things. Because love lacks the good and the beautiful, love of which it is, shall we believe it bad and ugly ? No, for, just as " true opinion, which cannot give a reason for itself " is intermediate between knowledge and ignorance, so love is intermediate between the bad and the good, between the ugly and the beautiful. It is one of the daemons or geniuses which serve as mediators between gods and men and, like the proportion described in the *Gorgias,* " connect the All with itself." In the arts, the man of genius, the " daemonic man " (δαιμόνιος ἀνήρ) owes his divine inspiration to them.

All that is contradictory and instable in the essence of love, and also all that is synthetic and active, is expressed by the myth of his birth. He was born of Penia, or Poverty, and so lacks everything, and Poros, the spirit of Gain, from whom he has inherited the never-satisfied desire for what is good, and for wisdom in particular, for Poros is himself the

---

Aristotle understands this (*Metaph.*, A. 6, beg. ; M. 4, 1078 b 12 ff.).

son of Metis, or Intelligence. "So he is a philosopher all his life." Having first seen the light while the gods were celebrating the birth of Aphrodite, he is naturally the love of beauty. Really, that of which he is more properly love, is "generation in beauty"—bodily generation, with a view to perpetuating the species, and spiritual generation, with a view to producing in others virtues and teaching such as will survive in the memory of men. Being the desire for the lasting and even eternal possession of what is good, love manifests the effort of the mortal being to make itself immortal as far as it can.

But this analysis of the effects of love is only the beginning of an "initiation," which ends in the "revelation" of a "mystery." It is accomplished by a "continuous" ascent, in which there is a series of "steps" or degrees—love of beautiful forms, of beautiful souls, of beautiful works of man, and beautiful laws in particular, and lastly of the beauty of knowledge. At all these degrees, but especially at the first, it must be remembered that beauty is not in one single object, but in many, and that in all it is "one and the same." Moreover, as one rises, one liberates oneself more and more from the individual; thought, "growing greater," never ceases to give birth "in an unbounded aspiration to wisdom." Having been thus gradually prepared, the initiate at last obtains, and "suddenly," the "revelation." Beauty, like the image of the deity in the Mysteries, appears to his eyes. It is one, unchangeable, outside time and becoming, pure and without mixture, "alone in itself and with itself, in the unity and eternity of its form, whereas all other things are beautiful by participation in this Beauty" (211 a-b), which remains independent of all the determinations and all the changes which occur in them. Then we become truly immortal.

No doubt, here the transcendental existence, independent of the sensible, is only that of the Beautiful. But one may suppose that there is a whole order of similar existences; each, having the unity of a kind, is nevertheless an individualized universal, from which the partial, changing individualities of becoming have all the reality which they possess. Moreover, the *Symposium* shows us a philosophic method by which certain passional elements of our nature, being a condition of the intuitions of genius, become the means of a favoured reminiscence which liberates us from time and contingent diversity. " Platonic love," the transfiguration of a sexual perversion to which some tried to give a specious nobility, intellectualizes passion ; it is a kind of dialectic and the revelation of an absolute. The racy, magnificent eulogy of Socrates which Plato puts in the mouth of Alcibiades at the end of the dialogue expresses in concrete form this theory of the ideal love as a philosophic discipline and a means of detachment or ecstasy ; the perfect " lover " (ἐρωτικός) is the true philosopher.

4. *Phaedon.* Whether the *Phaedon* was written before or after the *Symposium*, it is another idealized picture of the philosopher, rising, without pride and without effort, above the accidents and passions of the life of the senses, here, at the point of leaving it, no less than there, in the joyous liberty of an activity quick to seize, without pedantry, upon every opportunity of awakening reflection. The asceticism of the *Gorgias* reappears in the *Phaedon ;* the approach of death, far from frightening the philosopher, rejoices him. He condemns suicide, for we are the property of the gods and they are the best of masters, but he really aspires to death. By death he hopes to live in the company of virtuous men and of gods, the friends of men ; by death he will escape from what Orphicism called the " slough," he will be freed from the body which, with the constant alternation of its pleasures and pains, its desires and fears, hampers the proper function of the soul, which is to know the truth for which it longs. Our life must, therefore, be a kind of preliminary death, an " apprenticeship of death " (64 a, 67 e, 81 a), an effort to restore the soul to itself. The virtues, and especially true temperance, are nothing else than that " purification " (67 c, 69 c). Showing us the contradictions inherent in the life of the senses, they give our soul the hope, when it will be " concentrated " in the " purity " of its essence, of contemplating " by pure thought " its proper object, the " pure," true, eternal essence of each thing, that which the thing is " in itself apart from its accidents " (αὐτὸ καθ' αὑτὸ ὅ ἐστι)—the Just, the Beautiful, the Good, the Holy, Greatness, Health, Strength (65 c ff., 75 c-d, etc.). So, at once mystic and intellectual, this moral discipline, by purifying the intelligence, constitutes a philosophic " initiation " (69 c).

But can the soul possess a nature of its own, independent of the body, and survive in itself after the death of the body ? The *Phaedon* does not pretend to demonstrate the survival of the soul ; it " mythologizes " (61 e) and merely gives reasons in favour of a probability. There are three. The first contains two arguments. In the first argument, again a memory of Heracleiteanism, it is shown that, if becoming were not constituted by a " cycle of mutual exchanges " (ἀνταπόδοσις) between contraries, and if life were not reborn from death (palingenesia), all things, in the end, would be destroyed in death. But need one therefore believe that, before birth and after death, our soul always has its own *activity* and *consciousness* ? That is why the second argument is necessary (70 b, 77 c-d). It is based on reminiscence, and the exposition of the *Menon* is explicitly recalled, but with new developments which state more precisely what the *Menon* and *Cratylos* called the " truth of things." A present sensation awakens the thought, not only of what was joined to it before, but of what resembles it. Now, in this case we have a sense of what is lacking in that resemblance to make it complete. This is how the diverse and variable equalities of sensuous experience awaken in us the thought of a perfect, unchangeable, unique Equality, which exists " in itself, invisible (ἀειδές), apart from " equal things and as something " other " (74 a, c, 79 a). We must, therefore, have previously known this Equality, which sensible equalities imperfectly resemble, to which they " aspire " without ever " reaching " it, with which we compare them as with a pattern. In general, the existence of the soul is bound to the " previous existence " of such essences, " of which we are for ever talking " (76 d, 100 b)—a phrase which is significant of the place which they held in Plato's teaching.

These considerations lead immediately to a second reason for believing in the immortality of the soul. The essences are simple and indivisible in " the unity of their form." To know them, the soul must itself, as the old adage says, be like them, be " of the same family." Therefore, while the whole family of sensible things, including our body, is subject to change and dissolution, the soul, being akin to the intelligible realities, must be " indissoluble or something near it " (80 b). But it can only " come into contact with " that which it is like by delivering itself, by philosophy and by death, from that which is not like it, that is, its body. The transmigrations through which souls are made to pass are the consequence and punishment of their attachment to the body.

We have seen (above, pp. 66 ff.) the theories by which the Pythagoreans Simmias and Cebes manifested the doubts which they felt about this conception. The doctrine of the soul as a harmony is easily refuted. But the objection of Cebes is more profound, and requires a general examination of the causes of generation and corruption. Nothing, perhaps, is more representative of Plato's art than the famous piece of symbolic history in which he describes the stages of Socrates' thought, and thus explains what reasons there are for replacing naturalism by the philosophy of Ideas. The causes which Anaxagoras assigns to generation and corruption, and all similar causes, are merely conditions *without which* things would not occur, they are mere means. The true causes are ends—that is, as was required by the doctrine of Mind itself, they are the " notions " (λόγοι), intelligible, not sensible, which define the better and the good of each thing, or its " truth." These are really " sufficient," solid " reasons " (99 a-b, e ff., 101 e). What makes us call a thing beautiful is not the proportion of its parts or the brightness of its colours, but the " presence," or " communication," or " partaking " [1] of the essence of the Beautiful, however that may happen. But one must distinguish between two kinds of partaking : (i) the case of the relation of subjects to one another, as where A is large in relation to B and small in relation to C ; (ii) the case where the fact that one form partakes of another, Snow of the form of Cold, or Fire of the form of Hot, gives the first form an attribute which helps to make its nature. This partaking cannot occur between any two essences ; Snow-in-itself can only partake of the Cold-in-itself, and could not receive the Hot-in-itself without at once losing its nature, because the Cold-in-itself and Hot-in-itself are contraries. So the incessant succession of contraries concerns only empirical things, subject to change (102 b-105 b). This is an important theory, which will be further developed in the *Sophist :* attribution is legitimate, in so far as it is based on the very relations of being, on the eternally regulated participation of one essence in another essence.

---

[1] Παρουσία, κοινωνία, μετάσχεσις. Μέθεξις appears in *Parm.*, 132 d.

If we apply this to the soul, we shall have a third reason, " ontological " in a way, and this time decisive, for believing it immortal. The contrary of the form or intelligible essence of Life is that of Death. Now, what gives the Soul-in-itself its proper nature is its partaking of Life-in-itself. It therefore excludes Death. The same is therefore true of all our souls, since they are that part of us which receives into itself the essence thus constituted by its partaking of Life (103 b-107 b). Amidst the becoming in which everything comes into being and perishes, souls alone neither come into being nor perish ; they ensure perpetuity of becoming and prevent the final triumph of death. This conception, which is another evidence of their kinship with Ideas, should, perhaps, be examined more deeply. But this involves a " glorious risk " (114 d). For, if the soul proves to be immortal, it is our duty, during life, to " take care " of it and to think of the destiny which awaits it after death. Here we get the eschatology of the *Gorgias* further developed, and it is incorporated in a myth on the constitution of the earth and its place in the universe. The earth on which we live is an intermediate place between an underground region in which the souls of the wicked suffer punishment for their earthly life and an upper region reserved for the bliss of just men and philosophers. That is where the soul of Socrates will presently go. The simple, moving realism of the famous picture of the philosopher's death is, like the portrait at the end of the *Symposium*, a living illustration of the theory which went before it.

5. *The Republic.* The practical direction of Plato's thought, already visible in the dialogues which we have been considering, is more strongly marked in the *Republic*. Philosophic speculation is necessary to education, which is necessary to the constitution of the State. This vast composition seems to show that Plato, having come to a decisive stage, is now in a position to embrace the road already covered in a general survey and to define his end.

The subject—the nature and effects of justice—was laid down in Book I, and is resumed in Book II from an entirely new point of view. Justice, conceived as a relation between the classes in the State, is compared to the relation between the parts of the soul in the individual composite being. This is the ruling idea of the whole work. Now, on the one hand, the just State is that which achieves the greatest possible unity, and, on the other hand, that result can only be obtained if the government is in the hands of true philosophers. So Books V, VI, and VII, the keystone of Plato's philosophy, are intimately connected with the subject.

The first question is, what is the true philosopher. Like the perfect lover of the *Symposium*, he is the man who attaches himself to the Beautiful-in-itself, who does not confuse the reality of which things partake with the things which partake of it, and who does not refuse to follow the guide who will lead him to the end. He is contrasted with the *philodoxoi*, the lovers of opinion (*doxa*). Now, corresponding to this mode of knowledge, which, as we have seen, is " intermediate " between absolute knowledge and absolute ignorance, there is, as in Eleaticism, an infinity of " ambiguous " things, which the common man takes for realities, which are or are not at the same time, which " roll about " in the zone intermediate between absolute not-being and the absolute being of essence (475 d, to the end of Book V). The philosopher goes beyond this middle zone. He is none the less superior, even in *experience*, to those who cannot rise beyond it and reach the " pattern." But it is inevitable that, knowing the pattern, he should feel nothing but distaste for what is a lying image of it, and should shut himself up jealously in his own meditations. Now, he has no right to do so. For his business is to compare human nature, as it is, with the patterns, Justice, Beauty, Wisdom, in order to " combine " these two kinds of things and to make of them an " image of a man " which shall be " dear to the gods " (vi. 501 b). So the ascetic purification of the *Gorgias* and *Phaedon* is not a complete definition of the moral life, and already we have a foretaste of the doctrine of the *Philebos*.

Then comes the second question. Before the true philosopher can educate other men, how shall he educate himself —by what sciences and by what occupations (502 c-d) ? The object to be attained is " the highest object of knowledge, the Idea of the Good," to which everything beautiful, good, just, useful, owes its being and without which all other knowledge is vain (505 a). The Good, " with a view to which every activity of every soul takes place," is neither pleasure nor intelligence. Plato defers telling us what it is till later (506 d-e), and is content, for the moment, to consider one " fruit " or " generation " of the Good—the Sun. If we now collect under the intelligible unit of an Idea all visible things, objects of sight, on the one hand, and all intelligible things, objects of the intellect, on the other, we must say that the Sun is to the first group, " in the visible world," what the Good is to the second, " in the intelligible world." These are the terms of a proportion or analogy (508 b-c). But truth and knowledge are not the Good, any more than light and sight are the Sun ; they only resemble it. The Good is something far more beautiful. Like the sun, which not only gives light to things but causes them to be born and to grow, the Good not only produces the intelligibility of intelligible things, but gives them their " essence " and " existence." What is more, " it is not itself essence, but beyond essence ($\epsilon\pi\epsilon\kappa\epsilon\iota\nu\alpha$ $\tau\hat{\eta}s$ $o\dot{v}\sigma\dot{\iota}as$), surpassing it in dignity and power " (509 b). In short, between the Good and other Ideas there seems to be a gulf similar to that between sensible things and Ideas, or between the Beautiful-in-itself and the highest step in the erotic ascent. There is an exact parallelism between the different grades of rank in being and knowing (vii. 533 c ff.). Every degree in either scale is an " imitation " or " image " of the degree above. Between the absolute not-being of total ignorance and the absolute being of supreme knowledge there is a whole ladder of intermediate stages—fictitious copies of natural objects by the arts, copies of ideal realities by sensible nature, the symbolical objects of science *between* these copies and their patterns, and lastly the Good which rules the intelligible world and gives it life, the Good whose image in respect of the sensible world is the Sun. So, too, the illusive " fiction " imitates the perception which *believes* in the reality of its object, and, through the intermediacy of " reasoning thought " ($\delta\iota\dot{\alpha}\nu o\iota\alpha$), perception imitates pure intellectual apprehension.

All these relations are put in concrete form by the famous myth of the Cave (vii, beginning). With our thought in bondage to conditions of birth and upbringing, we are the captives, unable to move since our infancy, with our eyes perforce fixed on the back of the cave. The steep, stony path rising to the entrance symbolizes the difficulty of determining the nature and origin of our opinions. The great fire burning

outside, which illuminates the cave with a vague light, is the
sun, and the marionettes whose shadows are cast on the back
are physical objects, which are certainly artificial things. The
real actors remain hidden behind the screen. But the prisoners
hear the echo of their voices, and take it for the language of
truth, being chiefly intent on observing and remembering
how the shadows on the wall appear together or in succession.
When a prisoner drags himself or is dragged out of the cave,
his dazzled eyes can make out nothing. To use them, he has
to be content with the " reflected image " of things. This
symbolizes the ascent of the soul towards truth, by way of
mathematical notions. Many obscurities remain, chiefly in
reference to the existence of sensible things. When, later, in
the *Timaeos*, Plato tries to make his doctrine explicit, it will
still be in mythical form, the only one possible in a domain
which is not that of pure thought. Now, already, in Book X
(596–8), the celebrated example of the Three Beds (that of
" nature," the very essence of Bed, its Idea or form ; that of
the joiner, which is an imitation of it ; and that which is a
painted image of the second) introduces us to a craftsman god
or " Demiurge," but one who is the author of the essences,
and not, like the Demiurge of the *Timaeos*, of copies of those
essences. Could he be the very Idea of the Good ?

What the *Republic* describes very clearly is the stages of
philosophic education, and especially those which constitute
the " propaedeutic " (536 d) to dialectic. Above gymnastics
and " music," from which the traditional study of the poets
is severely excluded, as we know, there are forms of culture
which have an object only if they escape from the contradictions in which experience is entangled, and therefore make
it necessary to distinguish between the sensible and the
intelligible and to " awaken " the intellect. Now, that would
not happen if the collection of unities, or number, were an
immediate object of perception by the senses. For sense-
perception shows us " the same thing at once one and infinitely
many." To remove the contradiction, therefore, we must
consider unity in itself, and that can only be done by the
intellect (524 d ff.). Here, then, is a first science which can
elevate the soul—the knowledge of unity and number, provided, at least, that we detach it from its purely utilitarian
applications. But it is clear that, in this case as in that of the

following sciences—two-dimensional geometry, solid geometry (τρίτη αὔξη), astronomy, harmony—Plato means to go beyond the degree of abstraction to which the Pythagoreans had taken them. He will not be content, like them, to reduce experience to numerical relations or diagrammatical constructions. He regards this as merely the foundation for higher mathematical speculations, more fitted to liberate the mind. Astronomy and harmony merely furnish " examples " and " problems," by means of which one will rise to " true figures " and " true numbers," to " real " movement, to the mutual " consonances " of numbers.[1] If he attaches so much value to solid geometry it is doubtless because, under the guidance of a capable teacher (perhaps Theaetetos), he hopes for such fruits as these from it. It is in this sense, too, that Plato, contrary to Greek usage, constantly connects " logistic " or the art of reckoning, used only to deal with practical or amusing problems, with arithmetic, the study of the intrinsic properties of numbers (vii. 522-31).

Dialectic, the " coping-stone " of the philosophical education, is described by two images. It supposes a " regular progress " (μέθοδος), which is an " ascent " (ἐπάνοδος), and it procures a " vision," that is, an intuition. When Plato says that we must make " the whole soul " accomplish an " evolution," in order to turn it from the obscure vision of becoming to being and to what is brightest in being, he is thinking of scientific education. But, when this has been done, the " organ " in the soul made for seeing that bright point, the Good, must be " turned " upon it, and " the most effective manner " of producing such a " conversion " is dialectic (518 c-d). In this decisive act the scientific " arts " or specialities (τέχναι) merely " collaborate " ; they give the soul the attitude which it needs to obtain that " total vision " of which the dialectician alone is capable (σύνοψις, συνοπτικός, 537 c). So there are two different methods, although both remain in the sphere of pure intelligence and demand nothing of the senses. But, taking up an indication in the *Phaedon* (100 b ff.), Plato explains how the " hypothesis " is not used in the same way in both. In the symbols of truth which are

[1] The famous geometrical number of viii. 546 b, which has given rise to so much discussion (cf. **III**, 857, 1 ; **XXI**, ii, no. 34, ii, and iii, no. 78 ; James Adam, edition of the *Republic* ; G. Kaffa, in *Philologus*, lxxiii, etc.), may be an example of these speculations.

mathematics, it is a principle from which one comes down to the consequences ensuing from it. In dialectic, it is merely a starting-point from which one gradually rises to an " anhypothetic " term, which will then serve as a principle from which one will descend in the same way as in the other case (vi. 510 b ff. ; vii. 533 c ff.) ; it is a checking of the thesis by the agreement of the consequences with one another and with the thesis. This check is made by means of the dialogue, conducted according to definite technical rules, a skilled art, as the *Cratylos* says, of questioning and answering. But the procedure of Platonic dialectic is not yet fully elaborated.

This education of the philosopher, so different from the discipline of mortification of the *Phaedon* or the mystical elevation of the *Banquet*, leads Plato to regard the soul as an intermediate reality, which must touch the two extremes which it connects. A new idea, explicitly given as such,[1] appears in the *Republic*—that of the composition of the soul. This innovation is, moreover, connected with the fundamental postulate of Plato's political theory, namely, that a society is the image of the individuals composing it (iv. 435 e ff.). Consequently, the " letters," as it were, of the social whole, being writ larger, are easier to decipher than those of the unity composing it ; but in both the text is the same (435 a-b ; ii. 368 d). Now, the just State must be composite ; it must include a middle part intended to unite the two others. It requires the division of labour, " the appropriation of activity " (οἰκειοπραγία, 434 c) and capacity to their natural object ; otherwise men's energies are dissipated and expended uselessly.[2] This complex unity, consisting in a harmony, will therefore be that of the soul.

In the soul there are three distinct functions ; this is proved by the fact that each can be defined in its essence or its form apart from that of the others. By one function the soul is connected with the sensible ; this is the " appetitive part " (τὸ ἐπιθυμητικόν, sc. μέρος), the tendencies like hunger and thirst which the soul has from its body, and which aim at pleasure. Contrasted with this function is another which aims at the intelligible and the true, reflecting on the appetites

---

[1] iv. 435 b-c, 436 a-b, 440 e, 441 c. The vague indications in the *Gorgias*, 493 a-b, and *Phaedon*, 68 b ff., are only foreshadowings.
[2] ii. 369 b-374 e. Cf. *Charm.*, 161 e ff.

and combating them if necessary ; this is " the calculation of reason " (λογισμός, τὸ λογιστικόν). Between these two extremes is a third function, which effects a synthesis of them, giving to reason influence over that which has no reason, and making the latter obedient to its authority ; this is " the energy of willing " (θυμός, θυμοειδές). A savage monster, a man, and a lion—such is that threefold compound, the soul of a man (cf. ix. 588 c ff.). Therefore the evil of the soul will be that each function should not be appropriated to its object, that the function which ought to obey should command, or *vice versa*, and that the sovereign function should be betrayed by its natural auxiliary. This will be either intemperance, which overthrows the ordered harmony of the functions, or injustice, which upsets their relations, in any case, the principle of the worst misfortune (ix. 577 ff.).

In consequence of this conception, if the soul must be immortal, it is not, as it was in the *Phaedon*, because of its simplicity. Therefore new reasons are needed. Plato will therefore allege the beauty of the assemblage which unites two opposites by a harmonious mediation, or, again, the necessity that the number of composite souls should be constant, for an increase in their number would be at the expense of mortal nature and in the end would cause its total disappearance—a curious reversal of the first argument in the *Phaedon*. In truth, these souls are considered in their *present condition*—that is, united to a body which prevents us from seeing their true nature, just as shells and seaweed disguise the beauty of the sea-god Glaucos. But is this true nature, which " makes the soul akin to " the eternal and the divine, a " composite form " or a " simple form " ? Plato does not decide (x. 608 d-612 a). Once again, we are in the presence of a point of doctrine which calls for further development.

The celebrated myth of Er, the man who spent twelve days in Hades and, not having drunk the water of the River of Indifference (*Ameles*) in the Plain of Forgetfulness (*Lethe*), was able to tell of his great journey, contains a new attempt at eschatology. In it we find, closely bound together, a very obscure cosmology and a theory of the destiny of man. In the cosmology, there is talk of a column of light passing through the sky and the earth, connecting the poles of both, which is probably the axis of the universe ; of the Spindle of

Necessity, with its shaft, hook, and whorl, by means of which all the celestial revolutions take place ; and of the formation of that whorl out of eight whorls of different size and colour, fitted one into another, participating in the movement of the spindle at different speeds, and each giving off a different note, which represent the sky of the fixed stars, the five great planets, and the sun and moon, the earth being supposed to be at the centre.

In the eschatology, properly so called, the most interesting thing is the conception of the predestination of souls. Souls, in virtue of the penal code befitting them, are allowed every thousand years, unless their faults require longer expiation, to choose a new life on earth. " Specimens of lives," animal conditions or human conditions, are set before them, and the souls make their choice in turn, the order being determined by lot. But, since there are more lots than souls, the last soul does not suffer badly. They are told that " each is responsible for his choice," and that " God has no part in it," that each will have, to guide him in life, the " daemon " which he shall have taken for himself. While the souls were expiating the faults of their previous existence, they had not forgotten that existence. Therefore, those who have been damned before are cautious in their new choice. But those of the blessed who owe their bliss, not to philosophy, but to the chance virtues of which the *Menon* speaks, often choose without reflecting, and choose badly. Every soul, when it has made its choice, can read its whole destiny, and that destiny is irrevocable, being bound up with the very movement of the stars. For the Fates (Μοῖραι), the daughters of Necessity— Lachesis who presides over the drawing of lots, Clotho who spins them, and Atropos who ratifies them—play a part in the mechanism of the celestial revolutions. Also, the passing of each soul, with its " guardian " daemon, beneath the throne of Necessity shows clearly enough that henceforward it will merely carry out, without going back, the consequences of the choice which it made before entering upon life. What if it has chosen badly ? Then, it seems, its only resource is to learn from the philosopher to behave well under its present destiny and to be able, when the hour returns, to make a better choice.

The conception of the just soul, the education of the philosopher, all this is aimed at showing how a just State can be brought about. Since the middle of the Vth century, perpetual internal revolutions and an almost continuous state of war had aggravated social decomposition almost all over Greece. Thucydides has drawn a striking picture of this disorder, which, he says, was the same everywhere (iii. 82). It does not therefore seem that Plato's notion of reforming society can be put down to peculiar Utopian tendencies of his own. Some time before, two men, of whose philosophic connexions we know little, had had the same idea—Phaleas of Chalcedon and the celebrated engineer, Hippodamos of Miletos. Even some comedies, such as the *Birds* of Aristophanes (414) or his *Assembly of Women* (392), may perhaps be evidence that the hope of a better city haunted men's imaginations. The conviction that there had been a gradual degeneration led them to think that the remedy would be to turn back the clock and return to the institutions of the past or to those of backward peoples like the Hyperboreians or Sauromatians, among whom, as we know later from the Peripatetic Dicaearchos, the most positive minds did not hesitate to find vestiges of the Golden Age. And in Greece itself there were archaic social and economic systems, like those of Sparta and Crete, which exercised a veritable spell over the minds of aristocratic statesmen in democratic cities.

Plato starts by studying the general conditions of the development which has brought societies to corruption and injustice. Society is a natural fact, for it is based on need, which calls for co-operation and the exchange of services. For the multiplicity of the needs which a single man cannot satisfy " has brought a number of men together in the same dwelling-place, as natural associates and helpers." So long as " the community is confined to elementary needs," the division of labour established in it is a good for everybody. But as the necessary relations of this group with other groups develop, men set themselves to produce more than is needed, and for export. Then a general morbid inflammation causes a quantity of luxury-needs to sprout on the original social stem, and to satisfy them breeds as many useless people, the inevitable parasites of a sickly organism. The territory becomes too small for the increased density of the population, and they try to extend it by war. But, while the division of labour went on until it became a plague, men forgot to make fighting a special trade. Yet a society needs picked, trained men, appointed to guard it. But is there not a danger that guardians who are nothing but warriors will be as troublesome to those whom they should protect as to their enemies ? Therefore the real guardian must be a philosopher as well, combining courage with wisdom (ii. 369 b-376 c).

But the very principle of the specialization of functions demands that the function of governing should be distinct from that of fighting. It is, therefore, necessary that, first of all, the builders of the future city should be able to discern which of the children are best fitted by their natural bent to become good guardians, who will have the general good at heart. After that, a properly regulated system of tests will make it possible to select those who shall be " rulers " and those who shall serve them as " helpers " and " agents " (iii. 413 c ff.). Until they are about seventeen or eighteen, education is the same for all. To what has already been said of this, it will suffice to add that they receive this education with enjoyment, for constraint is excluded from a good education. But at this point their studies are interrupted by more intensive training in physical and military exercises. At the age of twenty, those who have shown themselves fit to go further study the sciences in their relations, and from a synthetic point of view. If they pass this test, which enables one to recognize the good dialecticians, they receive a further promotion. This takes place at the age of thirty, and five years are devoted to the study of dialectic. Then there begins for the learner the longest test of all. For fifteen years, he must go down again into the cave, mix with other men, and discharge military and administrative duties. Lastly, when they are fifty, those who have distinguished themselves both in speculation and in practice will be raised to the dignity of magistrates. But this is a duty which they only take, turn about, as a necessity, and they still remain philosophers (vii. 535 ff.). Let us note one last feature of the Platonic training of special faculties : it applies to women as to men, for, given equal aptitude, there is no reason why women should not perform all functions. The differences of individuals must only be considered in relation to what is to be done, and these differences are what decides the function which they shall perform, for the good of all (v. 451 b ff.).

Occupations so numerous and dignified as these do not give the guardians time to provide for their own sustenance. This will be supplied to them by a third class, which will have no other duty—farmers, workmen, and merchants of all kinds. This mass of the people has only one duty, to serve, and one virtue, to obey. But this does not mean that it is hereditarily bound to that servitude. For the principle of selection requires that children of the " Bronze Race " should, if their natural gifts make them fit for it, receive the education reserved for the Races of Silver and Gold, the warriors and magistrates. Conversely, degenerate children of these races will, if necessary, be reduced to the lower race. For the individual is the instrument of the one social function which he is fitted to perform ; there are neither several cities in one city nor several citizens in one citizen (iii. 415 ff. ; iv. 423 ff.). This solidarity of functions, each having its appropriate organ, is what gives Plato's State its complete unity and its justice and temperance, since each man is attached to the function of which he is the organ, the scale of rank of functions is established, and wisdom is the virtue of those who command and courage that of their helpers.

We know how Plato hoped to ensure this unity by a generalized, strictly regulated communism. The guardians will dwell in common on the portion of the State territory where they will be in the best position to do their double duty of guardianship, and will have no personal goods, for among friends everything is common. They will live together and have their meals together. In their hands there will be neither gold nor silver in any form whatsoever, coin, plate, or jewels. Individual property is allowed only to the lowest caste, which must pay tribute to the upper castes, and even among them it is kept within just limits. For, if that caste were over-wealthy, it would forget its duty, and if it were too poor, it would lack the capital needed for the practice of its industry ; and in the end the antagonism of rich and poor, the present curse of states, would soon make its appearance.

Like private property, the private family is forbidden, except to the lowest caste, where it, likewise, is controlled by the magistrates. The guardians are given women, who are their equals in education, by a drawing of lots which conceals a wise decision of the chiefs, and their unions are unmade and remade at the decision of the latter and subjected, in respect of procreation, to strict rules. Children born outside the prescribed time are exposed, and imperfect or vicious children are killed. For the population must always be kept at the right level, and, moreover, the lawgiver, like a good stock-breeder, takes care that his "herd" does not degenerate. A "common fold," with its special servants, receives all children born of these eugenic unions and their mothers suckle all indiscriminately. In this way, the undivided family seems to Plato to realize the most beautiful unity in the service of the general good and among those whose duty is to ensure it. It has been enough to replace kinship of blood by that form of kinship which the ancients had observed among certain barbarian peoples and modern students have called "kinship by classification," where relationship of age alone determines the kind and degree of kinship.

Lastly, there remains the question of the transition from present society to the just society. To bring it about, it is enough that philosophers should be invested, by a drastic measure of State, with absolute authority. Then they will send all inhabitants aged over ten away to the fields, and will keep by them only very young subjects, still uncorrupted, to train according to their principles. In this way, Plato concludes with disconcerting serenity, the ideal city will be established "as quickly and easily as can be" (vii, end).

This city, in his eyes, is, of course, the natural, normal city. All existing political forms are, in various degrees, degenerations of a perfect aristocratic government, that of the healthy city. Moreover, since a society is the image of the individuals composing it, an individual character will, reciprocally, symbolize a political type, and a human pedigree will symbolize the determined sequence of political degeneration. This is the idea which inspires the wonderfully vivid and colourful picture in Book VIII and part of Book IX of the "Timarchic Man," ruled by pride and ambition, pure will without conscience or heart, of the "Oligarchic Man," whom he begets, who knows only appetite for enjoyment, of the "Democratic Man" whom he begets in his turn, undisciplined and envious, and, lastly, his son, the "Tyrant." These, according to the *Republic*, are the four bad governments, each of which bears within itself the seeds of its inevitable corruption into a yet worse form. But how did the aristocratic State ever come to degenerate ? Because it required such exactly regulated conditions that the least misreckoning on the part of the magistrates sufficed to destroy the harmonious unity of the whole.

6. *Phaedros.* So far Plato's doctrine has been, even in his political theory, a Pythagorean interpretation of the ideas of Socrates. But his thought continues to develop, taking up the old themes to make them more explicit or to consider them from a new point of view. The *Phaedros* is an example of this ; it is a continuation of the *Symposium*, a more precise statement of the *Gorgias*, a completion and modification of the doctrines of the soul in the *Phaedon* and *Republic*, and a prelude to the teachings of the last dialogues.

A speech of Lysias on love is answered by Socrates with another speech, in which the same ideas are resumed following a better method. But the ideas developed cannot be chosen haphazard, for one must speak in accordance with the truth, not with illusory probabilities ; there is no rhetoric without a philosophy. Rhetoric by itself cannot be " a guidance of souls." To the external tricks on which the most famous masters pride themselves, as if they were marvellous discoveries, Plato opposes his dialectical method. But he does not define it only by the need for being in agreement with oneself and others on the subject discussed, as in the first speech of Socrates (237 b ff.), nor as a synoptical " bringing together " (συναγωγή) of a plurality under the oneness of the Idea. He lays stress, as he has not done before, on the details and order of the intermediaries which, thus brought together, unite the many to the one ; the unity of an essence, like that of an animal which you have to carve without hacking it about, must be decomposed, by a methodical " division, into its natural joints " (265 c ff.). Now, we shall see the place which this process holds in the dialogues of Plato's old age. Furthermore, the literary characteristic of those dialogues is indicated here : a writing, as is shown in the Egyptian myth of Thoth, the inventor of writing, is of value only if those who read it seek in it nothing but a means to recollect the lessons which they have heard. Infinitely more precious is the speaking of the true philosopher, which sows truth in men's souls and prepares an eternal harvest (274 b ff.). Lastly, in stating that the study of universal nature is a condition of knowledge of the soul, in regarding the soul as a thing which, moving itself and so moving everything else, is the unengendered and imperishable principle of becoming, and in finding in this a new proof of immortality (269 c ff., 245 c ff.), the *Phaedros* prepares the way to the *Timaeos* and the tenth book of the *Laws*.[1]

The brilliant myth in which Plato, making use of a traditional artistic theme of which we still have examples, depicts the soul as a team of winged horses driven by a charioteer, is another instance of the peculiar interest of the *Phaedros*. It takes up the conception of the composition of the soul, which the *Republic* associated with its present existence, and, transferring it to the existence beyond experience which preceded the fall of the soul into a body, he anticipates the *Timaeos*. The steeds driven by the intellect are will and desire. Now, in the circular revolution which our souls accomplish with those of the gods—that is, with the stars and the great elemental regions separating the stars from the earth—in the " supra-celestial place " above the astronomical sky, sometimes the driver is clumsy, and the steeds, especially the naturally indocile one, do not obey him. So an original fault sends the soul hurtling down from its divine abode. But, in thus falling into the materiality of the body, it brings with it its astral predestinations, which determine both its elective affinities and its place in the order of human values—the soul of the philosopher or the perfect lover in the highest rank and that of the tyrant in the lowest. It is true that the eschatology attached to this conception adds nothing to that of the *Republic*. But the *Phaedros* completes the elucidation of the part played by love, as an essential function of the soul and a condition of reminiscence. In its earthly life the fallen soul keeps, as a secret treasure, memories, some richer, some poorer, of the absolute realities which it once contemplated. If philosophic love is the highest form of " delirium " or enthusiasm, it is because it is able, in the emotion aroused by the sight of beauty, to awaken these slumbering memories.

---

[1] It is all these foreshadowings of his later philosophy, combined with other reasons, that have given rise to the hypothesis that the *Phaedros* was recast later (**XI**, iii. 27–9).

7. *Theaetetos.* The "midwifery" of the *Theaetetos* is a development of this conception. In connexion with the search for a definition of knowledge, Plato shows what "fruits" a well-guided love can produce in a well-made mind, which has been proved fit for that initiation by a preliminary examination. Just such a man is young Theaetetos, who, of all the pupils of the mathematician Theodoros of Cyrene, shows the fairest promise. This promise was upheld in his short life ; under Plato and in the Academy, he caused decisive progress to be made in the study of surds, the theory of numbers, and solid geometry. Now, this famous bringing to birth of souls, which appears only in the *Theaetetos* and will not be found in the later dialogues, is a new version of the doctrine of reminiscence, itself destined to disappear. Its interest lies in the fact that it defines the function of the educator and teacher, no longer as a function of generation, but as one of assistance and criticism, intervening to procure for souls the intercourse which will make them fruitful, helping them by presence and action to give birth at the right moment to the fruit with which they are pregnant, and judging the value of that fruit, whether it is normal and likely to live or only has a deceptive appearance of being so.

The "fruit" of which Theaetetos must be delivered and which will be subjected to the necessary test is his conception of knowledge. To define knowledge by sensation, like Protagoras and the Heracleiteans, is to condemn oneself to saying that everything that I seem to perceive, at any moment, is true for me. Since everybody can say as much, either truth must be a question of majority of opinions (171 a) or there must be, apart from truth on the human "pattern," a truth which depends neither on the judgement of each man nor on that of many, but on what things are by "nature" in "the property of their essence" and on the "divine pattern." Then, with the haughty picture of the philosopher as the only free man among a people of slaves, this statement of the duality of the sensible and the intelligible is accompanied by declarations in favour of an attitude which the *Republic* seemed to have abandoned. "There is the place pure of evils," whereas evil is inherent in earthly life, and we must escape thither from here as soon as possible, in order to achieve "identification with the divine" (171 d-177 b). We must, therefore, go beyond the senses. Now, how do we conceive of our senses—as our perceiving machines or as merely the " instruments " (ὄργανα) *by means of* which our soul perceives itself ? In the second way ; for from our senses the soul receives only a matter, the affections of the subject. And perception is properly the act by which the soul " co-ordinates " (συλλογισμός) these data and " brings them into relation " (ἀναλόγισμα) in universal judgements. In these judgements it states the existence or non-existence of a thing, which is what it is and other than its correlatives, is one or many, and is endowed with qualities by which it is like or unlike others. Without the " synthetic points of view " (τὰ κοινά)—being, relation, quantity, quality —which represent the first known attempt at a table of the " categories " of thought, there is no perception (184 b ff.).

Since knowing is not sensation, but the judgement of the soul on sensation, and certainly not false judgement, can we say that knowing is " true judgement " (δόξα ἀληθής) ? So the problem of error is propounded (187 b ff.), and the rest of the dialogue is taken up with discussing it. Now, whether we consider false judgement in its logical nature or as a psychological act, it appears equally inconceivable ; for it is impossible that one should, *at the same time*, not know what one knows, or know what one does not know. Can we explain it by a " misunderstanding " (ἀλλοδοξία) ? You " miss " what you were " aiming at." But if the act of thinking consists in " a silent conversation of the soul with itself," asking and answering it until it has " determined " the object which it has in view (189 e ff.), one cannot see how the soul could think anything but what it thinks. Let us then rather consider false judgement in its genesis. Let us suppose that Mnemosyne has placed a wax in our souls, harder or softer, purer or less pure, according to the individual. On this wax let us take the " impress " of everything which we want to keep in memory. So long as the impression lasts, we remember and know, and when it is rubbed out we do not. Now, it seems that error can only come when we try to make a present perception agree with one of the mnemonic " descriptions " thus stamped in the soul. It may happen, for example, that, seeing Theaetetos, I apply that sight to the description of Theodoros, or *vice versa*, as when you try to put your right shoe on your left foot. So error is not a false knowledge, but a false *recognition*, a disagreement between perception-knowledge and memory-knowledge (191 c ff.).

But if we say that error is the act of a synthesis like this, do we not commit ourselves to being unable to explain it when the elements of the synthesis are, not a perception on the one hand and a thought on the other, but both of them thoughts—as, for instance, when we say that 11 is the sum of 5 and 7 ? Perhaps we shall have a fair representation of what happens then, if we compare the soul to a dove-cot. To fill it, you must " obtain " the birds (κεκτῆσθαι). You possess them. But suppose you want to " have " (ἔχειν) one in your hand, in order to do something with it. That is another matter ; you want a turtle-dove, and you catch a ring-dove. So our soul caught 11 instead of 12 in the dove-cot of knowings which it possesses without having every knowing at its disposal when it is wanted. Yet this celebrated distinction between potential possession and actual possession, of which Aristotle was afterwards content merely to change the terminology, only revives previous difficulties ; for does it not thus happen that one knows what one does not know, and does not know what one knows ? It is, therefore, impossible to define error so long as we do not know what knowing is (197 a ff.). There are people (historians are not agreed who they were) who hold that, if knowing is " true judgement accompanied by its justification' ' (ἀληθὴς δόξα μετὰ λόγου), the only knowing is of the " syllables " of things—a knowing of the complexes which develop in speech, but not of the " letters " (στοίχεια) [1] or elements of those syllables, which elements are " unjustifiable " and " unknowable," perceived by intuition alone. But if the elements are not knowable, how will the compound be knowable ? Moreover, whatever meaning we give to this definition of knowing, in the last analysis it can only mean this : knowing is true judgement accompanied by knowing (201 c ff.)—a mere tautology. So, like the first dialogues, the *Theaetetos* comes to no end. But, even if none of the fruits borne in the soul of Theaetetos has appeared worthy of being nourished and reared, at least, thanks to this test, he has some chance of being happier another time.

8. *Parmenides*. The interpretation of this dialogue is one

---

[1] So it was that, in Plato's time, στοιχεῖον, the " letter " of the alphabet, began to take on the sense of " element." Cf. **XL**, 14 ff., 24 ff., and below, p. 227.

of the most discussed problems raised by Plato's philosophy. It is at least very probably related to the *Theaetetos*. The *Theaetetos* was a critical analysis of the notion of knowledge, which at the beginning evoked the Eleatizing Socraticism of Megara, but, from fear and respect, refrained from examining the properly Eleatic thesis (180 d ff., 183 c ff.) ; the *Parmenides* depicts that thesis and Socraticism, as Plato understands it, in conflict, and seems to be intended, symmetrically, as a critical analysis of the notion of Being.

Zenon's dialectic aims at showing that, if you admit the existence of plurality, the same thing contains opposite determinations in itself. Now, these contradictions in the sensible are what have led us to posit intelligible essences (γένη, εἴδη), of each of which a plurality of sensible things partakes. Shall we then find in one or other of these essences the same internal contradiction, so that Movement-in-itself, for example, becomes Rest-in-itself, or *vice versa* ? That is the starting-point of the *Parmenides*. But before Plato attacks that question he places a criticism of the theory of Ideas in the mouth of the aged Parmenides, speaking to a still young Socrates.

First of all, why hesitate to suppose that, by the side of the Ideas of the Good, the Beautiful, the Just, Movement, and so on, there are Ideas of empirical realities, and even of the vilest things, such as mud, filth, or hair ? There is no reason for this timidity, and a theory should follow its logical necessities to the end. There is a more serious difficulty in connexion with the existence of Ideas, not only apart from one another, but apart from the things which partake of them. For if that partaking absorbs the whole of the Idea, then the Idea, although one and simple, becomes immanent in a plurality of different things. If the partaking absorbs only part of the Idea, then the Idea loses its absolute simplicity. Can we say that it is the single form under which, for example, several men, specifically alike, are gathered ? But then, in order to gather these things under that form, there must be another formal unity, to make their mutual likeness, and then a third, and so on to infinity. So Plato has already happened upon the argument of the " third man," which Aristotle afterwards uses against him.[1] To represent that

---

[1] Polyxenos, to whom its invention is ascribed, is said to have been a disciple of Bryson the Megaric (cf. above, p. 137).

form as a " concept " (νόημα), existing only in our souls, would raise new difficulties ; for either, by partaking of the concept, everything becomes thought, or, on the other hand, nothing is thought, not being the concept itself. If, lastly, the Idea is a " pattern," the sensible thing a " copy," and its partaking an " imitation," either the Idea will cease to be an absolute and unlike anything else, or we fall again into the difficulties of the " third man."

After participation, we consider the consequences of the very notion of Ideas transcending the sensible. If Ideas are objects of knowledge to us, they are relative to us, they no longer are in themselves. Do they, nevertheless, exist in themselves, being relative only to one another ? Then the only relation between sensible things and Ideas is one of " identity of name," and things become true absolutes, relative only to one another. The world of Ideas (we find this objection again in Aristotle) is therefore a superfluous double of our world, and Knowledge-in-itself, the only kind adapted to Things-in-themselves, can belong to God alone, who, thus shut off in a sphere of another kind than ours, will be as unknowable to us as we are to him.

But does this mean that we must abandon the determination of essences ? If so, we shall not know what to take hold of, and it will be the ruin of all dialectical inquiry. The question is rather, " how one must conceive of the existence " of Ideas, and one must be in a position to follow one's opponent down to the very heart of his objections. Theory, the result of a magnificent " flight " towards the intelligible, should have been preceded by an " exercise " by which it was put to the test. So the object of the very much longer second part of the *Parmenides*, the dialectical part, is that indicated at the beginning of the first part : the application of Zenon's dialectic to intelligible reality (135 c ff.). Certainly we cannot here " play " with Plato " the complicated game " entailed by that application. But it furnishes such a significant instance of the agile subtlety of the Greek spirit that we must give at least an outline of it. Whatever the Idea considered may be, One or Many, Being or Not-being, Likeness or Un-likeness, Movement or Rest, Generation or Corruption, in respect of each in turn one takes up a " position," affirmative or negative, and one asks " what follows " from each of these positions, both for the Idea, when affirmed and when denied, in respect of itself and in respect of its opposite, and also, in the same way, for the opposite Idea in respect of the first. So, in each case, there are two positions and eight consequences. The fact that Parmenides undertakes to apply this method to his own thesis of Unity (137 b) seems to prove that Plato is now calling on Eleaticism to examine its conscience, as he examined his own a while ago. Nevertheless, the application of the method is more general, for, as we have seen, it concerns all Ideas, whatever they may be, and the very notion of partaking. The conclusion, then, would seem to be that Eleaticism is too narrow and the theory of Ideas too vague, but, if the former widens its point of view, it will prepare the way for a new theory of Ideas.

V

THE LAST FORM OF PLATO'S PHILOSOPHY

1. *His Oral Teaching, according to Aristotle.* The last stage of Plato's thought, to which we have seen him gradually travelling, is known to us not only from the last dialogues, but from the evidence of Aristotle, who entered the Academy about the time when they were written. This evidence is found chiefly in the first and the two last books of the *Metaphysics*. In addition, Aristotle, like other disciples of the school, wrote out the master's lessons *On the Good*, which he calls his " unwritten teachings." Lastly, he wrote a book *On Ideas*, which seems to have been a critical exposition of the doctrine. It is true that Aristotle's indications are often very obscure, and sometimes they may refer to Xenocrates, who was Scholarch of the Academy when Aristotle was directing the Lyceum. Yet they are of great interest, even if we confine ourselves to those in which Plato is named or quite clearly meant.[1] They give us information, imperfect though it may be, about doctrines which are hardly indicated in the last dialogues but help one to understand them, forming a necessary introduction to them. Even where the matter of the teaching is identical on both sides, they teach us that the vocabulary

[1] Cf. Bonitz, *Index Aristot.*, art. Πλάτων, and, on what follows, **CXX**.

of teaching had its special terms.[1] Lastly, the character of the last writings themselves becomes more precise when, in accordance with the conception of the written word set forth in the *Phaedrus*, we regard them as recalling or commenting on the oral teaching done inside the school.

When Aristotle analyses the " Platonists' " theory of Ideas, thinking chiefly, there is no doubt, of Xenocrates, he includes among the things of which there can be no Idea those which, involving " before " and " after," form an ordered series. So arithmetical numbers and geometrical figures do not presuppose an Idea of Number or Figure in general. What they presuppose is a definite plurality of such Ideas, themselves arranged in a certain order of rank. Now, the numbers and figures of the mathematician are only abstract notions, each of which can be repeated in an infinite number of examples. They are, therefore, " intermediate," as the *Republic* said (511 d). But they are intermediate (and this is expressly referred to Plato) between the sensible numbers and figures and the " Ideas " of Numbers and Figures. These Ideas, like all others, are true substances, each having its own nature and quality, unable to be divided into elements which could be transported hither and thither, and consequently " uncomposed." The " Ideal Numbers " are therefore the forms or types of the Numbers ; Three or the Triad is the form or type of all threes, Four or the Tetrad is that of all fours, and so on to the last Idea required to explain all possible numbers, Ten or the Decad, the perfect number of the Pythagoreans. The same may be said of the Ideal Figures, the Line, the Triangle, the Regular Tetrahedron, the individual patterns of all possible figures.

Every Idea results from two principles, one passive and material, the " Infinite " or Indeterminate, perhaps also called the " Unequal," and the other active and formal, the One, identical with Being or the Good, and perhaps called " the Equal." Of a truth, while the former of these principles allows of no specification (for the point, far from being a principle, is only a " geometrical fiction "), the latter certainly seems to involve distinct specifications, according as it is a matter of Number-Ideas or Figure-Ideas—the " indefinite Dyad of Great and Small " in the first case and that of " Long and

[1] E.g., *Phys.*, iv. 2, 209 b 11–16.

Short, Wide and Narrow, High and Low " in the second. The mysteries of this kind of " metamathematical " theogony are hard to penetrate. It will be enough to observe that in the case of Numbers the Dyad represents the indeterminate duplicative power of the plus or the minus ; that neither the Dyad nor One is part of the series of Numbers, the first term of which is Two, the first limitation of the double infinite by One, Three being thus the first odd number. Therefore the Ideas have matter in them, and are compounds and engendered products. Moreover, in the whole scale of Ideas, it seems that the Numbers and Figures are highest, and serve in their turn as patterns to the constitution of all the rest. Lastly, since, as we have seen, the matter of Ideas is partly extension, which even implies, in addition, an indefinite mobility, it seems that the Living-in-itself constituted by the action of the One on the primary Length, Breadth, and Depth is the Ideal Cosmos itself, the universe of Ideas.

Next, since the material principle remains fundamentally the same, that is, an " incorporeal " extension, a mobile indeterminate between contraries, a not-being which is the principle of evil, and the Ideas in their turn take the place of the One as a principle of determination, then another Cosmos, our sensible world, will result. For Aristotle says that, in Plato's view, since the modes of knowledge in our soul must answer to the degrees of its object in being, there must be an analogy between sensation and the number of the solid, 4, between opinion, which goes indifferently from the true to the false, and the number of the surface, 3, between reasoning knowledge and the single direction of the right line, whose number is 2, and between the intuition of the intellect and Unity. Now, Aristotle connects this theory with the doctrine of the *Timaeos* on the constitution of the " Soul of the world," which must have a natural sense of harmony, to introduce it into its own revolution round its objects and into the revolutions of the sky. Thus the soul is not only " the place of Ideas," but " what moves itself " and moves everything else. It does this according to geometrical figures and musical numbers, and therefore seems, with the whole of mathematics, to be the connexion between the world of Ideas and the world of sense.

Such, in a brief summary, is the mathematical symbolism

which, according to the evidence of Aristotle, constituted
Plato's teaching at the end of his life. Pythagorean inspiration is plain. But what is most significant is the idea of an
order of rank among realities ; the idea of their synthetic
construction, starting from two principles, one of which
determines the other ; the idea of a connexion between the
intelligible pattern and the sensible copy by the intermediacy
of a soul which is living mathematics, astronomy, and music.

2. *The Sophist and Statesman ; Philebos.* The impression
given by Aristotle's evidence is that the teaching of Plato is,
in its main lines, very much systematized. This impression is
confirmed by the scholastic rigidity of the last dialogues.
Therefore kinship of points of view is more important in them
than chronological order ; so it is desirable not to separate
the *Philebos* from the *Sophist* and the *Statesman* (*Politikos*).
Moreover, the two latter are explicitly given as sequels to the
Theaetetos, with which they form a trilogy. Lastly, by giving
the lead in the conversation to a stranger from Elea (without
however, excluding Socrates), Plato seems to want to connect
them with the *Parmenides*, so that, if the *Parmenides* aims at
a reformation of Eleaticism, it is in these dialogues that it
must be sought.

The *Parmenides* contained a definitive criticism of the
transcendent, mystical dialectic which had been extolled
chiefly in the *Phaedon* and *Symposium ;* the *Theaetetos* had
laid chief stress on the problem of the analysis of knowing ;
the *Phaedros* demanded, after the synoptic " bringing together " of plurality in the unity of the Idea, an analytical
" division " of that unity. This transformation of dialectic
is well brought out in the *Sophist* and *Statesman*. Have we
to clear up the confusion in which the essence of the Sophistic
doctrine is presented to us ? The appropriate method for
this inquiry may first be tried on a simpler matter, such as
angling. Is it an art, or not ? It is an art. So a first step
takes the mind at once to a very wide generality, in which it
sees, again all at once, whether the matter in question is
understood or not. But now we must know how it is connected with that generality, and what is its exact place or
rank in it. Are there two kinds of arts, some productive, such
as agriculture, tool-making, etc., and the others acquisitive,

such as hunting, the sciences, etc. ; or are there not ? Does not angling clearly belong to the second kind ? This point being granted, one at once sees the necessity for a further sub-division, between the two terms of which one must again choose, and so on until, from dichotomy to dichotomy, we come to a point where we can lay our finger on the kind of art which angling is. The same method is analysed and used in the same spirit in the *Statesman,* as being eminently fitted to safeguard us against ill-balanced classifications which oppose, on the same plane, a very small species and a huge, hastily constituted genus. Why does Plato consider technical activities of all sorts with so much attention ? Because they are systematized activities, in which the function of every tool and the part played by every operation or stage of an operation are exactly defined in relation to one another and to the whole, which is itself defined by the object to be attained (258 b ff., 279 a ff.).

Plato's predilection for the method of division, accompany-ing a new conception of dialectic, and the important place which he gave this process in the exercises of his school, are very well explained at the beginning of the *Philebos.* There he speaks solemnly of a method for which he has long been earnestly seeking, which is implied by every scientific or technical invention, and which, if properly understood, will at last settle the ancient conflict of the One and the Many. For in all things there are the One and the Other, " limit " ($\pi\acute{\epsilon}\rho\alpha\varsigma$) and " limitlessness " ($\acute{a}\pi\epsilon\iota\rho\acute{\iota}\alpha$). But we must be careful not " to make ' one ' haphazard " nor to pass im-mediately from one to the infinite. Consequently, after having discovered the unity of the essence to which the thing under consideration is attached, we shall look for two other essences, or more, which, as it were, " ensue " from it, and we shall treat each of them as we treated the initial unity. Thus, little by little, we shall have determined the number of unities which it contains. For we must not apply the essence of the Infinite to this internal multiplicity, before we have perceived " the number " which is that multiplicity, that is, all the " intermediaries " which separate the unity of the essence from the infinity of the individuals. This infinity is brought down to a definite system, each element in which is itself a definite object of knowledge and one of the classes or kinds into which the unity of the essence has been divided. To sum up, Platonic " Division," which is the methodical enumeration of the internal relations which constitute an essence, the exact measurement of these relations, and the application of the finite to the infinite by a regulated progression, has only the appearance of an analysis ; it is an attempt at a synthetic, progressive method. Whatever may be the force of Aristotle's objections to it, just as a logical process, at least it does not seem to have meant in his eyes an abandonment of the theory of Ideas. Regularly to " subordinate " every " form " ($\epsilon\tilde{\iota}\delta o_{\varsigma}$) to those under which it comes is, no doubt, to contemplate it as a " kind " ($\epsilon\tilde{\iota}\delta o_{\varsigma}$), but it is also to " isolate " it in its " nakedness " and to contemplate it " in itself " (*Pol.*, 304 a, d-e), that is, as a substantial type.

It is, however, quite true that the dialectic whose characteristic process is Division is something very different from the practical discipline of which Plato formerly spoke ; it is a translation into terms of intelligence of the ontological relations of the Intelligibles with one another. It is no more a question of connecting two worlds of different kinds, but of knowing how the realities of the same kind in the same world, that of Ideas, are connected or not connected with one another. So the theory of Ideas is transformed. Plurality and relation are introduced into the Eleatic logical theory—that is the essence of the reformation. Thus Plato opposes both the monism of the pure Eleatics and the logical atomism of the Eleatizing Socratics of Megara. As for his Pythagorean arithmology, it is perhaps not so predominant as one might be tempted to suppose ; it merely supplies the new theory of Ideas with a method of representation and expression.

The problem raised by the *Theaetetos* in the field of knowledge is raised by the *Sophist* in the field of ontology. It is the problem of illusion—of seeming without being, of taking the false for the true, of distinguishing doubtful opinion from knowledge. If Not-being is absolutely nothing, if one cannot make it " a something " without contradicting oneself, then false appearance and error are inconceivable. Against the Eleatics, therefore, we must allow that, somehow, Not-being is, and that, correlatively, Being somehow is not. Moreover, to define Being is as hard as to define Not-being ; either it is a pure indeterminate, of which one must deny all that is not it, or it is torn by the conflict of contrary determinations. Instead of blindly concluding from this that judgement and attribution are impossible, and so denying all discourse, we must rather show how Not-being is not separated from Being (237 b ff.).

Now, three hypotheses are possible regarding the " communication " of the kinds (εἶδος) with one another. Either none partakes of any ; thus Being is neither moved nor at rest. But to deny relation of Being is to posit relation—an internal contradiction. Or else any kind partakes of any kind. But then Movement is Rest and *vice versa*, and we have chaos for the intelligence. Or, lastly, certain kinds partake of certain kinds, while others do not. This is the right hypothesis. Therefore, just as grammar and music determine what letters or sounds agree or disagree with one another, so there must be a science which will say what essences suit each other and what do not, which are principles of union and which are principles of separation (251 c ff.). Therefore it is to a new conception of partaking that the new dialectic corresponds.

To explain this new sort of partaking, Plato is content to consider some of the " greatest " kinds, in other words, some of the highest in the scale of Ideas—Being, Movement, Rest. Between Movement and Rest no communication is possible. But separately both *are*—that is, both partake of Being. Moreover, each of these three kinds is " other " than the others, and " the same " as itself. They therefore partake of two new kinds—the Other and the Same. So we have five primary kinds. A subtle demonstration then establishes that each of them has a distinct " nature " and that, therefore, their number is irreducible ; they call one another synthetically, but they are not confused with one another. Now, if they are distinct from one another, each being itself, it is because they all partake of the Other, or, in other words, this last " nature " is found in all the kinds, as being " the not-being " of that which they are. Let us therefore say of Being itself that, as often as other things *are* by partaking of it, " just so often it is not." So, " in each of the Ideas, Being is much," since the Idea is what it is, " but Not-being is infinite in quantity," since the Idea is other than everything else (254 c ff.).

This dialectical analysis leads Plato to a result of considerable importance. In defining " the other than Being " as the total negation of Being, Parmenides had given the principle of contradiction an absolute sense. For Plato, on the contrary, the " not-being " of every " being " is, no less than that being, a reality, opposed to it ; Not-being is " the Other divided up among all things in relation to one another." So, before Aristotle, Plato gives the principle of contradiction its true meaning. If, with Not-being, we abolish the relation of essences, judgement and speech become impossible, and there is no longer any distinction between true and false. If, on the contrary, Not-being is mingled with judgement and speech, false discourse will be that which enunciates what is not as being, or the Other as the Same.

Now, on the one hand, every discourse determines a certain connexion of nouns and verbs, which has a meaning, and, on the other, every discourse is " the discourse of something." What it translates is the silent conversation of the soul with itself in which thought consists ; so the thought, before the discourse is spoken, is already true or false (?57 d ff.) It is, therefore, very important to obtain, by the use of Division, an exact knowledge of the real relations of the essences, in order that our internal dialectic may be a faithful image of the universe of Ideas. That is the solution which the *Sophist* gives of the problem of error which the *Theaetetos*, not having analysed the nature of Not-being, necessarily left unsettled.

On the constitution of that universe of ideas, the *Sophist* and *Philebos* give indications which are illuminated by the evidence of Aristotle on the Living-in-itself. Absolute immobility, Plato says in the former dialogue, is inconceivable in respect of " Being which is the All " and " which is wholly " (τὸ παντελῶς ὄν) ; for how could it not possess " intellect," and therefore a soul, and therefore how could it not be living ? Conversely, if it were incessantly moving, there would no longer be any permanence in the relations of things or in their modality or in their nature. It seems, too, that this living universe of absolute Being must be God ; against the mechanistic conception of a spontaneous cause, devoid of thought, Plato forcibly urges the divine cause, which is accompanied by " thought " and " a knowledge, the principle of which is in a god " (247 d ff., 265 c ff.). To these conceptions the *Timaeos* will give occasion to return.

The *Philebos*, no less enigmatic, furnishes even more abundant suggestions. It speaks (with examples all taken from experience, it is true) of five classes or kinds (εἶδος), as in the *Sophist*, the fifth being left to be determined later. But the classes of the *Philebos* are not classes of Being, but seem to correspond to some of the most important functions, active or passive, of which Being is capable—the Being defined in the *Sophist* (247 d-e) as acting and being acted upon—whether one considers it in its principles or as a reality. They are, first, those two principles of everything which we considered above—*Limit* and the *Unlimited*. Limit stops and fixes the oscillating movement of the Unlimited between the more and the less, the strong and the weak, the too much and the too little, so as to determine the " measured " and the " how much "—equal, double, triple, etc., in short, terms which have " proportion and agreement." This action of Limit on the Unlimited, so similar to that of the One on the double infinite of Great and Small in Aristotle, then produces " *generation into reality* (γένεσις εἰς οὐσίαν), effected by the measure introduced by Limit." These " realities which have come into being," these " mixtures," the " offspring " of the union of the highest principles, are surely (apart from sensible things, which Aristotle declares to be the products of the determination of matter by the Idea) the Ideas themselves. For there is in them something of the Same and of the Other, and the determination necessary on the edge of an ocean of indetermination. Fourthly, the *Cause* required by Mixture, what " causes it to be born " or " makes " it, is distinct both from these mixtures and from what is in them. Now, our world shows organization. Its body and the elements of its body depend on perfect elements and a perfect body, which are those of the universe, and the life of this perfect body supposes a soul, which is essentially " wisdom and intellect, a royal intellect " such as is required, in Zeus, by the proper " function " of the Cause. Must this function not be the thought of the Living-in-itself, the Mind of Anaxagoras at last given its true destination, or, what comes to the same thing, the action of the Ideas, reflected in a demiurgic thought ? The fifth class has as its function to *disassociate* the Mixtures. That is all that Plato says of it. But we may note that such an operation is that of Division, analysing the synthetic working which constitutes the Idea (23 b ff.).

The idea of measure has become the pivot of Plato's philosophy. Now, the *Statesman* (283 e ff.) distinguishes between two " arts of measurement." The science of measurement, with regard to " excess and shortage," can be considered either in the techniques of science and art, which measure their object by comparison with a unit of measure, or in an infinitely subtler form, in which it is taste in the arts or the intuition which inspires the philosopher even in his most exactly regulated processes. The more precise inquiries into " exactness " promised in this passage are probably those given in the last pages of the *Philebos*. The chief object of that dialogue (63 e) was to discover what is " the most beautiful mixture, that most free of sedition," and that which can best " enable us to divine what is the essence of good for man and for the whole universe." What is the " proportion," or law, of this mixture, what is the " incorporeal order " which makes its beauty ? Now, standing thus in the " forehall " of the dwelling in which the Good is hidden, we see first, as a condition of the conservation of the mixture, *measure*, then *Beauty* or *excellence*, as an expression of the " proportioned fitness " by which the mixture is perfect, and lastly *Truth*, the condition of ontological reality. These are the three Ideas in which we perceive the Good, the " cause " of the mixture and of the goodness of the mixture. Therewith we also see the scale of dignity of the other mixtures, according as they are more closely " akin " to that mixture or are more lacking in that which makes its inestimable value (61 a ff.).

These ideas also make a great difference to the conception of morality. It is no longer a matter, in the *Philebos*, of breaking with the body or mortifying life. The object, already indicated in Book VI of the *Republic* (above, p. 192), is to determine the elements of a " mixed " and " measured " life, putting each element in its rank. At the threshold of this life, let us place a door-keeper to admit those who have a right to enter and to stop others and prevent confusion. Thus the pleasures will go in last, and not all pleasures will be admitted, but only those which are both " true " and " pure " —that is, not mixed with pain, such as those given by knowledge or certain sounds, colours, or forms ; to these we shall add those which result from health and the moderate exercise of our various activities. If pleasure is not entitled to the first rank, which some would give it (doubtless Eudoxos, rather than the Cyrenaics), it is because its essence is " absence of measure " (ἀμετρία) and, since it always contains the more and the less, it is of the class of the Infinite and Becoming. To be a reality, it must tend towards a good, from which it is therefore distinct, and must, receiving a limit, be, contrary to its nature, " in possession of a measure " (ἐμμετρία). In that they bring this measure, intelligence and knowledge, in all their forms, will be welcomed in the mixture, but not all in the same rank. Their dignity will be the greater as their portion of the pure thought which calculates and measures is greater, and that of empiricism is less. In the first rank dialectic will enter, for its object is that which is most " exact," clearest, purest, and truest ; in the second rank—and doubtless in this order—will come the sciences, the arts and crafts, and lastly right opinions, that is, it seems, the whole gamut of " intermediaries " which lie between the highest knowledge and the contradictions of pure sense-experience (31 a ff., 59 e ff.). So for the scale of dignity of beings and their functions there is a corresponding scale of goods.

Lastly, this development of Plato's thought affects his political views. Certainly the *Statesman* retains from the *Republic* an idea which he never abandons—that " absolute authority in command " goes to him (he is thinking of Dion) who has true knowledge, whether he be the King himself or one governing behind him. It is he who, like the " divine shepherd " in whose keeping men born of the earth used to live, and even (less nearly) like the god who moves the universe by his own motion, gives the best guidance to the " flock " of which he has charge, and leaves that guidance to the flock when it is left to itself and is far from him. But there is a very much greater affinity with the *Laws*. Disappointments have prepared Plato to temper the rigours of his plan of social reform. Besides, the application of Division has made him see that the political mixture is made up of a greater number of intermediaries. He is ready to adapt the laws to the changes of circumstances and to balance contrary vices in order to obtain the least bad mixture possible. So he conceives of the relationship of the various constitutions in a manner quite different from that of the *Republic*. Good government, that of the true King, being placed apart, the value of the others is measured just by the equilibrium which they achieve. If they are subject to laws, democracy will not be so good as aristocracy, and aristocracy will be less good than monarchy or royalty, because the law of the relationship of parties, being determined by knowledge, is more exactly applied in the hands of a single man. But in states which have no laws the tyranny of a single man and oligarchy are the worst governments and democracy is the least disastrous, because the instability of the mixture constituting it allows harmful tendencies to cancel one another.

3. *Timaeos and Laws*. Between the *Timaeos*, although it contains a physical theory, and the *Laws*, although the Athenian Stranger speaks chiefly of legislation and religion, there is a real affinity ; in the *Timaeos* and in the *Laws* (particularly in the Xth Book) we find an almost identical theology, cosmology, and general doctrine of the soul.

In addition, in the *Timaeos* Critias sets forth in part the content of the dialogue which bears his name, which Plato did not finish—that the ideal State, whose constitution, as defined in Books II-V of the *Republic*, is recalled at the beginning of the dialogue, was, according to a tradition learned by Solon from the priests of Egypt, that under which the Athenians lived before the distant time when the city vanished in the flood which at the same time swallowed up their enemies the Atlanteans, who dwelled in a great island near the Pillars of Heracles, larger than Asia and Libya together.[1]

At this point we may define the function of the myth in Plato's philosophy. This form of the " story " (*mythos*), which had been the earliest language of science, Plato adapts to new needs. In this way the *Gorgias, Phaedon, Republic*, and *Phaedros* told the history of the soul before joining the body and after leaving it and its destiny in the course of its successive existences. The myth of the *Statesman* (269 a ff.), resumed in Book IV of the *Laws* (713 ff.), describes the happy

[1] Cf. Martin, *Études sur le Timée*, i. 257–333 ; K. T. Frost, " The *Critias* and Minoan Crete," in *J.H.S.*, xxxiii. 189 ff. ; L. Germain, " Le Problème de l'Atlantide et la géologie," in *Ann. de Géogr.*, 1913 ; P. Termier, " L'Atlantide," in *Bull. de l'Inst. océanogr. de Monaco*, no. 256, 1913.

condition of earth-born humanity in the reign of Cronos, before a social and political state appeared. The prehistory of mankind, as set forth in the myth of Atlantis, is bound up with the history of the earth itself, with the deluges and conflagrations, memories of which are preserved in the myths of Deucalion and Phaëthon, with all the great upheavals which from time to time compel the surviving men to re-commence all the creative effort of the industries necessary to life. But the *Timaeos* is a myth from beginning to end. It is so, because physical speculation is for the dialectician a sort of pastime, a relaxation for his thought when it has been reaching too long after eternal entities. He is then content with " verisimilitude " (εἰκός). By a fiction, of the rashness of which he is well aware, he sets himself to give " probable accounts " of the work of God himself, to whose knowledge and power the arrangements constituting our world and the all that it contains are due. But he is unable to make the " test " which would change his conjectures into knowledge (59 c-d, 68 c-d).

So we understand what is the function of the myth, and what is its rank among the processes of the method. It is not strictly an allegory or a fable, but is meant to represent a probable order of the succession and composition of the things given in experience. It is a first gleam of light shed on a dim region, a consistent symbolism, a system of images capable of representing that which is not intelligible and with which Dialectic cannot deal. But, if we are to link up the becoming which has at least had a beginning, which is going on under our eyes and has a past history and a future, with that existence without history by which, as we have seen, the eternal Ideas are constituted from all eternity, we must have a suitable intermediary. That will be another set of symbols, those of numbers and figures, with the sciences depending on them, astronomy and harmony. This symbolism brings with it a superior light, that of proportion and measure. In short, the *Timaeos* shows in decisive fashion that myth, that is, history, is for Plato a necessary stage of knowledge, and that it is not cut completely off from either intermediate, dis-cursive knowledge or the pure knowing of dialectic.

One principle dominates the cosmology of the *Timaeos* and Book X of the *Laws*, namely, that the world is a very beautiful work of art. The mutual arrangement of things, in general and in detail, is not merely the result of a chance concurrence of causes, but is due to an intelligence which aims at the general good and has arranged everything " according to a premeditated design " (πρόνοια), following a general plan which is as simple as possible, in order to avoid an infinite multiplicity of particular adjustments (30 c ; x. 903 e ff.). Moreover, one must distinguish between " that which always becomes and never is," the object of crude experience and the opinion based on it, and " that which always is, and has no becoming," always keeping the same constituent relations, the object of the intellectual perception which gives its reasons. Now, the latter being serves as a " pattern " to the former ; so the world once began to be, and is the image of the Intelligible produced by Intelligence. In other words, thought, with art and law, the products of thought, are by nature no less than Nature itself (27 d ff.; x. 890 d). Lastly (a development of an indication in the *Phaedon*, 99 a-b), we must distinguish two kinds of causes. Some are of the order of thought, and their operation involves premeditation of the effects to come ; in them it is thought which moves, and by itself. Now, this " divine kind of cause," which is that which is " most " cause, consisting in " primary operative movements " (πρωτουργοὶ κινήσεις), resides in the seat of thought, that is, in the soul. The other kind, on the contrary, is constituted by " subordinate " causes, which get their activity from something else, " auxiliary " causes, " severed from thought," which therefore operate " by chance and without plan," unless they are employed by the first kind of causes as " necessary " means and conditions, as a " that without which " in relation to " that with a view to which " these causes operate ; so they consist in " secondary operative movements " (δευτερουργοὶ κινήσεις), such as hot and cold, heavy and light, etc. (46 c-e, 68 e, 76 d ; x. 897 a-b).

Thus physical science is deductive, and is teleological ; the order of Necessity is subordinated to that of the Good or thought. If the circle of the Ecliptic is inclined on that of the Equator, if the stars have their revolutions, if there are four primary bodies, if every body in nature has such-and-such properties, if the head is at the top of the human body, etc., it is because it cannot be otherwise, that which the general good requires being granted. If, too, this doctrine of final causes is anthropocentric, it is still in relation to that general good ; for there must be a being capable of understanding the purposes of Intelligence (x. 902 b-c).

Thought, we have just seen, is the cause *par excellence*, and it resides in a soul. Now, the soul is a generated thing, but the most ancient of all (*Laws*, xii. 967 d). It must, therefore, have its cause in a thought which has made it. This thought is that of a " craftsman," a Demiurge. Being devoted to contemplating the intelligible, unchangeable pattern, it is good. Therefore it wishes, by introducing " order " (κόσμος) into that which lacks it, to produce a work which will, as far as possible, be a beautiful image of the pattern, but could not have all its beauty without being merged in it. Now, there is nothing more beautiful than what is alive. Therefore the universe, the work of the Demiurge and his most beautiful work, must be living. But what is most essential in what lives is the soul which makes it live. Therefore the first act of the Demiurge must have been to make a soul of the world. To unite the intelligible pattern to the corporeal, sensible copy, this soul must be a " mixture," into which the Demiurge will introduce " indivisible essence," or the absolute unity of every intelligible and " divisible essence," or the pure plurality characteristic of bodies and their becoming, and also an " intermediate essence " which appears to be composed in the same way, except that in it each of the two first elements is especially envisaged as being at once " same " and " other " —it is " existence," with its specifications by identity and difference, either in the order of indivisibles (Ideas) or in that of divisibles (bodies).

So the soul is a mixture, one of whose ingredients is itself a mixture. This complex mixture is then skilfully divided and combined by the Demiurge according to certain numbers and proportions, which are those of the musical scale. Then he spreads out the mixture in a band, cuts it in two longwise, coils it round so as to make a ring, and then separates the two parts, setting one " circle " inside the other, at an incline to it. The outer circle Plato calls " the circle of the Same," and it is undivided. The inner circle, the " circle of the Other," is divided into seven unequal circles (the orbits of the planets). Since the property of the soul is " to move

itself " (x. 896 a), the two circles start to revolve of themselves, the outer with a uniform motion, the inner with an
inverse motion which has not the same speed or direction in
all its parts, but is nevertheless governed by the supremacy
of the circle of the Same (34 c ff.). In short, in the constitution
of that mixture which is the soul there is everything which
we already know to be an intermediate thing—numbers and
figures, in accordance with which it brings about the movements of the heavens and musical harmony.

For the soul thus manufactured, which seems already to
have extension, constitutes a spherical envelope to the body
of the universe. Their centres coincide, and their movements
are but one and the same movement, the circular movement
of which the soul is the cause. Since that body must be
visible and tangible, the Demiurge makes it of fire and earth,
between which, for mathematical reasons, he inserts air and
water. Thus he makes use of materials not made by him.

How were they made, then ? To explain this, Plato
introduces, in addition to the intelligible pattern and the
sensible copy, a third term—a "universal receptacle " (ὑποδοχή,
πανδεχές), which he also calls a " malleable mass," or, again,
the kind of the " eternal place," or space (χώρα). It is hard to
imagine its nature, for it is neither sensible nor intelligible ;
we only come at it " by a bastard reasoning." In other words,
all that we know of it is that it is impossible to explain the
existence of a world of bodies and becoming without it. For
a becoming must be the becoming of a something, which has
no other nature than that of all becoming. It must be in itself
" without form," but, like an ingot of gold to which all kinds
of shapes can be given, it must be able to receive all forms.
It must not be such-and-such a movement in a given direction,
but mobility and instability themselves, or, as Plato says,
" the wandering cause." Lastly, it must not be a necessity
organized for purposes, but naked " Necessity." It has
rightly been regarded as an anticipation of the extension of
Descartes ; [1] its essence, always identical with itself, is
" to be " absolute indetermination. And yet it seems to
change incessantly, taking on a thousand " manners " of
being in turn, becoming hot here, wet there, solid somewhere
else, so assuming the " appearance " of what we call fire,

[1] On this question, see **CXXII**, pp. 39 n. 2, 44, 46 ff., 61 ff.

water, earth, and yet never being " this " or " that." Now, the " origin " of these states or changes of state of the formless mass is " external " to it, for otherwise it would lose its fundamental indetermination. Their origin is in unchangeable realities, intelligible forms, each of which " is in itself and depends only on itself," whose purity would be diminished by a receptacle which was not itself devoid of all form. By receiving from these forms (for example, from the Idea of Fire) an " impression," matter becomes all things, which are, therefore, " imitations of the eternal entities." So, in relation to that " mother " or " nurse of generation," the Ideas, Being, play the part of the " father." The universe, or Becoming, is their " image," the " child " who takes after them both (μεταξύ).

This exposition of the *Timaeos* (48 c ff.) represents one aspect of the new theory of partaking ; it attempts to account for the connexion of the sensible with the intelligible, and for their opposition, which is not properly one of nature, but lies in the manner or degree of being and between the dependent and the independent. Furthermore, Aristotle observes (cf. above, p. 211 n. 1) that the matter of the *Timaeos*, " the partaking " or " receptive," is what, in his oral teaching, Plato called " the Large and Small."

That, then, is the work of the divine Craftsman of the universe. Whether we interpret this cosmogony symbolically, with Xenocrates, Crantor, and others, or otherwise, at least the Demiurge, the organizing thought, doubtless residing in a soul, which would be the " place of the Ideas " which he uses as his pattern, seems to represent the power which causes and fructifies intelligible realities. But before he sets to work, brute Necessity, or pure mechanism, has already effected a certain sorting out in the mobile chaos of the primary matter. The shocks by which that material is constantly shaken produce in it, in the confusion of the determinations which it assumes by chance, separations and unions, as among the grains whirled about pell-mell under the winnowing-fan. So the first collocations of things take place of themselves, and by them fire, earth, air, and water are made distinct. Therefore the matter on which the Demiurge works has already started to organize itself, mechanically, and this secondary matter contributes to connecting the perfect order of the world of Ideas to its sensible image. In it, therefore, we should find the intermediate reality of mathematical things ; and, indeed, the first physical determinations form geometrically in pure extension. For, if, at least, we abstain from rising higher (53 d ; i.e. to the ideal Figures, apparently), the " elements " (στοιχεῖα) of things are not what we call elements. The true elements of every body, that is, of every solid, can only be surfaces, and, in particular, the simplest of plane rectilinear surfaces. They are, then, right-angled triangles, either isosceles or scalene, the latter allowing of great variety and being capable of grouping in equilateral triangles. From the composition of these triangles in each kind the " syllables " of things result, that is, regular polyhedrons, each of which represents the elemental molecule of one of these primary bodies and by its figure determines the physical and chemical properties of that body.

Thus, fire is the most mobile and penetrating of all, because it is made of regular tetrahedrons or pyramids, which are like arrow-heads. The body of air is the octahedron, or two pyramids on square bases, by which they are joined. That of water is the icosahedron. Earth is the cube ; hence its lack of mobility. But, since earth is the only solid made up of isosceles triangles, it is the only one which merely mixes with others and resists the incessant transformations of the others. The others, as a result of their reactions and by means of shiftings of parts which are easy to conceive, produce the most varied combinations, homogeneous in composition or otherwise, and in variable proportions. On the subject of the fifth regular polyhedron, the dodecahedron, which is closest to the sphere, Plato is very mysterious. God, he says, used it " to paint the picture of the universe." It does not, therefore, belong to the order of Necessity, but to that of Intelligence. The number of its pentagonal surfaces recalls the twelve signs of the Zodiac, which are like an " adornment " of the sky ; it may, therefore, constitute the body in which the stars move, namely, the ether (52 d-55 c).[1]

In addition to its motive function, the soul of the world has a function of knowledge, whose connexion with the other is indeed baffling to a modern mind. The circles of the Same and the Other, which, as we have seen, represent the celestial

---

[1] Cf. *Rep.*, vii. 529 b-c ; *Epinomis*, 981 c.

Equator and Ecliptic, within which the body of the universe is inscribed, are also the circles along which the operations of its thought take place. They bring it into relation, now with the sensible, that is, with the essence which is divided in accordance with corporeal becoming, and now with the indivisibility of the intelligible. In each case, it judges, under various relations or " categories," with what every object of its thought is identical and from what it is different; it makes specifications in the domain of things as well as in that of Ideas. From the revolution which touches the indivisible, pure thought and knowledge are born; from the other, sensation and opinion (37 a-c). This is a consequence of the intermediate nature of the soul, which unites two modes of being in virtue of its mathematical constitution. It is also a consequence of the principle, often asserted in the *Timaeos* and well brought out by Aristotle, that that which knows must be like that which is known. In virtue of this likeness, it seems that perfection of the relations within the object is correlative to a like perfection in the knowing it. Consequently, if the world, being included in the cosmic soul and being its very substance, goes wrong in its movement, the same must happen in its cognitive function.

So we have the distinction (*Laws*, x. 896 ff.) of a second soul of the world, which is bad and obeys " unreason " instead of obeying thought. But it does not seem to be the distinct, co-existent creation of a bad Demiurge, a kind of Satan; this hypothesis is explicitly excluded by the *Statesman* (269 e ff.). It is rather a second state of the soul of the world, into which it falls when, as is said in the same dialogue (273 b), it forgets the teaching of its maker. For movement can exist without the soul, since it exists wherever uniformity and equilibrium are absent (*Tim.*, 57 e); so there is no need for a soul, to explain the movement in brute necessity or the primary matter. The movement whose principle is the soul (in virtue of the diversity of the soul itself), is directed or governed movement. But its direction may be falsified and its good order impaired. Now, before Aristotle, Plato made important distinctions in this movement. On the one hand, there is spontaneous and natural movement, which seems to be perfect, circular movement, that which excludes change of place; on the other, there is communicated, dependent

movement. The latter includes five kinds—" transference,"
either by advance along a single axis or by revolution, collision
of a moving thing with a motionless thing and change of
direction, composition of movements, increase and decrease
pure and simple, and generation and corruption, which are
the two preceding kinds plus the substitution of a new manner
of being of the thing. The spontaneous, truly primary movement is that which is the essence of the universal soul. Now,
in this movement itself, by the side of determinations which
readily lend themselves to the authority of thought—the acts
of willing, reflecting and foreseeing, judging truly or falsely, all
the intermediate domain of θυμός and δόξα—there are other
determinations which belong to appetite and passion—joy and
pain, confidence and fear, love and hate (x. 892 a ff.). It is
because they exist, strange as it may seem, in the soul of the
cosmic living being, that that soul is able to disobey the rule
of Thought and, drifting about as Necessity drives it, to fall
into irregularities which upset the world and cause catastrophes
in it.

So we have, side by side, a blind mechanism of Necessity
and a teleological dynamism of Thought, the world being,
normally, the subordination of the first to the second, of the
body to a wise and good soul. We must now follow the
development of its becoming, of which only the main lines have
been drawn. Wishing to complete the likeness of his work to
the eternal pattern (37 c ff.), the Demiurge conceives a development of the becoming of the world in a " mobile image " of
undivided eternity, the image itself being capable of division
and enumeration—that is, time. So divided time, as contrasted with single duration, appears with the universe ; if
the universe were ever to perish, that time would end with it.
But to measure time the most useful " instruments " are the
movements of the stars. The Demiurge therefore proceeds to
make stars. They have a soul, there can be no doubt of it
(38 c, 40 a, 41 a ; *Laws*, xii. 967 a-b), with its two circles of
movement and knowledge. If Plato does not explain how
these astral souls are made, is it not because they are simply
the universal soul, but individualized in perfect bodies ?
That, no doubt, is the only plurality which the universal soul
can be given, since that plurality can be reduced to the unity
of the revolution of the intellect, or of the whole heavens

(x. 897 c, 898 c-d). To these souls he gives appropriate bodies, fiery and spherical. That being so, the uniform revolution of the heaven of the fixed stars on the circle of the Same (the Equator), accompanied by the rotation of the stars on their own axes, produces the succession of days and nights, the universal measure of time. Meanwhile, on the circle of the Other (the Ecliptic), the planets accomplish various revolutions, which are secondary measures of time, solar years, the year of each of the other planets, and the Great Year which brings all the planets back together to their common starting-point.[1] These are " the gods of the gods " ($\theta\epsilon o\grave{\iota}\ \theta\epsilon\hat{\omega}\nu$).

But in creating them the Demiurge has still produced the image of only one of the kinds which are in the Living-in-itself, his pattern. Then, taking the stars as auxiliary demiurges, he explains his " decrees " to them. If, in spite of their composition, they are to escape from death, it is not, as in Book X of the *Republic*, in virtue of the intrinsic goodness of the mixture constituting their souls, but because the goodness of the Craftsman who has made them cannot wish for the destruction of his masterpiece. Yet, " in order that the All may really be an all," and that every degree of being may be represented in it, there must be mortal living beings, but the Demiurge must not be the author of their souls, or they would be divine and there would be no degrees of inferiority. He therefore commits the making of them to his helpers. Nevertheless, since there must be something immortal in them, that is, something divine and " directing," he himself makes the seed of them with what is left over of the elements used for the soul of the world ; but he mixes them less exactly. He divides the mixture into as many portions as there are stars, and entrusts the gods of those stars with the task of placing a portion of this psychic substance in appropriate individual bodies, after adding two mortal souls to it, one volitive and one appetitive. When this compound, being the work of inferior demiurges, is dissolved, the immortal part, at last released from individuality, will be returned to the original sidereal store (41 a ff.). Here we have the outline of an astrology, other indications of which have already appeared.

---

[1] It is a difficult and much-disputed question, whether Plato at the end of his life abandoned the geocentric hypothesis and that of a motionless earth. Cf. **XXIII**, 174 ff., for the negative, and **XII**, 347 ff., for the affirmative.

But we also find here a conception which has a very important place in Plato's later philosophy—that of decreasing excellence from a higher form of Being through a long series of intermediaries.

Before considering other developments of this conception, we must dwell on the mechanical aspect of Plato's physics. For in them Necessity keeps an independent rôle, even after the Demiurgic thought has begun to act. That thought having given the world the shape of a sphere, the world " tends by nature to gather together upon itself." It therefore compresses the particles of the primary bodies and the composites formed by these particles. It is a general process of " compression," by which " emptinesses " are filled up wherever they exist. It determines, in relation to the volume of the molecules or their aggregates, a continual movement of " thrust," unions and separations, penetrations and expulsions, advances and retreats, risings and fallings, etc. (58 a-c). In fact, it determines an immense variety of necessary actions and reactions, by means of which Plato explains the transformations of the primary bodies, the qualities of things (among which, be it noted, he includes heaviness and lightness, purely relative qualities), the feelings of pleasure and pain, and the special sensations. But the mechanism of Necessity can also be made to serve the purposes of the Demiurge and his helpers. The operation by which these latter determine the functions and working of the organs in the bodies of mortal living creatures would, above all, furnish significant examples ; nutrition, circulation, respiration, etc., are explained in the same spirit as purely physical phenomena, such as the action of the cupping-glass or the magnet. Old age and death are likewise explained by mechanical action. These effects, lastly, are connected with the intentional placing of each soul in a suitable part of the body—the divine soul in the head, the volitive soul in the breast, and the appetitive soul in the belly, the neck and diaphragm serving as an isthmus and a wall respectively between them.

Thus, in order to account for all physical becoming, Plato's teleology throughout supposes movements of divisible extension in the successive moments of time. Yet his mechanism is quite different from that of the Atomists. For, first, he subordinates it on principle to the action of a providential thought, and always to the action of Form, to which all determination in the primary matter is due. Secondly, his primary elements are not solids, but surfaces, that is, geometrical rather than physical elements. Thirdly, in his view movement, far from having its condition in the existence of vacuum, takes place in a plenum, and in such a way as to eliminate all physical vacuum (58 a ff.). But there is, we should note, another vacuum, which might be called geometrical—that without which the surfaces which make up the primary polyhedrons would be flattened against one another.

When a portion of the psychic substance is united to a mortal body and provided with its two inferior souls, it is thereby plunged into the universal mechanism. The tumultuous onrush of empirical data and the seething of nutritive exchanges produce in it a disordered agitation, similar to that of the receptacle. This is the stage of brute sensation and ungoverned opinion. The circle of the Same comes to a standstill; that of the Other turns in wrong directions; "unreason" is complete. Then thought disentangles the chaos, little by little. The wise man is he who understands (as was said before in the *Apology*, *Symposium*, and *Theaetetos*) that, by "taking care of his soul," by "making himself immortal" as far as he can, by "imitating" the divine "pattern," he will safeguard his human essence (*e.g. Tim.*, 42 e ff., 89 d ff.). For at the beginning every soul is a human soul, and a male soul. What makes it lose its original virtue is its indocility towards its guiding daemon (90 a). A new order of excellence appears in the stages of the decline of guilty souls; at every generation, those which have not improved in their previous life take on a lower corporeal form, in relation to the nature of their faults. So, in succession, they inhabit the bodies of women, and then of other animals (76 d, 90 e ff.; x. 903 d ff.). In spite of some touches which look like sarcasm, Plato's eschatology is as serious here as elsewhere.

Indeed, it agrees very well with Plato's views on the suitability of the body to the soul and with his conception of our liberty. He still thinks that no one is wicked of his own free will. But he says that one becomes wicked as a result of the bad condition of the body or by faults of education or of the political constitution (86 b ff.). This does not dispense a man from the charge of guiltiness, especially when his action proceeds from evil intention (ix. 860 c ff.). The agent must therefore expiate the disorder which he has caused ; he is responsible for not having obeyed the " government of thought," for not having let himself be determined by it. He would have done so if he had taken more care, by hygiene and exercise, to preserve his body from the changes which, by excess or shortcoming, always constitute a " violent derogation of natural laws " ; if he had better maintained " balance " in the union of mind and body (81 e ff.) ; if he had not, out of idleness and obstinacy, clung to a system of education and government in which reason has no part. He cannot be guilty of " willing " evil ; that means nothing. But he is guilty of permitting evil, by negligence, to establish itself in him. He only had to let himself be moved, like a divine marionette, by the pliant golden thread which, in the hands of a god or a philosopher, can move other less delicate connexions (i. 644 d ff.). The mistake is always to imagine that you are freer, the more you break away from the whole in which you have your place (iv. 715 e ff. ; x. 903 b ff.). Now, in the whole, there are more goods than ills (907 b, 906 a). We have no right to complain of God ; he is good, he has not wished for evil. But he could not but permit it, as a shortage of being or a less good ; otherwise his work would not be an image, but would be confused with the pattern. God, it was already said in the *Republic*, is " innocent of evil." But that declaration was at the time accompanied by a pessimistic sentiment of ascetic inspiration, which seems to be wholly absent from the theodicy of the *Timaeos* and *Laws*.[1]

It is impossible here to go into the details of Plato's physics or his physiology. But the essential ideas of the *Timaeos*, to which the *Laws* as a rule add only a more vigorous formula or else a paraphrase, deserved our attention. The Latin Schoolmen knew them very early, chiefly by the translation and commentary of Chalcidios, and they exercised considerable influence on the thought of the Middle Ages and therefore, indirectly, on that of modern times. On the other hand, we can speak more briefly about the political part of the *Laws*, however interesting it may be from the point of view of ideas and that of history.

[1] For more copious references, chiefly to the *Laws*, see **CXXII**, 81–8.

In the *Laws* the ideal of the *Republic* seems to have been abandoned. There is no more mention of the education of philosophers, nor of their government, which makes laws unnecessary. On the contrary, as in the *Statesman*, Plato says that laws are necessary, and he lays them down in their most minute details, with a frequent search after mathematical exactitude. The division of classes in accordance with the division of the soul disappears, to make way for a classification which is likewise into three, this time the citizens with their slaves, the craftsmen, and the Metics, to whom all trade is confined. There is no common property, but there is family property, inalienable and indivisible ; there are as many lots as there are families, and the families number 5040, because the first twelve numbers, except 11, go into that number exactly. Of the produce of the soil, two parts are assigned to those who till it, and the rest is put into trade. There is no warrior caste, but a national army. Marriages and birth are still strictly controlled, but in a different spirit. The same is true of the common education of the young.

Yet, when Plato institutes this agricultural State on the basis of legal codes which are anti-progressive like that of Lycurgos or obsolete like the ancient law of Athens, he is far from having abandoned his old ideal, the ideal which the Catholic Church afterwards adapted to its own needs—that the " primary city " is that which has properly but one body and one soul, the almost eternal pattern, of which the " secondary city," that of the *Laws*, can only be an image (v. 739 b ff.). His legislation is only a practical expedient, for, as he said in the *Statesman* also, knowledge is better than all laws and all arrangements (ix. 875 c ff.). It is just because he has faith in that ideal, certain features of which he recalls at the end of the work, that he makes an effort to make it a reality, and will even be ready, if it proves necessary, to try a *third* adaptation (739 c) ; it is with that object that, by expositions of motives, he wants his laws to speak to men in the language of thought. He still appears to look to an absolute authority—here that of a tyrant endowed with every virtue (iv. 709 d ff.)—for the revolution needed to bring about a reform or a transition towards his goal. The failure and death of Dion have disillusioned him, and he now associates his monarchy of the " King " with the democratic principle of drawing lots, thus seeking to reconcile liberty with authority. In addition, a balance of powers and a whole hierarchy of Councils will make up what he expected of the " Scientist " as assistant of the King. Moreover, by strictly regulated discipline and very severe penalties which nip all danger of innovation and all independence of thought in the bud, he hopes to bring about, under the sovereignty of the law, the natural unity which is still the final object of his aspirations. Lastly, by connecting law and religion as closely as he does, he not only satisfies his profound belief in the universality of the divine order, but means to give the constraint of the law an additional efficacity, the authority belonging to a sacred thing.

This long chapter is very far from being sufficient to give a fair idea of the wealth of Plato's thought. It is fortunate that we have lost hardly anything of a body of writings which display in such abundance and with such brilliance the ordinary qualities of the Greek mind, which was at once bold and moderate, intuitive and rational, mystical and positive, artistic and geometrical. Indeed, only direct contact with his works can give a full sense of those qualities, without danger of presenting them in a hard-and-fast form. But, setting aside the incomparable art which they display, the historian of philosophic ideas also finds in them some of the greatest problems of thought, unravelled and prepared and established in their form for future speculation. Plato's influence was immense, and less external than Aristotle's, because the form of his writings did not lend itself so well to literal acceptation as an absolute authority. The living seeds which they sowed in the mind of those who meditated on them produced fairly different fruits, according to the soil, and few doctrines as well known as they have given rise to more divergent interpretations. Moreover, there seems to be in his reflection a combination of all the tendencies which had emerged in earlier philosophy—the geometrical mechanism of the School of Abdera and the abortive teleological dynamism of Anaxagoras, the pluralistic mobilism of Heracleitos and the monistic immobilism of the Eleatics, the mathematical formalism of the Pythagoreans and the conceptualistic formalism of Socrates. He always seeks the higher point of view which shall enable him to dominate contraries and to harmonize them by reducing artificial oppositions. At the same time as his thought reconciles philosophical tendencies or conceptions of life, such as intellectualistic asceticism and the aspiration to happiness, it strongly marks with its stamp the special techniques, scientific or otherwise, and especially rhetoric and poetry, medicine and politics. So the length at which we have studied Plato's thought seems to be justified.

Second Part—THE OLD ACADEMY

When Plato died, the Academy was already very influential and prosperous. Its influence may even have gone beyond the domain of speculation. For it is said that several cities had called upon members of the school to reform their laws, and there were little Platonic states in the Troad. The teaching was extremely varied. Plato had beside him a whole college of teachers, charged with special branches. Among these were Aristotle, Philip of Opus, Hermodoros, who wrote a book on his Master's doctrine, some fragments of which survive, Hestiaeos of Perinthos, Menedemos of Pyrrha, and others, more celebrated, of whom we shall now speak.

Eudoxos of Cnidos, a man about twenty years younger than Plato, was already the head of a school at Cyzicos when he entered the Academy. He left the Academy, but there is no proof that he did so because of disagreement with the Master's doctrine. In mathematics he studied the theory of proportions, and invented the celebrated method of " exhaustion," a curious application of Zenon's dichotomy, which consisted, without resorting to the notion of infinity, in bringing two unequal sizes as close together as was wished by " exhausting " their difference. But Eudoxos won even greater renown by his astronomical system, which enjoyed authority long afterwards and was propagated far and wide by the poem of Aratos, the *Phenomena*. How, it was asked, perhaps with Plato, can one " preserve appearances," that is, explain the observed inequalities of the movements of the planets, if we hold that they are circular, uniform, and concentric with the earth ? With an ingenuity to which justice has not always been done, Eudoxos invented a hypothesis, doubtless purely geometrical in his mind, which allowed one to represent the facts to oneself. He supposed the earth to be the centre of a system of eight concentric spheres, only one of which, that which gives the daily revolution of the whole heavens, has the same axis as the universe itself, the others having different axes. But since this was not enough to explain all the movements observed, he similarly constructed as many supplementary spheres as he needed, two more for the sun and moon respectively and three more for each of the other five planets, in such a way that everything took place as if each sphere obeyed the movement of the sphere immediately surrounding it. Twenty-seven spheres thus sufficed for Eudoxos to represent the movements observed in his day. Until the time of Kepler, astronomy continued to be based on this hypothesis, always complicating it more and more.

Heracleides of Heracleia, usually called Heracleides Ponticos, seems to have been one of the heads of the Academy, of which he was nearly made Scholarch on Plato's death. Geometry, astronomy, music, poetics, rhetoric, dialectic, ethics and politics, geography, history, legend, demonology, divination—he dabbled in them all, and, it seems, with such verve and originality that it is a misfortune that we have lost the romances of the man-in-the-moon who came down to earth and of the miracles of Abaris the Hyperboreian, and the dialogues in which animals talked together, or men of the people with philosophers. His physical theory, which was mechanistic like that of the *Timaeos*, introduced " uncomposed masses " (ἄναρμοι ὄγκοι) which, unlike the atoms, were regarded as centres of force. The theological atomism of Ecphantos and the theories of Hicetas of Syracuse on the immobility of the sky and the double rotation of the earth, the sun being the centre of the universe, may, perhaps, merely be the ideas which Heracleides placed in the mouths of those Pythagoreans as characters in his dialogues.[1] At least, in his view, Mercury and Venus went round the sun as satellites, and every planet was an universe with its own earth and atmosphere, the whole being in an infinite ether. Moreover, the stars were divine beings, and so was the soul, although it

---

[1] The hypothesis of P. Tannery, in *Rev. Ét. gr.*, xii. 305, rejected by **LXVIII**, note to ch. xxxvii, accepted by **XXIII**, 281 ff.

was a body of the nature of light and ether, descended from the sky and especially from the Milky Way.

After Plato, the two heads of the Academy were men on the threshold of old age—first Speusippos, the Master's nephew, and then Xenocrates of Chalcedon (339/8–315/4). Only the latter's doctrine is at all known to us. In both there is a tendency to place " metamathematical " speculations in the forefront of Platonism.[1] But, whereas Speusippos made mathematical number, as such and devoid of size, a transcendental number, Xenocrates, turning mathematics upside-down, as Aristotle says,[2] identified mathematical number with the ideal number of Plato, and geometrical size with atomic or indivisible size, the principle of which is " the uncuttable line." Thereby he sacrificed quantity altogether. Speusippos tried to remedy the difficulties of his own position by the possibility of taking different, but analogous, points of view on Being, making nature, as Aristotle says,[3] " a rhapsody of episodes," the systematic knowledge of which must, however, discover " similitudes." The scale of worth of these points of view he interpreted as an evolution in time, or " quantity in movement "—an evolution whose power lies in the principles, whose agent is the soul of the world, whose term is the perfection of being. The Good, then, is not something which is, but becomes and is made.

Although perhaps more orthodox, the philosophy of Xenocrates is like a caricature of that of Plato. The picture which he gives of it has none of its spirit, with its subtleties and shades of meaning, but only gives its letter, hardened and coarsened into school formulas, such as the celebrated definition of the substance of the soul itself as " a number which moves itself." The search for an order of dignity and intermediate degrees, which had such an influence on the thought of the old Master, becomes in the pupil a rigid, artificial schematism, full of divisions into threes. Moreover, although, as we have seen, Xenocrates regarded the manufacture of the world in the *Timaeos* as a device intended to show the order of the parts in what has eternity of movement and of time, he was none the less, in his own doctrines, full of mythology.

---

[1] Arist., *Met.*, A. 9, 992 a 32 : " Mathematics have become philosophy for people nowadays."
[2] **CXX**, 281, n. 263 (i).   [3] *Met.*, A., end ; N. 3, 1090 b 19.

In producing this hard-and-fast scholastic version of Platonism, Xenocrates succeeded, for a long time, and right down to the Neo-Platonists, in supplying the erudite with what seemed to them a faithful representation of it. That is partly the explanation of his great influence, of which early Stoicism bears the stamp. But he also owed the authority of his name to the austere loftiness of his moral theory, which reflected the gravity and nobility of his character.

CHAPTER V

FIRST PART—ARISTOTLE

I

HIS LIFE

ATTEMPTS have sometimes been made to explain the positive, technical bent of Aristotle's mind and the heaviness, which is so unlike the freedom and grace of Plato, by his race and education. But Aristotle was not a Macedonian. Stageira, his native town, was a very ancient Ionian colony in Thracian Chalcidice, and his mother came from Chalcis in Euboea. It is true that his father Nicomachos was a physician in the service of Amyntas II, King of Macedon, the father of Philip, and came of a family of physicians. But, since Nicomachos died while his son was quite young, it is very unlikely that he influenced him directly. At the age of eighteen (366–365) Aristotle entered the Academy. He stayed there twenty years, and taught in the school, perhaps in rhetoric. He was very much attached to the Master (notwithstanding tales which are suspect) and wrote a beautiful eulogy of him in his poem to the memory of his fellow-disciple Eudemos of Cyprus (Frag. 623), and Plato is said to have esteemed him for his penetrating mind and vast erudition. When Speusippos became head of the school, Aristotle left, with Xenocrates, for Lydia, and stayed at the court of Hermeias, the tyrant of Atarneus, an old fellow-pupil. Near-by, in the Troad, there were Platonic circles at Scepsis and at Assos, where, no doubt, Aristotle began to display an independent philosophic activity. Three years later, Hermeias having been surrendered to the Persians and killed, Aristotle took refuge in Mitylene, where he married his first wife, a kinswoman of the tyrant, named Pythias, of whom he seems to have been very fond. Shortly afterwards, he returned to Macedon at the request of King

Philip, who entrusted him with the education of his son Alexander, then aged thirteen (343–342). There he remained until 335–334.

At that date he returned to Athens and opened a school in the Lyceum, a gymnasium near the Temple of Lyceian Apollo. Like every gymnasium, it had a " walk " (περίπατος). So the name of " Peripatetic " given to the school of Aristotle probably refers to the fact that the Master gave at least some of his teaching while walking about (περιπατεῖν). We are told that the rhetoric courses were given in the afternoon and the philosophy courses in the morning. Alexander had regarded Aristotle with great suspicion since his nephew Callisthenes had been implicated in the plot against the King's life, but the prosperity of the school suffered chiefly from the anti-Macedonian reaction which took place on Alexander's death in 323. Aristotle was accused of impiety on futile grounds, and fled to Chalcis in all haste, leaving the Lyceum in the charge of Theophrastos. Shortly afterwards he succumbed to a stomach-trouble from which he had long suffered, being only sixty-three years old at the time (322).

II

His Writings

Strabo's *Geography* and Plutarch's *Sulla* contain, with a few discrepancies, a history of the writings of Aristotle. It is said that Theophrastos, when dying, bequeathed his library, including Aristotle's manuscripts and his own, to his fellow-disciple Neleus, whose father Coriscos had been a friend of Aristotle and head of the Platonic circle at Scepsis in the Troad. When Neleus died, the Attalid Princes of Pergamon were looking everywhere for books for their library, and his heirs, jealous of their treasure and wanting to put it in a safe place, rashly hid it in a cave. So the manuscripts were not only disarranged but very much damaged when, at least a hundred years later, they were sold to one Apellicon of Teos, a captain in the pay of Mithradates, who was at the same time an ardent book-lover and a shrewd man of business. He

hastened to have copies made—that is, to issue an edition—
but did not give the necessary care to the restoration of the
damaged passages. However, after Apellicon's library had
been seized by Sulla in the first Mithradatic War (87–84) and
transported to Rome, the work was resumed by the grammarian
Tyrannion, who had been taken to the city by Lucullus in 66
and was employed by Cicero as tutor and librarian in 57.
But he made no great improvement, and it was not till some-
what later that Andronicos of Rhodes, the eleventh Scholarch
of the Lyceum from Aristotle, at last gave the learned world
a correct edition, accompanied by "tables" and a book in
which he explained his method.

However, this story seems to be in large part a romance,
or rather the advertisement of an editor who wanted people
to think that Aristotle was practically unknown until he
himself took him up. For it is very probable that Aristonicos
is the source of the tradition. We can hardly suppose that
the library of the Lyceum contained no copies of Aristotle for
the use of students, and that there was none in the branches
of the Lyceum, such as the school of Eudemos at Rhodes.
Moreover, another tradition leads one to think that there must
have been some in the Library of Alexandria, since it was
founded at the time when the adviser of Ptolemy Soter was
the celebrated Demetrios of Phaleron, formerly a powerful
patron of the school. But there may be this much truth in
the romance, that, outside the schools and learned circles,
the cultivated public, from lack of easily obtainable instruments of study and also from lack of speculative curiosity,
had come to know almost nothing of Aristotle himself but
certain writings, such as those which Cicero praises for their
eloquence and graceful style, that is, the very works which are
totally unknown to us to-day.

Now, it is clear from Aristotle's own statements that, apart,
of course, from the "hypomnematic" writings, which were
mere notes for his personal use, his "works," properly so
called, were divided into two parts. One part included the
writings "given to the public," "in the common sphere," "in
circulation" (ἐκδεδομένοι, ἐν κοινῷ, τὰ ἐγκύκλια). They are
"exoteric," not in virtue of that fact, but in so much as the
form which especially (though not exclusively) suits them is
more "external" than demonstrative, more dialectical than

scientific.[1] The other part comprised the " philosophical " writings (οἱ κατὰ φιλοσοφίαν λόγοι), that is, scientific writings, lectures given to an audience of students, which, for that reason, were called " acroamatic " writings ; thus, φυσικὴ ἀκρόασις means *Lectures on Nature*. They were the " courses " or " labours " (μέθοδοι, πραγματεῖαι) of the school. These courses were written out, as seems to be proved by the frequent references from one course to another, and sometimes to a course which has not yet been given or belongs to a later stage in the programme of studies.[2] Of these courses the students must have had copies for their own use, and in this sense of being published inside the circle of students they are " esoteric."

By a singular chance, it is only the esoteric writings which have in part come down to us ; so we are in exactly the opposite position with regard to Aristotle to that in which we are with regard to Plato. We have only the literary writings of Plato and only the teaching of Aristotle. According to a good tradition, his whole works comprised a thousand books, whether complete works or divisions of works. Of these we have, in all, only a hundred and sixty-two, from which we must deduct apocryphal works. Also, the three catalogues of them preserved mention only five hundred at the most.[3] The most complete catalogue, in which we find almost everything contained in our collection, and which seems to be the remains of the " tables " of Andronicos, is that which two Arab writers of the XIIIth century ascribe to one Ptolemy, probably a Peripatetic of the Christian era. The two others, those of Diogenes Laërtios and the Anonymus Menagii, seem, for the part common to both, to come from the Peripatetic Hermippos, and it is not impossible that Hermippos, who was a pupil of Callimachos, copied the catalogue of the Library of Alexandria. In this part there are barely ten to fifteen of our books, and some of these are given under confused names and are divided differently from ours. But the Anonymus gives two appendices, which he is believed to have taken from the *Onomatology* of Hesychios of Miletos, one of which

---

[1] H. Diels, " Über die exoterischen Reden d. Arist.," in *Abhandl. d. Berl. Akad.*, xix (1883).

[2] Cf. Bonitz, *Ind. Arist.*, art. Ἀριστοτέλης.

[3] Published by V. Rose at the beginning of the *Fragments*.

completes or corrects the preceding list, while the other, much shorter, points out apocryphal writings.

When we compare our collection with these catalogues, we note that the books lost are, very unfortunately, all those which were written before Aristotle was head of the school, and which earned him his reputation as a good writer. At that time he belonged to the Academy, and it is not surprising that many of them should have been dialogues. But they were not like the dialogues of Plato ; they seem to have been, not so much free conversations as oratorical expositions in which, after a prologue in dialogue form, one of the characters expounded the author's ideas. In them Aristotle taught a fairly independent Platonism, as we can tell from the fragments of the most famous of them, *Eudemos* (*of Cyprus*), *or On the Soul*, a reply to the *Phaedon*, from those of the *Protreptic*, or, still better, from those of the dialogue *On Philosophy*, in three parts. To the same period, too, we should probably refer some of the Platonic expositions of which we have already spoken (p. 210 above), at least those which deal especially with Plato's oral teaching.

So our Aristotle is chiefly the Aristotle of the " acroamatic " books. Certainly, we have lost much of them, but chiefly among the documentary writings, often of a " hypomnematic " character, on which they were based, and among the technical treatises. On the whole, we have kept the most important. Since they are " lectures," the place to mention them is not here, but in connexion with the subject with which they deal in the encyclopaedia of knowledge. It was an ambition common to the great philosophic schools of that time to teach the whole of science. The Academy and Lyceum were both " universities " ; if we see this only in the work of Aristotle, it is not because he had a different conception of the function of a philosophic school, but because his activity as a writer had a different trend. We should also note three important points here. First, in his capacity of Scholarch, Aristotle seems to have organized the work of his collaborators thoroughly. Thus, we see from an inscription at Delphi that Callisthenes helped to write the *Chronology of Pythian Victors*. Therefore many of the special studies which we have under Aristotle's name may have been merely incorporated by him in the whole work. Secondly, since the " courses " and

" labours " of the school were its common property, the masters did not hesitate, after Aristotle's death, to make use of his writings for purposes of teaching, recasting them, completing them, combining lessons on the same subject by adding connecting passages, and sometimes even adding some writing of one of their number to such collections. Thirdly, to say nothing of the temptation to which an editor is exposed, of inserting references to some earlier or later part of the encyclopaedia, the systematic character of the work which we possess under the name of Aristotle makes it doubtful whether, for a general understanding of a system which is such a complex amalgam, it is of any great advantage, as it was in the case of Plato, to determine the development of his thought historically.

III

HIS DOCTRINE

1. THE PROGRAMME OF STUDIES. Whatever one may think of the real value of the Aristotelian division of the sciences, it does at least seem to represent a plan of studies in three cycles, the first two constituting the liberal education of the citizen and the third the training of the scientist. For the sciences are *poetic*, the knowledge of the " art " in obedience to the rules of which a work is " made " (ποίησις), or *practical*, when they consider the " activity " (πρᾶξις) of the agent in itself, independently of its external result, or, lastly, *theoretical*, where their object is knowing for knowing's sake, the purely " speculative " search (θεωρία) for truth. These last are the noblest. They are, moreover, the only ones which Aristotle is at pains to classify methodically, proceeding from that which is most abstract to that which is ontologically most real—first mathematics, which deal with numbers, figures, and movements apart from their subjects, although they are not really separate from them ; then physics, by which they get reality and, more especially, movement is connected with its internal principle, nature (*physis*) ; and lastly " theology," whose object is Being as being, apart from conditions which are merely particular and contingent, and the most real being, separate and motionless, or God.

This is also called " first philosophy," physics being " second philosophy," and mathematics also being a philosophy. So we have the whole of speculation, in three degrees of one same scale.[1]

Logic, we see, has no place in this classification. For it is not a science, but the " instrument " (organon) of science, as it was called in the school at an early date. Therefore the study of this instrument and of the ways of employing it can only form a general introduction to teaching. No doubt it was not taught, in its entirety, to all students. But those who learned only a part of it at least learned, in the limited sphere of their culture, the various general ways, legitimate or not, of producing verisimilitude, either in poetry or in eloquence ; they learned an art of those arts. This art, " dialectic," therefore belongs to the " poetic " sciences, not to logic. Yet, since the treatise devoted to it forms part of the traditional corpus of Aristotle's logical writings, the Organon, there is no harm, once we make this reservation, in studying it together with logic.

2. Logic. The most general conditions of thought are studied in the Categories, the five last chapters of which (10-15), usually designated by the title of Post-predicaments, are a very ancient addition to the original work. The Hermeneia (De Interpretatione) treats of the " enunciation of thought " in the proposition ; although perhaps recast in places, it is certainly authentic, except the last chapter (14). The object of the Analytics (Resolutions) is to set forth the method by which a given proposition or a given combination of propositions may be reduced to its causes, to the elements which are its necessary justification. The Prior Analytics deals with the syllogism, the Posterior with demonstration, each in two books. Lastly, quite distinct from the above body of writings, comes the Topics, which sets forth a merely probable method of arguing. The ninth and last book of the Topics is usually called the Refutation of Sophistic Arguments (Sophistarum Elenchi). It is very hard to say whether it is to the group of the logical writings that one should attach certain lost short treatises, several of which are quoted in the treatises preserved—The Choice of Contraries, On Opposites,

[1] Metaph., E. 1=K. 7 ; Phys., ii. 2 ; Nic. Eth., vi. 3-5.

On Negation, collections of " divisions " or " definitions," etc.

For Plato the method of science was the dialectical method. He expected too much from it, Aristotle protests ; dialectic is nothing more than the theory, the practical application of which is rhetoric ; it is a method for " discovering," about a " problem " under discussion, " arguments " whose premisses, being merely " opinions," are only " plausible," so that you can answer " Yes " or " No " to the question at issue " without contradicting yourself." So dialogue is implied in dialectic, even if it is not the expression of it. Dialectic is also called " topic," for it determines and groups the " places " (τόποι) which are the common " element " in which " oratorical arguments " on different subjects meet. When diverted from its legitimate object, it gives rise to " sophistry " and " eristic " ; the captious arguments or " sophisms " of the latter will be classified in minute detail and their tricks will be made plain. But, on the other hand, the normal use of dialectic has three functions. First, it is a *gymnastic* for the mind. Secondly, it is a *search,* or a *test* to which even a man who knows nothing of a science can subject one who pretends to be an expert—clearly a replica of the Socratic " examination." Lastly, where there is no scientific knowledge of an object, it serves for discovering the *first principles* of the science which treats of the object " philosophically," that is, scientifically ; this again it does by a test, but this time the object of the test is common opinions, or those professed by the learned. For a science cannot prove its own principles directly. Therefore the only way to open and clear the path for it is to *refute* illusory probabilities. Thus, a preliminary collection and examination of the evenly balanced conflicts of more or less reasoned conceptions, from which a " difficulty " or " question " (ἀπορία) results, prepare the mind to perceive intuitively the principles of a true science of the object in question.[1]

In using this dialectical method as the basis on which to build up the sciences,[2] Aristotle was the founder of the history of philosophy. He had prepared himself for it by a quantity of small special studies, mentioned in our catalogues, on the

[1] *Top.,* i. 1 beg. ; 2 ; 4, 101 b 28 ; vi. 6, 145 b 17 ; *Rhet.,* ii. 26, 1403 a 18.
[2] See *Phys.,* i ; *De An.,* i. ; *Metaph.,* A, B (i, iii).

Pythagoreans, on Alcmaeon, on Xenophanes, Parmenides, Melissos, and Gorgias (of which the apocryphal *De Melisso, Xenophane, et Gorgia* may preserve something), on Democritos, on Speusippos and Xenocrates, not to mention his books on Plato and extracts from the *Republic, Timaeos,* and *Laws.* But, great as is the value of his doxography, it is systematic, not properly historical, and is so obviously directed at establishing his own doctrine that sometimes his account of his predecessors' teaching is biased, whether he draws them on to his own side or unconsciously depreciates or even travesties them.

But the object of knowledge is not the " probability " of opinion, but truth. It is therefore based on " demonstration " (ἀπόδειξις) and is the source of a " conviction, which does not allow itself to be turned from its certainty by arguments " of mere likelihood. Now, the theory of demonstration is the final object of the *Analytics.* If that work lays down the limits of the domains of rhetoric and dialectic, it is just because it is analysing the conditions of a demonstrative knowledge. The proper object of logic, then, is to study the factors of demonstration—terms, propositions, and syllogisms.

Terms (ὅροι) are the elements, predicate (κατηγορούμενον) and subject (ὑποκείμενον), to which a proposition is reduced by the dissolution of their " connexion " ; they are, therefore, what is thought and enunciated " without a connexion " (ἄνευ συμπλοκῆς). Moreover, they are not mere words and nothing more ; for speech has something conventional and external to thought, and, by the side of synonyms, it has homonyms, identical words for different notions. Now, these " isolated objects of thought " (νοήματα) may be considered from several points of view, which Aristotle calls " categories." In its primary sense, a category is that which the subject can, as it were, be " accused of " (κατηγορεῖν, accuse), or the act of such accusation or the signification resulting from it. In a more restricted sense, the categories become especially all that can be " said of " a being, the " figures " of attribution, all the possible " kinds," primary and irreducible, of being— what, after Boëthius, were called " predicaments." Without seeking to deduce them, Aristotle empirically makes up a list of them by a method of grammatical analysis. In the most complete list there are ten possible senses of attribution :

substance or essence (man, horse), quantity (two cubits long), quality (white, grammatical), relative to (double, half, larger), the somewhere (on the square, at the Lyceum), the when (yesterday, never), attitude (lying, seated), possession (having one's shoes, or weapons), action and affection (to cut, to be cut). Each of these denominations has its meaning in itself and also, since they are outside all connexion, apart from all affirmation, and therefore without involving truth or falsity. Thus, the categories are the various kinds of " simple ideas," immediate and primary, the frames not only of thought but of reality.[1]

For it is in respect of a real subject that they represent every possible form of attribution. That real subject is called a " substance," just like essence. But, whereas the essence is only a " secondary " substance, the substance, as an individual and concrete existence, is " primary." It can only be a subject, never an attribute, except by an abnormal reversal. Essence is normally an attribute. " This " ($\tau \acute{o} \delta \epsilon$), the object of my present intuition, is " such " ($\tau \acute{o} \delta \epsilon \ \tau \iota$, $\tau o \iota \acute{o} \nu \delta \epsilon$) ; it is of a certain species and of a certain genus. Species and genera, therefore, are secondary substances, which " qualify " the primary substance, but in its essence. An essence may be imaginary, like the goat-stag, without being false ; it is only false when one connects it as an attribute with a real subject.[2] Lastly, the concept of a qualification, whatever that qualification may be, is absolutely simple only if it is considered as a last genus, or as a category in the strict sense. But the concept of a certain essence, of a certain quality or quantity, etc., may be made the object of an analysis. Thus the concept, the real but empty frame, is replaced by the concept, the content of that frame.

To analyse the content of a term, considered as a compound, and to " determine " it, is the object of *definition* ($\acute{o} \rho \iota \sigma \mu \acute{o} s$). The definition of an imaginary concept is a simple definition of a notion or " of a word." But an instructive definition must give information both about the nature of the concept of the thing and about its reality. So two very important elements of the reality of the concept appear. One, relatively

---

[1] Cf. especially, *Categ.*, i. 2, beg., 4 ; *Herm.*, 1, beg., and 2, beg. ; *Pr. Anal.*, i. 1, 24 b 16.

[2] Waitz, *Org.*, i. 288 ; Bonitz, *Ind. Arist.*, 495 b 40 ff.

indeterminate, is the " genus," that " of which " that reality may be made, or its " matter " (ὕλη)—logical or " intelligible " matter, that which the essence *is* in general and fundamentally (τὸ τί ἐστι). The other, which introduces a demarcation, is the " specifying difference " (διαφορὰ εἰδοποιός), determination, property, or " form " (εἶδος), " what it has been given to each thing to be " (τὸ τί ἦν εἶναι ἑκάστῳ). But, since difference implies the genus of which it is a difference, this second element by itself is the graded total of characteristics, what the Schoolmen called the " quiddity," and, as such, is truly the *logos*, the concept of the thing. But whereas the thing is in fact a natural reality, concrete or " by composition," the concept and its elements are " by abstraction," so that, as in the case of mathematical notions, what is not " separate " is treated " as if " separate. This manner, abstract or formal, of breaking up a reality, to define it, into what there is intelligible in it, whether matter or form, fully agrees with the point of view of the *Analytics*.[1]

What is thus separable or separated by abstraction, but not in reality, is " logically anterior," but not " chronologically " so, nor " in the nature of things." It is the " universal " (τὸ καθόλου), and Plato's mistake was that he confused the first and the last sort of anteriority in respect of it. Furthermore, we must distinguish several sorts of universal. First, universality of *genus* must not be confused with that of *analogy*, which is the result of a mere resemblance of relation—for example, the unity " man " should not be confused with the unity which brings together under the idea of the restoration of health all the different things which are called " medical " without distinction. Again, there is the universal which is merely the collective attribute *of the total* of individuals enumerated in a class, and there is also that which belongs *of itself* (καθ᾽ αὑτό), or necessarily, to some individual in that class, even to one at present unknown. Now, only this last universal belongs to the concept ; it is what gives rise to determinations of genus and, adding difference, of species. Even then one must make a condition —that it is not one of the properties regarding which, although they are no doubt essential, reasoning alone can show that they are " accidents which belong to the essence " (συμβεβηκός or

[1] Cf. opp. citt., ii. 399–401, 346 ff. ; 787 a 12, 19,

πάθος·καθ' αὐτό), such as, in the case of the triangle, the equality of the sum of the angles to two right angles. *Accident* in the strict sense (συμβεβηκός) and the *proper* (τὸ ἴδιον) are universals which *a fortiori* are excluded from the constitution of the concept ; it does not necessarily belong to the essence of man to be white, or to be a grammarian, although the latter attribute is proper only to a man. Thus Aristotle pays more attention to the necessity of an essence than to its generality, and, from this point of view, at least, to its " comprehension " than to its " extension." That is why the most general notions of all, like the One and the Being of Plato, are not categories in his eyes ; being empty of all content, the possible attributes of every notion, they are no longer genera of attribution, nor, therefore, " genera of being." Now, in the *Analytics* the term is what has a necessary content, really, if not logically, indissoluble, namely the concept, and it is also what, while still having a content, is absolutely simple, namely the categories.[1]

With the various kinds of *oppositions* which there may be between terms, we naturally pass from considering them abstractly in isolation to considering them as parts of one whole. The distinction of true and false here appears ; the relation of logic to ontology becomes still closer.

The opposites (ἀντικείμενα) which are most manifestly opposite are the *contraries* (ἐναντία), the terms " most opposed in one same genus," such as, to take examples from experience, high and low in position, starting-point and finishing-point in movement, heavy and light in weight, hot and cold in temperature, white and black in colour, and so on. But between these extremes there may be mean terms, such as tepid or grey. Certain contraries, it is true, allow of no such intermediate terms ; a number, for example, is always either odd or even. But, even where intermediaries exist, we sometimes find that one of the extremes is always inherent in some particular subject ; fire is always hot, snow is always white. Moreover, things themselves, their actions and privations, give rise to derivative contrarieties, by the fact that there is contrariety between their natural properties or between the natural effects of their actions and privations. Lastly, since

[1] *Post. An.*, i. 4, 73 a 28 ff. ; *Metaph.*, Δ. 30, end ; *Top.*, i. 5, 102 b 4 ff., a 18 ff.

the contrariety subsists, whichever way the change takes place, it is a reversible opposition.[1]

Another opposition, in many respects very like the above, is that between *privation and possession*. A given subject possesses a certain manner of being (ἕξις, Latin *habitus*, English " habit " in this technical sense), or it is deprived of it (στέρησις). In some cases this manner of being belongs to the genus itself, as sight to the animal, and it is a particular species which is deprived of it, as the mole. In other cases an individual is deprived of a " habit " natural to its species, and at a time and in circumstances in which it ought naturally to possess it ; in this sense blindness is opposed to sight.[2] This, then, seems to be the same as contrariety, but considered in a certain subject and in relation to certain conditions.

As Aristotle's logical tendency leads him towards more general forms of the opposition of privation and possession, we see that opposition approaching a certain sort of contrariety which, as he recognizes, is of a specific character among all the oppositions. *Contradiction* (ἀντίφρασις), according to him, is that limitation of contrariety which, as Plato had already clearly seen (*Rep.*, iv. 436 b-437 a), totally excludes one of the two opposites in respect of a same subject (individual or class), at least in the same relation and at the same time. Of all the principles, this is the most fundamental, and the principle of all the most general judgements. For it is the foundation of logical discourse, in that it absolutely opposes true to false and affirmation to negation, and that especially because it rejects the " middles " which experience sometimes compels us to admit between contraries.[3]

Lastly, there is the opposition of *relatives* (τὰ πρός τι), where each of the two terms is in relation to the other, and has its whole nature in that very correlation. Either they contain their correlative (as double contains half, and inversely, or a given aptitude contains the corresponding activity, and inversely) ; or the correlation is not reversible and, while one term depends on the other, the converse is not true (as in the

---

[1] *Cat.*, 6, 6 a 17 ; 10, 11 b 33 ff. ; *Metaph.*, I. 4 beg. ; Δ. 10, to 1018 a 38.
[2] *Ibid.*, 10, 12 a 26–13 a 37 ; Δ. 22 beg.
[3] *Metaph.*, Γ. 3, 1005 b 19 to end ; 4, 1007 b 18 ; 6, 1011 b 16 ; I. 4, 1055 b 7 ; 5, 1056 a 20 ; 7, 1057 a 34 ; *Herm.*, 2, 16 a 30.

relation of " before " to " after "). But in both oppositions the two terms are indissolubly bound to one another.[1]

But were they not already so bound in the case of contrariety ? That is the effect of the famous phrase, " The science of contraries is one and the same." At bottom, the graded scale of oppositions presents a progress of opposition of relation to increasingly negative determinations. However abstract and simplified the last, contradiction, may be, it does not, one should note, exclude all consideration of the real. For as soon as you are dealing, neither with the eternally necessary nor with the present, given real, but with a " contingent future," which is neither the one nor the other, then the determining function of the principle of contradiction disappears. That there will be a sea-battle to-morrow is true or false *indeterminately*.[2] All the more is it so with less abstract oppositions. Thus, for example, when we pass from the table of categories, where we have already met them, to the table of oppositions, relation and possession now concern truth and untruth, that is, the expression of the real and the unreal.[3] For how otherwise would formal, logical oppositions of propositions, other than contradictory, enable us, within certain limits, to recognize the true and the untrue, immediately and *a priori* ? Moreover, Aristotle started from experience in making up the logical framework of oppositions, and it was later, to the detriment of abstract strictness, that he corrected it in order to adapt its distinctions to the exigencies of reality.

Now, if opposition, in all its forms, thus inevitably introduces the consideration of truth and untruth, it confronts us, not only with terms as parts of one whole, as was said above, but with their connexion. This connexion lies in the *attribution of a predicate to a subject* in a judgement, a subsumption (ὑπόληψις) or proposition (πρότασις). It is only in this connexion, whether affirmative (κατάφασις) or negative (ἀπόφασις), that error and truth are opposed. In the case of simple notions, on the contrary, or notions treated as simple, and therefore isolated, either there is no room for error, as in the immediate intellectual apprehension of an essence, or in the immediate sensation by some sense of the quality which

[1] *Cat.*, 7 ; *Metaph.*, Δ. 15.   [2] *Herm.*, 9.
[3] *Ibid.*, 19 a 33 ; *Metaph.*, Γ. 7, 1011 b 25.

is its proper, specific object ; or there is no room for truth, as in the case of imaginary notions.[1] Therefore there can be true or false only if there are affirmation and negation. Now, this is what properly constitutes thought and discourse ; Aristotle is as severe as Plato on the philosophers who condemn attribution. But, if the opposition of contradiction enables us (except in respect of the indeterminate future) to discriminate completely, and without possible middle, between true thought and false thought, it is not so in all cases.

It is therefore useful to know in what cases operations on propositions (opposition and conversion) allow of a legitimate " logical calculation "($\sigma\upsilon\lambda\lambda o\gamma\iota\sigma\mu o\varsigma$).[2] But, although these rules may be verified, they cannot be proved. On such a foundation we cannot set up science. " We know absolutely ($\dot{a}\pi\lambda\hat{\omega}\varsigma$) when we know the cause " (or reason) " on account of which a thing is just what it is and cannot be otherwise than it is." [3]

Therefore scientific explanation is a necessary explanation. Consequently, and in virtue of a relation already pointed out, it is knowledge of the universal and of that which is always in the same manner, whether one be dealing with immediate necessary attributes or derived ones.[4] Moreover, since it explains universally, it is not, at least in itself, intuitive. For what an intuition apprehends is an individuality, concrete if it is sensible (like this circle of gold here), abstract if it is intelligible (like this geometrical circle). But neither of them, as such, is an object of explanation, or even of definition.[5] It is, however, quite true that science, to rise to what is " most knowable absolutely " and " by nature," or " the most intelligible," must start from an intuitive knowledge. For how could each science demonstrate its " principles " ($\dot{a}\rho\chi a\iota$), either those proper to itself or those which it has in common with others ? From demonstration to demonstration, we should go back to infinity, and nothing would ever be demonstrated. In our analysis it is therefore necessary to stop ($\dot{a}\nu\dot{a}\gamma\kappa\eta$ $\sigma\tau\hat{\eta}\nu a\iota$). But for science the term of this regression cannot be in contingent intuitions—neither in the natural sagacity

---

[1] Herm. 1, end ; De An., iii. 6, 430 a 27 ; ii. 6, 418 a 11 ; Metaph., H. 10, 1052 a 2.
[2] Bonitz, Index, 712 b 4 ff.　　　　[3] Post. An., i. 2, beg.
[4] Bonitz, Ind., 279 a 22, 47.
[5] Post. An., i. 31, beg. ; Metaph., Z. 10, 1036 a 6 ; 15, 1039 b 28.

which some men have from long experience and special
aptitudes, nor in the sensations, although they are what is
" most knowable in relation to ourselves " and, although, when
we perceive a concrete individual as such or such, we at the
same time perceive the universality of the species—for example,
man in Callias. Science finds its principles and starting-points
in *immediate propositions*, which have some claim to demand
acceptance—" singular " objects of a " last " intuition, which,
however, has nothing individual or contingent in it.[1] Thus,
the arithmetician will begin by enunciating that which he is
considering, unity, and defining it (position) ; then he will
state that unities exist (supposition). He will assert axioms
(τὰ κοινὰ ἀξιώματα), the judgements which every human mind
has, at least implicitly. He will demand (postulate) that his
pupil should accept certain principles which he cannot
demonstrate, but which constitute principles proper to his
science.[2]

Yet these undemonstrable principles, abstract and logical
as they are and without easily apprehensible relation to
experience, cannot suffice for demonstration ; demonstration
must therefore go to experience itself for other immediate
data. They are collected by *induction* (ἐπαγωγή), which parts
off the universal from the particular. For there is no science
of the singular (καθ' ἕκαστον) ; and the object of sensation,
from which induction starts, is singular. But in a sensation,
as we have seen, the universal is implied. Induction is, then,
a source of the universal premisses of the demonstrations of
science, and perhaps even their ultimate source, if, as Aristotle
says, the disappearance of a class of sensations, with the
corresponding inductions, must bring with it the disappearance
of a science. Moreover, since induction consists in discovering
what is common to the examples which it has collected, it is
in itself not very different from the Socratic induction which
we find in the earliest dialogues of Plato ; is it not one of the
most important objects of dialectic to extract the proper
principles of knowing ? It is not true that Aristotelian
induction, as some say, following Aristotle himself, requires
" the collection of all the singular cases " which constitute the

---

[1] Bonitz, *Index*, 159 a 33 ; *Nic. Eth.*, vi. 6 ; 12, 1143 b 4, 11 ; *Post. An.*, ii. 19,
100 a 17, 99 b 21 ; i. 3 ; *Phys.*, viii. 5, 256 a 29.
[2] *Post. An.*, i. 2, 72 a 14–24 ; 10.

extension of a class. It is much rather a condensation of experience, similar to that which takes place mechanically when sensations gather round one more intense sensation, thus preparing for the arrival of a notion. But it is a reflective, scientific condensation, which explicitly enunciates both the observations which have served to form it and the actual characteristics which, being verified in the cases observed, may for that reason be supposed to be inherent in the whole class.[1]

So induction seems to be very close to the process in which the endeavour of Plato's dialectic culminated—the method of division. Aristotle severely criticized the method, saying that it was based on a series of postulates.[2] Yet his own induction does not any more give us the reason of the relation which it establishes ; it is not scientific, because it is not demonstrative. The theory of demonstration, on the contrary, claims to be, as Aristotle readily shows for yet other questions, a return to Socratic thought ; for Socrates had seen quite well that the essence is the principle of demonstration. For demonstration is the syllogism, the logical calculation, which " expounds the cause " or reason of the attribution of a quality to a subject, the middle term ($\tau \grave{o}$ $\mu \acute{\epsilon} \sigma o \nu$) connecting these two extremes ; for " the middle is a cause." If the premisses of this calculation are necessary, the result must also be necessary. Therefore such an operation achieves what division, that " impotent syllogism," had not been able to do, and that for which the inductive syllogism had merely prepared the way. Moreover, Aristotle believes that his technique of reasoning truly symbolizes the rational art which nature is in his eyes —so much so, that, where this abstract symbolism is lacking, there will no longer be a science of nature. For let us suppose that we are standing above the moon, and when the earth passes between it and the sun we " see " the cause of the lunar eclipse. Such an observation is, for Aristotle, without scientific value, for in it the knowledge of the " why " ($\delta \iota \acute{o} \tau \iota$) is only a knowledge of the fact " that " ($\ddot{o} \tau \iota$), which has not universality. There is no true causality except in quiddity ; " man is begotten by man," and if Peleus is the cause

---

[1] Pr. An., ii. 23 ; Top., i. 12, end ; viii. 2, beg. ; Post. An., i. 18 ; ii. 7, 92 a 37 ff. ; 19. Bonitz, Index, 264 a 13–18.
[2] All the beginning of Pr. An., i. 31, and of Post. An., ii. 5.

of Achilles it is because he possesses the "form" of man.[1]

Aristotle's wholly logical conception of science, which we have been considering here, is very attractive in its apparent strictness, but it lay like a heavy weight on the later history of the natural sciences. It is therefore of advantage to establish the place which it holds in the whole of which it is a part. First of all, as Aristotle himself admits,[2] demonstration always tests a very general proposition, in the hope of discovering in it the particular proposition in question. In other words, like Plato's division, it starts from a postulate. Moreover, in doing so it does no more than artificially reverse the inductive syllogism, the conclusion of which has brought out a property, and thereby test that property as a "middle" or cause.[3] This is a singularly deceptive counter-check, for this change in the mode of exposition will not reveal an error in the induction, if there is one. This supposedly infallible knowledge confines itself to setting forth in the abstract the natural order previously extracted, somehow or other, from the empirical reality.

One must, it is true, admit that Aristotle was well aware how much the ideal of complete intelligibility described in the *Analytics* was hampered by conditions which have nothing to do with pure logic. After having, as we saw, made demonstration halt before an immediate, undemonstrated knowledge, he forbids it (what is still more characteristic) "to pass from one genus to another," for example, to apply the principles of arithmetic to geometry.[4] Furthermore, the form and conclusions of syllogisms depend on the "modality" of their premisses,[5] that is, on real determinations. For the relation of attribute to subject may be one of "mere existence" or "contingent possibility," or, on the other hand, it may be one of "necessity" of existence. There are yet other notions, still more markedly empirical in character, which it seems hard to incorporate, as Aristotle would do, in demonstrative science by the side of necessity based on essence ; such, for example, is the notion of what happens "usually," opposed to the

---

[1] Cf. above, p. 157 n. 1. *Post. An.*, i. 24, 85 b 23 ; 31, 87 b 29 ff. ; ii. 2, 90 a 6, 24 ff. ; *Pr. An.*, i. 4. 25 b 9 ; *Metaph.*, Z. 6, 1031 b 6 ff. ; Λ. 3, end ; 5, 1071 a 17–24.
[2] *Top.*, viii. 13, 163 a 1 ff.   [3] **CXXXIII**, 256 ff.
[4] *Post. An.*, i. 7, beg.   [5] On modal syllogisms, see **CXXXIII**, ch. xii.

contingency of pure accident.[1] Lastly, the different types of syllogism represent so many attempts to adapt the ambitions of theory to the need for reflecting about the concrete real. It is, for instance, impossible to reason a priori from cause to effect every time that you are dealing with a real becoming. Who can prove to me that a cause must produce its effect—that stones collected together as if for foundations must result in a house ? On the other hand, from the effect given in experience, or " supposed " (the house), I can, relying upon the " necessity derived from that supposition " (ἀνάγκη ἐξ ὑποθέσεως), conclude the necessary existence of the cause. Thus one reasons in the "enthymeme," or reflection on the " marks " of a causal connexion already known from experience.[2]

To sum up, Aristotle hoped for too much from demonstration, as if the logical form of mathematics could wholly satisfy all the needs of science. Secondly, by binding demonstration to the consideration of quality and of formal essence, as he did, he for a long time impeded the previous attempt of mathematics, in the Pythagoreans and in Plato, to give experience the degree of intelligibility of which it allows.

3. POETIC SCIENCES. When we pass from the general method of knowledge to its content, according to the encyclopaedic programme of the school, the most elementary subjects, as we have seen, are the poetical.

The works of Aristotle dealing with them are the *Poetics*, the second book of which is lost, the *Rhetoric*, which, especially the third and last book, is perhaps only a compilation of Aristotle's lectures, and the *Topics*, to which we need not return, having already defined its object. All these works were accompanied by treatises connected with them, some historical and others intended to illustrate the theory ; all these are lost. Students may also have used books which are said to have been written under the Master's direction by his friend Theodectes, who had great experience in all these matters. These are mentioned in our *Rhetoric* (iii. 9, end). The *Rhetoric addressed to Alexander*, which appears in our collection, is not authentic, nor is there any good reason for

[1] *Post. An.*, i. 30 ; ii. 12, 96 a 8 ff. ; *Metaph.*, K. 8, 1065 a 4 ff.
[2] Cf. L. Robin, in *Arch. f. Gesch. d. Philos.*, xxiii (1909), 18–21, 27 ff.

attributing it, as has been done, to a celebrated rhetor of the day, Anaximenes of Lampsacos.

There is no need to linger over these technical studies. That part of them which affects the history of philosophic ideas will be found in Aristotle's ethics and psychology.

4. PRACTICAL SCIENCES. Although there were many signs foretelling a new state of things, the strict dependence of the individual on the city remained a fundamental dogma for Aristotle. It is at the bottom of his general conception of human activity. Man, he says, is neither a god, sufficient to himself, nor a wild beast which resists social life, but a being made by nature for political life (ζῷον πολιτικόν). The city is first, not in time, but absolutely, in relation to the family and the individual. That being so, the end or good of man cannot be known and practically ensured either by " economics " (οἶκος, the domestic organism) or by " ethics," but only by the science which considers man in the specific achievement of his nature and in truly human perfection, namely, " politics." It is, therefore, from a very abstract point of view, remote from reality, that ethics will try to determine the essence and conditions of the good of man, apart from his domestic and social group. It is true that, as we shall see, this abstraction can take us to great heights. The fact remains that " morals " here have a place, minus the exactitude, analogous to that of mathematics in the theoretical order, and that politics is the " architectonic " science on which every other practical science whatsoever depends.[1]

A. *Ethics.* Of the works on this subject contained in our collection, one is of indisputable authenticity. That is the *Nicomachean Ethics*, in ten books, so called, not because Aristotle dedicated it to his son (as is suggested by the classical French title of *Ethics to Nicomachos*), but because Nicomachos doubtless edited it, after his father's death. The same must be said of the *Eudemian Ethics*, in seven books ; they were neither addressed to nor even, as has been supposed, written by Eudemos of Rhodes. It is probably an edition by Eudemos of old lectures of Aristotle, while the other *Ethics* is a publica-

---

[1] *Nic. Eth.*, i. 1, 1094 a 24 to b 27 ; 13, 1102 a 18–26 ; *Pol.*, i. 1, beg. ; 2, 1253 a 27, etc.

tion of much later lectures. In any case, one thing should
be noted : Book X of the *Nicomachean Ethics* belongs to that
work alone ; there is some correspondence between the first
four books of it and Books I to III of the *Eudemian Ethics*, and
between Books VIII and IX of the former and the last book
of the latter ; and the intermediate books of the two works
are completely identical. In all probability, these books were
added to the *Eudemian Ethics* later, and this work may be the
Ethics in five or four books mentioned under No. 38 in the
catalogue of Diogenes Laërtios. Lastly, the *Great Ethics* is a
school-résumé, of uncertain date. Our collection also contains
an apocryphal treatise, *On the Virtues and Vices*, an eclectic
work which has not even the merit of fidelity.

The notions which are the object of ethics are uncertain
and confused. One cannot hope to discover the " why " of
them, and must rely chiefly on a subtle judgement, the general
knowledge of old men, the customary moral experience of
healthy consciences (ἐθισμός)—in fact, on induction, based
on common opinion as well as on that of the learned. Now,
such a method of critical discussion does not rise beyond
probability (ἀπορίαι), and is essentially dialectical.[1]

The end at which the practical activity of man aims is a
final good, desirable in itself and " sufficient to itself," a
sovereign good, not transcendent, no doubt, like the Platonic
idea of the Good, and unrelated to action, but, on the contrary,
" realizable in action " (πρακτόν) by man. It is unanimously
called " happiness " (εὐδαιμονία), which means both living
well and acting well—a good which, if it did not comprise all
goods, would not be the greatest good conceived.[2] As to
knowing wherein it lies—in pleasures, in honours, in the
speculative life—there is no agreement among men, nor even
in the consciousness of each of us. We can, however, say that
man has " a work proper to man," like a particular artist or
organ, but it lies wholly in that very activity, in its " action "
or reality (ἐνέργεια, πρᾶξις), independently of an external
end ; that it does not belong to the nutritive life, that of the
living creature in general, nor to the sensitive life, that of
the animal in general, but to the life which includes thought
(λόγος). It is, then, the " actualization " of the powers of

[1] *Nic. Eth.*, i. 1, 1094 b 16 ff. ; 7, 1098 a 33 ff. ; vi. 12, end.
[2] i. 1, beg., and 1094 a 18–22 ; 2, 1095 a 16–20 ; 4 ; 5, 1097 a 34 ff. ; etc.

the soul of man, in accordance with the most complete
" excellence " (ἀρετή) of which that actualization is capable,
and the actualization must not be unstable or of short duration,
for " one swallow does not make a summer, nor does one day."
Lastly, against Plato (*Phileb.*, 11 d) and against Speusippos
and Xenocrates, we shall say that happiness, as here defined,
can only come of " use " (χρῆσις), and is not merely a
" possession " and a " manner of being " (κτῆσις, ἕξις). To
be happy without knowing it, when you are asleep, like
Endymion, or amid great misfortunes, like Priam—is that to
be happy at all ? [1]

Of the conditions of happiness, those which reside in
bodily goods, like health, or external goods, that is, goods
which do not belong to our essence, such as wealth and
honours, may no doubt contribute to it as " instruments."
Lack of them may spoil or hamper it, for it is absurd to say
(with Plato) that you can be happy on the wheel ; excess of
them may injure it. But the true conditions of happiness are
the goods of the soul and the excellent exercise of its activities,
" in accordance with its special virtue." Given these, a
mediocre prosperity, provided that it satisfies the requirements
of life, and even misfortune, provided that it is not too great,
become means for causing nobility of character to shine out.[2]

Therefore pleasure must not be separated from happiness.
Pleasure is not merely a " disposition " immanent in an action
and made real by the action, but rather that which, in the end,
crowns the action and " is added to it," like the bloom to
youth, without which youth would still be youth. It is,
therefore, equally wrong to refuse all worth to pleasure (with
Speusippos) and to raise it to the rank of the sovereign good
(like Eudoxos). But, for a man who places his happiness in
the realization of what is best in himself, pleasure, far from
being an artificial ornament, is always natural, and there is no
conflict between pleasures. Continual pleasure and everlasting blessedness are, indeed, the privilege of the being who
can " realize his essence continuously and without weariness,"
that is, of God, the simple, motionless, wholly active being.
At least, even in beings for whom " motionlessness " merely
marks the completion of a tendency, there is more " action,"

---

[1] i. 2, 1095 a 20–5 ; 3 ; 6 ; 7, beg. ; 9, 1098 b 31 ff. ; ix. 9, 1169 b 29 ff. ; x. 6.
[2] i. 7, 1098 b 12 ff. ; 10 ; 11, 1100 b 9 ; vii. 14, 1153 b 21 ff. ; x. 8, 1178 a 23 ff.

and therefore, more pleasure, in that motionlessness (ἐνέργεια ἀκινησίας) than in movement, which is an imperfect action, mixed with potentiality. Thus defined, happiness is obtainable by anyone " not infirm in respect of the virtue " of his normal being.[1]

So we see what virtue is, in the sense of morality and as the " form " or essence of the good actions which make a happy life. How shall these actions be effected ? The inquiry supposes, first of all, in the " irrational part " of the soul, a distinction between the functions of the vegetative soul, which are properly vital and have nothing to do with thought, and, on the other hand, the " impulses " (ὁρμαί), " appetites," or, more generally, " desires," which sometimes resist the authority of the " rational part " and sometimes listen obediently to its admonitions and counsels, " like a son to his father." In consequence we have two different kinds of virtues. On the one hand, there are the intellectual or " dianoetic " virtues, the fruits of teaching and reflective experience. These virtues organize our dispositions and conduct in a more or less completely rational fashion. They are, first, " art " and " science," the foundations of " prudence " (φρόνησις), and, secondly, " wisdom " and " intellect " (σοφία, νοῦς). On the other hand, there are the virtues concerning " morality " (τὸ ἦθος)—the affective dispositions and active tendencies of each individual, moderation, gentleness, or their contraries. These are the " ethical " virtues, those of morals, manners.[2]

But there is another reason for naming these virtues thus ; they presuppose " habit," " custom " (ἔθος). No doubt, one can in a sense speak of " natural virtues " (φυσικαί ἀρεταί), hereditary dispositions or idiosyncrasies. But, whereas in inanimate things the natural potentialities are not modified by exercise which either opposes or encourages them, and whereas the vital powers, such as sight, are immediately or almost immediately followed by their use, here we are in the presence of acquired manners of being, created by our very acts and by the repetition of those acts, and modifiable by education. By repeating acts of justice or injustice, you become

---

[1] i. 10, all the beginning ; 12, end ; viii. 14, 1153 b 14 ff. ; 15, 1154 b 24 ff. ; x. 2 ; 7, 1177 b 26 ff. ; 9, 1179 a 23 ff. ; *Metaph.*, Λ. 7, 1072 b 15 ff.
[2] i. 13, 1102 a 26 to end ; vi. 2, beg. ; 3, beg.

just or unjust, as you become a good or bad harpist by playing the harp well or badly. We must, therefore, control the quality of our acts carefully, and adopt good habits early. Furthermore, all virtue, being a unique manner of being, is a determination of pure power, which is ambiguous and equally capable of good and bad.[1]

The rational part of the soul likewise includes two functions, one " scientific " or " theoretic " (τὸ ἐπιστημονικόν, τὸ θεωρεῖν), whose object is the necessary, and one " logical " (τὸ λογιστικόν), the part of " reflective calculation," whose object is the contingent, that which can be other than what it is. Now, it is this latter class of things which are the objects of " deliberation " and " choice " (βούλησις, προαίρεσις), which is a " deliberative desire " (ὄρεξις βουλευτική), a preference of wish in respect of " things which depend on ourselves " (τὰ ἐφ' ἡμῖν), and principally in respect of virtue and vice. In its most general character, then, " ethical virtue " is a " disposition to prefer " (ἕξις προαιρετική) in respect of certain acts. Moreover, the " reasoning thought " (διάνοια) in the theoretic order, which distinguishes between true and false, which affirms and denies, has as its counterpart in the practical order another reasoning thought, sometimes even an intellectual apprehension (διάνοια πρακτική, νοῦς πρακτικός) which distinguishes between good and evil, desirable and undesirable, and pronounces upon what is to be sought or avoided. By it, truth of enunciation is righteousness of desire ; " right thought " (ὀρθὸς λόγος) is the same thing as " good practice " (εὐπραξία). For the choice " is the man himself," as a principle of his activity, and, in the famous phrase, " a desiring thought " or a thinking and " reasoning desire." [2]

It follows from this that, alone of the " dianoetic " or intellectual virtues, " prudence " is really in the domain of practice. The capital question, therefore, is that of its relationship to ethical virtue. Now, the prime motive of our choices is the desirable, which sets desire in motion, the former being a motionless motive while the latter is a moved motive, for in its turn it moves the body. This concatenation is, in Aristotle's eyes, analogous to that connecting a conclusion to its premises, and, since there is an analogy between the good or bad and the true or untrue, there must be a

---

[1] ii. 1 ; vi. 13, 1144 b 3–17.　　　　[2] iii. 5, end ; vi. 2.

" syllogism of the desirable." In the syllogism the desirable is the universal major, the minor is the perception which recognizes its presence and determines the actual desire, and the conclusion is the choice and act following on that desire.[1] Here alone, we see, is there room for deliberation. A physician, for example, does not deliberate about his own desirable, which is to cure his patient, nor about the recognition of that desirable in a particular case, which is done by his science. So, too, it being granted that the end of conduct is the improvement of our empirical character ($\mathring{\eta}\theta o\varsigma$), the task of prudence will be to choose the right means to achieve that end. Combined with that end, prudence is called " good will " ; without it, it is only " cleverness " or, if it is maleficent, " rascality." Prudence is the form without which the matter of natural inclinations remains unstable and ambiguous, and which determines the virtues by opposition to the vices. But without that matter prudence would be nothing but a purely intellectual function and (contrary to what Socrates held) it could not furnish a foundation for practice. It is prudence, however, that establishes " right thought " ($\mathring{o}\rho\theta\grave{o}\varsigma$ $\lambda\acute{o}\gamma o\varsigma$) in practice, that is, the exact relation of the elements which enter into the " syllogism of action," into calculation and choice, for beings capable of it. Prudence tells how a particular case will fit the general rule, " when, how, in respect of and with a view to what, and in respect of whom " one should do what, in general, it is desirable to do.[2]

It is not, however, enough to conform outwardly to right reason ; we must be inwardly united with it, we must act not only " according to " but " with " its bidding. Aristotle lays great stress on the value of right intention, provided that it is more than an isolated effort or an eloquent declaration. But since logic, as we have seen, has its place there, we must make an exact analysis of the sophisms of practice ; for error may creep into the major or minor of the " syllogism of action." False reasoning is very often used in the hope of justifying bad desires, and the incontinent man, he who does not master himself, is a man who reasons badly. Not so is the man who, in Aristotle's eyes, is the paragon of morality,

---

[1] vii. 5, 1147 a 25 ff. ; De Motu An., 7, beg. ; 6, 700 b 35 ; De An., iii. 10, 433 b 13 ff. ; 11, end.
[2] iii. 5, 1112 b 11 ff. ; vi. 13, 1144 a 20 ff. ; ii. 2, 1104 b 25 ; 5, 1106 b 21 ff. ; etc.

the " prudent man," who is " master of himself." In him
lustful appetite is merged in a right will, which is the same as
reason. The sovereignty of reason may even become greater,
if the man's practical activity involves dianoetic virtues higher
than prudence.[1]

Provisionally, it will suffice to keep to the point of view
which served to determine the distinction of the virtues, that
of a " composite " or concrete man, in whom reason and inclinations stand face to face. If, then, " ethical virtue " is
" excellence " of the irrational part of the soul, we must
discover what this virtue will be under the control of prudence.
Now, in every " functional disposition "—eating, drinking,
taking exercise, etc.—" well-being " ($\tau\grave{o}$ $\epsilon\tilde{v}$) is, as we see,
equidistant from the too much and the too little which are
alike bad for the health, whereas " right measure " ($\tau\grave{a}$ $\sigma\acute{v}\mu\mu\epsilon\tau\rho a$)
is good for the health. Of course, excess, shortage, and mean
are not absolutely determined terms, as 6 is the arithmetic
mean between 10 and 2, being as much smaller than 10 as it is
greater than 2. They vary with the subject and the circumstances ; a diet which will be too heavy for one starting on
athletics will be too light for Milon of Croton, and it is the
master of the gymnasium who decides. Now, a man's moral
character is composed of powers or tendencies, the particular
manifestations of which are emotions, " affections," " passions "
($\pi\acute{a}\theta\eta$), natural, sudden movements of the soul which are
followed by pleasure and pain, and which have no moral
worth because in themselves they are not objects of a choice
– lust, anger, fear and boldness, emulation and envy, joy,
love and hatred, pity.[2] The passions, then, are not in themselves good or bad ; what makes them so is their modality,
their " how." Thus, it is as bad not to be annoyed enough
by some things as it is to be too much annoyed by others. It
is this reasonable and right " how " which is established by
prudence, and virtue and vice lie in the manner, acquired by
a habit, in which we " behave in respect of " our passions and
" make our choice " in respect of them. The " quiddity " of
ethical virtue will consist in " choosing " and " aiming, by
preference, at the mean suitable ($\tau\grave{o}$ $\delta\acute{e}ov$) in respect of our-

[1] E.g., vi. 2 ; 13, 1144 a 1 to end.
[2] *Rhet.*, ii. 1–17, contains a very interesting analysis of the passions. Art is, in
certain conditions, a means to " purify " or purge the soul of them ($\kappa\acute{a}\theta a\rho\sigma\iota s$) by
giving it " relief accompanied by pleasure " (*Poet.*, 6, beg. ; *Pol.*, viii (v), 1342 a 4-14).

selves " and the circumstances, " as it is determined rationally, or as the judgement of the prudent man would determine
it "—the mean short of or beyond which " one misses the
aim " and commits a fault. Therefore the good will " which
aims straight at it has only one mode." That mean, which
can be missed in a thousand ways and hit in one alone, is
therefore like a roof-ridge, a " summit." [1]

It is no light matter to determine the mean in every
particular case. We should note, too, that it would be absurd
to hope to find one always. Sometimes one is in the presence
of an excess, like foolhardiness, or of a defect, like cowardice,
or of the mean itself, like courage. Nor will one ask what is
the right measure in the case of certain acts like murder or
adultery, which are bad in themselves. Lastly, one must
reckon with the poverty of language, which prevents one
from giving a clear, exact name to the extremes or to the mean.
What is important, then, is chiefly the method by which we
shall determine the virtues. Aristotle sometimes considers
passions or actions and their varieties in respect of the object,
and sometimes pleasures and pains. It is impossible here to
follow him through all the precise, concrete details of an
analysis which throughout bears witness to his anxiety to
keep in contact with moral experience. A few remarks may
suffice. The extremes, being contraries and themselves
relative to contraries, are at once excess and defect. For
instance, according as you are considering the acquisition or
the use of wealth, avarice and prodigality are at the same time
a too much and a too little. So, too, with justice ; injustice is
either the action which causes the injury or the injury
sustained. More, in this case even the mean varies, according
as the " equality " between the too much and the too little is
a proportional (geometrical) equality, that of " distributive
justice " (τὸ διανεμητικόν), or an arithmetical equality, that
of " corrective " justice (τὸ διορθωτικόν), and justice " of
exchange," commutative justice.[2] With justice, the most
important of the virtues of social life is friendship, with which
Aristotle deals at great length, as an especially important
example (Nic. Eth., viii.-ix.). His discussion also contains
(ix. 8) penetrating reflections on the place of " self-love " and
the egoistic sentiments in morality.

[1] ii. 2, 1104 a 10–13 ; 4 ; 5 ; 6 to 1107 a 7.   [2] ii. 6–9. Justice is discussed in bk. v.

The " composite man " is not, however, man in the perfection of his nature. Therefore ethical virtue, which for him is, under the control of prudence, all virtue, is not the only virtue. Nor is the happiness which can result from it the greatest happiness. The greatest happiness must lie in the excellence or virtue of what is best in man, namely, pure thought (νοῦς). For the inferior has the reason for its being in the superior, in view of which it exists. Now, pure thought is what is divine in us. Because one is a man, Aristotle asks, must one prefer to live as a man ? Because one is a mortal, must one prefer to live as a mortal, when one can " make oneself immortal " and is capable of a higher life ? That higher life is the " theoretic " life, the life of speculation or contemplation, whose virtue is " wisdom " or pure thought. Here we are in possession of a dianoetic virtue which can justify itself, free of diversity and uncertainty. For it is relative to the function by which we know the principles, and the knowledge of it is one and unchangeable. So there is no more question of the element of choice, which was inherent in ethical virtue and was the object of prudence. For the contingency implied by choice, the possibility of not preferring the preferable, was an evil. The only choice now is to submit oneself obediently to the necessity of reason.

This life, the complete achievement of the " proper work " of man, is the happiest possible, and is the only life which is fully " practical," for it is a life of leisure, a " scholastic " life (σχολαστικός), leisure being the immanent end of activity, complete in itself. For the same reason, this life is " self-sufficient " (αὐτάρκης), and only needs not to be hampered. But it will be easier to practise this life if several men living thus " associate " and " work together." In short, the semi-monastic life of the philosophical school is the ideal of human existence. There work which requires no relaxation raises pleasure to its highest pitch of exaltation and continuity. It is in no way different from the divine life, except that the latter has in absolute fashion what in the former is only relative to ourselves ; the scholastic life is an imitation, dear to the gods, of everlasting bliss. Without a doubt, the perfect city, in Aristotle's eyes, would be that which allowed the Wise to live on earth in the isolation and independence of God. In the meantime, however, we must resign ourselves to a compromise and merely accommodate the average and contingent conditions of experience to reason.[1]

In thus setting a morality of Wisdom and an empirical " ethology " and sociology side by side, Aristotle's ethical theory is a further evidence of the conflict which divides his mind between a concrete realism based on observation and a systematic, constructive intellectualism, which still aims at being realistic. Certainly he sacrifices the second point of view to the former, in the practical part of his teaching ; but whether he believed them reconcilable will be proved by what follows.

B. *Politics.* There is no harm in including in politics the study of the domestic sphere of activity, to which Aristotle attaches the acquisition and use of wealth. Besides, of the *Economics* of our collection, the second book is certainly apocryphal, while the first is only a summary of what is said on the subject in Book I of the *Politics.* But what is now the Introduction may originally have been a separate treatise. For our *Politics* certainly seems to be a collection of independent researches, put together by an editor who may have been Theophrastos, and at an early date it was supposed that the books are not in their natural order. Books VII and VIII seem to follow on III, while IV-VI form one whole, and there are connecting chapters and lacunae. This group of writings, like the others, included special studies, such as the *Manners of Barbarians* and the collection of *Constitutions* (Πολιτεῖαι) of a hundred and fifty-eight Greek and barbarian cities, probably including Carthage and Rome. Our *Constitution of Athens*, discovered by Kenyon in 1891 in a papyrus of the British Museum, is a precious fragment of this collection, which may give an idea of the rest. It is in two parts, one historical, taken from the most varied sources, and one descriptive, apparently based on official records.

Man, we have seen, is a political or social animal. But others of the more intelligent beasts share this characteristic with him—cranes, ants, and especially bees. They are distinct alike from those which live in isolation and those which live gregariously. Now, what makes them political or social creatures is the fact that there is " community of work "

---

[1] x. 7–9 ; vi. 7 ; 9, 1142 a 23 ff. ; 13, 1145 a 6 to end ; *Pol.*, i. 2, 1253 a 27 ff. Cf. *Metaph.*, Λ. 6, 1071 b 17–22 ; 8, 1074 a 35 ; 9, 1075 a 5–11.

among all the individuals. Moreover, since the end of all activity conforming with nature is the good of the creature and the achievement of its essence, the good of the highest creature in the scale, man, must be the greatest good possible. Therefore between the human political society and those of the animals there is only a difference of degree, in the worth of the end and the complexity of the means.[1] The first characteristic of Aristotle's politics is that society is supposed to be natural, not artificial.

Now, first of all, *community*, the specifically political form of natural activity, is not mixture or combination, for the parts in it keep their differential individuality ; it is a " composition " ($\sigma\acute{v}\nu\theta\epsilon\sigma\iota s$). Secondly, the individuals of which the composite is made up must represent different values in it, which correspond to needs and may be a *matter of exchange* between the associates. There is no community, for example, where there are only women, or only men, or only physicians ; a community must be of men and women, or of physicians and farmers. Lastly, between these component individuals, different but united, there must be a *similarity*, which lies in the fact that they unite with a view to " something common," such as procreation or the restoration of health. In other words, there is division of labour and there is unity of labour, as in a ship's crew where every sailor has his own job.[2]

The most important of all possible human communities, the ultimate realization of what is contained in our essence, is the *polis*, the State. Historically, it is derived from a combination of villages, which are themselves combinations of families. But from the point of view of nature, of the essence of things, the converse is the case ; family and village are only stages in the progress of the individual man towards his ultimate end. For these communities are not yet capable of exercising a sufficient constraining force, organized according to justice, without which the habitual practice indispensable to virtue is impossible. The State, on the other hand, is essentially " law " and the establishment of an " order." For, although it is true that the association of individuals for procreation in the family and that of families for food and defence in the village already tend towards the perfection of

---

[1] *Hist. An.*, i. 1, 487 b 33 ff. ; *Pol.*, i. 1, beg.
[2] *Nic. Eth.*, v. 8, 1133 a 16–25 ; *Pol.*, iii. 4, beg. ; 3, 1276 b 6 ff. ; i. 1, beg.

life, and towards its "self-sufficiency" (αὐταρκεία), which is the same thing, yet these communities contain only the potentialities and the "matter" of social nature. This tendency is only achieved and determined in the right measure, neither too much nor too little, in the State, the "form" of that same nature. With the State we go beyond the limits of instincts and needs ; a moral order is constituted ; there is community, not only with a view to living, but with a view to "living well," that is, with a view to the happiness, identical with the virtue, of the whole and of the parts. So far as this common end is lacking, there may be unity of territory, exchange of services, military alliance, commercial union, mutual engagement not to injure one another, but there is no *political* community. But without this last, since he cannot be a god, man would sink lower than the social animals, whereas the existence of moral notions and that of a language which can express them proves that his nature destines him for a richer and worthier sociality than theirs. What makes the specific nature of his sociality, is the fact that it needs a truly civic education, in the widest sense, to prepare and preserve its characteristic, the existence of a moral order determined by law.[1]

Although the State is other than the family, it includes the family in itself, and therefore cannot ignore what goes on in the family or refrain from extending its authority over the moral relations of husband and wife, the education of children, the relation of slave to master, and the properly " economic " phenomena which belong to the family. Now, although the hybrid expression " political economy " is not found in Aristotle's writings,[2] the fact remains that he regards the problem of wealth, considered in relation to the State, as one of especial importance. It seems, indeed, to be the capital problem, the solution of which must determine our views about everything else, and it must be attacked first of all.[3]

A *possession* (κτῆμα) is a " distinct instrument of life," or, what is the same thing, a " distinct instrument of activity." *Property* (κτῆσις) is a whole collection of such instruments. They are not the same as the " instruments of production "

---

[1] *Pol.*, i. 1, 1252 b 27–30 ; 2, 1253 a 7–18, 30, and end ; iii. 1, 1274 a 36–8 ; 9, 1280 a 31 ff. ; 16, 1287 a 16–24 ; *Nic. Eth.*, x. 10, 1180 a 14–22.
[2] It is found in the apocryphal bk. ii of the *Economics*.
[3] *Pol.*, i. 7, 1256 a 12 ; 13, 1260 b 8–20 ; v (viii). 9, 1310 a 12–25 ; viii (v). 1, beg.

(ποιητικά), which are tools, properly so called ; for their end is specifically " use " or " activity." The study of property or wealth (κτητική, χρηματιστική in the wide sense) gives the first place to the acquisition and possession of the foodstuffs necessary to life, in relation to the various kinds of life—hunting, fishing, stock-breeding, agriculture, and even brigandage and piracy. In all these cases, even if the activity is not always " spontaneously productive," at least it is derived from nature. This primitive form of property constitutes the natural and normal form of wealth, because, although it does not exclude " laying up provisions," it is limited by the actual end to whose requirements it answers. For wealth is " a finite quantity of economic and political instruments." But with *exchange*, not, more generally, of services, but of *wealth*, there ceases to be an exact and direct relation between the end and the things which serve to bring it about. It is true that in the elementary form of barter, which survives among some savage peoples, this relation may continue to exist. But, since barter implies that the social group, having grown larger, a village instead of a family, is no longer sufficient to itself, we are already on the verge of an abnormal " chrematistic." For the principle of this deviation lies in a new extension of the group. More things are needed, and have to be imported ; more are produced than are consumed, and have to be exported. The transition from natural economy to monetary economy is the effect and the sign of this deviation, which causes the need for coin to arise.[1]

Thus it was the exchange of wealth which led to the determination of *value* (ἀξία, τιμή). No doubt, everything which is useful to a man is valuable to him. But he does not need to measure his wealth until the day when he undertakes to exchange it. Value is measured, in proportion to utility, by comparing the labour of production. Corn and a pair of shoes both answer needs, and the former will be to the latter what the farmer's labour is to the cobbler's. In the case of barter, so much corn is worth so many pairs of shoes. But when barter has become impossible, it is more convenient to express the value of utility by money, which is thus " a kind of unit of measure " of values, a " middle term " between different values, a " common factor in the exchange of utilities." [2]

[1] *Pol.*, i. 8–9. [2] *Nic. Eth.*, v. 8, 1133 a 5-b 28 ; *Rhet.*, i. 7, 1364 a 23–30.

Aristotle carefully distinguishes between the different forms of this perverted economy. First, there is *trade in goods* (τὸ ἀγοραῖον), where buyers and sellers fix the price of goods on the market, and all the branches and sub-branches of trade —retail trade, hawking, wholesale trade, transport by land and sea, warehousing. Then there is *trade in money and usury* (τοκισμός), a signal example of the perversion of " chrematistic," for it is monstrous that money, a purely conventional thing, should " breed money " and so imitate the productive work of nature or art. Another example of this perversion is *salaried labour*, an important point to which we shall return presently. Industry, as soon as it ceases to be merely agriculture or stock-breeding, also becomes artificial and abnormal—even the exploitation of mines or forests. But what is most important, is that this perversion brings with it a general deterioration of social life. As money ceases to be a symbol and becomes a separate end, and industrial production seeks its end in itself and not in the satisfaction of real needs, it follows that the end will no longer be the life which is happy in the realization of moral excellence, but the life of pleasure, and that, the means having been transformed into ends, it will become impossible to assign an ultimate end to the means. Thus, the desire to acquire has no longer any limits. That is why Aristotle is hostile to industry but is in favour of the agricultural State, where the source of production is natural and limited to needs, and trade is reduced to a minimum. That State alone can, if properly governed, approach the ideal of the State which is self-sufficient and which must therefore remain small in order to satisfy the requirements of a closed economy, without imports or exports.[1]

Very significant evidence of Aristotle's state of mind is afforded by his attitude to the problem of labour and to that of population. First, the population—at least the free population—must remain almost constant, and proportionate to the extent of the territory and to the food-supply. Otherwise pauperism and the subversive tendencies of which it is the principal cause will become general, internal cohesion will be destroyed until the law cannot make its influence felt, and the State will be unable to suffice to itself.[2] Secondly,

[1] *Pol.*, i. 10–11 ; 4, 1254 a 1–8 ; iv (vi). 4, 1291 a 4 ff. ; vii (iv). 4, end, and 5, beg.
[2] ii. 6, 1265 a 38-b 16 ; 7, 1266 b 9-14 ; vii (iv). 4, 1326 a 5 to end ; 16.

" workman's labour " (βαναυσία) is regarded as degrading to the human being. The handicraftsman, mechanic, and labourer are examples of the *banausos*, the man who is dominated by his task and the pay which he expects from it. This would also be the case, we should note, with a brain-worker, if he was so much the slave of his special subject and (like the Sophists) of the demands of his clients that he no longer knew leisure or freedom of thought. Aristotle regrets that workmen, merchants, and farmers can be free citizens, and in his ideal State only slave workers are admitted.[1]

Therefore Aristotle's position on the question of slavery, his opposition to the theory that it is an unnatural state, is based on profound reasons. For him, the slave is a possession, but a living possession, an instrument, but an animate instrument among mere tools, as a pilot has a steersman with his rudder. The slave is superior to the other instruments, in that he does not only serve for doing one thing or another, and, if he does not directly affect activity itself, he is truly an auxiliary of it. Lastly, while he is like an organ to the subject of the activity, that is, to his master, he is at least a separate organ, unlike the organs of the body.

But how can one justify that a human being should be thus reduced to belonging to another instead of to himself ? By the right of war ? But that is a conventional right, often derived from an initial injustice. By nature, which made some men inferior to others, thereby destining them to be the instruments by which their betters act ? Now, that is just what the barbarians are in relation to the Greeks ; they are their slaves by vocation. There are, Aristotle says, other examples of this natural subordination—that of the body to the soul, of the wife to her husband, of the domestic animal to man. Slavery is, then, a particular case of the " despotic " relation, and the slave is to his master what the plough-ox is to a farmer. Like the ox, he has no reason, except what is implied in sensation, and no deliberative will. He is only valuable for his physical constitution, which is not even that of a free man. Moreover, if a shuttle could be made to run on the loom automatically (absurd supposition !), one would not need a slave worker to throw it. Lastly, the master's right is a moral and even a metaphysical right. He is the

[1] iii. 4, 1278 a 6–9, 17–21 ; vii (iv). 9, 1328 b 39 ff. ; viii (v). 2, 1337 b 11 to end.

good, the end, and the sole reason of the relation connecting him with the slave ; he is really the whole with a view to which the part, which is only a part, exists.

Consequently, in spite of some ambiguous expressions, Aristotle cannot allow that there is " community," in the exact, defined sense of the word, between the two. Although they complement one another, they have no common aim. One is an end, while the other is a means and a chattel. There is, therefore, no room here for a moral relation. What justice does a ploughman owe to his ox or a workman to his tools ? A possession, however useful, cannot become a " member " of the political association, and slaves united among themselves could not form such an association, being only means. Yet, in relation to his end, which is his master, the slave has his own " virtue," whereas in Aristotle's eyes there is no virtue in the handicraftsman, the monstrous product of abnormal " chrematistic," the " specialized slave " without a master. So Aristotle's economic ideal seems to be an association of land-owners, having slaves and foreigners to work at all the industries necessary to their leisure, and exchanging their products direct, all free industry and trade being abolished.[1]

For him, therefore, the capital problem of politics is a practical problem, that of the organization of the State (τὸ πολίτευμα) or its constitution (πολιτεία, πόλεως τάξις).[2] He is opposed to plans of radical reform, and we know that he criticized Plato's at length,[3] especially in respect of the abolition of the family and private property. These measures would not make the State as united as possible ; on the contrary, they would rob it of a natural bridle to the passions and a stimulus to activity. He also condemns every exaggerated attempt to reinforce the principle of a constitution, whatever it may be ; a prudent opportunism, composed of concessions and hypocrisy, seems to him the best method of government. Besides, the question is not so much, who shall have the power, as how wealth shall be distributed. Equal distribution is impossible, and before you can make one in proportion to worth you must find a criterion by which to

---

[1] *Pol.*, i. 2, 1252 b 5–12 ; 3–7 ; 13, 1260 a 2–24 ; vii (iv). 8, 1328 a 28–37 ; 9, 1328 a 37 ff. ; 10, 1330 a 24 to end. Cf. *Nic. Eth.*, viii. 13, 1161 a 32 ff.
[2] iii. 6, beg.   [3] E.g., ii. 1–4.

determine worth. Yet, if you want a stable State, it is essential to regulate equality or inequality of wealth, and correlatively of power, among the citizens. The form of polity varies with the manner in which this problem is solved. The principle of democracy is " arithmetical equality " in respect of power, implying an equalization, or at least a neutralization of differences, of wealth. All other systems are based on inequality, either of birth, with the principle of heredity, in certain monarchies and oligarchies, or of strength or wealth, in most oligarchies, or of personal worth, in the sense of virtue, in aristocracies.[1] Since the existing governments in Greece are democracy and oligarchy, Aristotle chiefly tries to establish an ingenious compensation between honours or employments and allowances or taxes, so as to deal lightly with the rich in democracies and with the poor in oligarchies. He controls and limits ownership even more than Plato did in the *Laws*, he constitutes a national property, and he restricts the power to dispose freely of one's goods and the right to bequeath them. In sum, in politics as in morality, he seeks to realise a just mean. Therefore the preponderant position must be given to the middle class. Moreover, if the data of the problem are economic, the solution is, in his eyes, chiefly moral. Although education is always made appropriate to a given political constitution, it must counterbalance its vices, by combating the unchecked play of desires and unbridled individualism.[2]

How far do the various constitutions satisfy these general requirements ? Aristotle says that there are three natural types of government—kingship, aristocratic oligarchy, and republic (πολιτεία in the strict sense), according as the sovereignty is in the hands of one man, of the few, or of all, and according as its essence is authority, worth, or freedom. All three are " right " if the object of the governors is " the common interest," but " defective " if their object is " personal interest." Hence there are three corresponding " deviations " —tyranny, oligarchy of wealth, and demagogy, which carry the normal principle to its absolute extreme and have as their essence, respectively, despotism, plutocracy, and licence or arbitrary power in the interest of the poor. Here we clearly

[1] Especially vi (vii). 2–3 ; iv (vi), 1293 a 12 to end.
[2] *Nic. Eth.*, v. 4–5 ; *Pol.*, ii. 7, 1266 b 28 ff. ; 10, 1272 a 12 ff. ; iii. 4, beg. ; 10 ; iv (vi). 11, 1295 b 35 ff. ; v (viii). 8, 1309 a 20 ff. ; vi (vii). 4, 1319 a 6 ff. ; 5, 1320 a 33 ff. ; etc.

recognize the teaching of Plato's *Statesman*. But Aristotle regards even the right types as departures from an ideal constitution, " according to our aspirations," freed by abstraction from all obstacles. Failing it, we shall be content to study historically certain existing governments, their development, and the revolutions which have ruined them, and, " starting from that," we shall determine what could have saved them, and what, consequently, is of a nature to give the State the greatest possible stability—that is, doubtless, as we have seen, a happy compromise between oligarchy and democracy.[1]

Interesting as it is for its wealth of evidence, Aristotle's *Politics* at the same time shows a strong tendency to systematize in the abstract. Whatever empirical adjustments his instinctive opportunism may inspire, this tendency prevented him from seeing properly the great events which were happening or brewing before his eyes in the Greek world. His eyes, like Plato's, were turned on the past, on the small self-centred republic, and he sought its future, blindly, in a reinforcement of that concentration.

5. THEORETIC SCIENCES. The elementary discipline in the order of speculation is mathematics. But Aristotle's mind tended rather to the logic of discourse and to scientific erudition or truly philosophic speculation, and he does not seem to have had the same mastery of the subject as Plato. Although he often makes use of it, it is rather to draw examples from it, or to present the results of an empirical analysis with an outward appearance of simplicity. He is an opponent of the mathematical theory of Xenocrates, and is more interested in the object treated by mathematics, to which, according to one of our catalogues, he devoted a book. In any case, the treatise *On Indivisible Lines* in our collection is not by him, but by Straton or Theophrastos. Our *Mechanics* may be the work of Aristotle which Simplicius mentions together with *Geometrical Books*. No doubt, he was chiefly interested in the physical part of mathematics—optics, harmony, astronomy. He certainly wrote on the last subject, and is said to have entrusted his nephew Callisthenes with the task of collecting the astronomical tables of the Babylonians.

[1] iii. 6–7 ; iv (vi). 1–13.

A. *Physics.* Aristotle makes physics a single science, in which a theoretical, general study of nature may be distinguished from an analytical, special study of natural beings, and in the latter study animate, or living, beings may be separated from others.

The first subject is the theme of the eight books of the *Physics* and the two *On Generation and Corruption.* The first four books of the *Physics* are often described by Aristotle as a treatise *On Principles* and the rest as one *On Movement* (although the seventh, with its double version, seems to be a school text-book, introduced into the collection of "lectures"). The general point of view of the work *On Generation and Corruption* is found again in the second half of the tract *On the Heavens,* in four books, the two first of which treat especially of the stars, and also in Books I-III of the *Meteorology,* the fourth book of which, sometimes attributed to Straton, deals especially with terrestrial nature. Our collection also contains several works which are certainly apocryphal, although some at least may be derived indirectly from Aristotle *On the World,* a work probably of the end of the Ist century B.C., which is interesting as clearly bearing the stamp of the influence of Poseidonios, *On the Breath* (περὶ πνεύματος), *On the Positions and Names of the Winds, On Colours, On the Qualities of Sounds,* the *Problems,* a collection of 262 " Whys," followed by many answers, not all of them about nature, and the *Marvellous Historics,* the most ancient example of the treatises in which rare facts, regarded as inexplicable " paradoxes " of nature, were collected in classes.

(a.) *General Principles of Physics.* The fundamental notion of physics is the notion of *nature, physis.* It is not a soul, but it is something analogous, a principle in virtue of which, " essentially " or " immediately," certain things of themselves commence or cease movements and changes. Nature is a spontaneous art, " immanent in " the thing which is at once its subject and its agent (ἀρχὴ ἐν αὐτῷ ᾗ αὐτό), without any distinct, outside cause being necessary (ἀρχὴ ἐν ἄλλῳ). It is something like a physician who heals himself, with the difference that in that case the coming together of the morbid state and the curative action is purely accidental, and not essential to the being in question.[1] What chiefly distinguishes the nature

---

[1] E.g., *Phys.*, ii. 1, all the beginning ; *Metaph.*, Λ. 3, 1070 a 7 ff.

of Aristotle from that of the Physicists is that it is not only matter, the formless subject and necessary seat of future determinations ; it is also, and chiefly, form, inseparable from its matter as snubness from a nose, and end, an essence which requires and effects its own achievement. For nature, like human art, is "thought directed at an end " (τὸ ἕνεκά του καὶ ἀπὸ διανοίας), "providence " (προνοοῦσα) without deliberation or choice, finality by the attraction of a good which is to come yet is anterior in the order of being. In its work nothing is " in vain " (μάτην) or random or an " episode," unconnected with everything else, or lack, or absence of measure ; for, having good for its end, it is irreconcilable with infinity.[1]

The movement which, for all that exists " by nature " (φύσει), is as an " immortal and unceasing life " is not merely movement in the strict sense ; it is all " natural passing from one state to another," all change (μεταβολή). Now, for such a passing there must be a " matter capable of being one of these states and the other." Therefore the change is " from what is potentially (δυνάμει) to what is actually " (ἐνεργείᾳ). More precisely, the change or movement is an " imperfect action," the very action " of what is potentially, in so far as it is potentially." Thus, so long as an edifice is being built and is not completed, movements are going on which will change the possibility of an edifice into a reality. Therefore movement requires something " mobile," whose mobility it makes actual, and a " mover," which is within the mobile thing in the case of the natural movement which is the object of physics. For otherwise movement is " against nature " or " forced." This does not mean that an outside cause is not sometimes necessary to remove the obstacles which oppose that movement, as in the case of the tendency (which is, however, in accordance with nature) of bodies having weight to go downwards. It is none the less true that in every moving thing there are (i) a privation of movement in fact by the side of the possibility of being moved, and (ii) an immanent and truly motionless form, which is called a " mover " because it turns that potentiality of movement into a real movement. Consequently, movement is nothing

[1] *Phys.*, ii. 2, 194 a 12–14 ; 5, 196 b 21 ff. ; 8, 199 a 30–2 ; *De Caelo*, ii. 4, end ; 9, end ; 11, beg. ; etc.

apart from that " composite " of matter and form, that is, apart from things which " act and are affected." There is no " movement of movement," no speed except that which is expressed by the speed or slowness of a moved mobile thing. There is no trace of the point of view of orthodox kinematics in Aristotle's mechanics, and he has no idea of a composition of movements other than the play of acting substantial forces. So, too, we shall not say that a thing moves when, in consequence of the movement of its correlative, it changes its state or place ; " there is no movement of relatives." Lastly—a conception very characteristic of Aristotle's dynamics—the continuation of the movement of a projectile after it has ceased to be in contact with the mover is explained by a transference, renewed in a discontinuous manner, of the original impulse to the space traversed by the moving thing. By a phenomenon comparable to magnetic action, an aptitude to move is awakened in that space. That aptitude decreases with distance because of resistances which lie in the mass of the moving thing, namely, its natural weight. Aristotle is very far from the law of inertia.[1]

With movement and change in general several other important notions are connected. First of all, they are *continua*, not indivisible totals. A continuum is something consecutive or something contiguous, the boundaries of whose parts not only lie side by side so as not to be outside one another, but " make one." [2] Secondly, they get this continuity from the extended " size," whether it be full or not, which is their seat all through or the place of the trajectories, and they in their turn communicate it to time, which expresses their development without end. Extension, vacuum, time, and infinity are fundamental notions of physics.[3]

Now, what is interesting in extension is not the vague localization of a thing in that " common place," or universal, which is the whole world, but the determination of the " special place " of that thing. Moreover, it is certain that, in the universal place of the world, there are " natural places," an above and a below, and, in relation to them, a right and a left. These are not merely parts of a homogeneous space ;

[1] *Phys.*, iii. 1, 200 b 28 ff. ; 201 a 8 ff. ; iv. 13, 222 b 16, 21 ; v. 1, 225 a 1 ; 2, beg. ; 4, 228 b 26 ff. ; vi. 5, beg. ; viii. 4 ; 5, esp. 258 a 1 ; 10, 266 b 25 ff.
[2] v. 3, 226 b 21 ff.=*Metaph.*, K. 12, 1068 b 26 ff.
[3] *Phys.*, iv. 11, 219 a 10 ff.

they are specific local " properties," the formal essence of which is, for the two extremes, to be the abode of fire and earth, and, for the middle, to be that of air and water. So space appears to be bound up with things. But it is not a thing. Nor is it, as Plato thought, formless matter, for it sets bounds, nor form, for then it would be inseparable from the thing. Yet, although it is not a thing, it is a size, a real size, not a purely intelligible one, and, although it is not that which contains other entities (for then it would itself have to be contained), it is a " container." It must be defined as " the first limit of the container, immediately contiguous to " the contained and not forming a continuum with it. It is a motionless limit. It may be comparable to a pail, but the pail is at least a place which can be moved about. Yet it is a limit which can move on itself without changing its place, as is proved by the example of the First Heaven, which is the limit contiguous to the universe which it envelops. So space is both bound to things and independent of them, and in such a way that they move in it, just as a pail remains what it is when the water has been emptied out of it and air fills it instead. In relation to space, then, movement is (as Plato said) a phenomenon of " replacing " (ἀντιπερίστασις); cold, wet exhalations, for example, " take the place " of hot, dry ones, and *vice versa*, or, as Straton says, the fish and the water in which it moves take each other's place in turn.[1]

So vacuum is not, as the Atomists thought, the fundamental condition of movement and change. On the contrary, it would make movement incomprehensible. For if place had no natural local property, what reason would there be for a body to move in any direction ? How, too, should we explain the fact that its movement grows quicker as it comes near its " natural place ? " If you thus do away with the proper dynamic activity of nature, you will not be able to substitute mechanism even in the order of " forced " movements, for they are only an artificial diversion of natural movements. Moreover, since movement can only be conceived as the relation of two opposing substantial forces, active and passive, and since, by hypothesis, vacuum has no force of resistance, the moving thing would move in it with infinite speed, or in no time ; and also two moving

[1] iv. 1–5.

things of different weights would cover the same distance at equal speed. This would be as much as to deprive bodies of their own weight, that natural property which determines the acceleration or, where the impulsion comes from outside, the slowing-down of their movement. It is, then, on a substantial quality, and not on " mass," that Aristotle's mechanical theory makes " force " depend. Moreover, vacuum, being defined as the absence of all content, is contradictory to the very nature of place, the qualitative limit of a real content. Lastly, rarefaction and condensation, which some people believe to be unexplainable without vacuum, are likewise qualitative modifications of substance, but modifications which change its size.[1]

The qualitative tendency of Aristotle's physics becomes still more marked when he considers the dependence of *time* on movement. Movement is, above all things, a covering of distance ; the moving thing goes from a point behind to a point in front. Now, these two terms, considered in their succession and as a " before " and an " after," are time. Time is not movement, but " something of movement," a property of what is itself a property of the mobile thing. This property of a property has, moreover, a definitely subjective quality. For without the soul, which reckons the successive moments of movement and is alone capable of doing so, there would be neither duration nor time, because then there would be no consciousness of change, as in the case of the legendary Sleepers of Sardinia, who thought that the moment of their falling asleep and that of their waking were the same. So time is created by thought as " the number of movement in respect of ' before ' and ' after '." This creation gives time its own reality ; for the instant of " now " ($\tau\grave{o}$ $\nu\hat{v}\nu$), which merely separates past from future, is nothing more than the " limit " of a perceived duration. Also, being something other than the two instants which bound it, time is distinct from movement ; it is the same everywhere and for all movements, neither faster nor slower. But it shares in the double eternity of movement, and is therefore eternal, infinite in its past as in its future.[2]

This statement raises the problem of the *infinite*, and great

---

[1] iv. 6–9 ; viii. 5, 250 a 8 ff. ; 9, 265 b 13 ff.
[2] iv. 10–14 ; viii. 1–2 to 253 a 2.

difficulties with it. For Aristotle regards the infinite as nothing more than "the possibility of dividing and subdividing without end." It is, then, the absence of limitation, that is, of form, in the continuum, what there is negative and "vanishing" in it, its endless divisibility. Far from being a thing, it is "that outside which there is always something," that which is always unfinished and imperfect, in contrast to the perfect, which is the finite. It is true that it is like movement ; both, "like a fight or a day," have all their being "in their perpetual becoming." But, whereas movement goes towards its term, "privation" is always bound up with that potentiality, the infinite. So, when Aristotle condemns "infinity of composition," he means to condemn every claim to "realize" the infinite ($\dot{\omega}\varsigma$ $\dot{\alpha}\phi\omega\rho\iota\sigma\mu\acute{e}\nu o\nu$), in size, in movement, or in generation (for, without being infinite, generation can be circular). It is, therefore, surprising that, alone of all physical continua, time is infinite, and still more so that it should get that infinity from movement, of which it is the number ; for movement is not infinite, nor is number, because it is impossible "to finish the course covered by the infinite." Yet there is an infinite movement, and it is a perfect movement—that of the First Heaven. Why is it perfect, although infinite ? Because it is an absolute unity and not a discontinuous series of movements ; because it describes a circular trajectory, on which it is impossible to distinguish starting-points and end-points ; because, lastly, it is a movement of which there is no number. Therefore the time which corresponds to infinite movement is a time which is neither distinction nor number ; for divided time "neither contains nor measures eternal things in so far as they are eternal," that is, the stars in so far as they move with the circular movement.[1] So the fundamental generalizations of physics cannot be determined without introducing other generalizations, which concern the system of the world, and even ontology.

Aristotle distinguishes several kinds of movement and change. Moreover, movement itself is, to speak strictly, a kind of change ; it is a passing in the thing "from one contrary to another." Now, there are various kinds of being, which are the categories. Therefore there should be as many kinds of movement. But there will be none corresponding to the

[1] iii. 4–8 ; iv. 12, 221 b 3–7 ; viii. 6–9.

categories of action and affection or of relation, for in that case there would be either movement of movement, or movement without movement, which, as we have seen, Aristotle considers unreasonable. We must also leave substance on one side, at least for the moment, and time, which is a property of movement, and some minor categories. So we have left movement in quantity, or increase and decrease, movement in quality, or alteration (ἀλλοίωσις), and movement in place, locomotion, " transference " (φορά). Of these kinds, which Plato had already partly distinguished,[1] the last is implied by the two others ; for alteration to take place, the agent must approach the affected, and in increase and decrease the body, changing in size, must change in place, but never beyond a certain term. Similarly alteration, even if it occurs at once and " all over," like freezing, modifies the thing's qualitative constitution only within certain limits. This is because the locomotion supposed by these finite movements is in a straight line, and is compelled to recommence unceasingly. Now, if movement is to be really continuous and one, there must be a perfect locomotion, without beginning, middle, or end—in fact, circular.[2]

Connected with this first condition, and therefore with the movement of the First Heaven, is a process which plays an important part in physics, and which Aristotle usually regards as the fourth kind of movement—" generation and corruption," or coming into being and passing away (γένεσις, φθορά). A thing begins or ceases to exist. But that passing from not-being to being, or vice versa, takes place between contradictories, not between contraries. It is not therefore strictly a movement. In any case, therefore, the circle of generations mentioned above can only be a broken reflection of the circular movement ; and, if the process is capable of a certain continuity, it is certainly not in its form or its essence. Besides, Aristotle has the greatest difficulty in exactly defining this important essence. Between relative generation, or alteration, where the subject persists and becomes other in quality, and absolute generation, where the subject gives place to another subject, which, however, the first already was potentially, there seems to be only a difference of degree. In the presence of the facts, Aristotle himself

---

[1] *Theaet.*, 181 c-d ; *Parm.*, 138 b-c. See also above, p. 229.
[2] *Phys.*, v. 1–2 ; viii. 7–8.

endeavours to soften the rigidity of the structure of his own scholastic teaching. That is shown also in his study of mixture. Mixture is more than mere aggregation, for it gives birth to a new body ; yet it is not corruption of the elements, for, if they lose their own nature, they keep it potentially and only " alter " one another. Nor is it a generation for the resulting " mixed thing," for, even if this latter is a new substance, at least it never has, like a living creature when born, specifically distinct parts, adapted to different functions ; on the contrary, all its parts will be like one another and the whole—that is, it will be homoeomerous.[1]

Natural changes or movements being such, the physicist may consider their *cause* from different points of view.. A first superficial distinction can be made between immanent causes and external causes. In the first rank of these latter is the " motive " or " efficient " cause, " that from which the movement comes " ($\tau\grave{o}$ $\acute{o}\theta\epsilon\nu$). We explain the existence of a child by its parents, and that of a quarrel by an insult. So, too, we explain by an external cause when we say with a view to what or for what something happens. You go walks in order to keep well ; that is causality of the end or object ($\tau\grave{o}$ $o\hat{v}$ $\acute{e}\nu\epsilon\kappa a$). But we can also explain by a principle inside the thing itself—either that from which it springs or the materials of which it is made ($\tau\grave{o}$ $\acute{e}\xi$ $o\hat{v}$—seed for the plant, bronze for the statue), or as the chief part and " that without which " ($\tau\grave{o}$ $o\hat{v}$ $o\grave{v}\kappa$ $\acute{a}\nu\epsilon\nu$), or necessary condition (the heart for the animal, the foundations for the house). This is, in general, the material cause. But, if we go deeper into this distinction, we see that the outwardness of the two first causes is purely apparent, and that what makes them causes and principles of explanation has been neglected. For an efficient cause is a cause because it is a part of the essence of its effect, and a final cause is a cause because it is that essence itself, considered as a pattern. The walk is part of a good health which aims at perfecting itself, the begetter is contained in the begotten as the type which the latter shall realize, the architect is implied by the idea of the house. Being outside, being before or after—all these distinctions in space or time are valueless except in relation to experience and the preparation of knowledge. In relation to the true order of

[1] *De Gen. et Corr.*, i. 2–4 ; 10 ; ii. 10.

nature, or of art as an image of nature, all that matters is the order of rank of notions and their dependence on the whole essence. That essence is the end, and the concatenation of determining antecedents is merely a translation, in the reverse direction, of the order in which analysis of that essence reveals the attributes which make it up. In short, it is an immanent causality that the two forms of external causality reveal, more or less immediately ; it is " causality of form " or of " idea." The quiddity of the thing, its nature or own function, is its true reason for being, and in what we call cause and effect there is only a difference of point of view about the undivided unity of the essence.[1]

There is, however, as we have seen, another immanent cause—matter. Consequently, Aristotle does not regard physical causality as purely conceptual. Indeed, matter is a *reality*. It is negation and " privation " of the future form, but it " possesses " the contrary form which will be followed by the future form. It is the permanent subject of what changes and the substance of the modifications (τὸ ὑποκείμενον). Have we here, not alteration, but generation or corruption, *subjects* which come into being or pass away ? In that case, it will be noted that these subjects are " composites " (σύνολον), that the old and the new still have a common basis, whether it be a matter, which is first one composite subject and then becomes another, or a necessary condition. The matter of water becomes that of fusible things, the matter of marble becomes that of the statue, the female principle becomes the embryo, the food becomes nourishment for an animal. Moreover, except, perhaps, in the case of differences of sex and those dividing beasts from men (for beasts and women are degenerations of men), the matter is the principle of the *individuality* only, of the purely " numerical," not " specifically " differential plurality. Lastly, just because it is indeterminate and ambiguous, the *power* of becoming or doing this or that, which is proper to matter, is not realized in all cases or for ever, or it is realized wrongly ; from matter come contingency, the imperfections and perishableness of our works, and the errors of nature.[2]

[1] *Phys.*, ii. 3 = *Metaph.*, Δ. 2 ; cf. 1, 1013 a 7–10, 16–19.
[2] *Phys.*, ii. 8, 199 a 33 ff. ; *De Caelo*, i. 9, 278 a 15 ff. ; 12, 283 b 4 ff. ; *Metaph.*, E. 2, 1027 a 13 ff. ; I. 9, end ; *Part. An.*, iv. 10, 686 b 2 ; *Gen. An.*, i. 2, 716 a 18 ; ii. 3, 737 a 27 ; iv. 8, 777 a 5 ff. ; 10, 778 a 6 ff.

But, when matter thus seems to have a force of resistance of its own, we are justified in asking whether it is not rather energy which is lacking in the agent. Everywhere else, in any case, it is plain that matter is nothing in itself and apart from form. A certain form requires a certain matter and cannot accept any other. " The carpenter's art cannot descend to flutes "—that artistic truth exactly symbolizes what happens in nature. Matter and form are therefore correlatives, which, in the natural order, are never separated, and they are not interchangeable correlatives. A certain determination is correlative to a certain indetermination, a privation to a possession, an activity (ἐνέργεια) to a potentiality, and *vice versa*. So a physical reality cannot be defined by the matter alone nor by the form or end alone, but by the matter together with the form. So, too, to know a physical cause is to know what is the quiddity of the natural composite which you are studying, and, since this quiddity is the ordered whole of the qualities of the composite, it is to know what their order is, rising from those which are antecedents or material conditions to the essence which holds them together and is their end.[1] So the cause is always inside the thing ; to explain the thing is to analyse the notion of it. Therefore, in so far as it is science and not a preparation for science, Aristotle's physical theory does not accept the consideration of experience.

An ordered series of causes—that, in the last analysis, is what constitutes the determinism of nature. In the scale of forms, the rank of each is marked by the richness of its content, that is, by the number of essences which it rules and unites. Moreover, since matter never exists except in the composite, and as a potentiality of that of which the composite is the activity, every composite will serve as matter to a form in whose essence it is contained ; the scale of matters corresponds to that of forms. We must, therefore, mark the degrees of rank in these two scales. Certain causes are proximate, " nearest," immediate or " first " in relation to the thing in its individuality. Others are more remote, but they too are " first," as being fundamental conditions—hot and

---

[1] *Phys.*, i. 7, 191 a 4–12 ; 9, 192 a 3–6 ; ii. 9 ; *Metaph.*, Δ. 4, 1015 a 3–11 ; Z. 9, 1034 a 30 ff. ; H. 1 ; 4, 1044 a 25 ff. ; Θ. 6–9 ; *De An.*, i. 1, 403 a 29 ff. ; *Part. An.*, i. 1, 646 a 29 ff.

cold, which are more remote than the matter of an animal, or the form of man, which is more remote than Peleus, the father of Achilles.[1]

But in neither series can the progression be indefinite. In the order of matter, it stops before total absence of determination. " Primary matter " is a pure abstraction, and cannot be anything else, since, even when united to a form, matter is never knowable in itself, but only " by analogy " with artificial fabrications.[2] In the order of form, the series stops before total determination, and, since form is by itself the real and the knowable, this last term must be that which is most real and must exist wholly *in action, apart from* all which, preceding it, nevertheless depends on it and is explained only by it. Therefore physics, being the science of movement and change, demands a first cause of them, a " first mover." Now, that demand will only be satisfied if the mover is not a moved mover, but a motionless mover, and is eternal, and is unextended. For every force, in Aristotle's view, has an extent for its seat. If the infinite force required to explain incessant movement has its seat in an infinite extent, it follows, in virtue of the theory of projectiles (above, p. 279), that the speed will be infinite and that the movement will take place in no time ; which is absurd. Therefore the first mover must be outside space, as it is outside movement and time. So— an important observation—in the first mover, and in it alone, the efficient cause and the final cause are external causes, and that for the very reason which prevented them from being so really in the order of nature—their identity with the formal cause. For in the first mover the formal cause is separate, not immanent. So even now, and without waiting for " first philosophy," we see that, for the principle of nature and of its movement, even physical theory is compelled to go to a supernatural form, lying outside its own domain.[3]

(b) *Cosmology.* After these generalizations, we can attack the content of physics, first of all leaving out living beings.

The *world,* the universe (τὸ πᾶν), is often called the

---

[1] *Metaph.*, H. 4, 1044 a 20 ff., b. 1 ff. ; 6, end ; Λ. 5, 1071 a 20 ff. ; *Phys.* ii. 3, 195 a 29 ff., b 1 ff. ; *Gen. An.*, iv. 1, 765 b 4 ff.

[2] *Phys.*, i. 7, 191 a 7–14 ; *De Gen. et Corr.*, ii. 1, 329 a 9 to end, and very often ; *Metaph.*, Z. 10, 1036 a 8.

[3] *Phys.*, viii. 5–6 to 259 b 31 ; 10, end ; *De Caelo*, 4, end ; 9, 279 a 28 ff. f. **CXXXIII**, ch. xviii.

" heavens " by Aristotle, since the heavens embrace the " whole " of things. This universal place of natural things and their movements is the first of the " moved movers." It is necessarily single, since the " first mover " is single, and, since the first mover is eternal, the universe has neither beginning nor end. Since there is nothing outside it, it is perfect, and therefore finite, and forms a sphere moving with the most perfect movement, the circular. But, since all directions of rectilinear movement are included in it, a first qualitative diversity is thus manifested in the sphere of the universe—that of *natural places*, which are bound up, as we know, with fundamental oppositions of quality. Above is the place of absolute lightness, below is that of absolute heaviness, and the region between is that of relative lightness and heaviness. So there are four simple or elemental bodies, fire and earth, water and air, which Aristotle also calls the four " matters," for outside them there is only the primary matter. But, in virtue of the same reasoning, there must also be a more perfect matter corresponding to the eternal circular movement. This fifth essence of matter, the ether, allows, therefore, of no contrariety or any kind of change ; it is truly something divine.[1]

In consequence, the universe must be divided into two great regions, profoundly different from each other. In one, movements are perfectly simple, regular, and eternal, and therefore circular. The only indetermination or potentiality which it admits is that of the mobility inherent in the ether, the element of which the bodies in that region are made ; this is what Aristotle calls " local matter " (ὕλη τοπική). Since, moreover, this indetermination is that of an eternal movement, which cannot be other than what it is, the necessity reigning there excludes constraint, because its principle does not lie in conditions imposed by something inferior. This region is the heavens properly so called, and extends from the First Heaven, that of the fixed stars, which envelops the universe, to the moon, the star nearest to us ; it is the region above the moon. The heaven of the fixed stars is the first of the moved movers, that nearest the first mover, an animate and truly divine body. The stars, like it, are animate spherical bodies, whose life and practical activity are, by their impassi-

[1] *De Caelo*, i. 2 ; 7, 275 b 12 ff. ; 8–10 ; ii. 1 ; 3 ; iv. 5, 312 a 30 ; *Phys.*, iii 5.

bility, eternal unchangeability, and superior sufficiency, incomparably excellent. Now, it is the degree of this excellence which, according to Aristotle, should account for all the facts of observation. Thus, since the infinite force of the first mover weakens as it is passed on, and can no longer be communicated to so many mobile things, it is reasonable that there should be fewer stars the farther you go from the sphere of the fixed stars. Or, again, since perfection is no longer realized immediately, it is reasonable that the single revolution of the First Heaven should be replaced by many complicated sidereal revolutions.[1]

All these revolutions must be conceived in the same manner. For the planets are just as motionless as the fixed stars. It is proved, *a priori* and *a posteriori*, that they have no movement of their own, neither rotation on themselves nor circular locomotion. What is moved in a circle is only the transparent sphere which bears the star, although it is impossible to know whether it is moved by the soul of the star, or has a soul of its own, or is moved with the ether and merely guided by the star. The star, being thus conveyed at great speed, grows hot with the motion and becomes luminous. But, whereas all the fixed stars are borne by one single sphere, each planet has its own sphere, or even spheres, as many as are needed to " give the phenomena " attested by observation. Here we recognize the astronomical system of Eudoxos. To account for certain appearances neglected by Eudoxos, a contemporary of Aristotle named Callippos of Cyzicos had raised the number of the spheres to thirty-four. Aristotle further increases the number, but, it seems, for physical reasons, not for the needs of geometrical representation. For his heavens are solid heavens. That being so, if the proper movement of each planetary sphere is not to be affected by that of the sphere immediately surrounding it (which would destroy the unity of this physical system), it is necessary to insert between them as many " compensatory " spheres as are required. There will be twenty-two of these, so that the total number of heavens, contained concentrically in the First Heaven (which is also counted), will be

---

[1] *De Caelo*, i. 9, 279 a 19 ff. ; ii. 1, 284 a 14–16 ; 2, 285 a 29 ; 3, 286 a 9–12 ; 12, 292 a 20 ff., b 1 ff. ; *De Gen. et Corr.*, ii. 11, 337 b 35 ff. ; *Meteor.*, i. 3, 340 b 6 ff. ; *Metaph.*, Θ. 8.

fifty-five, or forty-seven, if the sun and moon are set apart from the other planets and one deducts the heavens lying between Venus and the sun and between the sun and moon.[1]

The sublunary region is far less extensive. The earth is quite a small sphere,[2] and is in the middle, for we see that all bodies having weight tend towards its centre, and it serves as a motionless pivot to the whole system. Being farther away from the first moved mover, this region is very different from the other. In it there is change, the generation and corruption of substances, instead of unchangeable, eternal existence. Instead of things, all animate, which possess their own good immediately or almost so, it contains a majority of inanimate bodies, and even the animate things in it often lack the good at which they aim (diseases and monstrosities), or are obliged to deliberate about it and err in their calculations. So in this region intelligible necessity, which comes from form, is opposed by inferior necessities, which come from matter, not from a perfectly determined matter like that of the sidereal world, but from a matter which is essentially indetermination. Discontinuity will be the rule of movement, even of circular movement. Mere frequency will take the place of absolute regularity. Lastly, this sublunary region is the domain of the contingent, of the accidental and chance. The *fortuitous* ($\tau\grave{o}$ $a\dot{v}\tau\acute{o}\mu a\tau o\nu$) is, for Aristotle, that which occurs exceptionally and without finality in a sphere of activity, such as our conduct or the work of nature, which normally allows of finality. Digging the ground, going to the market-place, going to sea—these are human actions which usually have an end. But happening upon a treasure, meeting your debtor unexpectedly, and being cast up by a storm on Ægina, which was not your destination, are facts of chance, but more especially of *fortune* ($\tau\acute{v}\chi\eta$), good or bad. Now, when speaking of the works of nature, we shall not assert fortune, for want of a possible choice, but merely chance in general, the fortuitous—as in the case of the production of a monster, for nature of itself was aiming at the achievement of a normal being. Fortuitous facts, then, are not facts without a cause,

---

[1] *De Caelo*, ii. 7–8 ; 10–12 ; *Metaph.*, Λ. 8.
[2] Its circumfa1ence is estimated at 400,000 stades, or about 46,000 miles (*De Caelo*, ii. 14, end.

but facts which result from an unforeseen or abnormal coming together of causes. In short, in the sublunary region, the energy of form issuing from the first mover grows steadily weaker ; it is applied to matter with less and less exactness and allows the indetermination of matter free play.[1]

It is, therefore, reasonable that the only elements of this region should be those inferior to the ether. Now, they can be explained, not, as above, in relation to their " natural places," but by qualities relative to the most fundamental of our senses, that of touch. Hot and cold, dry and wet, are opposites which exclude one another, but only in those pairs. So four combinations are possible, which produce dry, hot fire, dry, cold earth, wet, hot air, and wet, cold water. Moreover, the first two qualities are active and the second two passive. Therefore the elements are never apprehended except in these mutual relationships, and can only mingle with or be transformed into one another. So the sublunary world is properly the region of mixtures. But there is an order of rank among these.

Some are temporary manifestations of the preponderance of one element, and are destroyed as soon as formed. Such are all the very various phenomena of the circumterrestrial region, which Aristotle puts together under the name of *meteora* (winds, clouds, rain, snow, hail, ice, rainbow, thunderbolt, lightning, thunder, various celestial fires, shooting stars, comets, Milky Way, etc.) in a group whose constitution was respected for centuries afterwards. The others, which are more stable and are the true mixtures, belong to earth.[2] For, on the one hand, the envelope of the sublunary world is a sphere of fire, or, more exactly, of inflammable matter, which turns with the First Heaven. It surrounds the air, which surrounds the water, which covers the earth. The movement of this envelope heats and dries the air, to which dry, smoky exhalations rise from the earth. At the same time wet, vaporous exhalations rise from the water. The conflict of these two kinds of exhalation and their mutual proportions give rise, by condensations, rarefactions, compressions, ex-

[1] *Phys.*, ii. 4–6 (chance. Cf. *Metaph.*, Δ. 30) ; 8, 198 b 34 ff. ; 199 a 33 ff. ; b 19 ff. ; *Gen. An.*, iv. 3–4 ; *De Caelo*, i. 9, 278 a 28–30.
[2] *De Gen. et Corr.*, ii. 2–3 ; *Meteor.*, iv. 1, beg.

pulsions, and projections, to all *meteora*. Since the hot wetness of the air is transformed by cooling into the cold wetness of water, we understand why the study of springs, rivers, and the sea belongs to meteorology. So does that of earthquakes, because there are hot exhalations in the cavities of the earth which endeavour to escape, to reach their natural place.

The terrestrial mixtures, composites which division does not reduce to their elements, are homoeomerous bodies, some inorganic and derived chiefly from earth (stones, crystals, salts) or chiefly from water (the metals), and some organic, constituting the various organs of animals and plants, or else derived from them, namely the tissues and humours (flesh, blood, sap, bones, viscera in general, marrow, fat, tendons and cartilages, various membranes, horns and nails, hair, secretions and excretions, etc.). Now, to know all these compositions one must make a general study, which is Aristotle's chemistry—the study of the secondary qualities, derived from the dry and from the wet (hard and soft, compact and loose, brittle and viscous, smooth and rough) and the study of the action of heat and cold on those qualities (cooking, with digestion and ripening, dissolution and fusion, putrefaction, etc., and their contraries, rawness, coagulation, induration, etc.).[1]

(c) *Living Things and the Soul.* Living things, in their reproduction and nutrition, in their growth and some in their movement, are the most evident example of the spontaneity which is the definition of nature. The study of life and of the soul which is the principle of it is therefore a chapter of physical science.

It is a considerable part, a third at least, of Aristotle's whole works. Most important is a general treatise *On the Soul*, in three books, with some fragments of another version for the second. Animal morphology, physiology, and embryology are the subject of special treatises—the *History of Animals*, in ten books, the last of which is doubtful, *On the Parts of Animals*, in four books, *On the Generation of Animals*, in five books, *On Walking*, and *On the Movement of Animals*, a contested work. The name of *Parva Naturalia* is used to designate several small special works, some of which are very remarkable

---

[1] For the terrestrial mixtures, cf. *Meteor.*, iv.

—*On Respiration, On Life and Death,* to which the treatise *On Youth and Age* is an introduction, and to which that *On Length and Shortness of Life* is attached, *On Sleep and Waking,* with the *Dreams* and *Divination by Dreams, On Sensation and Sensible Things,* and *On Memory and Recollection.* Treatises belonging to this group were lost at an early date—an *Anatomy,* accompanied by illustrations, *On Nutrition, On Plants.* The work which we have under this last title is a forgery, and so is our *Physiognomics*

We have just seen how the organic tissues and fluids are connected, as mixtures, with elemental conditions. These homoeomerous parts are in their turn material conditions of the anhomoeomerous parts of the living creature, the differentiated " instruments " of his life, which are *organs,* each having its form and its function. Thus equipped with tools in order to live, a body is an *organic* body, or immediately capable of living, which is the end and *raison d'être* of its material conditions. Now, these conditions are the potentiality of a form, life, which makes them actual by using them in relation to itself and so makes the natural body an organism. So there are three degrees : the indeterminate power or potentiality of a matter of life, or its necessary conditions ; the determinate potentiality or habit (ἕξις), the aptitude to live ; and the complete exercise of that aptitude, when it manifests itself by one of its activities and is not benumbed by sleep or inaction. The soul is the second of these degrees, which is the *first* degree of life *in action.* It is therefore defined as " the first actualization of a natural body, which potentially has life." It is not a reality separate from the body, nor is it a body ; but it is " something of the body," its quiddity, by which the body is one living thing or another, and without which it would be a mere aggregate. Their union is the very unity of the " proximate " matter and its form. No doubt, we cannot strictly say that the soul " abides in " its body, " like a skipper in his ship." But it is for the body what sight is for the eye—its aptitude to accomplish its function. As the formal and final cause of the life of the body, too, the soul is the " mover " of the body, and even a motionless mover, but it does not move it continuously. Moreover, since certain of the movements of which it is the cause, such as respiration and nutrition, presuppose conditions outside it, we may say that this motionless mover is never-theless " moved by accident " with the body which it animates.[1]

The soul is not a kind, divided into species, but it is a function which has three modes, arranged in order. At its lowest, and therefore most fundamental, degree, it is *nutritive and generative*, and therefore common to all living things with-out distinction. At a higher degree of determination, it is capable of discerning by sensation the qualities of things, and then of bringing about in general suitable changes of place, according to its desires and aversions ; at this degree it is *sensitive, appetitive, and motive*, and is common to all animals alike. Its highest function, with a view to which all the others exist, belongs to man alone ; this is the *reasoning function and intellect*. This scale, which also includes intermediate degrees, determines, at least broadly, the natural series of types of living things. For the soul, as a form, is what determines the constitution of the body and the functions of which it is capable. Thus, the lowest of living things, the plants, have organs which are but little specialized, because almost their only vital function is to grow and to produce their seed ; they can reproduce themselves without the distinction of sexes and some are even born by spontaneous generation ; their only movement is upwards ; their life is a sleep without waking ; their corporeal unity is almost that of a mere aggregate, because their soul is of a low form, and, much rather, potentially a number of souls, each of which can, from a cutting of the plant, make another like itself. With a some-what higher soul, very simple animals, sponges and oysters, have similar characteristics, but some rudiments of sensitivity and motivity. Moreover, the embryonic life of the higher animals is, at first, a purely vegetative life, like that of the larva of an insect. Looking at things the other way round, we shall say that the animals are degradations from human perfection ; the more the internal heat decreases and the earthly element predominates, the more they are weighed down, attaching themselves to the ground by many legs, and finally becoming completely fastened to it. This regression takes us as far as the plant, a completely inverted animal, since

---

[1] *Gen. An.*, i. 1, 715 a 8–11 ; 18, 722 b 30–3 ; *De An.*, i. 3 to 406 b 15 ; ii. 1 ; 2, 414 a 19 ff. ; 4, 415 b 8–28 ; *Metaph.*, H. 6, end.

it carries its seed where the animal has its head, and its mouth is its roots.[1]

But in all this (let us make no mistake) there is no suggestion of evolution in time, or from one species into another. The species are eternal, like the earth, the centre of an eternal universe. There is only a static progression of these " forms," which is also continuous. They vary in the wealth of their determinations, and, since each requires an appropriate matter, they give rise to organizations of varying complexity. The end of this progression of nature is the most perfect organization which we know, that of man. Man, therefore, represents the whole plan of nature, which all living things reproduce in various degrees, and often in conditions more favourable to observation. The differences of the secondary plans, thus arranged in stages, lie either in the size or position of an organ or in the qualitative properties of the tissues or humours. But these outward differences do not destroy the unity of a particular plan nor of the whole plan. For among all, and among the varieties of each, there are common features or, failing them, analogies. Organs, tissues, or humours, although differently placed or constituted, may have the same functional relation to the whole. What the wing is to the bird or the hand to man, the fin is to the fish and the claw to the lobster. Since the function of the lungs must be found in the aquatic animals, the gills are analogous to lungs. The hoof is analogous to the nail, the fish-bone to the bone, and so on. The envelope of the foetus in viviparous creatures, the egg of the oviparous, the cocoon of insects are all analogous. For these views Aristotle doubtless owes much to his predecessors. But in organizing their observations into one system, he perhaps deserves to be regarded as the founder of the comparative method in biology.[2]

Other more particular principles are brought into play, more or less explicitly, by Aristotle. Thus, he regards correlations of organs, or their modifications, as " consequences " of the influence of a " dominant " organ, or of a change in

[1] De An., ii. 3 ; Part. An., ii. 10, 655 b 32 ff. ; iv. 10 ; Gen. An., iii. 2, 753 b 27 ff. ; 9, 758 a 32 ff. ; Hist. An., viii. 1 ; etc.
[2] Ioid., and i. 1 ; 16, beg. ; iv. 1 ; Part. An., i. 4–5 ; iv. 5 ; 10 ; Gen. An., ii. 1, 731 b 35 ff. ; 4, 737 b 26 ff. ; etc.

that organ by which the whole biological type is commanded ; such dominant organs are those of generation and nutrition. The adaptation of a part to a special function, e.g. of the mouth to defence, prehension, or only feeding, determines its size and structure. Lastly, if the whole effort of nature concentrates on one part, it is often at the expense of another. But that other part, belonging to a system of correlatives, does not disappear altogether ; it survives in miniature, " by way of indication." [1]

Aristotle's biological writings would be inexplicable if we did not regard them as a *summa*, doubtless prepared by collaborators, of all the knowledge possible for the poorly-equipped investigators of his time. We cannot here make up a balance, even of a summary kind, which we can put all down to his credit. There is, therefore, little use in pointing out certain famous errors, such as the theory that the lungs and gills, by means of air or water, cool the blood which has been heated in the " hearth " of the heart, or the attribution of a similar function to the brain, sensitivity depending mainly on the heart, and so on. What is more important, is the method on which Aristotle conducted his work of systematiza-tion or chose between the hypotheses of his predecessors. Now, it is quite certain that his curiosity was truly scientific ; there is no thing or function in nature but deserves to be studied for its own sake. In studying monsters, as departures from the finality of nature, he showed how even his theory of finality could usefully inspire research. If he often relied on the observations of others, they were at least the observations of specialists—physicians, veterinary surgeons, stock-breeders, hunters, or fishermen. It is possible, too, that he sometimes investigated for himself, for example, the development of the hen's egg or that of the human foetus.[2] But it was inevitable that he should be led by the requirements of his didactical calling, no less than by the postulates of his philosophy, to resolve a number of problems dialectically.

His classification of animals has perhaps been praised rather more than it deserves. Certainly, he saw that the

[1] *Gen. An.*, iii. 1, 749 b 7–9, 750 a 3 ff. ; iv. 1, 764 b 22–5 ; *Part. An.*, ii. 14, 658 a 35 ff. ; iii. 1, 662 a 22–5 ; *Hist. An.*, viii. 2, 589 b 31 ff.
[2] *Part. An.*, i. 5, 645 a 5 ff. ; *Gen. An.*, iv. 1, 764 a 34 ; 3, end ; 4. Cf. Bonitz, *Index Ar.*, 104 a 4 ff., 328 a 13 ff.

determination of groups should be based on essential characteristics, and that these should be judged comparatively, so as to place the groups in a scale. But he certainly did not usually succeed. Although his descriptions of species are sufficiently precise for it to be possible to identify most of the five hundred which he has analysed, it must be admitted that the principles of his classification lack strictness and consistency. In looking for criteria of specific differentiation and position in the scale, he accepts, by the side of truly profound and general characteristics (such as the presence or absence of blood in relation to the degree of vital heat, or the manner of generation),[1] some very superficial characteristics. For example, he distinguishes fresh-water aquatic creatures according as they live in rivers, ponds, or swamps. Sometimes he classifies by the degree of intelligence, so that the ants and bees, which, as insects, are in the lowest rank of the creatures whose lack of blood reveals their imperfection, stand, as social or " political " creatures, almost at the level of man. What makes man a distinct species among the viviparous animals is his upright stature and power to tell right from left. He does not know where to place the monkey, or the bat, or the crocodile (because a saurian must be terrestrial and even troglodytic). He breaks up the group of serpents into oviparous and viviparous, because the viper is, at least in appearance, viviparous. The frog is characterized simply as a swampdweller. And so on.[2] In sum, Aristotle's logical ambition seems to have been overwhelmed by the mass of facts which he tried to systematize.

Of the functions of the animal soul, the most characteristic is the discriminative aptitude manifested by the sensations. According as we place ourselves at the point of view of the object or of the subject, of power (potentiality) or of activity, of indeterminate potentiality or of potentiality determined into a habit or function, and, lastly, of the exercise of that function, we can distinguish : (i) that which is sensible or felt, colour or a colour ($\tau\grave{o}$ $a\grave{\iota}\sigma\theta\eta\tau\acute{o}\nu$) ; (ii) that which is sensitive or that which feels, sight or that which sees ($\tau\grave{o}$

---

[1] Spontaneous generation is ascribed to certain plants, as we have seen, and is also found in animals, e.g., the oyster, the cuttle-fish, and several species of insects and even fish.

[2] See, e.g., Hist. An., i. 1–6 ; ii. 1, beg. ; 15, beg. ; iv. 1, beg. ; Part. An., i. 4, beg. ; iv. 5, beg. Cf. **IV**, 553–65.

αἰσθητικόν, τὸ αἰσθανόμενον), with sensation itself as the activity of the sensitive, seeing in relation to sight (ὄρασις, ὄψις); (iii) the sensorium (τὸ αἰσθητήριον), the eye, for the soul has the organs of its functions in the body. Consequently, if sensation is passivity and alteration of the subject (since the subject is modified by an agent outside itself), it is so only in a particular sense. The sensible, far from destroying a manner of being of the subject, makes it actual. Moreover, the sensible is not taken in like food, the matter with the form, but the sensitive receives the form without the matter, as wax receives the impression without the metal of the die. In short, the sensible becomes felt at the same time as the sensitive becomes sentient, just as the mobile becomes moved at the same time as its mover becomes moving (active verb). Hence the classical formula : sensation is the " common action " of the sensible and the sensitive ; for one single act, Aristotle says, assumes two different quiddities in sensation, e.g. colour and the seeing of colour.[1] This is an example of irreversible correlation.

The nature of sensation being thus defined, we shall distinguish in the sensible, and correlatively in the sensitive, between what is common, what is proper and special, and what is accidental. Thus, if this whiteness here is such-and-such a man, it is an accident for that sensible, and for my sensation, and the latter may be false, judging of something which is not within its province. It is the same, and for the same reason, with the sensation of the " common sensibles " —movement and rest, extension and figure, unity, number and time—which can be perceived in bodies by all the senses without distinction, but especially by sight and touch. Therefore only the special sensations are infallible, when they have as their object their " proper sensible," which is not the object of any other sensation (De An., ii. 16).

The necessary basis of all the special senses, the sufficient condition of a sensitivity and an animal life, is touch, a sense which is but little specialized. It has as its object the contrary qualities of the body as a body, that is, the elemental qualities, hot, cold, dry, wet, etc. But, if they are to be the object of sense, the sense must, first, be a " middle term " between these contraries, capable of discriminating one from the other and

[1] De An., ii. 1, 412 b 28 ff. ; 5 ; 12 ; iii. 2, 425 b 25 ff. ; 8.

of assimilating itself to one or the other. They themselves must also be " middles," neither too weak nor too intense. Moreover, since immediate contact makes sensitive discrimination impossible, touch needs a " medium " which shall both separate the sensible from the sense and unite them. This medium is the flesh, and, since it is part of our body, some people suppose that it is the sensorium of touch. On the contrary, that sensorium, as is right, lies very deep, where the principle of all sensitive and animal life resides, in the region of its central organ, the heart. Lastly, the organ of touch will be, in its contexture, an appropriate mixture of elements—of earth, since earth is the proper matter of vegetative life, and of fire, since the heart is the hearth of animal life.[1]

This analysis holds good for the other senses, of which it will suffice to note the special determinations, which are increasingly complex and rich in intellectuality. Taste, although closely connected with touch and having the same sensorium, is already a middle term between less general contraries, sweet and bitter, and has for its medium a special part of the flesh, the tongue. There is the same kinship between taste and smell (and smelling), as between their sensibles. But here the medium is outside the body, and so it is with hearing (the sense and the action) and with sight and seeing. By the example of the medium of sight, the " diaphanous," we shall understand the part played by the other mediums, which the commentators call *diosmos* and *dieches* (conducting smell, conducting sound). In itself, the " diaphanous " is invisible ; as an indeterminate possibility of sensible light, it is darkness. But if every adverse circumstance is removed, it passes to action under the influence of fire or even of the ether, and instantaneously determines itself as light. If, lastly, it limits itself in bodies of definite shape, it becomes the " carrier of colour." Since, too, there always remains in it a part not actualized, which is darkness, the variously proportioned mixture of black and white will produce seven different colours. The sensoria of these last senses will doubtless be mixtures of elements in relation to their sensibles (air and water, perhaps with fire, for smell), one element being markedly

[1] *De An.*, ii. 11 ; iii. 1, 425 a 3–8 ; *De Sensu*, 2, end ; *De Gen. et Corr.*, ii. 2.

predominant for the higher senses (air for hearing and water for sight).[1]

Above these five special sensitivities, which are the only ones possible, given the qualitative elemental oppositions, there is a " common sense," that is, not special. First, it perceives the " common sensibles." Secondly, since each special sense has its own individuality, it would be impossible to distinguish and compare the sensibles of one and another if there were no higher sense, whose unity was " mean " between two separate genera of special sensibles (e.g. between a taste and a colour), just as the special senses are middles between their contraries. But if this common sense were not implied in different sensations, mediation between them would be inexplicable. So the common sense is, thirdly, " sensation of sensation," what was afterwards called consciousness. So this " first and universal sensitivity," being immanent in all " differentiated sensitivity," effects a synthesis of a hetero-geneous multiplicity, to make of it a world of experience, the various aspects of which it constantly attaches to the subject. This common sense must have a common sensorium, which can only be that of the first sensitivity, and also, it seems, a common middle, the " congenital breath," which has its source in the heart and circulates in " passages " ($\pi \acute{o} \rho o \iota$), by which the peripheric sensoria are connected with the heart.[2]

In addition, when the special senses are impeded or wholly inactive, this consciousness keeps an activity of its own, to which dreams belong, and which connects the sensitive function with the *imaginative function* ($\tau \grave{o}$ $\phi a \nu \tau a \sigma \tau \iota \kappa \acute{o} \nu$) and the memory. The picture given by sense and that given by the imagination ($a \ddot{\iota} \sigma \theta \eta \mu a$, $\phi \acute{a} \nu \tau a \sigma \mu a$), sensitivity and imagina-tivity, or their actions, in any order of sensations, differ only as a " strong " state and a " weak " state, and by their quiddity, but not in themselves. First of all, after the external stimulus has ceased to act, the sensorial movement continues, growing weaker, in the special sensorium and into the common sensorium. Secondly, as these delayed sensations are re-inforced by like sensations, a whole permanent stock of images is formed, and this stock, always in close relation with

---

[1] *De An.*, ii. 10 ; 9 ; 8 ; 7 ; iii. 1, beg. *De Sensu*, 2, does not agree with 5.
[2] *De An.*, iii. 1, 425 a 14 to 2, 425 b 25 ; *De Sensu*, 7, 449 a 16–20 ; *De Somno* 2, 555 a 12–22. Cf. **XXX**, 328–36.

the life of the body, becomes a proper object for the activity of the imagination. Normally, the imagination is never freed, even in dreams, from a corrective reaction of the perception and reasoning, and delirium is an exception. So imagination is the condition, not only of experience (ἐμπειρία) and the intuitive perception which it involves, but even of pure thought, for pure thought can hardly take place without an image to support it. The fact that imagination creates works of art and the fact that it is deliberation and calculation are accidents relative to use, and in the end do not alter the nature of imagination. Its relation to the common sense appears clearly in memory and expectation. For these differ from imagination only in the introduction of a " common sensible," time, without which memory and foresight are only images. Besides, the illusion of the *déjà vu* (where you feel as if your present situation had all happened before) proves that it is the aspect of the image which suggests to us not to refer it to the present. When the habitual " consecutions " according to contiguity, resemblance, or contrariety, already analysed by Plato, do not operate spontaneously, a man sets out in search of the lost trail ; this is " recollection " (ἀνάμνησις). This effort to re-establish the broken continuity of memory is also connected with the deep-seated organic life, so that it sometimes goes on in spite of ourselves, and often attains its object after we have ceased to make it.[1] All that was best in orthodox psychology down to the end of the XIXth century is contained, in sum, in a few pages of Aristotle.

The motivity and appetitivity which, by the side of the sensitive function, likewise characterize the animal soul, have been considered in their relation to the intelligence in respect of ethics. Here it will suffice to call attention to the fundamental unity of these three modes. Desire and aversion are connected with pleasure and pain, which are inseparable from the sensations ; they are different quiddities of one same function. Moreover, while the movement following on desire or aversion is always such as it is determined by the organs of the animal, conversely an accidental state of the body can profoundly modify the affections of its soul, intensifying or diminishing desires or aversions in an unexpected manner.

---

[1] Principally *De An.*, iii. 3 ; 7, 431 a 16 ff. ; 8, 432 a 3–10 ; 11 ; *De Mem.* ; *De Somno ; De Insomniis.* Cf. *Rhet.*, i. 11, 1370 a 28 ; *Post. An.*, ii. 19, 99 b 34 ff

So pleasures and pains become for the animal " indications,"
often illusory, of the value of the relation established by its
sensations between its environment and itself. The common
sense and the imagination then give these passing indications
a borrowed individuality, which fixes them, both in the consciousness and in the very depths of the organism, as permanent
objects of appetition or repugnance.[1]

Lastly, the mental act by which one rises from the sensitive and imaginative functions to the *intellective* function is
the accepting of an object of belief or opinion ($\dot{\upsilon}\pi\acute{o}\lambda\eta\psi\iota\varsigma$,
$\pi\acute{\iota}\sigma\tau\iota\varsigma$, $\delta\acute{o}\xi a$)—in short, judgement, however elementary it may
be. Prudence and science are higher forms of it. In all
there is already intellection, the action of the intellect. Now,
if this function and this kind of soul are not contained in
those previously mentioned, these latter at least serve it as
material conditions and necessary antecedents. Ethical
theory has, moreover, shown how the intelligence moves us,
by associating itself with desire, and how pleasure is realized
in it in its most perfect form. In a sense, however, these
lower necessities signify that thought cannot suffice to itself,
that it is hampered and limited in the composite of which we
consist. For by itself, just like a sense in its own sphere,
it is theoretically infallible, in so far as it comes " into contact with " the intelligible, its object. But the indeterminate
ingredient in its material conditions introduces contingency
and fallibility into it. Would not the absolute dominion of
rational necessity be better for it than a liberty which is
always capable of choosing wrong ? Moreover, the intellect
cannot be " the form of forms," a " sovereign " kind of soul
and what is " most divine " in us, unless it is intimately
bound up with what is below it. For how could it cause
" intelligible forms " to emerge from sensible forms, if the
latter were not already extracted from extension by
sensation ?[2]

Now, if the intelligibles, which are here the mover of the
function and make its power or potentiality actual, are forms
parted off from sensible matter, simple and indivisible, there
can be no question here, as in the case of sensation, of a

---

[1] E.g., *De An.*, i. 1, 403 a 16–25 ; 2, 403 b 25–7 ; ii. 2, 413 b 23 ff. ; iii. 3, beg. ;
7, 431 a 10–14 ; 9, beg. ; 10.

[2] *De An.*, iii. 8, 432 a 2–6 ; i. 4, 408 b 29 ; *Nic. Eth.*, x. 7, 1178 a 2 ; *Part. An.*
iv. 10, 686 a 27–9 ; *Metaph.*, Λ. 7, 1072 b 20 ff.

common action of the agent and the affected. The action is single ; to receive certain forms and so to make one's own potentiality actual is to *become* them. Apart from that, intellect is only potentiality or receptivity, and, not being, like the sensitive, a concrete composite, it is properly " impassible " when in contact with form. It is therefore " without mixture," because, to receive simples and all simples, it must be simple itself, and, like the " receptacle " of the *Timaeos*, it can have no previous determination which might alter what it receives. Lastly, it is separate from the body, for an organ would only disturb it. It is, in short, like wax spread out on a tablet—absence of all writing and possibility of receiving it. Or it is " the place," not real, but possible, " of all forms." [1]

But, it will be asked, if the intelligibles are bound up in sensations and images, how will an intellect, which is absolutely nothing but receptivity, extract them ? Are they, on the contrary, eternally actual ? Then they are Plato's Ideas. There is only one way to evade the difficulty, and that is to imagine, as Aristotle does, that above the intellect which *becomes* intelligibles, and which has rather incorrectly been called " passive " (by Aristotle himself, indeed), there is another intellect which *makes* them, what is called the " creative " intellect.[2] All the characteristics possessed by the lower intellect as a potentiality are possessed by the higher as an action, and, above all, it is really separate. It eternally sheds light on the intelligibles, to enable the other intellect to come out of its potentiality and apprehend them, when, at the same time, they likewise come out of the matter in which they were embedded. Yet all difficulty has not been removed. For the various kinds of soul exists potentially in the male semen, which is the only carrier of form. But, whereas the two lower kinds, brought with the heat of the *pneuma*, become actual in turn in the human foetus, " the divine kind of intellect comes into it from outside " (θύραθεν), and exists there in actuality. How, then, will it become individual without being something of the body, since the principle of individualization resides in matter ? If, unlike the other souls, which, being born with the individual

[1] *De An.*, iii. 4 ; 6, beg. ; *Metaph.*, Λ. 9, 1075 a 3–5.
[2] *De An.*, iii. 5.

body, must perish with it, this alone has the privilege of immortality, it will be in so far as it is *not* individual, and, correlatively, as it is eternal.[1] So the potential intellect would be the eternally actual place of eternally actual intelligibles. This return to Platonism does not agree at all well with the empirical aspects of the theory of the soul, and clearly embarrasses Aristotle. Hence the reticences and obscurities of his exposition, and hence the vain attempts of so many interpreters, ancient and mediaeval, to give that exposition the unity which it lacks.

B. *First Philosophy.* Speculation on the creative intellect takes us out of the plane of natural things. We leave the domain of physics for that of " first philosophy " or " wisdom," the highest degree of " theoretic " science and the main theme of the collection known to us as the *Metaphysical Books*, from which the subject treated in those books has taken its name. This designation is a mere verbal trick, referring to the position of the books " after the physical books," *meta ta physica*, in the tables of Andronicos. It is first found in Nicolaos of Damascus, who was rather younger than Andronicos. It is an extremely artificial collection, from which one must at once take away the second piece, α,[2] a kind of introduction to physics, written by a pupil, perhaps Pasicles of Rhodes, the nephew of Eudemos. We shall also separate Book Δ, which Aristotle often describes as a distinct work, *On Manifold Acceptations* (περὶ τῶν ποσαχῶς λεγομένων), a school vocabulary in which the chief technical terms of philosophy are explained, sometimes in a rather summary fashion. The bulk of what remains consists of an introduction to the science of *Being as being* (A, history of the problem ; B, the problem and the " questions " or ἀπορίαι ; Γ ; E), a study, in part a mere sketch, of the nature of that being (Λ), and a treatise on substance (Z, H), completed by a dissertation on potentiality and activity (Θ). Books M and N, on the principles, are connected, one with A and B and the other with I, which treats of the one and the many. Certain parts of M and A are almost identical. But if, in A and B, Aris-

---

[1] *De An.*, i. 4, 408 b 24–30 ; ii. 2, 413 b 24–7 ; iii. 5, end ; *Gen. An.*, ii. 3.

[2] When the books of the *Metaphysics* are numbered from I to XIV, this is the second in the series. But, since it is sometimes not included, there is an ambiguity in the designation of the books which is best avoided by using the Greek letters.

totle sets forth and criticizes the Platonic doctrines, it is as a member of the Academy. " We prove that Ideas exist " —a remarkable peculiarity, which recalls the celebrated passage in the *Ethics* (i. 4, beginning) which tells how he is obliged, hard as it is for him, to sacrifice the friendship which ties him to the friends of Ideas to devotion to truth and impartial criticism. About the relationship of the books in question, we can only make conjectures. Lastly, Book K is, in its first eight chapters, another version of ΒΓΕ, and in the rest a compilation of the *Physics*.

The theoretic sciences considered so far are based on abstractions, which, as it were, cut out a point of view in the whole of reality. There will be infinitely more explanatory value in a knowledge which will have for its object Being itself, *as being* (τὸ ὂν ᾗ ὄν), explained in its nature and in its attributes by means of causes and principles which are the highest which we can discover.[1] In the solution of this problem which he has sketched, Aristotle opposes both the pure mechanists, like Democritus, who deny the problem, and especially, among the Socratics, the Platonists. Now, on the whole, what is his quarrel with the latter ? First, he blames their theory of Ideas for raising universals to the rank of substances and giving to quiddities an existence independent of the thing whose quiddity they are, so uselessly doubling things on the pretext of explaining them. Secondly, he says that they cannot account for the causality of their Ideas, whether these are partaken of or are patterns, and cannot explain movement and change by these unchangeable realities. Lastly, he accuses them of having arbitrarily closed the world of Ideas to certain universals (artificial things, relatives, etc.), and of having, on the other hand, allowed into it certain things which, like the One, Being, the Good, are not universals.[2]

Therefore there are two chief questions. What are the relations of the universal and the individual ? What is a substance ? To answer them, Aristotle has recourse to the general method of explanation by form and activity, matter and potentiality, of which there are already many examples in the other parts of his philosophy. Thus, the first problem will be solved if we observe that the universal, being merely

[1] *Metaph.*, Γ. 1 and E. 1. [2] Cf. **CXX**, bk. i.

the " common attribute of a plurality of things (ἐν κατὰ or
ἐπὶ πολλῶν), represents only an indefinite " possibility " of
repetition ; that it cannot therefore be isolated, like a thing,
" apart from that plurality " (ἐν παρὰ τὰ πολλά) ; that it is
posterior to essence and constitutes an *accident* for it. The
individual, on the contrary, is that which is not an attribute,
and cannot exist in a number of subjects, but is the very
reality of each, with the attributes required by that reality ;
it is *activity*. If, then, matter is the principle of individualization, it is so in so far as, by it, individuals can be " numerically
many." But what causes each of them, apart from the rest,
to be just what it is, is its form or quiddity, and the individual
is then truly the " last species." Consequently, all the
particularities in the sensible which affect it have nothing to
do with what it is ; they merely situate its body in the midst
of a multiplicity, and, coming from matter, they in no way
serve to explain the individual.

And now for the second question : which of the acceptations of substance fits the individual ? Not that of " composite," a form immanent in a matter, nor that of permanent
" support " of qualities and of the successive substitution of
contraries, i.e. that of logical " subject " of attributes. These
two senses hold good only in respect of the sphere of generation
and corruption, and for empirical thought, which is not
explanatory. The only sense which fits is that in which
substance is form or quiddity. Therefore the universality of
a genus, or of a species other than the last species, cannot in
any sense be substance, except by analogy and, as we have
seen, as a " secondary " substance.[1]

By presenting Aristotle's philosophy thus, and by carefully
distinguishing two planes, we free his ontology of many
difficulties and many contradictions. But, since forms are
unengendered, since each of them is at the same time matter
in respect of a higher form, since all that is eternal is actual,
in action, and since there is an intellect, actual and truly
separate, which is the forms or intelligibles in action, will not
these unengendered forms in action also be separate ? It is
therefore vain for Aristotle to forbid us to believe that they
are identical with Plato's Ideas. To explain our thought at

[1] E.g., *Herm.*, 7, beg. ; *De An.*, i. 1, 402 b 5–8 ; *Metaph.*, Z. 1, 1028 a 23 ff. ;
7, 1032 b 1 ff. ; H. 1, 1042 a 26–31 ; 6.   Cf. Bonitz, *Index*, 219 a 47 ff., 544 b 46-60.

work, he needs a supernatural plane, and that is the plane of *Being as being.*[1]

What is the nature of this "supremely real" being ? If it is not the intellect itself in action,[2] it is at least the pattern of it. For Aristotle's *theology* presents us with a God who is "a thought eternally thinking itself," an entirely intelligible thought of intelligibles, which are intelligence. Being thus the form of the separate forms, he is himself separate, and the individual *par excellence*. He transcends the world, he is not its providence, he does not even know it, for it is better not to know the imperfect, but he is none the less the mover, without extension, not only not moved, but absolutely immobile, of this world. For otherwise there would be matter or potentiality in him, however little. It is, therefore, as a "desirable" and external end that he moves all nature and every perishable natural thing, by the movement of the First Heaven and the eternal natural things. So, in the last analysis, the movements of perishable things signify only their aspiration, satisfied or thwarted, to the Good and the Perfect, more or less clearly desired. Everything "hangs from him" and depends on him ; he alone is self-sufficient. Lastly, in the undivided, timeless eternity of his contemplative life, God, "the thought of thought," pure action, enjoys perfect bliss.[3]

Shall we say that the beautiful simplicity of this construction hardly disguises its ambiguity ? Shall we ask Aristotle, the critic of Plato, why the notions which he uses in it "ring hollow" and are only "poetical metaphors" when Plato uses them ?[4] That, perhaps, is why Aristotle is so sparing of justifications in respect of his own doctrine. It was easier to point out the weaknesses of Plato's intellectualism than to protect himself against similar dangers. One remark will suffice : if there is, in Aristotle's view, a science of *Being as being*, it is because all beings resemble one another in their common "relation of dependence on a single nature" which is independent.[5] But the important thing was, having

---

[1] *Metaph.*, Z. 8, 1033 b 5–26 ; 9, 1034 b 7–16 ; Θ. 8, 1050 b 7 ff. ; Λ. 3, beg. and 1070 a 5–17 ; N. 2, 1088 b 25 ff. ; etc.

[2] As Alexander of Aphrodisias says.

[3] *Metaph.*, Λ. 6–9 ; *Phys.*, viii. 10   *De Caelo*, i. 9, end ; *Nic. Eth.*, x. 7 ; etc. Cf. above, pp. 261, 267.

[4] *Metaph.*, A. 9, 991 a 21 ff.   [5] *Metaph.*, Γ. 2, beg.

asserted this universal analogy, to deduce it from its principle. Now, in refusing to follow Plato in making mathematical relations the basis of what there is intelligible in quality, in isolating form and action without providing any transition, other than astrological, between the intelligible and the sensible, Aristotle's qualitativism deprived itself of all possibility of representing the existence of sensible things, their scale of degrees of perfection, their becoming, except in terms of pure empiricism.

It would, perhaps, be a fair description of Aristotle to say that he was too much and too little of a philosopher. He was a skilful and tricky dialectician, but was neither deep nor original. The invention which is most clearly his consists in well-coined formulas, verbal distinctions which are easy to handle. He set up a machine whose works, once set in motion, give the illusion of penetrating reflection and real knowledge. The misfortune is that he used this machine to attack both Democritos and Plato. So he for a long time turned science away from paths in which it might fairly soon have made decisive progress. On the other hand—and that is what justifies this long chapter—he was a mighty encyclopaedist and a master teacher. He possessed all the knowledge of his day, and was able to systematize it with great art in lectures and treatises. The amount and variety of his works and his undeniable gifts of elaboration and presentation, although they are not the same thing as the very spirit of inquiry in science and philosophy, are, apart from special historical circumstances, what have earned his philosophy and name their incomparable authority.

SECOND PART

THE IMMEDIATE DISCIPLES OF ARISTOTLE

One of the most striking characteristics of the Lyceum is its thorough organization of scientific erudition, in accordance with the ideal of knowledge as Aristotle conceived it. It was probably at his inspiration, if not under his direction, that Theophrastos of Eresos (the Scholarch of the school at a troublous time, from 322 to 288–287, and, it is said, until his eighty-fifth year) composed the great history of the *Opinions of the Physicists*, the importance of which has been mentioned (above, p. 11) ; that Eudemos of Rhodes wrote a *History of Geometry, Arithmetic, and Astronomy*, the fragments of which are of infinite value, and probably, too, a history of the early cosmogonies ; and that Menon wrote a history of medicine, Phanias of Eresos, a history of poetry and a history of the Socratic schools, Dicaearchos of Messana, a *Life of the Greeks*, which was a history of Hellenic civilization, and Aristoxenos of Taras, a history of music.

In addition, Dicaearchos wrote a *Voyage round the World*, a truly scientific geography in which determinations of measure, particularly altitudes, figured largely. Aristoxenos composed a treatise on *Musical Instruments, Elements of Rhythm*, of which a fairly long fragment survives, and *Elements of Harmony*, which we possess, perhaps in an altered form, and which shows a keen desire to observe accurately, not to " turn one's back on sensation " to lose oneself in mathematical speculations. Theophrastos also wrote his *History of Plants* (description, classification, cultivation, use, geographical distribution) and his treatise *On the Causes of Plants* (structure and functions). These last two are precise works, based on good observation and solid evidence, and are invaluable records of ancient botany. Of Theophrastos, too, we have fragments *On Fatigue, Sweat, Vertigo, Fainting, and Paralysis, On the Winds as Signs of the Weather*, and *On Stones and Fire*, not to mention a multitude of similar works of which we have only the titles. His immense output also included writings on logic, on general physics, on first philosophy, and many on politics, rhetoric, etc., to which one must add the curious essay in descriptive psychology known as the *Characters*, and literary compositions whose elegance called forth the admiration of the ancients. All these early Peripatetics have the same taste for special monographs and collections of observations, in which personal studies are inserted, and the same dislike for premature speculative synthesis.

All take the teaching of their Master as their basis. But, with the exception, perhaps, of Eudemos, whose only ambition, almost, is to interpret him scrupulously, they do not refrain from expanding his ideas or from criticizing or correcting them. Thus Theophrastos, aided by Eudemos, considerably develops the logical theory of modality and gives the formula of hypothetical and disjunctive syllogisms. He criticizes the doctrine of movement and that of place, and asks whether we should not define space as " the order and position of things according to their natures and their properties." He slightly alters the theory of the elements. A very close discussion of the theory of the intellect leads him to a conception which makes one think of the monads of Leibniz. The " questions," which are all that is left of his *First Philosophy*, refer chiefly to the first mover and its teleological action. All these criticisms, and his corrections of Aristotle's moral theory, are inspired by the desire to take facts into account and to limit the part played by transcendence. As for Eudemos, on the other hand, if it is true, as we have seen (pp. 259-60), that the *Ethics* which bears his name is not by him, but is a youthful work of Aristotle, we cannot look to it for evidence of a divergence of his moral tendencies from his master's. Furthermore, in Aristoxenos and Dicaearchos, the relation of the soul to the body is of a definitely phenomenal kind ; the soul is merely the unity of the body and the natural relation of its functions—what Aristoxenos, the musician, could not fail to call their " harmony," like Simmias in the *Phaedon*.

Theophrastos was succeeded by Straton of Lampsacos, " the Physicist," who had lived in Alexandria at the court of Ptolemy Soter as tutor of his son Philadelphos, and managed the Lyceum until 269. Because he follows the demands of Aristotle's naturalism to the end, and places the supernatural mover back in nature, he has been regarded as a heterodox Peripatetic. Yet he keeps qualitativism, since Hot and Cold are principles and all the effects of bodies are due to " natural properties." But he establishes a connexion between the qualities and the measurable determinations of weight and movement. There are no " natural places." The soul is a material *pneuma ;* none of the arguments of the *Phaedon* proves that it is immortal. All its functions, without exception, are explained by movement. Thought, which resides at the base of the forehead, is merely a weakened sensation, to which a corporeal impression can restore liveliness. So, without it being necessary to suppose the influence of Epicuros, Straton comes near to Democritos. But although he appeals only to mechanical causality, or, as he says, to *fortune*, excluding all finality, he rejects the " dreams " of the Atomists. His qualified matter is infinitely divisible. Vacuum does not exist save inside bodies or the universe (he allows it there only in order to explain the transmission of heat and light), and nature always has a tendency to fill it up. To tell the truth, this experimental and mathematical tendency in physics was an isolated episode in the development of Aristotelianism. But it seems to have had great influence in the technical domains of mechanics, medicine, and astronomy.

BOOK FOUR

MAN IN THE UNIVERSE. THE IDEAL OF THE WISE MAN

HELLENISTIC PHILOSOPHY

THE foundation of the Empire of Alexander and that of the great kingdoms into which it split up, the vassal position of the Greek cities and the final ruin of their ancient organization, a reflux of the Hellenized East on to the Greek mainland, the creation of new centres of culture in that same East, Alexandria, Pergamon, Rhodes—these are some of the facts characteristic of the " Hellenistic " age. Rome inherited the ambition of Alexander, extended it, and realized it in stable form ; Rome would become the capital of the world. So the field of mutual actions and reactions gradually widened. And, as Greek thought grew weaker, it came more and more under influences alien to its spirit.

The political and social circumstances which immediately preceded and followed the death of Alexander had intensely aggravated urgent needs to which philosophy had to supply new answers. In the great centralized state of which he was now a subject, the citizen of the old small city asked himself what attitude he should take up ; he felt lost. Then he turned upon himself, considered his inner salvation, asked to be told what was the object of life, to be given an ideal in pursuing which he would find his lost liberty, with a view to his own happiness. The ideal might be different in every school, but it would always be the ideal of the Wise Man, who belongs to no age or country ; all would conceive him in the same resolutely pragmatic spirit.

As a fact, this pragmatic tendency was already over a century old. It had been started by the Sophists, and still more by Socrates. It was with a view to the moral renovation of society that Plato instructed a few elect ones in the sciences and dialectic ; in organizing the study of rhetoric and politics in the Lyceum, even Aristotle showed that he was not neglectful of this point of view. But the thinkers who did most to turn post-Aristotelian philosophy in this direction were the other Socratics—Cynics, Cyrenaics, and even Megarics —uncompromising pragmatists, for whom knowledge was nothing if it did not serve action, if it was not the knowledge of action itself. No doubt, among the philosophies of their successors, many preserved the framework, now become classical, of philosophic education, and therefore comprised a logic, a physical theory, and a theology. But all this is valueless except in relation to the organization of conduct. Besides, the constant trend of the sciences towards technical specialization was bound to encourage this kind of ethical depolarization of philosophic speculation.

A last characteristic of post-Aristotelian philosophy is a more marked return to pre-Socratic doctrines. No doubt, they had never been forgotten. But the vigorous personalities of men like Antisthenes, Eucleides, and, above all, Plato had transformed what they adopted from them, assimilating it. Now things were different ; theories were merely set forth side by side and harmonized ; one system was inserted in a quite different system, as a complete part of it. This was a result of the predominance of practical interests in thought and a sign of indifference to pure speculation.

CHAPTER I

SCEPTICISM

IT is very difficult to say how much of the whole Sceptic doctrine is due to its first representatives. For the only Scepticism about which we have abundant information is late Scepticism, and even there we know more of its history than of its tenets and arguments. But can it be proved that the essential part of these does not come from the tradition of the school ? It is, therefore, safer, since we cannot discuss the evidence here, not to separate the two phases of Scepticism, so long as we remember that they are divided by about three centuries, and that the second phase is in part contemporary with the last period of the history of Greek thought.

Scepticism is the earliest in date of the great post-Aristotelian philosophies. Pyrrhon, whom the Sceptics unanimously regarded as their founder, was about forty years old at Aristotle's death. He was a contemporary of Theophrastos and Xenocrates. At Elis, where he was born, he may have known the last philosophers of the school of Phaedon, and it is certain that he was initiated by the teaching of Bryson, the pupil of a pupil of Eucleides, into Megaric dialectic, the most illustrious professors of which belonged to his time. So his mind was partly trained in one form of the Socratic tradition. But, on the other hand, he attached himself to Anaxarchos, with whom he followed Alexander into Asia, and so he also owed something to Democritos and another Socratic tradition, that of the Cyrenaics.

Anaxarchos of Abdera [1] is an original figure. His master, Diogenes of Smyrna,[2] was a pupil of an immediate disciple of Democritos, namely Metrodoros of Chios, one of the heads of the school, and had perhaps already attempted a reconciliation of physical atomism with a complete subjectivism

LXVIII, ch. 59.   [2] *Ibid.*, ch. 58.

like that of Protagoras and a practical attitude recalling Aristippos the elder. At least, this last tendency would explain the paradoxes of Anaxarchos's character—his approval of Alexander after the murder of Cleitos and his proud courage under awful torture. In his view, was not the only wisdom " to know the limits of the right moment " ? Our sentiments are like the scenery of a theatre or the illusions of delirium ; to convince ourselves of this gives happiness more surely than knowledge. So the Wise Man is he who is superior to all circumstances, a supreme judge of all situations, and always happy for that very reason. Perhaps this conception would not be different from that which we find in other philosophers of the time, if it were not that Anaxarchos went to India, and there saw the impassibility of the fakirs, whom the Greeks called Magi or Gymnosophists. One of them, whom the Greeks called Calanos, mounted on a pyre before the whole army, and endured a voluntary death without weakening. There is no doubt that these examples, and the friendship of Anaxarchos, had great influence on the thought of Pyrrhon.

Like Socrates, Pyrrhon wrote nothing. We know of his personality and teaching only through the evidence of others. First, there are the writings of the school. But those of Sextus Empiricus (about 180–210) were written four centuries later than Pyrrhon, at a time when a complex development of the original doctrine had reached its term. However, they owe much to Timon of Phlius (315 ?–225 ?), the " Sillographer." Timon, after an adventurous youth, had gone through the School of Megara, and finally lived at Elis with Pyrrhon, who was already old. It was to extolling his master and his teaching, at the expense of other philosophers and philosophies, that he devoted a great part of his literary output—his poems, the *Silloi*, in three books, and the *Images*, with a prose dialogue, the title of which, *Python*, may be a pun. This was the source on which our later witnesses drew—Antigonos of Carystos, rather later than Timon, in his lives of Pyrrhon and Timon, which are largely used by Diogenes Laërtios ; Aristocles of Messana, in a clear, precise exposition of the doctrine ; [1] and, lastly, Sextus Empiricus. Cicero, who regards Pyrrhon only as a moralist, speaks of him on the strength of the

[1] Cf. **LXVI**, pp. 175–81

statements of Antiochos of Ascalon, who was little capable of appreciating the originality of Pyrrhon's speculative thought, and the Neo-Academicians, who were interested in concealing it.

Of Timon's Pyrrhonian writings we have, unfortunately, barely a hundred and fifty lines, which betray imitation of Xenophanes, with more brutal vigour and sometimes, too, the same nobility of tone. In the *Images* he denounced the tyranny of appearances and the vanity of distinctions between good and evil; [1] he asked Pyrrhon to reveal his secret : " How, being but a man, do you lead a life full of ease, in tranquillity, indifferent to everything . . . never surrendering to the eddies of a smooth-voiced wisdom ? " He alone is the Sun-god who guides mankind. And Pyrrhon uttered " the word of truth," the word which tells " the eternal nature of the divine and the good," which is the " right rule " of " the most equal life." [2] The *Silloi* [3] began with a Homeric combat of the philosophers, all smitten with a common ailment, a " verbal diarrhoea," which degenerates into a " verbal fight." The army of the Dogmatics is routed. Arcesilaos claims the credit, but the true victor is Pyrrhon, " the invincible," who, however, does not let his mind be troubled by the " fumes " (ἄτυφος) of pride, and has relieved his fellows of the heavy burden of subjective " affections " and " illusory conventions." [4] Then the theme changed. In the great preserve of the Academy, a shoal of fish come and go, with Plato in the forefront. The biggest of all is Pyrrhon ; beside him, Mene-demos, and Diodoros, Arcesilaos shelters when the fishermen (the Stoics) cast their net.[5] In the second book there was a *Nekyia* of philosophers. Among the shades called up, Timon spared only the Eleatics, but especially Xenophanes. " Old man," says Xenophanes to Pyrrhon, " how, and by what way, didst thou find escape from the bondage of opinions and the empty-mindedness of scientists ? . . . Little didst thou care, what winds blow on Hellas, nor what are the origin and end of all things ! " [6]

If we take the other evidence together with what Timon tells us, we can form a fairly consistent picture of Pyrrhon's personality. First of all, he set out to be a Socratic, but the

---

[1] *Ibid.*, frs. 69–70.   [2] Frs. 67–8, 63 ff.
[3] According to Diels's reconstruction, *ibid.*, 182–4.
[4] Fr. 9.   [5] Frs. 30–2   [6] Fr. 48.

sturdiest child of the family, with the strongest likeness to its ancestor. He alone broke away from the seductions of a pretended wisdom, and shook off the yoke of individual impressions and that of prejudices. For neither our sensations nor our judgements can speak truly, nor yet err ; everything is " equally indifferent, balanced, vague." He will, therefore be " without opinion, without inclination, without vain agitation of mind "—" no one thing more than another " (οὐδὲν μᾶλλον), " Yes," quite as well as " No," or rather neither " Yes " nor " No." " Suspension " of judgement (ἐποχή) leads in the end to silence (ἀφασία).[1] Pyrrhon does not write, because he is not vain enough to want to have his say in the disputes of the philosophers ; he triumphs over their subtleties because he soars above them. This speculative indifference is the principle of his practical indifference. The actions of ordinary life are of no importance. Pyrrhon looks after his pig and sells his hens and sucking-pigs at market, and does not refuse to be high-priest of his city. He affects humility and " gentleness " (πραότης). If a man goes away while he is speaking to him, he pays no heed ; he is indulgent to men, because he knows that nothing is in itself noble or shameful, just or unjust, but everything is sometimes one and sometimes the other. So, too, his " impassibility " (apatheia) must be complete. He does not distinguish between sickness and health, and endures a cruel operation without wincing. Unlike the Cyrenaic, he does not even enjoy physical pleasure, for in his eyes the ideal of the Wise Man is " to shed the man completely." That is the perfect " equilibrium " of a soul " which nothing can trouble " (ataraxia). That is what Timon calls the " rule " of life and the " essence " of the good and the divine. So there is only one truth, namely, that, in the order of sensations and opinions, everything is indifferent, and nothing is of absolute worth, except " tranquillity " of mind. Pyrrhon preached this " fight against things," which is to liberate us, much more by his example than by his words, and that, doubtless, is why he died, at the age of ninety (about 275), surrounded with the wondering respect of all who had seen his life.[2] He introduced the Greeks to a version

---

[1] Cf. Aristocles and Diog. Laërt., in **XIV**, nn. 446, 449, 451.
[2] Diog. Laërt., 61 ff., 64, 66–8, 106 ; Aristocles (in Euseb., Praep. Ev., xiv. 18. 4) ; Cic., De Fin., ii. 13. 43 and Acad., ii. 42. 130.

of the Hindu ideal of absolute renunciation, in speculation and in practice.

Later we shall find traces of the influence exerted by Pyrrhon.[1] Did his chief disciple, Timon, have successors ? In spite of many obscurities, it is probable that the school was handed down continuously.[2] In any case, Sextus distinguishes between the early and late Sceptics. The former were those who recognized ten " modes " or " tropes " of suspension of judgement ; the latter recognized only five.[3] From this point of view, early Scepticism is represented by Ænesidemos of Cnossos, and late Scepticism by Agrippa. It is a wonder that the latter's name should have survived at all ; Diogenes Laërtios only mentions him in passing [4] and does not give him in his catalogue, and Sextus never speaks of him. We know absolutely nothing about him. Of Ænesidemos, all that we are told is that he taught in Alexandria and dedicated his *Pyrrhonian Discourses* to L. Tubero. But who is this Tubero ? Since we do not know, we must be content to say that Ænesidemos lived somewhere in the first centuries before and after Christ. Among the other Sceptics, three names emerge, all of physicians—Menodotos of Nicomedeia (known chiefly from the attacks of Galen), Sextus Empiricus, and his pupil Saturninus, who lie between A.D. 150 and 250. The *Pyrrhonian Hypotyposes* (*Sketches*) of Sextus are a remarkably lucid account of the Sceptic doctrine in three books. He wrote a much larger work, *Against the Dogmatics* (logicians, physicists, or moralists, in five books) *and Theorists* (professors of grammar, rhetoric, mathematics, etc., in six books).[5] The first part, which is a discussion of other philosophies, is one of our most valuable monuments of ancient erudition. On the edge of the Sceptic tradition, one should also mention the rhetor Favorinus of Arelate (between 120 and 150), who taught in Athens and Rome and was the master of Aulus Gellius.

The ten " tropes " of Ænesidemos seem to be a methodical classification of all the arguments of past philosophers which should deter one from dogmatic assertion and denial. The

---

[1] See the following chapter.   [2] Diog. Laërt., bk. ix, end.
[3] *Pyrrh.*, i. 36, 164.
[4] 88. From 69 to 108, Diog. Laërt. speaks of Scepticism in general, not of Pyrrhon.
[5] The usual title is *Against the Mathematicians* (abbreviated to *Math.*) ; books vii-xi are probably the first.

list owes much, no doubt, to the polemic of the New Academy and also draws without discrimination on all thinkers whom the Sceptics wanted to regard as forerunners—Heracleitos, the Eleatics, Democritos, Protagoras, Diogenes of Apollonia.[1] Perhaps Ænesidemos thought it no treason to his principles to regard the inventory of contradictions in appearances as a preparation for a Heracleitean conception of universal contradiction in the hidden foundation of things.[2] At least, there is no ambiguity about the meaning of the tropes. It is impossible, the Sceptic said,[3] to know what things are in themselves, since they appear very different to different animals, to different men, to different senses, and in different circumstances—state of health, age, etc. After these first four tropes come three others, based on the variations in perceptions due to position, distance, situation, mass ; perceptions are always modified by their combination with some factor other than the object itself, or simply by the quantity of the object. Thus, the scrapings of a black horn are white. The eighth trope, which covers all the first seven, concerns relativity—the relation of the subject to the object, of things or notions with one another. With this one may connect the criticism of causality ;[4] for that criticism consists, essentially, in denying that there is a causal power in the agent, since all causality is a relation, of which the thing affected is itself a term. The ninth trope shows that we do not see what is frequent and what is rare in the same light. The tenth, which deals with the diversity of moral judgements and customs, should lead us to place happiness in *ataraxia*, or in the *metriopatheia*[5] which maintains our natural passivity in " measure," if it be granted that nothing of what is necessary according to nature can be an evil.

Agrippa, if, indeed, the credit is due to him, not merely classified the reasons for doubt more methodically ; he added to them. Instead of confining himself to sense-perception and moral judgement, he considers, in a more general way, the sensible on the one hand and the intelligible on the other. Now, on neither of these do " the voices of men harmonize " (διαφωνία), whether they be philosophers or not. This is

---

[1] In Diog. Laërt., ix, they go before Pyrrhon and Timon.
[2] *Pyrrh.*, i. 210.   [3] *Ibid.*, 36–163 ; Diog. Laërt., 79–88.
[4] *Math.*, ix. 195–276 ; good summaries in **VII**, ii. 324–7, or **CXLIII**, 350–2.
[5] *Pyrrh.*, i. 25–30, iii. 235 ff.

not surprising, for the sensible and the intelligible are always relative, to a sensitivity and to an intelligence respectively ; they are never apprehended in themselves. Thus all the tropes of Ænesidemos are merged in the first and third tropes of Agrippa. Moreover, if, in either of these two orders, one tries to prove anything at all, one must " go to infinity," without ever coming upon evidence. But, the Dogmatist will say, are there not principles to which evidence is subject ? Perhaps, but only by hypothesis ; and your hypothesis is no more evident than the contradictory hypothesis. These are the second and fourth tropes. The last is the famous argument in a circle ; in order for instance, to prove the sensible by the intelligible (or *vice versa*), you prove " the one by the other " (δι' ἄλληλα), and if you try to escape from the circle you fall once more into indefinite progress.[1] In short, nothing is evident, yet nothing can be demonstrated —that, in two tropes,[2] is the last version of the Sceptic theory. So nothing is true, in the sense which the word has for Dogmatism. If by any chance a truth of this kind did exist, there would be no " distinctive sign " or " criterion " by which it could be recognized and made indisputable.[3]

Salvation in Wisdom was the object of Scepticism in its original form ; but gradually its dialectic assumed a significance which was mainly methodological. To the Dogmatic scientist, who thinks that science can be based on the demonstrative syllogism, the Sceptic, anticipating John Stuart Mill, points out, for instance, that the inductive major term of a syllogism supposes complete enumeration and therefore depends on the truth of the conclusion.[4] It may be said that manifest (πρόδηλα) things indicate (ἐνδεικτικά) the nature of concealed things (ἄδηλα), and so are signs. This, the Sceptic objects, is a particular case of the general illusion of Dogmatism ; the sign is only a fact, which recalls (ὑπομνηστικόν) another of which it was formerly the concomitant, so that, one or the other of these facts being given, one can infer from it, as past or as future, that which is not at present given.[5] Understood thus, the study of signs is the basis of good practice and a great number of very useful

---

[1] *Pyrrh.*, i. 164–72 ; Diog. Laërt., 88 ff.   [2] *Pyrrh.*, i. 178 ff.
[3] *Pyrrh.*, ii. 15–94 ; *Math.*, vii. 25 to end (bk. i of *Against the Logicians*).
[4] *Pyrrh.*, ii. 195–7.   [5] *Ibid.*, 97–133 ; *Math.*, viii. 143–58, etc.

322 THE IDEAL OF THE WISE MAN

arts. But, where there is only " consecution," the Dogmatists seek a causal action, and construct an aetiology. Now, the very search for these alleged causes is exposed to faults, which Ænesidemos enumerated in eight special tropes.[1] Medicine is a special example of the attitude taken by the Sceptic in this matter. He condemns the " logical " physician (ὁ λογικός). Even the pure " empiric " is, in his eyes, only a Dogmatist turned round, almost as narrow as the other. He himself is a " Methodist." That is the essence of his doubt ; he " observes concomitances " (τὰ κατάλληλα) and " consecutions " (ἀκολουθία τηρητική) with a view to foreseeing and acting, but he is not so arrogant as to believe that he has in this way discovered causes.[2]

Strict and untiringly exhaustive analysis of every aspect of a problem, unequalled dialectical skill, uncompromising honesty of a mind which refuses to dupe itself, determined hostility to theory and foregone conclusions, whatever they may be, respect for the pure fact, with anxiety to observe its relations scrupulously and to make use of it for practice— these are some of the features characteristic of Greek Scepticism at the end of its development. At its origin, its method was a moral discipline, the aim of which was a tranquil life ; later it became, in addition and chiefly, a discipline of the scientific spirit. It never played the insurgent or sought to create a sensation ; it was led by its humble quietism to accept life as it is, and by its respect for fact to treat collective facts, such as customs and laws, as facts of nature. In the face of doctrinal intolerance and the tyranny of the prejudices of schools, its critical attitude expressed a bold attempt to make science independent, by making it confine itself to strictly determining its technical methods with a view to useful practice. In this respect it was, as has been rightly said,[3] a forerunner of the positive spirit.

[1] *Pyrrh.*, i. 180–5. Cf. **CXLIII**, 266 and n. ; **CXLV**.
[2] *Pyrrh.*, i. 236–41 ; *Math.*, viii. 288. We see from this that Sextus himself disowns the epithet of " Empiric " bestowed on him by tradition.
[3] **CXLIII**, 298, 375–9.

CHAPTER II

EPICUREANISM

THE doctrine of Epicuros seems to have been a new elaboration
of Democritean and Cyrenaic ideas, after they had been
transformed by the teaching of Pyrrhon. The first master of
Epicuros is said to have been Nausiphanes of Teos. Now,
Nausiphanes had been a pupil of the Democritean Hecataeus
of Abdera, who is said to have heard Pyrrhon, and he may
have known him himself. At least, tradition says that
Epicuros often went to him to learn about the old master.[1]
Moreover, the first time he went to Athens, about his eighteenth
year, he heard Xenocrates, and he heard Pamphilos, another
member of the Academy, at Samos. We must note these
connexions with Platonism, the influence of which, although
in an altered form, is often to be seen. Epicuros passionately
denied all his debts to the philosophy of others and heaped
coarse insults on those who were declared to be his masters or
forerunners.[2] He wanted his doctrine to be regarded as a
wholly original creation of his own genius

About 307-306, Epicuros, then aged nearly thirty-five,
returned to Athens and settled there permanently. Although
born at Samos, where his father, an Athenian immigrant, kept
a school and his mother was an exorcist, he legally kept his
citizen rights. No doubt, his doctrine was by that time
established, for he had been teaching for three years at
Colophon, Mitylene, and Lampsacos. He bought a piece of
ground and opened a school, which came to be called the
Garden, while the Epicureans were called the Philosophers
of the Garden. He seems to have had an extraordinary
ascendancy over those whom he gathered round him. He was
one of the exceptional beings to whom men are grateful

[1] **LXVIII**, ch. 62, A. 1-9. Cf. ch. 60, A. 2-3 ; ch. 63, A. 3.
[2] **CXLVI**, 231-41.

because they condescend to behave as men and who inspire enthusiastic devotion. For his philosophy is not a teaching, but " an activity, which by reasons and reflections procures the happy life." [1] His school is an association of brothers or friends who wish to practise that activity in common (συμφιλο-σοφεῖν).[2] The society is open to anyone who wishes to find his salvation in the new faith, without distinction of culture (for it is sufficient to be able to read),[3] race, or condition. The names of Leontion and Hedeia tell us that courtesans went there for peace of heart and found it. The courage with which Epicuros died (270), suffering agonies from stone, remained a sublime example in the eyes of the faithful. He became a god, who had brought men a liberating revelation.[4] Thenceforward, the common meals of the school, on the 20th of every month and on the anniversary of the Master's birth, the 10th Gamelion (Jan.-Feb.), were religious celebrations and acts of worship, held with more or less solemnity.[5] We can understand, therefore, that there was an Epicurean orthodoxy, and, although there were changes of detail in the doctrine, and some foreign elements were introduced into the main fabric of its principles,[6] there is no doctrine in respect of which there is less question of later development.

Epicureanism quickly spread far and wide. As the head of a semi-religious community, Epicuros wrote epistles to the " churches " of Mitylene, Lampsacos, Egypt, Asia. The abundant correspondence which he kept up with distant members of his flock is always of a catechetic nature ; he dictates to them an attitude towards questions which trouble their conscience. When the Master died, the organized cult of his memory held the sect together and perpetuated and helped to propagate the doctrine. It seems to have been the first of all the Greek philosophies to enter Roman Italy, at first, apparently, among people of modest condition.[7] But the inward resources which it offered amid the disorder and perils of political life also attracted the great men and the cultivated men of the last period of the Republic—L. Piso,

---

[1] Sextus, *Math.*, xi. 169. [2] Cic., *De Fin.*, i. 20. 65 ; *Test.*, 18, 20.
[3] **CXLVI**, 117, 227 ff.
[4] Lucretius, esp. v, beg. ; i. 62–79 ; iii, beg. and 1042–4 ; vi, beg.
[5] **CXLVI**, Ind. Nom., p. 405 b.
[6] E.g., the theory of friendship, *De Fin.*, i. 20, or in many passages in Lucretius.
[7] **V**, 383 (4) ; Cic., *Fin.*, ii. 4. 12.

the protector of Philodemos, L. Manlius Torquatus, C. Velleius, C. Cassius (who murdered Caesar with the Stoic Brutus), C. Vibius Pansa, T. Pomponius Atticus (Cicero's friend), and others. A rich villa in Herculaneum has already given up the remains of an Epicurean library. Perhaps as early as the end of the IInd century, the first philosophic treatise in Latin was devoted to Epicureanism by C. Amafinius, and had a success which, being followed by imitations, must have spread the influence of the doctrine all over Italy.[1] Probably, therefore, Lucretius only means to boast [2] of being the first to set forth in Latin the matter of Epicurean physics. Epicureanism maintained its vitality until the beginning of the IVth century after Christ. In the IIIrd, the refutation of its physical theory by Dionysios, Bishop of Alexandria, and the ferocious attacks of Lactantius prove that it was a dangerous rival to Christianity. It continued to be so, until the day when the Christians had the political power on their side.[3]

Epicuros wrote much—over three hundred rolls, it is said. These included the *Canon* or *On the Criterion*, a *Physics* in thirty-seven books, of which he composed a *Large Abridgement* and a *Small Abridgement*, which may have been the model of Lucretius, treatises *On Atoms and Vacuum*, *On the Gods*, *On the End*, *On the Things to be Sought or Avoided*, *On Justice and the Other Virtues*, *On Holiness*, polemical writings, letters, etc. Of all these works, which were rather rude in literary style, but robust and grave, little remains—three letters, the second of which is of doubtful authenticity (*To Herodotos* on physics, *To Pythokles* on meteorology, and *To Menoeceus* on morality),[4] a collection of *Principal Thoughts* (κύριαι δόξαι),[5] a collection similar to which has been found in a manuscript of the Vatican, various fragments of papyrus, and the *Testament* of Epicuros. Our information is supplemented by fragments of other Epicureans, particularly of Metrodoros and Philodemos, by the six books of Lucretius's poem *On the Nature of Things*, by the Life of Epicuros in Diogenes Laërtios (Book X), by the great inscription which Diogenes of Œnoanda (in Lycia) caused to be engraved in the middle of the IIIrd century on the

---

[1] Cic., *Tusc.*, iv. 3. 6 ff. ; cf. *Acad.*, i. 2. 5.
[2] v. 336.   [3] **CXLVI**, pp. lxxv ff.
[4] Indicated in the notes by i, ii, iii, respectively, with the number of the paragraph in Diog. Laërt., bk. x.
[5] Also in Diog. Laërt. Abbreviation, ΚΔ.

portico of his city for the edification of all, and by abundant expositions, with translations or quotations, in non-Epicurean writers such as Cicero, Seneca, and Plutarch.

" It is never too soon or too late," Epicuros used to say, " to pay heed to the health of the soul." [1] On that happiness depends, and it is the end of philosophy. Therefore nothing in philosophy which does not contribute to it is of any use, and everything else should be valued in relation to that end. Now, what prevents us from attaining it is the "hollow opinions" by which the soul is "troubled" and, as it were, poisoned, and which have nothing corresponding to them in the nature of things—the fear of the gods and of death, the wrong appreciation of pleasure and pain. Therefore, of the three parts of philosophy, logic, physics and morality, the two first are to the third what hygiene or medicine is to health— means, which must not be made ends.

Scientific logic, consequently, does not interest Epicuros. His logic aims at being chiefly a criticism of knowledge, a discrimination of what it contains which is incontestable as being "evidence" (ἐνάργεια, perspicuitas, manifestum). Thus we obtain the "signs," starting from which we shall be able to infer what is not evident, especially in the matter of physics. On this basis, finally, we shall be able to establish the "rule of life." [2] Now, the first source of all our ideas is representative sensation (φαντασία) and the affective state (πάθος), pleasure or pain,[3] which is likewise sensation. For sensation can never be convicted of error—neither by reasoning, for reasoning itself comes from sensation, nor by opposing sensations to one another, for each is shut off in its own sphere.[4] Besides, representation and affective state would be inexplicable without a reality (ὑπάρχον) capable of producing them, as an agent.[5] For, as we shall see, every state of the subject is part of a natural mechanical process which starts from the real object, and it is what the whole movement allows it to be. It is always, therefore, what it must be, and consequently always true, even if it is the principle of a false judgement, even in dreams and delirium.[6] That, then, is the "first certitude" (fides prima), the "foundation and corner-stone" of all truth.

[1] iii. 122. [2] Cic., Fin., i. 19. 63 ff. [3] Diog. Laërt., 34.
[4] Lucr., iv. 485–99 ; Diog. Laërt., 31 ff.
[5] Diog. Laërt., 32 ; Sextus, Math., vii. 203–5.
[6] Ibid., 208 ff. ; CXLVI, 252–4. Cf. Cic., Acad., ii. 25. 80.

To say, like Democritos, that the sensible qualities are pure convention, to deny, with the Sceptics, that there is a truth, is to wish " to walk head downwards," or to shake the very base of our salvation.[1] We have there an indisputable " evidence," a first " rule " or " canon " of truth (*regula, norma*), a " criterion " to distinguish true and false (*indicium*).

But there is another evidence, and therefore another criterion—anticipation (προληψις) or " prenotion " (*notities* in Lucretius). It is a kind of " universal thought which has formed in us, that is, a recollection of what has often presented itself to us from outside." If someone says " man," " snow," " heat " in my presence, I at once know what is talked about, even before perceiving it ; but I should not know it if I had not often perceived it in the past.[2] The transformation of particular sensations into notions is in great part mechanical, without, however, excluding the collaboration of reflection, and takes place by concomitance (περίπτωσις), analogy, similarity, or fusion. Of this analysis, unfortunately, only an obscure outline is preserved.[3] By the study of language we come to know the natural notions. For words, far from being the product of a convention, or, as the pure Nominalists say, class-names empty of all real content, condense and translate the most ancient effect of things upon us and the " primitive notions " in relation to our natural means of expression and differently according to regions and races.[4] But anticipations do not merely precede things ; by the application of thought (ἐπιβολὴ τῆς διανοίας, *injectus animi*) they seem to constitute a true intuition of principles (στοιχεῖα), an empiricistic plagiarism of the intuition of Aristotle. No doubt, it is not, as some Epicureans have said, a fourth criterion ; it is, at least, " a guide for all our inquiries." Thus, we perceive immediately that nothing comes from nothingness or returns to it ; that there are simple bodies, and that they must be indestructible and indivisible ; that the gods, of whom we naturally have a conception, can only be immortal and blessed ; that pleasure is the true good,[5] etc.

Whereas evidence, in whatever form nature impresses it

---

[1] Lucr., iv. 462–79, 502–12 ; Sextus, *Math.*, vii. 216.
[2] Diog. Laert., 33 ; **CXLVI**, 255 ff.   [3] Diog. Laert., 32.
[4] i. 37 ff., 75, beg. ; Diog. Laert., 31, beg. ; Cic., *Fin.*, ii. 2. 6.
[5] Especially i. 38 ff., 50 ; ΚΔ. 24 ; Diog. Laert., 31 ; Cic., *Fin.*, i. 9. 30 ; Lucr., ii 740.

328 THE IDEAL OF THE WISE MAN

in us, leaves no room for error, error appears with " opinion "
—in other words, with the inferences which we base on the
present and immediate data (τὸ παρὸν ἤδη) of evidence. Here
we have a veritable " interpretation of signs " (σημείωσις),
either in relation to the " object of our expectation " (τὸ
πρόσμενον)—" Is the tower which I see over there round ? "
—or in relation to " hidden things " (τὰ ἄδηγα)—" Does
vacuum exist ? " Now, all wisdom consists in not confusing
the opinion thus defined with intuitive evidence, and in being
able to " bring down " what is not now perceived or what
could only be seen if our means of perception were stronger,
to the criteria of evidence. In the former case, the facts may
confirm or invalidate my judgement (ἐπι- or ἀντιμαρτύρησις),
and I must consider the conditions on which that can happen.
In the latter case, confirmation by experience is obviously
impossible, but the facts may contradict my hypothesis ;
therefore my hypothesis will be true if nothing in the facts
invalidates it (οὐκ ἀντιμαρτύρησις).[1]

It seems, however, that this negative verification, if it is
not strictly governed, can only be a matter of divination in
the Wise Man, and of faith and a revelation in others. So
certain Epicureans of the IInd and Ist centuries B.C., Demetrios of Laconia and Zenon of Sidon in particular, tried, so
far as we can tell from the fragments of Philodemos's treatise
On Signs and their Interpretation, to define the exact technique
of the method.[2] Interesting as these attempts may have
been, they were only a rough outline of an experimental
method. For in respect of natural phenomena the Epicurean
is indifferent to the truth of the explanation given of them.
It is enough for him that the explanation should satisfy certain
very general conditions, logical or moral, which alone need to
be defined exactly. The Master's contempt for culture
embraces all the sciences. Even if it were based on true
principles, a knowledge whose only end is itself and which
does not serve to make us happier is worthless.[3] " To flee
from science," Epicuros writes to a disciple, " hoist sail with
all speed ! "[4] No doubt, in confining science to the mechanical
explanation of phenomena, Epicureanism did it a negative

---

[1] i. 50–2 ; ΚΔ, 24, 22 ; Lucr., i. 423–5 ; ii. 121–4 ; iv. 464–6 ; Cic., Acad , ii.
14. 45 ; Sextus, Math., vii. 211 ff.
[2] Cf. LIII, 237–55, and CLI.   [3] Cic., Fin , i. 21. 71 ff
[4] Diog. Laërt., 6.

service. But the originality of its point of view lies much
rather in the strange principle that, in all the details of physics,
" it can be thus quite as well as otherwise," that, in this
domain, " our need of exact knowledge " will be fully satisfied
by " a number of possible explanations," provided that, by
all excluding the arbitrary action of the gods, they equally
contribute to delivering us from empty terrors. On this
condition, we are free to believe what we like about the size
of the stars, the real nature and cause of their risings and
settings, etc. What is important, is to reduce these imposing
phenomena to the dimensions of our most familiar experience.[1]
By stating with such decision that the winning of salvation
is more important than knowledge, Epicureanism was bound
to gain converts ; but one cannot fail to see how alien it is to
the true scientific spirit.

The interest of Epicurean physics, therefore, lies in the
practical intention which in it determines the choice of
general theories.[2] The gods must be banished from nature ;
therefore nature cannot be a work of the spirit and a finality.
So the Epicurean adopts a materialism, and not a vitalistic
materialism, but a mechanistic, that of the School of Abdera.
Nothing comes from nothingness, for in that case everything
could come from anything. Nor does anything become
nothing, for then there would long ago have ceased to be
anything. Reality is twofold—bodies and vacuum. Vacuum
is either absence of body, " space " where there is nothing
(ἡ χώρα), or the extension where a body takes its " place "
(ὁ τόπος). Unlike vacuum, a body is what acts or is
affected. Among its modes there are some without which
there would be no body—the three dimensions, resistance
(ἀντιτυπία), etc. (in short, what results from corporeity
itself and is bound to it ; συμβεβηκότα, conjuncta)—and
others which are " eventual accidents " of it (συμπτώματα,
eventa). Now, these latter are always relative to perception,
and belong to the body in so far as it is a composite, a sensible
aggregate. But the composite implies the simple, and, in
virtue of the fundamental principle, these simple things will
be indestructible and irreducible ; they are the atoms, or
" primary bodies." [3]

[1] i. 78–80 ; ii, passim ; Lucr., v. 509–770 ; vi, passim.   [2] Cf. ΚΔ. 11.
[3] i. 38–41, 68, 70 ff. ; Lucr., i. 146–634. Cf. Sext., Math., x. 2.

We should especially note the critical points on which Epicuros disagrees with his forerunner Democritos. First of all, he gives the atom an essential weight ; this seems to be an original conception of his. Therefore the atoms move downwards ; this does not, of course, refer to the infinite void, but to the relative direction of their movement.[1] Secondly, the shapes of the atoms are finite, not infinite, in number, although we cannot count them. Although indivisible in practice, the atom, having extension and shape, is theoretically divisible. To realize an infinite number of shapes it would be necessary to increase the number of these parts of extension endlessly, and so the atoms would at length become large enough to be perceived. Moreover, if there were an infinite number of shapes there would be an infinite variety in nature, and the negation of all stable order. Now, the facts contradict these two consequences of the hypothesis.[2] Lastly, the existence of aggregates of atoms and of a system of those aggregates, our world, would be inexplicable if the atoms always fell parallel, in a medium without resistance, all at the same infinite speed, the hypothesis of an oblique descent of bodies being, furthermore, belied by the facts. So, too, the spontaneity of actions in animals and in man contradicts the hypothesis of any such determination and " fatal " concatenation of movements. For these two reasons we must suppose that the atoms possess, in addition to gravity, a second cause of movement, an entirely indeterminate capacity of " diverging " spontaneously, but " infinitely little," from the vertical line of descent. This is called their " inclination " or oblique motion ($\pi\alpha\rho$-$\epsilon\gamma\kappa\lambda\iota\sigma\iota\varsigma$, clinamen).[3]

So the atoms fall in the infinite void, being infinite in number for every kind of shape. By reason of the essential indeterminateness of their inclination, the meeting of any two of them is a pure matter of chance. However small the aggregate so formed may be, it creates a barrier against the fall of the rest. The heavier ones become fixed, the lighter bound off them when they collide with them, and a rotation sets in, which is the first nucleus of a world, which

[1] i. 43 ff., 60; Lucr., ii. 184–215; Cic., Fin., i. 6. 17–19, etc. Cf. above, pp. 113–15.
[2] i. 42, end ; Lucr., ii. 478–521.
[3] Lucr., ii. 216–93 ; Cic., Fin., i. 6. 18 ff. ; De Fato, 10. 22 ; Nat. Deor., i. 25. 69 ; Diog. Œn., fr. 33 W ; and other texts in CXLVI, 281.

is, as it were, " walled round " by burning ether.[1] In the same way other worlds, similarly limited, are formed, " infinite in number." Now, in the eternity of past time, which is a third infinity, all possibilities of meeting and combination have been able to come about (this is what justifies the method of multiple explanations), until, still by mere chance, that combination was obtained which was capable of persisting and developing.[2] The normal and the good are, therefore, a result of contingent combinations, not their cause. The natural order of causality cannot be " inverted " without absurdity. There is no final cause.[3]

Even if our world showed itself kinder to man, it would still, by the fact that it is a composite, contain the principle of its decomposition and destruction. It cannot, therefore, be regarded as a divine work, any more than another world.[4] So, to remove the gods from inevitable risks of destruction, Epicuros places them (a curious adaptation of the theology of Aristotle) in " the spaces between the worlds " (μετακόσμια, intermundia).

Epicuros's statement that the gods exist is not a prudent concession to public opinion, as is the advice, coming from the opponent of " impious " superstition, to take part in religious ceremonies. The reality of the gods is clearly an integral part of his doctrine. First, they are the object of a " prenotion " common to all men, and for a prenotion there must be the influence of a reality. Secondly, they answer to our intuition of an " immortal and blessed existence." [5] In this we find the chief application of a law which plays a great part in Epicurean physics, the law of " compensation " or " equilibrium " (ἰσονομία), aequilibritas, aequalis tributio), in virtue of which our painful mortal life must have something to counterbalance it in the whole of nature, and, in general, everything must be counterbalanced by its opposite.[6] What is most beautiful in us gives us an image of the nature of the gods ; their bodies are " a sort of bodies," " holy " or " glorious " bodies. Although they are aggregates of atoms of the most subtle kind, they are not subject to the limitation

---

[1] E.g., Lucr., v. 454–9.   [2] E.g., Lucr., i. 1021–37 ; ii. 1048–76.
[3] Lucr., iv. 823–57.   [4] Lucr., v. 146–234. Cf. **CXLVI**, 367–83.
[5] iii. 123 ff. ; Lucr., vi. 68–79 ; v. 1198–1203. Cf. Cic., Nat. Deor., i, end ;
CXLVI, 12–13, 387.
[6] Cic., Nat. Deor., i. 19. 50 ; Lucr., ii. 569–80 ; cf. i. 524–6.

of concrete individuality. They are like " outlines " or " silhouettes," constantly moving and infinite in number.[1]

Since the fear of death is, with the fear of the gods, the chief obstacle to inward peace, we must know what life is. A thing is living when the aggregate of atoms constituting its body is such as " to serve as a house " to another aggregate of atoms, which is its soul. So long as the thing is alive, the two aggregates are in constant correlation and interaction. But when the containing body becomes seriously broken up, the contained body becomes free, and, since it owed its cohesion solely to its inclusion in the other, it is scattered abroad, and the atoms which composed it separate. Death, therefore, is " nothing which concerns us," for once the soul has left the body we cease to feel. The illusion of a future life is dispelled. Moreover, the soul-composite has a twofold function. It spreads life through the organism, and, having its seat in the heart, it is the principle of sentiment, thought, and will. The elements composing it, which make its organic or " un-thinking " function (τὸ ἄλογον, anima in the strict sense) possible, are very tenuous and very mobile, fiery (calor, vapor), airy, and of the nature of breath (aura). For the properly psychic or " thinking " function (τὸ λογικόν, animus, mens) there are atoms of even greater subtlety, doubtless those of which the gods are made, which have no equivalent in our experience; therefore this fourth element is " nameless." The first function, as we have seen, is the condition of the other; but the " soul of the soul " is sufficiently independent to be capable of happiness, whereas the organic soul suffers with the body with which it is mingled.[2]

For the rest, sensation, thought, and will can be explained by purely mechanical processes. Every real thing constantly " emits simulacra " (εἴδωλα), a kind of hollow envelopes which keep its general structure and qualities, whether these be superficial like colour or are capable of rising to the surface like odour. These proportionate miniatures of objects move with extreme rapidity. When received by the sensoria, they penetrate to the heart, where they produce sensation. There is an infinite number of them floating in the air; they come

---

[1] ΚΔ, 1 and Schol. Lucr., v. 146–55, 1161 ff., etc.; Cic., Nat. Deor., i. 18–19; Div., ii. 17. 40. Cf. **CXLVI**, 352–66.

[2] i. 63–8; iii. 124 ff.; ΚΔ, 2; Lucr., iii (the whole book).

not only from what encounters our senses, but from objects which have ceased to exist and others beyond the range of our senses, either at the present moment or by their nature, such as the gods. In this way all images are formed, the phantoms of dreams and delirium and the apparitions which have given rise to the prenotion of the gods. In their long journey, these frail atomic pellicules may become altered, or fuse with others more or less completely. This is how the simulacrum of the square tower has its corners rounded before it reaches me, or images of fabulous animals which have never existed, chimeras, centaurs, etc., are formed. This explains and confirms the absolute value of the criterion of sensation.[1]

The operation of the will is analogous. When the simulacrum of an object of desire or aversion, or that of the subject in one of his actions or manners of being, is present, it moves the thinking soul, which in its turn sets the organic soul in motion, and muscular movement is accordingly provoked or stopped. So, when Epicuros revives, in his own fashion, Aristotle's theory of the logical indeterminateness of future contingents, and attributes " personal independence " to us (τὸ παρ’ ἡμᾶς ἀδέσποτον), he is not thinking of liberty at all in the spiritual sense, and as something of the consciousness. In our organization, liberty is the result of the contingence of the atomic inclination. But it is sufficient, in his eyes, for the simulacrum of the happiness of tranquillity to be able to act on the soul and, as we shall see, to determine fitting movements or inhibitions in the body.[2]

On the appearance of living creatures from the earth, their mother and nurse, there are no important ideas in Epicureanism which we have not already met in Empedocles or Democritos. The transformism which some have seen in it refers only to the period of groping in which nature, seeking at random for a combination capable of surviving, tries experiments. But, once that combination has turned up, out of all the shufflings and dealings of chance, " the pacts of nature " (*foedera naturae*) are signed for good. Specific characteristics are fixed and reproduce themselves without variation, until the species grows old and dies with the world to which it belongs.[3]

[1] i. 46–53 ; Lucr., iv. 26–268, 722–822, 962–1036, etc.
[2] iii. 133 ff. ; Lucr., iv. 877–906 ; ii. 251–93 ; Cic., *De Fato*, 10. 21 ; 16. 37 ; *Acad.*, ii. 30. 97 ; *Nat. Deor.*, i. 25. 70.
[3] Lucr., i. 584–98 ; ii. 865–901 ; v. 780–924.

But another problem of origins had long exercised men's minds, that of the prehistory of mankind. Hecataeos of Abdera had written about the Hyperboreians and the Egyptians, and it may have been indirectly from him [1] that Lucretius got what he says of the life of the earliest men and the invention of the arts, by which man sought to preserve or adorn his life—speech, social life based on contract, political organization, the production of fire, metal-working, agriculture, the training of useful animals, the weaving of clothes, house-building, the division of time, writing, music, poetry. Epicuros himself defined the conditions of technical progress in connexion with the invention of speech. External nature, he says, " presses on " us, and its action, when reflection has been applied to it, engenders our inventions with time.[2] Yet this progress, at least in Lucretius, is not really an advance. It is a remedy for real evils—a less kindly nature, a diminished power of resistance. The evils which it has begotten— religion, war, and the like—are more numerous and greater than those to which primitive man was exposed in the primitive state of the world.[3] The pretended benefits of civilization are, therefore, so many dangers for wisdom, and wisdom lies in approaching the state of nature.

For the Epicurean seeks the foundation of his ethics in nature. The sole object of his " canonics " and physics is to enable him to discover it with certainty. Now, we see that all living things, in so far as they obey their natural tendencies, seek pleasure as their good. Pleasure is " the beginning and the end of the happy life " ; it is " our principle of all preference and all aversion," and therefore is the supreme affective criterion to which all our judgements on our good refer. But, on the other hand, " we need pleasure only when pleasure is absent and we suffer from its lack ; but when we do not suffer we do not miss pleasure." That is why " the term of greatness in pleasures," their maximum, is " the elimination of all suffering." Where pleasure is, and so long as it exists, there can be no pain or sadness.[4]

---

[1] The accounts of Lucretius and of Diodoros Siculus (*Bibl. Hist.*, i. 7 ff.) agree on the whole. Cf. K. Reinhardt, " Hekataios v. Abdera u. Demokritos," in *Hermes*, xlvii (1912).

[2] i. 75 ff. ; Diog. Œn., fr. 10 W ; Lucr., v. 925 to end.

[3] Cf. L. Robin, " Sur la conception épicurienne du progrès," in *R. de Métaph. et de mor.*, xxiii (1916).

[4] iii. 128 ff. ; ΚΔ, 3. Cf. Cic., *Fin.*, ii. 3. 9.

Now, this is what people forget when, like the Cyrenaics, they define pleasure by movement. No doubt, " in movement which is being accomplished a joy and a satisfaction are manifested "—as, for example, when you are in the act of quenching your thirst. But true pleasure is to have thirst no longer ; then the object of the movement is attained. So the reality of pleasure exists only in " stabilized pleasure " (ἡδονὴ καταστηματική, voluptas in stabilitate), not in " pleasure in movement " (ἡδονὴ ἐν κινήσει, voluptas in motu), which is merely the former in the process of becoming.[1] This distinction leads to a very important practical consequence. Whenever, having come to the term of the movement which prepares our pleasure, we try to prolong that movement, we really cause the final realization of our pleasure to recede. No doubt, we " vary " it (ποικίλλειν) by thus perpetuating the " ticklings " of our sensibility (γαργαλισμοί, titillationes). But these extra embellishments, in which men delight, do not increase pleasure, since they do not increase the satisfaction of the need from which we were suffering. Pleasure is the elimination of that need, nothing else and nothing more. " Absence of pain " (ἀπονία, vacuitas doloris, indolentia)—that is perfect, achieved pleasure. It is not a state of passing from past pain to future pleasure ; it is a positive term, where we should stop and settle.[2]

Moreover, since the body and the soul are two distinct aggregates, but one part of the soul gives sensibility to the body, while the other is relatively independent of it, it is legitimate to distinguish between pleasures of the body and pleasures of the soul, that is, of the thinking soul. But we must not be misled regarding this distinction. The pleasures of the body are not only pleasures in movement, for they consist, on the contrary, in " a stable equilibrium of the flesh "—this is, in the strict sense, " absence of pain." The thinking soul, too, could not obtain " absence of disturbance," ataraxia properly so called, without having had the enjoyment of the internal movements which bring about that final tranquillity.[3] Moreover, the pleasures of the soul are not superior in quality to those of the body, for one pleasure is

[1] CXLVI, 1–2 ; Cic., Fin., loc. cit., and 5. 16. Cf. above, pp. 261–2.
[2] ΚΔ, 18 ; Cic., Fin., i. 11 ; ii. 3. 9 ff. ; Nat. Deor., i. 40. 113 ; CXLVI, 411.
[3] Ibid., 68, 424–8 ; iii. 131, end ; cf. 128 ; Sen., Ep., 66. 45.

as good as another. We should have no quarrel with the debauchee, Epicuros said, if his pleasures were able to satisfy him, if they delivered him from the fears which trouble the soul, if they were free of what is the only evil—pain.[1] But, each of the two kinds of pleasures has its own function. Those of the body are fundamental, as Epicuros declared frankly, to the great indignation of his opponents. " The principle and root of all good is pleasure of the belly." [2] But " the flesh is so made that it perceives the limits of pleasure as infinite, and would that it should last to all infinity." The soul must, therefore, set its limits for it " by reflection " ; for " the soul knows that pleasure is as great in a finite time as in an infinite time, and that one does not need an infinite time in order to be happy." [3] The soul also measures the pains of the body. If they are chronic, they are not very keen, since I continue to live, and in an incurable infirmity like blindness the soul still finds some enjoyment. If they are acute, they cannot last long, or else death will presently deliver me from them.[4] Lastly, thanks to the personal power which is in me, I can summon to my aid so many images of my former joys that they will " drive away " my present pains, forcing them " to retire," so that I no longer even feel them. " I am spending a happy day, and it is the last of my life," Epicuros wrote in the midst of the awful pain of which he was to die ; for all these sufferings were " faced by the tranquil contentment of my soul, bent on the memory of our old conversations." [5] This is a haughty attitude, which has its parallels, but the Epicureans alone tried to connect it with the very conditions of experience.

Ignoring this aspect of the doctrine, the detractors of Epicuros laid stress on his defence of pleasure, which was easy to misinterpret. " When we say that pleasure is our end," Epicuros answered, " it is not the pleasures of debauchees . . . that we are considering." [6] For there is a rule, born of the reflection of the mind which estimates the " wealth " of the virtual pleasure which exists in our pains as well as in our pleasures, their *quantity*, not their quality.

[1] KΔ, 10. Cf. Cic., *Fin.*, ii. 7. 21.
[2] **CXLVI**, 67, 409.   [3] iii. 126 ; KΔ, 19 ff. Cf. **CXLVI**, p. 397
[4] iii. 133 ; KΔ, 4. Cf. **CXLVI**, p. 395, nos. 446 ff., 503.
[5] **CXLVI**, 138 ; cf. 601 ; Cic., *Tusc.*, ii. 7. 17 ; iii. 15. 33 ; Sen., *Ep.*, 9. 3.
[6] iii. 131.

" It is just because pleasure is the first and natural good that we do not seek every pleasure. On the contrary, sometimes we pass over a number of pleasures, when a greater quantity of pain must ensue for us. On the other hand, we prefer a number of pains to pleasures when a greater pleasure will be the result for us. . . . So every pleasure, in virtue of its own nature, is a good, and yet not every pleasure is to be sought. So, too, every pain is an evil, but not every pain is such as to be always avoided." What is ordered, then, is a " comparative measurement " (συμμέτρησις), with pleasure for its unit and the strict demands of nature for its standard. Now, among our desires and among our aversions there are some whose object is outside these demands. Therefore Epicuros divided the desires into three classes (and the aversions correlatively)—those which are " neither natural nor necessary," such as that of obtaining honours, those which are " natural but not necessary," like that of every refinement by which a natural pleasure is " varied " without being increased (" Send me a little pot of curds," Epicuros wrote to a friend, " that I may have a feast when I feel inclined "), and, lastly, those which are both " natural and necessary," such as those of eating when hungry and drinking when thirsty, which can be satisfied with black bread and water. We shall do well, never to yield to the first kind of desires. The second we shall only obey exceptionally, for their rarity is what makes their value. The last are the easiest to satisfy, and are always " within our reach " (εὐπόριστοι, parabiles). " Thanks be given," said the Master, " to blessed Nature, for having placed within our reach the things which are necessary, while those which are not easily within our reach are those which are not necessary ! " To keep oneself " within the limits of nature " is to possess self-sufficiency (αὐτάρκεια), and is the " height of wealth." [1]

All the traditional virtues, temperance, courage or strength of soul,[2] prudence, therefore have their place in the Epicurean conception of individual conduct. But none of them is of value except in relation to pleasure. " I spit on morality " (τὸ καλόν), Epicuros said,[3] " and on the hollow admiration

---

[1] iii. 129-32 ; ΚΔ, 15, 29 ; Cic., *Fin.*, i. 13. 44 ff. ; Lucr., v. 1116–18. Cf. **CXLVI**, 181 ff., 456, 468–77, 602.

[2] Cic., *Fin.*, i. 14. 47 ff. ; 15. 49 ; **CXLVI**, p. 269, note on l. 19.

[3] *Ibid.*, 512 ; cf. 504, 506.

which is bestowed on it, when morality does not produce any pleasure ! " Of all the virtues, understood thus, the fundamental, perhaps the only virtue, is prudence (φρόνησις), for the discernment of the true pleasures is the work of reflection. Therefore it is not unlimited sensual enjoyment which creates an agreeable life, " but a sober calculation, applied to knowing the reasons of every preference and every aversion and to driving away the opinions which are the chief source of the trouble which seizes men's souls." For prudence teaches us that " we cannot live agreeably, if we do not live in a reflective, moral, and just manner, nor can we live in a reflective, moral, and just manner if we do not live agreeably." [1] Epicuros even goes so far as to say that prudence is of value by itself, and independent of success, for success is sometimes due to fortune.[2]

Refined as this egoism was, it led to theories of repulsive brutality. Thus, for example, in the mutual renunciation on which society and justice are based, each of the contracting parties has only his own interest in view ; therefore injustice is an evil only because there is more to be lost than gained by breaking the undertaking not to harm one another. Even if the unjust act were " ten thousand times secret " and practically certain to go unpunished, the soul is poisoned by the dread of final chastisement.[3] The value of friendship is that it is necessary to the security and pleasantness of life ; you love yourself, not your friend. Since this theory aroused indignation, some Epicureans modified it. Some said that my friend is another myself ; he is, therefore, not the means of my happiness, but an element of it. Others, whom J. S. Mill may have remembered, said, more subtly, that there is a true disinterestedness in friendship, for, with habit, the initial egoistic motive has come to be forgotten.[4]

Although in practice this conception of life was exposed to a number of difficulties and inconsistencies, for example, in the matter of family relations,[5] we seem to be able to extract from what has been said a fairly definite figure of the Epicurean

---

[1] iii. 132 ; cf. KΔ, 5, and Cic., *Fin.*, i. 18, beg.   [2] iii. 135 ; cf. KΔ, 16.
[3] KΔ, 31–8. Cf. Cic., *Fin.*, i. 16 ; ii. 16. 53 ff. ; **CXLVI**, 523, 531.
[4] Cic., *Fin.*, i. 20 ; ii. 24–6.
[5] This and similar difficulties are the theme of the book of διαπορίαι or *Uncertainties*. Cf. **CXLVI**, 18–20. The family cares revealed in the *Testament* may refer to the spiritual life.

Wise Man. Two paradoxical features must first be pointed out. This Wise Man is an ascetic. He subjects the pleasure of the flesh to a severe discipline. He reduces it to a minimum —on the pretext, it is true, of not spoiling it. He turns to a meditation which takes him away from the present for a means to drive suffering away. Secondly, he is a coenobite, for the only society for him is that of men who have gathered together to make their salvation in common. " Live hidden," Epicuros orders,[1] and he himself withdrew from the world. He is not bound by laws ; it is the wicked who are bound by the laws in their treatment of him. Unless the interests of his own protection compel him, he abstains from public affairs, and scoffs at those who have sacrificed " the crown of *ataraxia* " to the interests of their country.[2] He is, lastly, a spiritual healer. Against the four errors which corrupt life, regarding the gods, death, pleasures, and pain, he has found the " fourfold medicine " ($\dot{\eta}$ $\tau\epsilon\tau\rho\alpha\phi\acute{\alpha}\rho\mu\alpha\kappa\sigma\varsigma$) whose magical virtue calms and cures.[3] So he has in himself all the defensive resources which he needs in order to give himself the most positive of all happinesses. In the midst of a depraved civilization he has had the wisdom to return to good old Nature, and by this return to native simplicity he is able to be self-sufficient. He does not cease to be " amid pleasures," even when he is shut up in the red-hot bronze of the bull of Phalaris. He is " as a god among men, for there is nothing less like a mortal being than he whose life, though he is a man, passes in the midst of immortal goods." In blessedness " he vies with Zeus himself."[4] The emancipation of the Wise Man, " the equal of the gods," is, in short, the highest realization of individuality. Wholly centred upon itself, ruling itself by thought and imposing the law of thought on the flesh, it detaches itself from all the net of circumstances which surrounds it on every side. The independence of the Wise Man is the culmination of the individualistic tendencies which strongly mark Epicurean philosophy. That philosophy may be called a generalized atomism.

Historically, Epicureanism is an attempt to give more

[1] **CXLVI**, 551. [2] *Ibid.*, 187, 530, 556, 559 ff.
[3] *Pap. Herc.*, 1005, col. 4. Cf. iii. 133 ; Cic., *Fin.*, ii. 7, end ; 29. 94. These are the four first $\kappa\acute{\nu}\rho\iota\alpha\iota$ $\delta\acute{o}\xi\alpha\iota$.
[4] iii. 135 ; Diog. Œn., fr. 63, cols. 3–4 ; Diog. Laërt., 117 ; Lucr., iii. 322 ; Cic., *Fin.*, i. 18 ff. ; **CXLVI**, 601 ff.

coherence to Cyrenaicism and a dogmatic justification to the asceticism of Pyrrhon. It was not so much a philosophic school as an organized religious society, in which every member received the talisman of his deliverance and the rule of his salvation. The Epicureans may themselves have been partly responsible for the misunderstanding of the spirit of their doctrine by the uninitiated. But they were neither the " swine " of whom Horace speaks nor even refined, delicate voluptuaries. Seneca, Stoic as he is, judges them fairly when he observes the " sadness " which is at the bottom of the Epicurean life, by the side of its " holiness and righteousness." [1] It is possible, too, that the doctrine owed its enormous success to that very variety of its aspects, which constitutes its originality. It declares pleasure to be the highest good, and diminishes it by asceticism ; it places resignation side by side with beatitude, and melancholy with optimism ; its thorough sensualism is supplemented by a reasoned calculation of pleasures ; it is materialistic, and seeks its foundation in thought ; it is scornful of scientific truth, and bases conduct on the knowledge of nature ; into mechanism it introduces liberty ; it combats superstition, and preaches a faith.

Since Metrodoros of Lampsacos, that " second Epicuros " [2] and dearest of the disciples, died seven years before the Master, the management of the school passed to Hermarchos. Colotes, another disciple of Epicuros, is known from the treatise in which Plutarch attacked Epicureanism in connexion with one of his writings. In general, we know hardly anything of its most illustrious representatives down to the Ist century B.C. Philonides of Laodicea and Demetrios the Laconian are little more than names to us. Zenon of Sidon, Phaedros, Patron, and especially Philodemos of Gadara are somewhat better known, thanks to the papyri of Herculaneum, and thanks to Cicero, who knew and esteemed them all. After them there is total darkness, as far as we are concerned. It would seem that the life of the school was altogether dispersed in local brotherhoods, and the Garden was no longer the " holy place " of the community.

---

[1] *Vit. Beat.*, xiii. 1.   [2] Cic., *Fin.*, ii. 28. 92.

Chapter III

EARLY STOICISM

The philosophy of the Stoics is like that of the Epicureans in its final intention, the definition of the notion of the Wise Man, and in the problems which it considers ; they are the same problems, and on all of them it adopts an attitude exactly opposite to that of the Epicureans. The opposition runs all through. In the domain of materialism, it is vitalism as against mechanism ; as a pre-Socratic patron of their cosmology, Heracleitos is chosen instead of Democritos ; there is teleology instead of chance combinations ; godhead lies in the heart of the world and not outside the worlds ; there is one single world, not an infinity of worlds, and it is not wholly destroyed, but is reborn ; the division of matter does not stop at the atoms, but goes on to infinity ; all is full, and vacuum only exists outside the world ; there is a generalized solidarity, with fatalism, instead of generalized atomism with contingence ; there is complete fusion, instead of an aggregation of simple units. These are not so much differences as reactions ; two philosophies are engaged in hand-to-hand combat.

Now, it certainly seems that this obstinate, methodical contradiction must be put down to the Stoics. Epicuros had already been teaching for several years when Zenon of Cition opened his school, about 300, in the Painted Portico, *Stoa Poikile*. Previously he had been feeling his way. He had come to Athens for the first time between 315 and 312 (by the chance of a shipwreck, according to one tradition), and had heard, in succession, Theophrastos, perhaps Xenocrates, certainly Polemon, Crates the Cynic in particular, in whom he had sought a living image of Socrates, and lastly, among the dialecticians of Megara, Stilpon, Diodoros Cronos, and his disciple Philon. It therefore seems that the early success of the Garden led Zenon to undertake a symmetrical and opposite work with other methods. When Timon and others sneered at him as a " Phoenician," they doubtless referred to his sham originality. Moreover, even if the Porch started before the Garden, it would none the less be true that a very striking characteristic of early Stoicism was its continual development, so unlike the unchangeableness of Epicureanism, and an ingenuity which endeavoured not so much to open new paths as to follow its opponents on to their own ground, laboriously adapting defence to attack, without appearing to yield anything. At the service of their tactics these men, almost all from Asia, placed all the resources of their mystical tenacity and of a verbose, tricky subtlety, to which Greek dialectic only furnished its modes of expression.

When Zenon died, at the age of seventy-two (by his own hand, it is said), revered by many disciples, the direction of his school passed into the hands of one of the oldest and most devoted of them, Cleanthes of Assos. According to the story, he was a retired pugilist, and used to draw water for a market-gardener at night, in order to pay his fee at the school next day. Whether the story is true or false, it at least tends to show that the " second Heracles," as he was called, was a man for whom philosophy was a religious matter, concerning his life's salvation. But he was more serious than versatile, and during the long years in which he managed the school (264–232) it steadily went down. Against the attacks of the Epicureans or of the New Academy, Cleanthes could only oppose the solid weight of his own principles. Fortunately he found an able helper in Chrysippos of Soli (or Tarsos). When Chrysippos succeeded Cleanthes, he restored the prosperity of the Porch, and was called its " second founder." In his teaching and by his immense literary output (over 705 books), he waged war on the rival schools with untiring courage until his death at the age of more than seventy (208–207).

But this was not the only aspect of the earliest Stoicism. Instead of turning away from public affairs, like the Epicurean, the Stoic strove or condescended to be a factor in Hellenistic politics. Aratos of Soli, whose metrical adaptation of the *Phenomena* of Eudoxos has been partly preserved in Cicero's quotations, Persacos of Cition, and Sphaeros of the Bosphorus

were like ambassadors of the school at the courts of princes—
Aratos and Persaeos with Antigonos Gonatas, King of Macedon,
and Sphaeros with Ptolemy Euergetes and later with Cleo-
menes III, King of Sparta. Moreover, while the aim of the
mother-school was to preserve the orthodox tradition, while
developing, there were some more uncompromising, like
Herillos of Carthage, who has been wrongly supposed to have
had a tendency towards Peripateticism, and Ariston of Chios,
both disciples of Zenon, each of whom declared that his own
school represented the Master's true spirit. They were, no
doubt, heretics, rebels against the official discipline, but they
were not heterodox. For it is remarkable that this Stoicism,
which had principally retained the Cynic influence, while
purging it of its element of charlatanism, was that to which
the revival of the doctrine in Imperial times was attached.
Lastly, it is perhaps an instructive fact, that one Dionysios
of Heracleia, not having found in Zenon's philosophy the
peace of mind for which he sought, went in pursuit of it to the
Cyrenaics or the Epicureans.

After Chrysippos, the Porch showed a more marked
tendency to accommodations and concessions, although the
doctrines which represented the special character of the school
were still proclaimed for the benefit of the public. Zenon of
Tarsos and Diogenes of Seleuceia in Persia, called the
Babylonian, were pupils of Chrysippos. The latter was with
Carneades and Critolaos the Peripatetic on the celebrated
embassy which the Athenians sent to Rome in 156–155 to
obtain the remission of a fine. The tradition of Diogenes was
carried on by Antipatros and Archedemos of Tarsos, Apollodoros of Seleuceia, and Boëthos of Sidon, with whom Middle
Stoicism begins. At the same time, we find men trained in
the school devoting themselves to special studies, some of
which, such as rhetoric and grammar, were held in great
honour there—the grammarian Crates of Mallos, Zenodotos,
the librarian of Alexandria, Eratosthenes (276–194), who
perhaps came from the school of Ariston, Apollodoros of
Athens, who wrote the *Chronica*, the famous critic Aristarchos,
etc. Stoicism was already tending towards philosophical
doxography.

Stoic literature was considerable. Ariston and Herillos
seem to have confined themselves to morals, the former having

a preference for the Cynic method of practical instruction by example or typical anecdote (χρεία). Zenon, Cleanthes, and Chrysippos, on the other hand, not to mention their polemical writings, dealt with all the " domains " (τόποι) or branches of the teaching of the schools of philosophy—logic and rhetoric, physics and theology, morals and politics, the philosophical explanation of the poets. The works of Chrysippos were the richest example of such a complete collection. He also devoted special books to Providence, Fate, divination, and the problem of the possibles. Of all this we have, unfortunately, only general summaries, like that of Diogenes Laërtios (*Zenon*, vii. 1), or arbitrarily chosen quotations. Few passages of any length have been preserved—forty lines of a hymn of Cleanthes to Zeus, important extracts from Chrysippos's treatises *On the Soul* and *On the Passions* in Galen's book *On the Dogmas of Hippocrates and Plato*, and mutilated fragments of the same author's *Logical Questions* and a passage on the dialectical virtues of the Wise Man on papyri.[1] Having no direct documentary evidence, it is only exceptionally that we know what each philosopher contributed to the progressive constitution of classical Stoicism. As a rule, our classical Stoicism seems to be the Stoicism of Chrysippos, that is, a doctrine which had been compelled by the objections of the New Academy to change its form. What Cicero tells us bears the mark of the successors of Chrysippos, and also of Middle Stoicism, or else it has become distorted in passing through the academic eclecticism of Antiochos of Ascalon. In Plutarch (*The Contradictions of the Stoics, On Common Notions against the Stoics*), in Galen, in commentators on Aristotle, like Alexander and Simplicius, or, again, in Plotinus or Sextus Empiricus, we are dealing with enemies of Stoicism. Even the Stoics Seneca and Epictetos are not certain witnesses ; their Stoicism is far removed from the thorny dialectic of the maturity of the Old Stoa, and sees nothing in it but a historical curiosity.[2] It is impossible to discuss the evidence here. We must therefore take the history of the earliest Stoicism in one mass, and roughly in the form in which tradition presents it.

[1] **CLIII** (this reference will not be repeated), ii. 180, 131. The Letronne Papyrus (on negative propositions, ii, 298 a) is a school work.
[2] E.g., Epict., *Ench.*, 49 ; *Diatr.*, i. 4. 6 ff.

For the Stoic, philosophy is the " exercise " ($\mathring{a}\sigma\kappa\eta\sigma\iota\varsigma$) of an art whose special object is Wisdom, the science of divine and human things, or the supreme " perfection " ($\mathring{a}\rho\epsilon\tau\acute{\eta}$), which is divided into three kinds of " perfections " or studies— one logical or dialectical, discourse, one ethical, human life, and one physical, the world. Although this division, which doubtless came from Xenocrates and the earliest Peripatetics, was accepted by Zenon,[1] Ariston regarded it as a concession contrary to the spirit of the doctrine. Physics, he said, go beyond our range, and dialectic is only the mud on the road which impedes the wayfarer, or again, as when one is eating crabs, little meat for much shell.[2] But when the three parts were kept, the great question was, how they were related. Philosophy was compared to an orchard, to an egg, to an animal (Poseidonios). Logic was invariably the fence of the orchard, the shell of the egg, the bones and muscles of the animal. But the relative positions of physics and ethics varied according as the first place was given to fundamental conditions or to what results from them.[3] In any case, physics being the condition of logic and ethics, these two can only be properly understood if we know the general principles of physics, in relation to the world and in relation to man.

All that is real is *a body*, having its own individuality distinct from every other individuality. This being so, it acts and is affected. For, on the one hand, it has an essential motive spontaneity, entirely actual, a " tension " ($\tau\acute{o}\nu o\varsigma$), which, starting from its centre, endeavours to spread and then returns inwards to condense into a unity. On the other hand, what is thus extended or condensed by the active force is a passive matter, which is likewise the body, but the body in so far as it is unqualified and amorphous, or unindividualized. Matter, form, and mover are all one. In their turn, the *qualities* ($\pi o\iota\acute{a}$) of a body are themselves bodies, co-existent with one another and with the body. The body represents only the " proper quality " ($\mathring{\iota}\delta\acute{\iota}\omega\varsigma\ \pi o\iota\acute{o}\nu$) which subsists through the changing of the others and, by its tension, unites in a natural solidarity what would otherwise be a mere aggregate.[4] So we already have two of the Stoic

[1] i. 45 ff. ; ii. 35, 38. [2] i. 351–7, 392 ff.
[3] ii. 38–44 ; cf. iii. 68. [4] i. 90 ; ii. 301–3, 336, 363, 380, 386 ff., 395–7.

categories, *substance* and *quality* (ὑποκειμένον, ποιόν) ; they represent what is corporeal or real in the " something " (τι). The two others, *manner of being* taken by itself and taken *in relation* (πως ἔχον, πρός τί πως ἔχον), correspond to the something in so far as it is incorporeal, that is, to that which neither acts nor is affected, and in contrast to what is " not even something " (οὔ τι), such as a general qualification (κοινῶς ποιόν), or idea, which is only an " object of thought " (ἐννόημα).[1] So the categories here have quite another meaning than in Aristotle. They signify what is real, and alone real, in the individual, whether it be profound or superficial, whether it come from itself or from its environment. The incorporeal aspects of an entity are its events or its acts, mere manifestations of the causality which is in it, effects whose whole reality lies in their " enunciation " by a verb (λεκτόν, κατηγόρημα). To the incorporeals already mentioned we must add the place which the entity occupies, the time or interval of its movements and (in respect of the world only) the void in which it extends or contracts.[2]

Now, to be understood, this doctrine of the individual must be considered in relation to the pattern individuality of the world. If, instead of the " universe," the " all " (τὸ πᾶν), that is, the infinite void and the world which is virtually inside it, we consider the world itself, we have the " whole " (τὸ ὅλον), the totality of the corporeal and the incorporeals, all the real, the aspects of which are the categories. Since the infinite void is outside it, the world is finite and excludes vacuum ; it is single and perfectly one ; on every side it tends towards its centre, and is spherical. Now, if this is so, the world is also the very " organization " of the " system " which unites the heavens to the earth (διακόσμησις), and is also the divine principle which acts and organizes.[3] The matter thus organized is not amorphous, but already qualified by the active principle. The four elements, therefore, each constituted by a single quality of its own, themselves have both activity (fire or heat, air or cold) and passivity (water or wetness, earth or dryness).[4] Now, either in God or in the elements, activity is always the " tension " of a body in order to maintain its

---

[1] i. 65 ; ii. 329 ff., 361–3.   [2] i. 89–95 ; ii. 331, 341, 501–21.
[3] i. 99 ; ii. 526–30, 535, 550.
[4] ii. 418, 408, 410, beg., 439, end, 440, middle, 444.

constitution (σύστασις). That body is the " breath " or
pneuma, vital principle or spirit, which is made of fire and
air, or, more precisely, of what acts in the very activity
of those elements. It " goes through " (διήκει) the world
and penetrates even into its lowest parts. It makes it
live and maintains its unity. It " administers " it by its
" providence " (διοίκησις, πρόνοια); for it is a " thinking
breath," an " intelligent, craftsman fire," which " methodically advances to the generation of the world." So the
Stoics want to be both pantheists and monotheists, for the
force immanent and diffused in the world is a single " reason,"
an individual demiurgic principle, which makes the world " a
living thing full of wisdom."[1] We must not regard it as a
creator. But it is the craftsman of the wonderful finality
by which, in proportion to their kinship with that principle,
things which are find instruments of their good in the things
below them, and even in what might be taken for an evil in
respect of them. I need not quote the facile examples and
childish arguments by which the Stoics, from Chrysippos
onwards, tried to demonstrate the universality of this teleological relativism.[2]

What it expresses is, at least, a capital fact : the world is a
solid order of ranks, of which it is itself the end. There are
several degrees of individualization, since there are several
degrees of " tension." At the lowest degree, the *pneuma*
produces only qualified individuality, the consistency of the
body (ἕξις) — stone, metal, wood, etc. If this manner of
being also includes the spontaneous movement by which the
thing makes its being, what the *pneuma* then produces is a
growth (φύσις). It is, lastly, a *soul*, when in addition to all
this the thing has sensation and " motive impulse," or the
instinctive tendency to act (ὁρμή).[3] But, if things are divided
into ranks, they are also intimately bound together. For, to
explain the causality of the *pneuma*, in general and specially
in every being, Chrysippos, perhaps following Zenon, advanced
the theory of " total mixture " (κρᾶσις δι' ὅλου), a materialistic equivalent of Plato's participation. Mere juxtaposition
(παράθεσις), or a mixture which fuses two things together
(σύγχυσις) and, taking away their distinctive individual

---

[1] E.g., i. 171 ff. ; ii. 300, 441–4, 1107 ff., 1134, 1141 ff.
[2] ii. 1152 (Cic., *Nat. Deor.*, ii).   [3] i. 111 ; ii. 633, 458 (cf. 449, 716).

quality, annihilates them to produce a new thing, does not explain how two bodies, of which one acts and the other is affected, keep their individualities, although the action of the one penetrates and modifies the other. But this can be understood if the penetration (without a vacuum being necessary) is total, if one thing really mixes with another (σύμμιξις), as a drop of wine mixes with the whole sea. This presupposes the infinite divisibility of matter. Now, if fire and air are what act most, if God, " the burning breath," is the supreme agent, it is because, in virtue of their extreme mobility, they lend themselves best to that infinite diffusion.[1]

And now, how does the generation of the world and of the things in it come about ? There are no chance meetings and aggregations ; our fundamental postulate is a " seed " which develops, following an alternating rhythm. For fire, the most elemental of the elements, which at the beginning exists alone in the infinite void, would not satisfy the " love " and the generative impulse which are in it if, its tension diminishing, it were not extinguished. So it condenses and becomes air, and then air becomes water. But this water, penetrated by the breath of burning air, gives birth to a central seed, which is the " seminal reason " (λόγος σπερματικός) or law of the world. Then the living cosmos organizes itself, all at once, in distinct parts, each having its own function and seat. In the centre of the infant world part of the water condenses into earth, while another part remains on the surface. Under the action of heat, exhalations rise and, according to their degree of lightness, form surrounding spheres of air and of the ether where the stars are, the most intelligent living things and those most capable of a perfect movement. The seed also contains in itself all the seminal reasons, or laws of organization, of all living things, so that every individual is a " total mixture " of its whole pedigree.[2] After a fixed period, the living thing in its turn becomes capable of producing the seed of a new being like itself ; and so, too, after a " great year," when the stars have returned to their original conjunctions, the world must be capable of producing a seed from which a new world will issue, the exact image and full heir of the old, with the same individuals and the same events. For this eternal

[1] i. 92 ; ii. 338–40, 470 ff., 473, 480, 482. Cf. CLXII, 128.
[2] i. 102, 107, 120, 128, 497 ; ii. 413, 558, 579–84, 622, 684, 741, 747, 1027.

return there must be a process the inverse of the preceding process, a " pouring out " (χύσις), which destroys the world by taking it back, under the ever-increasing action of the internal fire, to the dilated tension of the original fire. In this conflagration (ἐκπύρωσις), which heralds rebirth, God, or Zeus, gathers together his sundered attributes, which are manifested symbolically for different regions or in different forms by the popular gods, and revives all his ordering power in its entirety.[1]

The law which Zeus, who is reason and providence, gives to the world is fate (εἱμαρμένη), a " concatenation of causes," such that even departures from the natural order are comprised in the eternal order ; for chance is only a word, which conceals our ignorance of the real cause.[2] Yet, in relation to a future event, fatality is not absolute. The event is in itself a possible contingent ; it will fatally become real only *if* no outside circumstance fatally comes to prevent it. It is, therefore, merely the result of a coming together of " co-fates." So the " inactive argument " (ἀργὸς λόγος) is invalid ; for my efforts to preserve or restore my health are written down in the general and eternal order of the world just as much as their result. One may blame the Stoics for conceiving of the " sympathy " of all things, and their " blowing together," in the same absolutely abstract way as the total mixture, or, again, for holding that the best form of relative necessity, or of universal determinism, was astrology, of which Poseidonios was afterwards the most active preacher.[3] But in asserting the governed interconnexion of things and facts they made a revolution. Causal connexion was no longer regarded as the logical development of an essence, but the " consecution," contingent in itself, of two stages in the fated development of the world—in other words, a real determination and a natural law. That particular fatalism, which Chrysippos strove, with great subtlety, to distinguish from the necessitarianism of the Megarics and to oppose to the freedom of the Epicureans or Carneades, none the less claimed to preserve the spontaneity of will. But this spontaneity was compelled to accept what the Cynic Œnomaos neatly called a " semi-

[1] i. 109, 510 ; ii. 596, 601, 616, 618, 623, 625, 1049, 1076.
[2] i. 175 ff. ; ii. 913, 919, 939, 954, 965, 973.
[3] ii. 543, 912, 952, 956 ff., 959, 962, 998 ; Cic., De Fato, 4–6.

slavery." A cylinder, Chrysippos said, is compelled by a blow from outside to roll down an incline, but its manner of rolling is independent of that compulsion ; it rolls as a cylinder. So, too, the internal spontaneity of my own nature is alone a " principal cause " of my actions ; in it lies my power of determining myself.[1]

The human microcosm, body and soul, is an image of the macrocosm. All that can be said of the divinity which is the soul of the world must likewise be said of our soul, which is a material " breath of a fiery nature," endowed with intelligence. As soon as this breath is moistened and then cooled by the air blowing on it, it causes a body to be born and live. It goes all through the body, having in the heart its own Zeus, its " directing principle," its *hegemonicon*. This principle, rather as Zeus has the gods of the seven planets under him, exerts its power by seven special functions—the five senses, speech, and generation. By its " tension," the breath of the animal's seminal reason is transmitted to the generative organ ; the breath of " immanent speech " (λόγος ἐνδιάθετος), which the breath of God speaks in the world or in our soul, in proportion to their tension, goes to the organs of speech and produces " uttered speech " (λόγος προφορικός) ; by its tension, too, the *hegemonicon*, like a spider on the watch in the centre of her web, provokes the various sensations in the appropriate organs.[2]

Now, the impression of a " real thing " (ὑπάρχον), passively received by the soul as a " stamp " (Cleanthes, and perhaps Zenon), or rather as an " alteration " (Chrysippos), produces a *representation* (φαντασία, *visum*) in the soul, which is, in Zenon's famous comparison, like a wide-open hand. A slight contraction of the fingers inwards will now be the symbol of the *assent* (συγκατάθεσις, *assensus*) given to the representation by the directing principle ; by the side of the representation, which is a *proximate* cause and in a sense external, and has its own weight and mark, we have a *principal* cause ; by accepting the representation we confer " evidence " on it. Then the hand closes altogether on its " capture " ; this is *comprehension* (κατάληψις), and the representation is now comprehensive, it is a perception. Lastly, to keep what

[1] ii. 344, 351 ff., 915-74 (*De Fato*), 978, 1000.
[2] ii. 134 ff., 605, 774, 778 ff., 806, 827, 836, 879, 885 ff., 891.

I have thus apprehended, I can clasp my closed hand in the other hand ; this is a symbol, not of opinion, the fruit of a " weak " assent, but of *art* and *science*, " systems of comprehensive representations," the former being empirical and directed at an end, while the latter is " sure, firm, and irrefutable."[1] So logical thought has its basis in the sensations. These are elaborated by the *hegemonicon* by various processes, similar to those of which the Epicureans spoke, to which one must add a " rational comparison," i.e. by analogy, and they produce naturally, and also by technical education, " common notions " or " anticipations " (κοιναί ἔννοιαι, προλήψεις) which, as we see, are very different from abstract concepts, which are empty of all reality. Those which are natural (ἔμφυτοι) constitute reason, which all men alike possess, but only men. The good employment of this is " right reason " (ὀρθὸς λόγος). In themselves, they are notions—whiteness, the good, god, man, etc. But the assent which they require is only found in judgements, sometimes based on demonstrations—this is white, good, a man ; the gods exist.[2] The process is the same with the appetitive and motive function. The representation of " something fitting " or an end provokes a spontaneous " motive impulse." If we give it our assent, it becomes a " motive thought " (λογικὴ ὁρμή), or a judgement which translates desire in beings capable of rational activity (πρᾶξις).[3]

The part of this physical theory which concerns human knowledge is an immediate condition of logic, and allows one to describe it briefly. What logic claims to be is a translation of the real into words. If, then, we pass over rhetoric, which is the art of " discoursing well," logic consists essentially in a dialectic, or science of correct discourse by questions and answers, capable of discriminating true and false in relation to *truth*, that is, the real, which is distinguished from the *true* as the corporeal from the incorporeal. The founder of Stoic dialectic was Chrysippos, who seems to have wanted to follow all the demands of his realistic conception to the end, without allowing himself to be deterred by the excesses of the most subtle formalism. Whereas Aristotle's logic was

---

[1] i. 58–60, 66–8, 72 ff., 484 ; ii. 53–6, 59. Cf. Cic., *De Fato*, 18. 42.
[2] ii. 81, 83–5, 87 ff. Cf. Epict., *Diatr.*, ii. 11. 2–3.
[3] ii. 836, 839 ; iii. 169, 171, 173, 462.

the "instrument" of science, this dialectic is a "part" of philosophy. It treats of the "signified" as well as of the "signifying" ; it is one of the "virtues" of the Wise Man. It is not enough, therefore, to say that the criterion of truth consists in "comprehensive representation" (Zenon), even if we add the "prenotion" derived from it (Chrysippos). What matters chiefly, is to find what "perfect enunciations," or enunciations forming a complete sense, that is, what judgements and *propositions* (ἀξιώματα) necessarily, in accordance with what has been said above, translate the action of one individual body upon another individual body. Then, we must find what rational system of such singular propositions translates *a priori* the rational system of the world and the "succession" of its single phases.[1] Nothing could be further from the logic of Aristotle.

Consequently, the most interesting propositions are those which, by means of a distinction introduced into a "simple" proposition, show its connexion with another. The various types of these connexions must correspond to the real connexions of things. The connexion of an antecedent and a consequent (ἡγούμενον and λῆγον) is a *connex* or conditional proposition (συνημμένον) : "*If* this man is wounded in the heart, he will die." A cause enunciated by the antecedent is a *causal* proposition : "He died *because* he was wounded in the heart." The mere co-ordination and disjunction of facts are *conjunctive* ("Both . . . and . . .") and *disjunctive* ("Either . . . or . . .") propositions. Lastly, there is the *comparative* relation of more to less. The first of these connexions, which the second merely makes explicit, especially deserves attention. For in it the relation of signification is such that the perceived antecedent is the "revealing sign" of a "hidden thing," which however, has been, or will be, or could have been an object of experience. No doubt, the antecedent being posited, the consequent cannot be denied without contradiction. But the logical contradiction is here only the expression of a real and fatal "consecution," that is, one contained from all eternity in the rational order of the world. Therefore the consequent is not, properly speaking, the result of the antecedent ; both are conjointly the results of that universal order, so that a

[1] i. 47–50, 60, 489, 491 ff. ; ii. 49, 105, 124, 130.

conjunctive proposition might take the place of the conditional proposition. When organized into a system, these propositions will become the theorems of a science or of an art—medicine, divination, astrology, etc.[1]

So, among the innumerable kinds of syllogisms which Chrysippos distinguished, only five were at once " formally " sound and " materially " true, at once demonstrative and needing no demonstration, and therefore such that all the others must be reduced to them. They are disjunctive and chiefly hypothetical syllogisms. If the connexion between two terms is one of conditioning and conditioned, the existence or non-existence of the one entails that of the other. Conversely, if they are incompatible or alternative, the existence or non-existence of the one entails the non-existence or existence, respectively, of the other. We must also have *inference*, which draws conclusions from some fact not immediately sensible, to enrich our knowledge.[2]

In sum, the nominalism and formalism of the logic of the Porch are only an appearance, behind which we find the naturalistic realism which was already revealed in the transformation of the Aristotelian categories. But, since they regard nature, at bottom, as a reason in action, this naturalistic realism can only be pure empiricism. For experience is the unceasing creation and expression of reason. The rôle of dialectic, therefore, is to discover the articulations of that creation and to enunciate them faithfully.

The object of morals is similar—to find the natural reason in ourselves and to express it in acts. Now, what has made us lose our clear vision of it is our *passions*. So the Stoics said that the passions should be extirpated, that is, torn up by the roots. But, whereas Zenon regarded them as merely an exaggerated or perverted movement of the motive impulse, what Chrysippos chiefly condemned in them was an error of judgement, which he put down to the too weak tension of the *hegemonicon* of a reasoning being. " All the passions," then, " are equally wrong " ; they allow of degree only in their accompaniments or physical consequences. Moreover, since the good or evil towards or from which our natural impulse drives us is a good or an evil which the agent represents to

---

[1] ii. 181, 193 ff., 203 ff., 207, 221. Cf. Cic., *De Fato*. 8. 15.
[2] ii. 239, 241 ff.

himself, of which he forms an opinion, either in relation to the present or in relation to the future, we can distinguish between several kinds of passions. Four will be fundamental —pleasure and pain, desire and fear. But beneath these the Stoics, who loved subdividing things minutely, recognized no less than seventy secondary passions.[1]

Under the empire of their passions, men (as the Cynics had already said) are " fools " (φαῦλοι, insipientes, stulti).[2] So, conversely, the first virtue of the Wise Man is impassibility ; nothing can afflict him or beat him down. This does not mean that he has no active tendencies ; far from it. But the judgements which he forms in respect of these are the " strong " assentings of a soul which spontaneously " stretches " (" tension ") towards agreement with the rationality immanent in nature. Consequently, his good affections, his " eupathies," are themselves agreements (constantiae) ; for pleasure he substitutes joy, for desire, will, for fear, precaution. So the Wise Man is assured of always being the happiest of men, as happy in his limited life as eternal Zeus. The fool, on the contrary, is always plunged in misfortune. For virtue, by itself alone, is sufficient to give happiness. Now, Wisdom unites all the virtues in their indivisible mutual consecution, and gives soul and " life " to them all. Therefore the Wise Man never errs or deceives ; having no needs, he alone is always rich ; being delivered from the passions, he alone is free ; he alone is beautiful with the supreme beauty of the soul ; a " citizen of the world," from which all fools are " banished," he in theory forms a society with all his peers, and therefore with the gods themselves ; since he dictates his law to himself, he alone is " dictator " and king.[3] In sum, the Wise Man is he who carries in himself the very reason of nature, and, if he seems to be outside nature, it is just because he alone is a faithful image of it amid the universal folly.

This famous paradox is the foundation of all the other paradoxes of the Stoics. If progress is unintelligible, it is because Wisdom is a complete, absolute perfection, without any relativity, particularly to time, and therefore immediate, and equal in all Wise Men. Is this not accordance with nature ?

[1] i. 205, 209 ; iii. 228, 377 ff., 380, 384 ff., 387, 393 ff., 397, 401, 409, 414, 443 ff., 468.
[2] i. 216 ; iii. 657 ff., 661-4.
[3] iii. 49-51, 54, 295, 305-7, 336 ff., 548 ff., 567 ff., 582 ff., 589 ff., 671-4, 677 ff.

Accordance either is or is not ; it admits of no more and less. If, on the contrary, it is possible to be more or less a fool, still one is a fool, and it does not much matter whether you are drowned at the bottom of the water or near the surface. Therefore, just as " all the virtues are equal," so all the vices are equally vices.[1]

For there is an *end* (τέλος) of our activity, immanent in it and ultimate. It is a sovereign good, desirable by itself and for itself. For it is identical only with the beauty (*honestum*) of our activity at work. That an advantage ensues from it for us is certain, just as it is a superiority for a dancer or a navigator to do all that his art includes magnificently well, even if he gets no profit in addition. Success is related only to aiming at a " target " (σκοπός). Now, this is something outside the modality of the activity, something partly subordinate to external factors. A good bowman is the man whose activity is in accordance with what is his internal law, whether he hit or miss the target. So, for morals, or " the art of living," the end is " to live in accordance and consequently with oneself " (Zenon), or, rather, " in accordance with nature " (Cleanthes), taking into account the " consecutions " which experience teaches us (Chrysippos). Virtue is a " disposition " appropriate to that end.[2]

But between good and evil, between virtue and vice, there is always a middle region, in which are the " targets " or aims and " progress." " Indifferent things " are really indifferent only in relation to good and evil. In themselves, they differ. Some are absolutely " neutral," such as the fact that you have an odd or an even number of hairs on your head. Others are " preferable " or " not preferable " (προηγμένα, ἀποπροηγμένα, *producta, reducta*). The former are, first, the aims to which we are aware of being " naturally appropriate " in virtue of our constitution, primary inclinations which, contrary to the Epicurean theory, do not aim at pleasure, but get it " in addition." More generally, they are " all that befits " our nature or our condition, our proper " functions " (καθήκοντα, *officia*). But these relative preferences cannot be the supreme object of a being capable of reasoning about nature and with it. He therefore rises to " the perfection of suitables, what is

[1] i. 566 ; iii. 221, 524–40.
[2] i. 179, 552, 554 ; iii. 2, 4 ff., 11, 13–16, 18, 29 ff., 34 ff., 75–8, 93, 197 ff.

fitting " ; " achieving " what was only " sketched," he creates " right actions " (κατορθώματα, *perfecta officia, rectae actiones*).[1]

Is it fair to join the opponents of the Stoics in charging them with a dual sovereign good, the natural end of our inclinations on the one hand and the end of moral righteousness on the other ? The truth is rather that, without leaving the domain of nature, the latter is the achievement of the former, and the former is a matter to which the other gives, in us, rational form. On the other hand, by trying to place " right action " so high that one single right action is enough to confer that miraculous Wisdom (whose acknowledged place is among mythical things), the Stoics were in danger of sacrificing, in fact, Wisdom to prudence, " right action " to the merely fitting, inward accordance with universal reason to wholly external conformity with our " functions." Now, the successors of Chrysippos (Antipatros, at least, for certain) had come in the end to define morality as " a reflective, continuous, unfailing choice of natural preferables." So its domain was henceforward the region of indifferent things. It was not that the previous Stoics had completely closed that region to the consideration of the Wise Man. But when the Wise Man made it the object of his " examination," it was, to the great scandal of Ariston, to draw up a body of " casuistry " for the use of the fools, or to establish a " paraenetic " in which they should find appropriate " advice " with a view to their various " functions." So, for example, while declaring that fools have no more reason for remaining in life than for leaving it, he nevertheless determined the *cases* in which it is least absurd for them to leave it voluntarily. For himself, in these matters, he does what he thinks good in the sovereignty of his Wisdom ; Wisdom sanctifies everything which it decides and makes it a " right action." If he considers it necessary, the Wise Man will turn three somersaults for money, and incest and cannibalism will seem indifferent things to him.[2] This was bringing in Cynicism by the back door, and adding one more paradox to many others.

The influence of Stoicism was perhaps less general than that of Epicureanism, but it was very great. It impressed

---

[1] i. 191–4 ; iii. 117–22, 127–30, 178, 182, 188, 190, 195, 491–4, 497 ff., 500–2.
[2] i. 249 ff., 358–69 ; iii. 18 ff., 658, 668, 757 ff., 743 ff. (688). For Antipatros, see 57–9.

men by its grandeur of scale, its lordly assurance, and its inexhaustible defensive resources. Its very contrasts enabled it to satisfy the most different tendencies—pedantry by the refinements of its scholastic methods, conservative respect for tradition by its opportunism and its skill in giving a philosophic cloak to a venerable stock of beliefs, and the widest religious sentiment by its theological naturalism. It was rationalistic and dogmatic, but at the same time very empirical; it had room for fate and the independence of the person side by side ; its ethics combined practical catechism with the most paradoxical mysticism. Such a hybrid was bound to revert, but by way of eclecticism, to the elements which it had by a miracle amalgamated for a moment. But what survived was its universalism, and, shorn of the pride of its submission to God, its moral mysticism. Cultured souls would turn to it for the refuge which those of the simple whose aspirations had not been satisfied by Epicureanism would seek in Christianity and other religions of salvation.

CHAPTER IV

THE NEW ACADEMY

THE successors of Xenocrates at the head of the Academy were Polemon, whose teaching was chiefly concerned with morals, and Crates of Athens, with whom Crantor was connected. Crantor was perhaps the earliest commentator on Plato ; with his famous book *On Grief* he founded the literary form of the " Consolation," which was afterwards so popular. None of these thinkers seems to have departed from the Platonic tradition, at least in the form established by Xenocrates.

But with Arcesilaos of Pitane, who succeeded Crates in 268–264, the school became, as it is called, a *New* Academy. As against the general dogmatism, it was akin to Scepticism, with which, however, it must not be confounded. The fact that both sides were at great pains to deny the kinship is certainly not enough ground for not accepting it. Moreover, when the Sceptics accuse their Academic doubles of being hypocritical doubters, who are Dogmatists within the walls of their school, their good faith is suspect.[1] But in fact, as we shall see, the spirit of the two sects is quite different.

Arcesilaos had at first studied mathematics with the celebrated Autolycos, gone through the school of Theophrastos, and known Sceptics and dialecticians of Megara or Eretria, at least in their writings. But his moderate and elevated mind seems to have been keenly alive to the barrenness of dogmatic disputes and the need for finding a better foundation for conduct than custom, with which the Sceptics were content, or the eloquent exhortations in which the Academy delighted at that time. Forgetting Xenocrates, he remembered that Plato had exalted the personality and the method of Socrates. To Socrates he would return. In the image which he formed

---

[1] Sextus, *Pyrrh.*, i. 233 ff. ; *Math.*, vii. 153 ff. Cf. Cic., *Acad.*, ii. 18. 60

of him, critical dialectic and the statement of ignorance held the first place, and it was in the same sense that he understood the doubt-expressing formulas and mythical expositions of Plato. Like Socrates, he wrote nothing, and like him he never dogmatized. He asked the opinion of his interlocutors, and started a lively conversation with them. Not the authority of the master but their own reason should guide them. Even his answers were new questions.

For every opinion has at least two faces. We must, therefore, refrain from judging ($\epsilon\pi o\chi\acute{\eta}$).[1] Whether this technical expression is his own or not, he is with the Sceptics in the notion. But he differs from them in that he is a dialectician ; he does not assert, but he discusses. The comprehensive or " cataleptic " representation of Zenon and Cleanthes (whose contemporary he was) never had a nimbler opponent than Arcesilaos. By examples drawn from fact, he showed that there are in nature " indiscernible " things, that there is nothing indisputably evident, nothing which one can assert without danger of confusion, that evidence is really based on assent, and that therefore, if one would not lightly accept a suspect evidence, one must be " acataleptic." Now, that consists in examining the reasons for and against, and " pleading," as in a law-court, for that which you can justify by reason to yourself or others ($\epsilon\H{v}\lambda o\gamma o\nu$), for that which " seems to us approvable." It is in this sense that Arcesilaos is a " probabilist." [2] So Ariston's witty sally, " Plato in front, Pyrrhon behind, Diodoros Cronos in the middle," is not a fair description of Arcesilaos. Far from being indifferent in the matter of morals, like the pure Sceptic, he seeks by his dialectical scepticism to base moral conduct on a positive test. For he, like the Stoics, holds that there are " right actions." [3] But one can only hope to find motives for them, not to demonstrate their accordance with an unknowable reality.

Lacydes, who succeeded Arcesilaos in 240 and is the source of our knowledge of his ideas, is for that reason the only Scholarch of the Academy who deserves mention down to Carneades of Cyrene. When Carneades, already renowned,

[1] Cic., *Acad.*, i. 12. 44 ff. ; ii. 18. 59 ; 21, beg. ; Sextus, *Pyrrh.*, i. 232.
[2] Sext., *Math.*, vii. 150–5 ; cf. *Pyrrh.*, i. 234.
[3] Sext., *Math.*, vii. 158.

went to Rome with the embassy of 156–155, his speech in the Senate and, still more, his lectures, in which he showed, in succession, the contrary aspects of moral notions, had such a dazzling success that the aged Cato hastened the departure of a guest who was such a danger to reverence for tradition. Unfortunately, Carneades wrote nothing, like Arcesilaos. Only in scattered remarks of Cleitomachos, who succeeded him in 129 and is said to have reflected his views faithfully, do we catch a glimpse of the figure of that skilful dialectician. After the great attempt of Chrysippos to restore the shaken Porch, he succeeded on attacking his opponent with his own weapons, and even with his language. While maintaining the critical attitude of Arcesilaos in respect of comprehensive representation,[1] he allows the reality of the sentiment of evidence. But he wants to determine its internal movements exactly, in order to give more guarantees to practice. It is a rope, *I think*, that I see there ; it does not move, and therefore " nothing draws my belief in a contrary direction " ; but if I examine it more carefully, " if I walk round it," I perceive that the rope is a snake.[2] So it is we ourselves who create truth, by successive gropings. Correlatively, the consciousness of our liberty means the possibility of our statement about such-and-such a future event coinciding with what will really happen.

The " critical " interpretation of certitude, a " prag-matistic " conception of moral conduct—that is the last word of the New Academy. Therein it is an anticipation of the most modern forms of thought.

---

[1] Cic., *Acad.*, ii. 26. 83 to 28. 90 ; Sext., *Math.*, vii. 159–64, 401–14. Cf. Cic., *ibid.*, 13. 40 ; Plut., *Stoic. Rep.*, 10, 1036 b.

[2] Πιθανόν, ἀπερίσπαστον, περιωδεύμενον. Cf. Sext., *Pyrrh.*, i. 227 ff. ; vii. 166–9, 176, 181 ff. ; Cic., *Acad.*, ii. 11. 35 ; *De Fato*, 9. 19 ; 11, beg.

BOOK FIVE

THE DECLINE OF GREEK THOUGHT

Chapter I

SCIENTIFIC SPECIALIZATION. ECLECTICISM. REVIVALS

An immense period of nearly four centuries—that is the subject of this short chapter. Although much of our evidence comes from that time, and it saw great progress in the sciences, philosophical thought developed little. While the sciences became more and more specialized, the natural rationality of the old Greek spirit yielded more and more to the invasion of Oriental superstitions. It employed what vigour was left to it in working over its past achievement, or in mixing it all together in an alleged eternal philosophy, a pure negation of the individual efforts of thinkers, or in resuscitating it in another form. Certainly, there were still remarkable personalities, but they were remarkable chiefly for the intensity of their moral sentiment. Greek thought, as such, had exhausted its powers of invention. It became science, that impersonal thing, or it tended to founder in a turmoil of religiosity

Here we can only mark by a few names the principal stages or directions of the scientific movement. In mathematics, pure and applied (geodesy, optics, mechanics, astronomy, etc.), three men shed glory, in different degrees, on the Alexandrian age (end of the IVth century and all the IIIrd). The chief merit of Euclid, without doubt, is that he put in order and systematized the geometry, or rather the kind of geometrical algebra, on which others had worked before him. Archimedes, certainly a more original and wider genius, perfected the " exhaustion " of Eudoxos and extended the horizon of mathematical physics. Apollonios of Perge, taking up the work of Euclid, and of Menaechmos and Aristæos before him, treated the problem of conic sections by a method curiously similar to our analytical geometry.

Heron of Alexandria (probably Ist or IInd century after Christ) had less breadth of view, but was a careful investigator of numerical applications and a most ingenious mechanic. In the IIIrd century, in Alexandria, Pappos and Diophantos were not so much original mathematicians as makers of collections, but the latter gives us some information about the works which had dealt with the theory of numbers since the Pythagoreans.

After Eudoxos, two astronomers have a place by themselves—Aristarchos of Samos (IIIrd century B.C.), whose heliocentric theory, anathematized by the philosophers and defended among the specialists by Seleucos (IInd century) alone, was to remain in oblivion until Copernicus, and Hipparchos of Nicaea (IInd century), the most accurate of ancient observers and the founder of trigonometrical methods. In the IInd century of our era, Theon of Smyrna and Claudius Ptolemaeus (Ptolemy) merely expounded existing science, the latter in the famous encyclopaedia which deals with far more things than astronomy and was revered in the Middle Ages under its Arabic title of *Almagest*—ἡ μεγίστη (πραγματεία), *The Greatest (Treatise)*.

Medicine, which has to interpret facts and has to take so many psychological factors into account in practice, remained more within the orbit of philosophy. It was divided between its sects—the Dogmatists or rationalists, who claimed to follow Hippocrates, the Empirics, and the Methodists. The antagonism of the two last really began in the Alexandrian period with Herophilos of Chalcedon on the one side and Erasistratos of Ceos on the other. It developed on the occasion of the attacks of the Stoicizing Pneumatics of the Ist and IInd centuries of our era (Athenaeos of Attaleia, Archigenes, Aretaeos) on the school of Asclepiades, a contemporary of Cicero and an Epicurizing mechanist, whose pupil Themison was, in the Ist century, the true father of Methodism. Others, much better known, were chiefly compilers, like Celsus [1] (Ist century), or eclectics, like Galen of Pergamon (IInd century).

[1] Not to be confused with the Platonist of the same name combated by Origen.

We should also mention the explorers, whose voyages to fabulous lands, by widening the Mediterranean horizon of early Greek thought towards the Ocean and towards India, perhaps helped to disturb it as much as to enrich it— Nearchos, Alexander's admiral, the extraordinary Pytheas of Marseilles, and others. Lastly, Poseidonios and all those who have pillaged information from him, the geographer Strabo, Pliny the Elder in his stupendous encyclopaedia, brought the results of countless attempts to know or make use of nature and to represent the shape of the earth within the reach of all, not without confusions and discrepancies.

In philosophy, the IInd and Ist centuries were the age of eclecticism and erudition. In the Academy, after the death of Cleitomachos about 110, Philon of Larissa, and still more Antiochos of Ascalon (died about 68), to whom Varro and Cicero owed so much, gave probabilism a strange twist in the direction of dogmatism and, leaving the Epicureans out altogether, reconciled Plato with Aristotle, and the Academy, thus widened, with the Porch, reducing the most profound oppositions to mere differences of vocabulary. So, too, the Middle Stoa assumed a Platonic form with Panaetios of Rhodes (about 180–110), whose presence, with Polybios, in the circle of Scipio Africanus and Laelius was decisive for the establishment of philosophy in Rome. It inclined more towards Peripateticism in Boëthos of Sidon and Poseidonios of Apameia (died about 51), the latter of whom, however, returned to the orthodox views of the school, especially in physics. He was a great traveller, of unrivalled erudition, and the second father of doxography, after Theophrastos, and he enlarged and modernized Aristotle's encyclopaedia. If we methodically take Cicero, Lucretius, Strabo, Seneca, Pliny, and others to pieces, check their information from other sources where necessary, and examine the pseudo-Aristotelian *De Mundo* or the book of Cleomedes (IInd century after Christ) *On Circular Revolutions*, we shall, little by little, gather together the scattered fragments of the immense mass of material which for centuries constituted scientific tradition. In morality, as we see from the example of Cicero's *De Officiis*, which is derived from them, Panaetios and Poseidonios completely sacrificed the absolute morality of the early Stoics to the search for the " fitting," through all the winding ways of a subtle casuistry.

Of all the forms then assumed by philosophical syncretism, none is more significant than that which was so abundantly interpreted by Philon the Jew (first half of the Ist century after Christ). In Alexandria Judaism had long ago begun to Hellenize, and in the IInd century B.C. the ingenious Aristobulos had, in order to combine Greek wisdom with the revelations of Jehovah, provided himself with evidence, notably by fabricating Orphic poems. Moreover, on the fringe of orthodox Judaism, under mysterious Stoic and Pythagorean influences, the sects of the Essenes had formed, and those of the Therapeutae, who practised the contemplative life. Finally, Philon started the method of allegorical interpretation, using the rationalistic philosophy of the Greeks, especially Platonism and Stoicism, to discover between man and the transcendent God " intermediaries " neglected by the exalted mysticism of the Therapeutae. Under this God, who is both personal and the indeterminate One, there is a whole hierarchy of intermediaries—first, the Word or Logos and the Ideas which are the patterns of things, with Wisdom below them, then the Man of God, or the first Adam, and the Angels below him, then the Breath of God, and lastly the Powers, by which he places himself still more completely within our reach. To transform oneself by asceticism, and especially by inward worship, is to raise oneself, " coming out of oneself " ("ecstasy "), to the highest intermediary, the Word or revelation of God. Now, this seeking in the religious conscience, and with a view to salvation, of the real principle of an explanation of things was a novelty quite alien to Greek thought. Born of the mystery religions rather than of Judaism, this novelty came to establish itself in Hellenism with the increasing diffusion of Eastern cults.

With eclecticism went that work of compilation and exegesis, already mentioned in connexion with our sources, which was done by the makers of " manuals " and the commentators on Plato and Aristotle. These commentators were the keepers of the tradition of the schools. The Peripatetics maintained their tradition more faithfully, while the Platonists, having a doctrine which was less definitely laid down, were naturally inclined to introduce alien elements. Among these we may mention Potamon, in the middle of the IIIrd century of our era, in Alexandria, who is regarded as the father of eclectic Platonism, Plutarch of Chaeroneia (about 50–125), the Sophists Maximus of Tyre and Apuleius of Madaura in the second half of the IInd century, then, rather later, the physician Galen, Celsus, whose *True Discourse* can be partly reconstructed from the virulent refutation of it by the Christian Origen, Numenios of Apameia, who found Moses at the back of Plato, and Albinus and the so-called Alcinoos in their expositions of Platonism. All these men either interpret Plato in a theosophical spirit, in the smoky light of Oriental mysteries, using the allegorical method and overloading it with astrology, demonology, and magic, or, at the very least, bring him close to Peripateticism, or to Stoicism, or even, like the first Apologists, to Christianity. So the way was prepared for the Neo-Platonic revival.

Long before, the Neo-Pythagoreans had claimed to revive the secret teaching of Pythagoras. The founder of this sect is said to have been P. Nigidius Figulus, a contemporary of Cicero. But the most noteworthy, or best known, representatives of this arithmological mysticism, strongly tinged with Platonism and Stoicism, were, in the Ist century after Christ, Apollonios of Tyana, whose miraculous personality was set up as a rival to that of Jesus in an extraordinary biographical romance by Philostratos, and Moderatus of Gades, and, in the IInd century, Nicomachos of Gerasa, the author of the *Arithmetical Introduction*. The element of moral asceticism in the old Pythagoreans seems to have inspired a little-known variety of Cynic Stoicism, founded in Rome, about the same time as Neo-Pythagoreanism, by Quintus Sextius and his son. The Sextian school did not last long. One of its masters deserves mention—Sotion of Alexandria, whose teaching had a profound influence on the mind of Seneca. Seneca had also studied Stoicism with Attalos, and had learned, perhaps from him, the noblest moral maxims of the Epicureans. These combined influences were what gave its special character to the Neo-Stoicism which was started by Seneca. If we leave aside the *Natural Questions*, a mere compilation, he appears to be little interested in physics and still less in dialectic ; he often shows, not without a certain force, a keen sense of moral obligation and of its religious value. Rather later than

Seneca, we have L. Annaeus Cornutus, who wrote in Greek, and influenced Persius, and Musonius Rufus, who seems to have wished to return to the original tradition of Zenon, or rather to the purified Cynicism which had been defended by Ariston of Chios. But the real greatness of Musonius has been eclipsed by Epictetos the Phrygian. The *Manual*, if not the *Conversations* (*Diatribes*) collected by Arrian in the school of Epictetos at Nicopolis, and the admirable meditations of Marcus Aurelius *On Himself* are works whose content has passed through so many intermediaries into the modern mind that it will suffice to have mentioned them in their place.

The lofty sentiment of the spiritual life which we find in these last representatives of Stoicism is of religious inspiration. But this sentiment comes from a rational conception of the universe. That conception, which had been the essential element of Greek thought, is more and more effaced with the advance, favoured by the Imperial power, of a religious spirit which overturns the order of ancient values and, in the service of a confused mysticism, uses the vocabulary of the old philosophy, emptying it of its meaning. The profound decline of philosophical thought was not only seen in the multiplication and conjunction of religious cults. There were philosophical expressions of it, such as the religious syncretism of the so-called Hermes Trismegistos (Thrice Greatest), whose book appears to belong to the IIIrd century, or the doctrine of the Gnostics, which started at Antioch in the IInd century, spread chiefly among the Christians, and was combated by Plotinus (*Enn.*, ii. 9), whose mysticism, as we shall see, was of quite another quality. With its Pleroma and its generations of Æons, Gnosis, which claimed to come from Zoroaster, threw Greek thought ten centuries back, to the wildest of cosmogonies. Revelation had put down the endeavour of reason.

CHAPTER II

PLOTINUS AND THE END OF NEO-PLATONISM

OF all the attempted revivals of the first centuries of our era, only one is of real interest for the history of Greek thought, and that is Neo-Platonism, and, indeed, that of Plotinus alone.

From the mystery in which Plotinus deliberately wrapped his origins a few indications emerge which give one an idea of his personality. When he left Lycopolis, the distant city in Central Egypt where he was born, to come to Alexandria, he was already twenty-eight years old (232). He had therefore, doubtless, had time for personal meditation, and aspirations which he wished to define. So, for a long time, he looked in vain for the master who should give them a direction, until he met Ammonios Saccas. The original method of this teacher held him for about ten years, and later he was to introduce it, we are told, into his own teaching. The progress which he made in philosophy with Ammonios inspired him, we should note carefully, with a desire to know the philosophy of the Persians and the Indians, and he only left him to follow the Emperor Gordian on his disastrous expedition (242).

In Rome, where he settled about 244 after a stay at Antioch, and remained almost until his death (270), his activity seems to have been that of a philosopher and also of a spiritual director. On a text of Plato, Aristotle, or one of their more celebrated commentators, on a Stoic theory, on a difficulty raised by a pupil, on fashionable doctrines such as the Gnostic philosophy, the Master would utter reflections, and the questions or objections put to him served as a starting-point for further developments. The rule of his thought was adherence to the philosophy of Plato. In it the best tendencies of the past were made explicit, but it needed to be made explicit itself and to be cleared of the distortions to which it had been subjected. But, in addition to the hearers of these philosophical " lectures," some of whom were notorious opponents, there were " zealots," men and women, Romans and Orientals, who asked Plotinus for a rule of life, the perfect observance of which seems to have been total renunciation, asceticism, living in a community. Children were placed in his guardianship. In the exaltation of the spiritual life which he recommended, physicians appear to have seen a therapeutic method. His character attracted the attention of the Emperor Gallienus and the sympathies of the Empress. Lastly, to his followers he seemed to be endowed with supernatural intuitions and powers. In short, in a tired world in which the place of the old Orphicism had been taken by the many beliefs of the East, he was like another Pythagoras or Empedocles, but one whose thought was stocked with five centuries of dialectical elaboration of philosophical concepts.

The fifty-four treatises of Plotinus reflect the conversations and discussions of his school. After the Master's death, Porphyry of Tyre (whose real name was Malchos), the disciple who, with Amelios (Gentilianus of Etruria), had been on the most intimate terms with him, decided to publish these writings, in order to prevent an incorrect promulgation of his doctrines. But, instead of arranging them chronologically in the three periods into which their composition had been divided, he arranged them systematically, and, as it were, in order of profundity, and moreover, placed them, in accordance with the sacred rites of arithmology, in six groups of nine treatises each—the *Enneads*, or *Nines*. At the head of the edition stood a picturesque biography of Plotinus. It may be said, summarily, that the first *Ennead* is about the individual, the second and third deal with his environment, the sensible world, the fourth raises us to knowledge of Soul, the fifth, to that of Intelligence, and the sixth to that of Being and the One. But each treatise, considering its special subject from the point of view of the whole system, contains at least an outline of the system, which gives Plotinus an opportunity to dispose of difficulties which he has first discussed. Thus, by a very deft and very vivid critical or dialectical exegesis,[1] the reader is gradually taken to a higher point of view and is given a suggestion for an inward meditation in which the truth is revealed. The movement of thought and the force of sentiment are often quite irresistible.

Such a doctrine is hard to translate in terms of the intelligence, when it is separated, for purposes of exposition, from the images which are intended to create a sentimental attitude in the soul. It transposes all the old conceptions of Greek thought to a new plane. When Socrates made himself the apostle of " Know thyself," he gave to the reflective method as its final object (at least, that is what the historical development of his philosophy shows), the determination of essences and their mutual limitation. The Socratic schools, for all their differences, all set out to draw the main lines, with their intersections, of a reality which lies outside the subject but is fundamentally identical with thought in its purity. It was a humanizing of the old naturalism. No doubt, the Stoics had had a livelier and clearer sense of the dynamism of life, but it was of a life governed according to reason, a life of which the individual was only a part. Perhaps the earliest Scepticism was the only doctrine before Plotinus which, under the influence of Indian ideas, had a glimpse of the liberation of the subject as an annihilation of the mind in the indeterminate. But this negative position had no religious signification, and, consequently, the Sceptic criticism of rationalism aimed only at creating a scientific empiricism. Plotinus, on the other hand, broke with the tradition of Greek thought. The body is a tomb, the sensible world is a cavern or a slough, our earthly existence is a fall of the soul—in brief, Plato's Pythagorean Orphicism, his conception of love, all has a new meaning in Plotinus. It is no longer a matter of liberating the free gaze of the intelligence, but of restoring to the Ego all the wealth of its internal life. Moreover, the object of philosophy is not the finite, neither the rational nor the empirical finite ; it is a soaring to the infinite. Thus the infinite, which for Plato or Aristotle or the Stoics was a

---

[1] E.g., the criticism of the doctrine of the Categories in Aristotle and in the Stoics (*Enn.*, vi. 1), the criticism of the distinction between potentiality and action and of the notion of movement in Aristotle (ii. 5), and the interpretation of the five kinds of intelligible in Plato's *Sophist* (vi. 2, 8–18)

sign of unreality or of resistance to the order of reason, becomes for Plotinus the fullest and most perfect power of the Ego. His dialectic does not seek to define or to concatenate essences, but to make the subject capable of going beyond the finite and so realizing absolute unification in himself.

" More than once," Plotinus says, " when coming to myself out of a sleep of the body, having thus become external to everything else but internal to myself, I have perceived a marvellous beauty " (iv. 8. 1, beg.). But this vision, in which the fullness of my internal life manifests itself, supposes a series of stages. While the diversity of bodily activities is translated in my sensible life, I see that they all depend on a certain unity which directs them and binds them, my soul. The analysis of the powers of my soul reveals a new plurality ; while the soul, as it were on its lower side, specifies and organizes the diversity of sensible nature, it also directs the eye of contemplation upwards at the intelligible. When the intelligible, in its turn, is analysed, it is seen to be the correlation of a simple possibility and an effective act of intellection, which is itself a higher power of the soul. But, from a higher point of view, I see that all similar correlations are connected with one another, and that there is a universal thought which is as the substance of intelligible being. " It is as a plurality .hat this god (thought) exists in any individual soul, which is the very cohesion of that plurality, provided that it does not wish to go away from him. When, therefore, it has come close to him, and has so become a kind of unity, it asks, ' Who, then, is the father of this god, he who is single and anterior to his plurality, he who is the cause of his being and of the multiplicity of his being, he who makes number ? ' For number is not first, for before two there is one, and two only comes second " (v. 1. 5, beg.). It is, therefore, impossible that thought, which, like number, is the unity of a multiplicity, should be the last term to which the soul aspires, and where, its ascension completed, it will find rest. That principle must, therefore, be a unity absolutely devoid of all plurality (v. 9. 14). These are the regressions, or successive " reductions," by which the Ego at last discovers, under the deposits which have accumulated on the top, the truth and purity of its being.

That is the method for coming at the true, or, what is the same thing, for satisfying the aspiration of the soul to the divine. Outwardly, it recalls the " erotic " of Plato's *Symposium*. But that " erotic " was directed at the beautiful, and aimed at knowing intelligibles. Plotinus wants to go beyond intelligibility. " Detachment " (ἀπόστασις), which Plato also preached, would not bear all its fruits, if it did not lead to an " ecstasy," that is, to a state of rapture, which simplifies and unifies the soul, liberating it from everything which is limitation (vi. 9. 10 ; iv. 8. 1, etc.). It is a state which only a few privileged souls can know, and they only as a rare experience. " To that God who has no shape or form, who stands above thought and above everything thinkable, I, even I, you must know," says Porphyry, " have only once come near, so as to be one with him, in the sixty-eighth year of my life." As for Plotinus, " four times, during all the time when I was with him, he approached that end in an ineffable act, and not merely potentially " (23). It is no longer a question of merely " following God " or resembling him but of uniting with him in love, feeling his much-desired " presence," blending with absolute unity. It is not enough to compare philosophy to the revelations of the Mysteries, as Plato did ; for Plotinus, the mystery itself is the last word of philosophy. Plato's One was certainly the summit of a hierarchy, but it was so as being measure and limit ; the One of Plotinus is the absence of limit, infinity.

But it is not enough to show the soul the way to salvation ; we must explain its fall, say why there are sensibles, evil, and error. This theoretical part of the philosophy is the inverse of the other, descent as against ascent. To call this descent a " procession," as Proclos does, is perhaps to misrepresent Plotinus's thought. For the word suggests a progress, a cortège. Now, when Plotinus speaks of the onlookers at a royal show who are content to have seen the crowd of great dignitaries and do not wait for the sovereign to appear (v. 5. 3), what he is describing is the progress of the soul towards the One. But the One, or the " First," does not need to progress ; it is the absolute and the perfect, it lacks nothing, it always rests in itself, and it never departs from itself. Nor has everything else gone away from it, for it is not divided and it is present everywhere and always near us. But other things receive the fullness of it in various degrees of imperfection ; what we take for the successive moments of a procession are the simultaneous degrees of an unequal receptivity (vi. 5. 3). For the causality of the One does not go on in time, since it is " eternity " (αἰών, iii. 7. 11), but it is immanent. It is " a fullness of power which overflows," not like a basin which empties, nor like successive waves, but in absolute continuity. It is a light or a voice which is seen or heard everywhere, but of which an eye or an ear only takes in what it can, although none of it is lost. Between emanation and immanence there is no preference ; it is only a difference of image. What best expresses Plotinus's sentiment is the comparison of the One to the common centre of a number of spheres (vi. 9. 8). What, at least, is quite clear, is that things are not enriched by the multiplicity of their determinations, for they thus become more and more relative and dependent. This is proved by the evolution of organic things ; the more they lose sufficiency of life, the more numerous and the more differentiated are the organs which they need (vi. 7. 9, end).

By why do things grow more powerless as " one descends into multiplicity " and the proportion of " otherness " becomes greater (v. 3. 16) ? Here a postulate is necessary, to confirm the experience of the soul's journey and of its desire to return, namely, that " everything which departs from itself grows weaker " (v. 8. 1). Besides, one must come out of the infinite to be aware of it and to be able to speak of it. For in itself it is " formless," like Plato's " receptacle " or Aristotle's potential intellect, in order to be all forms. It is, therefore, not a unity and not a being ; it is the One and " What is. " Or rather, it is " beyond and above Being," but not in the same way as Plato's Good, for it is also " above the Good." Lastly, being thought, but without any relation of object to subject, it neither knows itself nor is ignorant of itself. Thus, the only way to qualify it is to say what it is not. " Really it is ineffable " (i. 7. 1 ; v. 2. 1, 3. 13, 4. 1, 5. 6 ; vi. 7. 17 and 32, 9. 3 and 6). If, therefore, we would know something of the universal " substance," or, in the language of Plotinus, of the fundamental " hypostasis," which gives itself substantiality (vi. 8. 16), we must seek out and follow its " traces." Then, going backwards along the road which we have already followed upwards, we see that there must be " ranks," some-

thing immediately " after " the One, and then something else
—that is, several " hypostases."

Only two are necessary—Thought and Soul, which are
principles, no longer single, but unifying principles, of the
intelligible world and of the sensible world. Thought, or,
more exactly, Being " enunciating its being " and so thinking
itself, causes the One to become immediately knowable and
knowing, in a multiplicity of things, which are correlatively
objects and subjects. For every Idea or form is, at the same
time, an intelligence. The connexion of them all together,
similar to that uniting the propositions of a science, at once
constitutes an intelligible universe and a universal mind.
Everything in it is distinction and fusion together, so
that " all are each, and each is all " (vi. 8. 9) ; " everything
in it is transparent, without anything obscure or resistant
. . . it is light illuminating light " (v. 8. 4). Soul in its
turn serves as a middle term between the intelligent intelligible, from which it proceeds, and sensible and corporeal
nature, which it produces in accordance with " seminal
reasons " which imitate the Ideas. A body is, really, what
there is material in a soul (iv. 3. 22). Therefore, below the
two last hypostases, there is nothing but pure multiplicity,
unorganized and unknowable. Each hypostasis, as we learn
from the experience of the return, exists there where it is
possible for the light emanating from the One to be reflected
upon it. The first mirror of the One is Intelligence, and
its first image is the Intelligible. Then the light is reflected
on to Soul, that " borrowed intelligence," which is as the
moon to the sun. This last reflection of the One is the world,
with science, and a whole vast system of souls which, spread
everywhere, at once separate and united, live in greater or
less darkness the life of the soul of the world, as citizens
live the collective life of the city.

So, after rising from the Ego to the One, I now find the
Ego once more, and in that Ego the infinite One, if I wish.
But if I turn from it to determine my own domain and to give
myself the illusion of independence, then I become only a
part isolated from its whole, and am truly reduced to slavery
(vi. 5. 7). My Ego is in reality an eternal aspect of the One.
True individualization is not brought about by matter.
Developing Plato's thought to its very term, Plotinus re-

cognizes the Ideas of individuals themselves, which Ideas are, in Thought, refractions of the light of the One. Liberty, then, is not a freedom of choice, but, as it were, one of receptivity ; it expresses the very necessity which is in the Principle, and which only a " shameless pride " (τόλμα) prevents us from obeying. Evil is a consequence both of this pride and of the seeds of death which are introduced into becoming by a matter which has " fallen from reason," the matter which Plotinus compares to a " decked-out corpse." This matter is very different from that which, in the Intelligible, is like " an illuminated essence," and introduces into it, not limitation, but only distinction (vi. 37 ; ii. 4. 5).

What gives the philosophy of Plotinus its incomparable charm in our eyes is not only the breath of internal life which animates it, but the fact that it deals with the essential interests of the modern mind. He constantly makes one think of Spinoza, and often of Leibniz. Yet he was very much a man of his time. The needs which his meditation was intended to answer were those for which satisfaction was sought in Epicurean quietism and in the salvationist religions which, from every quarter of the East, were spreading over the Roman Empire, favoured by the mixture of races, social calamities, and growing dread of the morrow. But, on the other hand, his meditation looked beyond these immediate needs. With startling clearness, it raised a new philosophical problem, of which Plato had had an inkling in his theory of Love—that of the relation of the individual consciousness to the universal mind. So Plotinus satisfied the cultivated minds of his day in one direction, by adapting the traditional notions of Greek philosophy to the religious modalities of contemporary reflection. But he also gave thought a new direction, the true sense of which would not be understood till later.

The genius of Plotinus lay in the intensity of his spiritual life. There was nothing like it in later Neo-Platonism. His successors only desiccated the Master's thought and organized it into a learned scholastic method. Against the Christians they pleaded the cause of rational culture, from which they claimed that their religious philosophy was derived. They methodically interpreted classical philosophy in conformity with their principles. Lastly, on those principles they based a philosophic occultism and sorcery.

Porphyry, for example (died 304), who went through the school of the rhetor Longinus before he joined Plotinus, was a philologist and professor even more than a philosopher. He devoted himself to laying down the orthodoxy of Plotinus's doctrine, but saw in it nothing more than the common philosophy of Plato and Aristotle. He wrote a *History of Philosophy* of which his *Life of Pythagoras* is a significant part. He commented on all the great dialogues of Plato and on the ethics, physics, and theology of Aristotle. He defended the latter's logic against Plotinus's criticisms in a sort of catechism of the *Categories* and especially in his famous *Introduction to the Categories* (*Eisagoge*), the treatise of the " five voices " (genus and species, difference, property and accident), which was to provide much of the material of mediaeval thought, Arabian or Christian. In another direction, after having, in his *Philosophy of Oracles* and *Images of the Gods*, expounded his conception of mysteries and salvation, and elaborated a whole " theurgical " ritual of purifying magic, he then adapted these views to the mysticism of Plotinus, and wrote his great work *Against the Christians*, of which the Christians, after a century and a half of polemics, at last obtained the destruction. All this part of his work, too, is dominated by his moral preoccupations. Thus, if he recommends abstinence from meat, it is because that ascetical practice has an ethical value as a purification. The same is true of his interpretation of the poets in his *Cave of the Nymphs.*

Iamblichos, a pupil of Porphyry, born in Coele-Syria and dying about 330, founded what is sometimes called the Syrian School. It is characterized by its attempt to maintain, in the face of the advance of Christianity, a ghost of rational philosophy, and to interpret the cults of the East and Egypt symbolically, by its accentuation of practical mysticism, by its Pythagorean affinities and love of religious arithmology (*Theologumena Arithmetica* attributed to Iamblichos) as against " common " mathematics,[1] by its tendency to multiply the formal divisions in Plotinus and to organize the degrees of the " procession " in triads, and by a systematic alle-

---

[1] In the IVth century, Macrobios and Favonius Eulogius commented in the same spirit on Scipio's Dream in Cicero's *Republic*. It is an interpretation of the harmony of the spheres (cf. above, p. 64).

gorism in the interpretation of the dialogues of Plato, each of which was treated as a sort of word-puzzle, in which you had to seek the whole of his philosophy. No doubt, we must not judge the philosophers of the school from the childish biographies of Eunapios, one of their number. It included several clear-minded men. Of Dexippos we have a commentary on the *Categories*. Libanios was an ingenious and fertile rhetor.[1] The book of Sallustius *On the Gods and the World* describes clearly how Neo-Platonic philosophy can serve as a basis for traditional religion. Lastly, the Emperor Julian was a man of remarkable intelligence and character, whose work deserves attentive study. The so-called " Apostate," who had been forced to be a Christian, hoped to restore the Hellenic worships, rejuvenating them with the breath of Oriental mysteries, and to regenerate the world by school arguments or decrees inspired by philosophy.

Except for violent popular reactions, such as that to which the learned Hypatia, the daughter of the mathematician Theon, fell victim in Alexandria in 415, triumphant Christianity tended not so much to fight Neo-Platonism as to absorb it and to feed its own theology with it. The Bishops Synesios and Nemesios (IVth-Vth centuries) are examples of this. Independent philosophy was pent up in the schools of Alexandria and Athens. In the latter city, which since the reign of Marcus Aurelius had been the official university town, a new school was founded, which, through Theodoros of Asine, was connected with the school of Iamblichos. Close relations existed between it and the school of Alexandria. Thus, Hermeias, who commentated on the *Phaedros*, and Domninus, the mathematician, were pupils of Syrianos, who was head of the School of Athens after its founder, Plutarchos, son of Nestorios. Asclepiodotos, the great Alexandrian physician, and Ammonios, son of Hermeias, were pupils of Proclos. With him, too, were connected Asclepios and the Christian John of Alexandria, surnamed Philoponos. Of these last two, and of Ammonios, we have useful commentaries on Aristotle. The School of Athens lasted about three hundred years, until 529. Then Justinian, who had for a long time been pursuing the

---

[1] We may mention here another Sophist, Themistios (IVth century, second half), who made a clear and intelligent paraphrase of the *Posterior Analytics*, *Physics*, and *On the Soul* of Aristotle.

" Hellenizers," that is, the champions of the ancient culture, issued the famous Edict which ended its precarious existence. Following the example of the masters of the Syriac School of St Ephrem at Edessa (middle of the IVth century), which had been closed in 489, the Athenian Damascios the Successor (Diadochos) and his fellow-workers, Simplicius of Cilicia, Priscian of Lydia, and others, sought a refuge at the court of Persia, with a king who befriended philosophers, Chosroës Anushirvan. It was to resolve " difficulties " which troubled that prince that Priscian wrote a short treatise which we have, and perhaps also his paraphrase of Theophrastos. Perhaps, too, it was under his patronage that Simplicius wrote his commentaries on Epictetos and especially on Aristotle, in which he displayed the resources of an extensive and intelligent erudition.

The most illustrious philosopher of the School of Athens is Proclos (Vth century). He was the pupil of Olympiodoros in Alexandria and of Plutarchos and Syrianos in Athens, and like them he wrote commentaries, especially on Plato. Some have been preserved—those on the *First Alcibiades*, *Cratylos*, *Parmenides*, *Timaeos* and *Republic*.[1] He also commented on the *Elements* of Euclid and Ptolemy's astronomy, and composed historical manuals, such as his *Elements* of physics and theology. He employed his gifts as a professor in pouring the theory of Plotinus into the mould of a metaphysical theogony. Things are generated by a sort of spiral descent, and by means of a series of triads, in which two terms, one being unity and determination and the other plurality and potentiality, give birth, by their very opposition, to a third term, which is the child of the first two. What Plotinus regarded as the mere external articulation of the phases of spiritual life becomes a whole history, and philosophical method, as we see, for example, in Isidoros of Alexandria, a pupil of Proclos, becomes a code of theosophical practices. Lastly, Damascios, in his book *On the Principles*, discovers in the old mythologies of Greece and the East, by a dialectical exegesis, a secret foundation, which is no other than the eternal truth of which Neo-Platonism is the interpreter.

---

[1] With which we may take the commentaries of the second Olympiodoros on the *Phaedon*, etc., and on Aristotle's *Meteorologica*, etc. Elias and David, from whom we have commentaries on Aristotle, were his pupils.

This kind of metaphysics, at once realistic and full of confused aspirations, was what Christianity wanted, in order to graft a philosophy on to the Revelation. The Latin translation of Marius Victorinus, a Christian philosopher, introduced Plotinus and Porphyry to St Augustine. The writings ascribed to Dionysios the Areopagite, the *Divine Names*, *Mystic Theology*, *Celestial Hierarchy*, *Ecclesiastical Hierarchy*, are Christian works of the beginning of the VIth century, which gave the men of the Middle Ages, through the translation of Johannes Scotus Erigena, the most mystical version of Proclos. To these we should add the *Book of Causes* and the *Theology*, other Neo-Platonic writings wrongly ascribed to Aristotle. Lastly, it was from the Neo-Platonic tradition that the Middle Ages received their education in logic and a part of the science acquired by Graeco-Roman antiquity—through Martianus Capella (second half of the Vth century), the author of nine books on the *Nuptials of Mercury and Philology* and on the *Seven Liberal Arts*, an encyclopaedic work, and through Boëthius, Theodoric's minister, who wrote a *Consolation*, imbued with Platonizing Stoicism, an *Arithmetic*, a *Music*, and commentaries on the *Interpretations* of Aristotle and on the *Introduction* of Porphyry.

CONCLUSION

MODERN philosophic thought can be fully understood only in the light of Mediaeval thought. Now, Mediaeval thought, through Cicero and other Latin writers, through the Fathers, and through the continuations of Neo-Platonism, took on the heritage of Greek thought. For Greek thought had its own middle age, which prepared and determined our own Middle Ages, and an old age which nevertheless bore within it the presage of a revival of speculation.

But before it undergoes this transformation, truly Hellenic thought itself appears as a phase in a whole evolution. It is connected with the civilizations of Egypt and Asia by bonds which must be estimated impartially, without preconceived desire to tighten or relax them. But it is not illegitimate to detach it, by abstraction, from the tradition of which it forms a part. For it represents for us the first systematization of a science and a philosophy. Moreover, both by the way in which it made use of its mythical and technical material, wherever it may have obtained them originally, and by the way in which it afterwards lost its distinctive individuality, it very clearly shows well-defined characteristics.

It is a rational, even a reasoning thought. It is so from its historical beginnings, in virtue of its effort to understand the order of things and to organize beliefs intelligibly. This is a general characteristic, affected by social conditions and varying with them. Whether democratic or aristocratic, the politics of the Greek city were always the subject of reasoned debate. Later, the break-up of the city at once compelled the individual to find a more exact consciousness of himself and set him face to face with the universe. Then the logical tendency of the Greek spirit seems to turn back upon itself. The analysis and arrangement of concepts take on an independent value, draw a picture of the real *a priori*, and impose on it the abstract form of mathematics or the image of a life ruled by reason. Of the transposition of Orphicism to the plane of present life, too, the mystical ideal of Wisdom is born. But side by side with this mysticism there still goes, as is shown by the example of Socrates, the Cynics, and their heirs, an argumentative intellectualism. Thenceforth the Greek spirit in philosophy is often made of violent contrasts; it is no more afraid of excess of asceticism than of excess of dialectical subtlety. It is a miraculous equilibrium. Once the intelligence loses the vigour of its sap, the break-down of that equilibrium is detrimental to it. To bring that about, an offensive movement of Oriental religiosity is sufficient.

We have seen, in the very first pages of this book, the obstacles which check the historian of Greek thought at the threshold of many regions of his domain, and the gaps in our knowledge have been mentioned in their place. If Plato and Aristotle have been discussed at length, it is because in them we obtain in full what we have elsewhere to reconstruct laboriously. But the work of methodical exploration, which has shed a new light on the pre-Socratic period, should be carried out in other fields. A systematic plundering of the authors who have the least pretension to philosophic originality would lead us to discover many of the pieces missing from our mosaic. Lastly, there are periods, the surviving productions of which have been too much neglected, when they were of no interest to erudition. This is true of Neo-Platonism after Plotinus. Yet it is through it that our thought is connected with the true thought of Greece.

BIBLIOGRAPHY

THE literature concerning the history of Graeco-Roman philosophy is considerable. The books and articles which I mention are, for the most part, either
indispensable instruments of study, or treatises likely to arouse curiosity and
reflection. In general, the bibliographical information which I have had to
sacrifice here will be found in them.

[Certain English and other editions are added in square brackets. The foot-
notes do not refer to the pages of these editions unless it is so stated. TRS.]

I. GENERAL BIBLIOGRAPHY

1. PERIODICALS

The *Archiv für Geschichte der Philosophie* (1888 onwards), the *Revue d'Histoire
de la philosophie* (1927 onwards), and *Isis* (1913 onwards) are special reviews of the
history of philosophy and that of the sciences, publishing articles in the author's
own language. It is very important to add to these the periodicals of philological
or historical erudition of all countries. The *Jahresbericht über die Fortschritte der
Altertumswissenschaft*, founded by BURSIAN, is of capital importance, on account of
the reviews in it which deal with all the works written about an author or a group
over a period of several years. In the *Revue de Synthèse historique* (xiii, 1906),
G. RODIER has done a work of this kind for the history of Greek philosophy between
1880 and 1904. Lastly, there are several reviews devoted entirely to philosophy,
science, or religion, which publish articles on ancient philosophy and should be
consulted.

2. DICTIONARIES AND REPERTORIES

PAULY and WISSOWA, *Realencyclopädie der klassischen Altertumswissenschaft* (1st ed., 1864, etc., 8 vols.), 2nd ed., in progress, 1894, etc.
(A-L, R-S, 18½ vols.) (Original articles, with copious bibliographies)   **I**

In addition to the very full special bibliography in **VIII**, it is generally useful
to consult repertories of general literature.

3. GENERAL WORKS ON THE HISTORY OF GREEK PHILOSOPHY

ZELLER (Eduard), *Die Philosophie der Griechen in ihrer geschichtlichen
Entwicklung dargestellt* (1st ed., 1844-52) :—

Part i. *Allgemeine Einleitung. Vorsokratische Philosophie*, 6th ed.,
by F. LORTZING and W. NESTLE, 2 vols., Berlin, 1919-20. French
trans. from the 4th ed. by E. BOUTROUX, 2 vols., Paris, 1877-82.
[Eng. trans. by S. F. ALLEYNE, *A History of Greek Philosophy
from the earliest period to the time of Socrates*, 2 vols., London, 1881   **II**

Part ii, sec. 1. *Sokrates und die Sokratiker. Plato und die alte
Akademie*, 4th ed., 1888. French trans. from the 3rd ed. by
G. BELOT of the first subdivision. [Eng. trans. by O. J. REICHEL,
Socrates and the Socratic Schools, London, 1868 ; by S. F. ALLEYNE
and A. GOODWIN, *Plato and the Older Academy*, London, 1876]   **III**

—— sec. 2. *Aristoteles und die alten Peripatetiker*, 3rd ed., 1879.
[Eng. trans. by B. F. C. COSTELLOE and J. H. MUIRHEAD,
Aristotle and the Earlier Peripatetics, 2 vols., London, 1897]   **IV**

382   BIBLIOGRAPHY

Part iii, sec. 1.   *Die nacharistotelische Philosophie*, 4th ed., by
E. WELLMANN, 1909.[1] [Eng. trans. by O. J. REICHEL, *The
Stoics, Epicureans, and Sceptics*, London, 1870]   V

—— sec. 2. *Die nacharistotelische Philosophie*, 4th ed., 1903.[2] [Eng.
trans. by S. F. ALLEYNE, *History of Eclecticism in Greek Philosophy*, London, 1883]   VI

RENOUVIER (Charles B.), *Manuel de philosophie ancienne*, 2 vols.,
Paris, 1844 [3]   VII

UEBERWEG (Friedrich), *Grundriss der Geschichte der Philosophie :* pt. i,
Das Altertum (1862), 11th ed., by C. PRÄCHTER, Berlin, 1920.
[Eng. trans. by G. S. MORRIS, *A History of Philosophy from
Thales to the Present Time*, 2 vols., London, 1872-4   VIII

BENN (Alfred W.), *The Greek Philosophers* (1882), 2nd ed., London, 1914   IX

WINDELBAND (Wilhelm), *Geschichte der antiken Philosophie* (1888),
3rd ed., by A. BONNHÖFER, Munich, 1912 (in I. MÜLLER'S
Handbuch ; cf. **XV**)   X

GOMPERZ (Theodor), [*Griechischer Denker* (1893-1902), 2nd ed., Leipzig,
1903-9 (stops at Straton).   French trans. by A. REYMOND,
Les Penseurs de la Grèce, Lausanne and Paris, 1908-9.] Eng.
trans. by L. MAGNUS and G. G. BERRY, *Greek Thinkers*, London,
1901-12   XI

BURNET (John), *Greek Philosophy :* pt. i. *Thales to Plato* (only this
part has appeared), London, 1914   XII

JOËL (Carl), *Geschichte der antiken Philosophie*, i (to Socrates and the
lesser Socratic schools), Tübingen, 1921   XIIa

BRÉHIER (Émile), *Histoire de la philosophie :* i. *Antiquité et Moyen
Âge :* 1. *Introduction, la période héllenique.* 2. *Période hellénis-
tique et romaine*, Paris, 1926-7   XIIb

RENOUVIER (Charles B.), *Philosophie analytique de l'histoire*, i and ii,
Paris, 1896-97   XIII

4. SELECTED TEXTS FOR THE HISTORY OF GREEK PHILOSOPHY

RITTER (Heinrich) and PRELLER (L.), *Historia philosophiae Graecae*,
9th ed., by E. WELLMANN, Gotha, 1913 [4]   XIV

5. WORKS ON THE HISTORY OF SCIENTIFIC THOUGHT IN GREEK ANTIQUITY [5]

GUENTHER (Siegm.), *Abriss der Geschichte der Mathematik und der
Naturwissenschaften im Altertum* (Appendix to the 2nd ed. of **X**),
Munich, 1894   XV

HEIBERG (Johan L.), *Naturwissenschaften und Mathematik im klassischen
Altertum*, Leipzig, 1912   XVI

TANNERY (Paul), *La Géométrie grecque*, Paris, 1887   XVII

—— *Recherches sur l'histoire de l'astronomie ancienne*, Paris, 1894   XVIII

[1] To the end of the Ist century after Christ.
[2] Later history of the various schools, Judaeo-Hellenic philosophy, Neo-
Platonism.
[3] Excluding Neo-Platonism ; gives the history of the sciences.
[4] An excellent collection of texts and testimonies, with notes.
[5] See also **VII** ; **XI**, i, bk. ii, ch. 6, bk. iii, ch. 1.   On the religious and literary
forms of Greek thought and its connexions with social, political, and economic
conditions, see *The Formation of the Greek People, The Religious Thought of Greece,
The Greek City*, and *Macedonian Imperialism* in this series, and histories of Greek
literature.

TANNERY (Paul), *Mémoires scientifiques* (published by J. L. HEIBERG and H. G. ZEUTHEN); *Sciences exactes dans l'antiquité*, 1874-93, vols. i-iii; *Philosophie ancienne*, 1880-1904, vol. vii, 4 vols., Toulouse and Paris, 1912-15, 1925   XIX

MILHAUD (Gaston), *Leçons sur les origines de la science grecque*, Paris, 1893   XX

—— *Les Philosophes géomètres de la Grèce : Platon et ses prédécesseurs*, Paris, 1900   XXI

—— *Nouvelles Études sur l'histoire de la pensée scientifique*, Paris, 1911   XXII

HEATH (Sir Thomas L.), *A History of Greek Mathematics*, 2 vols., Oxford, 1921   XXIII

—— *Aristarchus of Samos, the ancient Copernicus : a history of Greek astronomy to Aristarchus, together with A.'s treatise of the sizes and distances of the sun and moon. A new Greek text with trans. and notes*, Oxford, 1913   XXIV

DUHEM (Pierre), *Le Système du monde : histoire des doctrines cosmologiques de Platon à Copernic.* i. *La Cosmologie hellénique*, Paris, 1913   XXV

BERGER (Hugo), *Geschichte der wissenschaftlichen Erdkunde der Griechen*, 2nd ed., Leipzig, 1903   XXVI

GILBERT (O.), *Die meteorologischen Theorien des griechischen Altertums*, Leipzig, 1907   XXVII

BOLL (Fr.), *Studien zur Geschichte des antiken Weltbildes und der griechischen Wissenschaft*, 6 vols., Leipzig, 1914-21   XXVIII

CHAIGNET (A. E.), *Histoire de la psychologie des Grecs*, 5 vols., Paris, 1887-92   XXIX

BEARE (J. I.), *Greek Theories of Elementary Cognition, from Alcmaeon to Aristotle*, Oxford, 1906   XXX

RIVAUD (A.), *Recherches sur l'anthropologie grecque* (*Revue Anthropolog.*, 1911)   XXXI

DIELS (Hermann), *Die antike Technik*, 2nd ed., Leipzig, 1915   XXXII

BOUCHÉ-LECLERCQ (Auguste), *L'Astrologie grecque*, Paris, 1899   XXXIII

BRUNSCHVICG (L.), *Les Étapes de la philosophie mathématique*, Paris, 1912 (repr., 1922)   XXXIV

—— *L'Expérience humaine et la causalité*, Paris, 1922   XXXV

REYMOND (Arnold), *Histoire des sciences exactes et naturelles dans l'antiquité gréco-romaine : exposé sommaire des écoles et des principes*, Paris, 1924   XXXVa

A *Corpus Medicorum* (Greek and Latin) is being published by H. DIELS, J. ILBERG, G. HELMREICH, J. MEWALDT, M. WELLMANN, Fr. MARX, etc. (Leipzig, 1908, etc.). There is an edition of Hippocrates by LITTRÉ, with a French trans., 10 vols., 1839-61, and one of Galen by KUHN, 20 vols., 1821-31.

6. HISTORIES OF SPECIAL NOTIONS AND OF PARTS OF PHILOSOPHY

KRISCHE (August B.), *Die theologischen Lehren der griechischen Denker : eine Prüfung der Darstellung Ciceros*, Göttingen, 1840   XXXVI

ROHDE (Erwin), *Psyche : Seelenkult und Unsterblichkeitsglaube der Griechen* (1894), 4th ed., Freiburg i. Br., 1907. [Eng. trans. from the 3rd ed., by W. B. HILLIS, *Psyche : the cult of souls and belief in immortality among the Greeks*, London, 1925]   XXXVII

DIETERICH (Albrecht), *Nekyia*, Leipzig, 1893 (anastatic repr., 1913)   XXXVIII

384 BIBLIOGRAPHY

HEINZE (Max), *Die Lehre vom Logos in der griechischen Philosophie*, Oldenburg, 1872   **XXXIX**

DIELS (Hermann), *Elementum : eine Vorarbeit zum griech. und latein. Thesaurus*, Leipzig, 1899   **XL**

BAEUMKER (Cl.), *Das Problem der Materie in der griechischen Philosophie : eine historisch-kritische Untersuchung*, Münster, 1890   **XLI**

RIVAUD (A.), *Le Problème du devenir et la notion de la matière dans la philosophie grecque, depuis les origines jusqu' à Théophraste*, Paris, 1906   **XLII**

HIRZEL (Rudolf), *Themis, Dikê, und Verwandtes : ein Beitrag zur Geschichte der Rechtsidee bei den Griechen*, Leipzig, 1907   **XLIII**

HARRISON (Jane E.), *Themis : a study of the social origins of Greek religion*, Cambridge, 1912   **XLIV**

ROHDE (Erwin), *Der griechische Roman* (1876), 3rd ed , Leipzig, 1914   **XLV**

HIRZEL (Rudolf), *Der Dialog*, 2 vols., Leipzig, 1895   **XLVI**

PRANTL (C.), *Geschichte der Logik im Abendlande : i. Die Entwicklung der Logik im Altertum*, Leipzig, 1855 (repr.)   **XLVII**

WUNDT (Max), *Geschichte der griechischen Ethik*, 2 vols., Leipzig, 1908-11   **XLVIII**

BARKER (Ernest), *Greek Political Theory : Plato and his predecessors*, London, 1917   **XLIX**

TREVER (A. A.), *A History of Greek Economic Thought*, Chicago, 1915   **L**

BRUNSCHVICG (L.), *Le Progrès de la conscience dans la philosophie occidentale*, 2 vols., Paris, 1927   **La**

7. COLLECTIONS OF ESSAYS ON VARIOUS SUBJECTS

BOUTROUX (Émile), *Études d'histoire de la philosophie*, Paris, 1897   **LI**

BROCHARD (Victor), *Études de philosophie ancienne et de philosophie moderne*, collected by V. DELBOS, Paris, 1912   **LII**

NATORP (Paul), *Forschungen zur Geschichte des Erkenntnisproblems im Altertum*, etc., Berlin, 1884   **LIII**

TEICHMUELLER (Gustav), *Studien zur Geschichte der Begriffe*, Berlin, 1874   **LIV**

—— *Neue Studien zur Gesch. der Begr.*, 2 vols., Gotha, 1876-79   **LV**

—— *Literarische Fehden im IV. Jahrhundert v. Chr.*, 2 vols., Breslau, 1881-84   **LVI**

RODIER (G.), *Études de philosophie grecque*, Paris, 1926   **LVIa**

8. ORGANIZATION OF SCHOOLS AND SOCIAL POSITION OF PHILOSOPHERS

ZUMPT (C. G.), *Über den Bestand der Philosophenschulen in Athen und die Sukzession der Scholarchen* (*Abh. der Akademie der Wissenschaften zu Berlin*, 1842), Berlin, 1843 (cf. **LVI, LX, LXIII**)   **LVII**

USENER (Hermann), *Organisation der wissenschaftlichen Arbeit bei den Griechen* (*Preuss. Jahrb.*, liii, or *Kleine Schriften*), 1884   **LVIII**

DIELS (Hermann), *Über die ältesten Philosophenschulen* (*Philosophische Aufsätze Ed. Zeller gewidmet*, pp. 239-60), Leipzig, 1887   **LIX**

POLAND (Friedrich), *Geschichte des griechischen Vereinswesens*, Leipzig, 1909   **LX**

II. SOURCES

At present the best and most complete collection of texts is Teubner's *Bibliotheca scriptorum Graecorum et Romanorum*, Leipzig. Only a few philosophic texts have as yet appeared in the *Collection des Universités de France, publiée sous le patronage de l'Association Guillaume Budé* (with French translations) and in the Oxford *Scriptorum classicorum bibliotheca Oxoniensis*. Certain volumes of Didot's Greek collection (with Latin translations) are still useful. This series includes MULLACH, *Fragmenta Philosophorum Graecorum*, 3 vols., 1860, 1867, 1881, a mediocre collection, very much out of date, the last two vols. of which may, however, be useful. The most important editions of the chief philosophers and collections of texts and testimonies will be mentioned in their place. Here one may mention only the following :—

Poetarum philosophorum fragmenta, ed. by H. DIELS (in WILAMOWITZ-MŒLLENDORFF's *Poetarum Graecarum fragmenta*, no. iii, pt. 1) (Xenophanes, Parmenides, Empedocles, Timon, Crates, etc., with critical or explanatory notes and collected testimonies), Berlin, 1901 **LXI**

DIELS (Hermann), *Doxographi Graeci*, Berlin, 1879 (the capital work for the critical study of the sources of the history of Greek philosophy ; the "Prolegomena," 263 pp., are especially important) **LXII**

WILAMOWITZ-MŒLLENDORFF (Ulrich von), *Antigonos von Karystos* (lives of Pyrrhon, Timon, Polemon, Crates, Arcesilaos, Menedemos, Zenon, extracted from Diogenes Laërtios), with : i. *Die Philosophenschulen und die Politik ;* ii. *Die rechtliche Stellung der Philosophenschulen* (KIESSLING and WILAMOWITZ, *Philol. Untersuch.*, no. 4), Berlin, 1881 **LXIII**

JACOBY (Felix), *Apollodors Chronik : eine Sammlung der Fragmente* (same collection, no. 16), Berlin, 1903 **LXIV**

COBET'S very defective edition of Diogenes Laërtios in the Didot collection has already been improved by all who, in special treatises, have published extracts from the work (e.g., **LXI, LXIV, LXVIII, LXXVIII, CXLVI, CXLVIII, CL**) ; bk. iii (Plato) was published separately at Basel in 1907. A new edition by P. von der MÜHLL is in course of preparation (cf. below, §11).

There is a very good edition of Stobaeos by WACHSMUTH and HENSE in 5 vols., 1884-1912 (cf. **LXII**).

III. SPECIAL BIBLIOGRAPHY

1. ORIGINS

MAZON (Paul), *Hésiode, Les Travaux et les jours ; nouvelle édition* (with commentary), Paris, 1914 **LXV**

KERN (Otto), *Orphicorum fragmenta*, Berlin, 1922 **LXVI**

DECHARME (Paul), *La Critique des traditions religieuses chez les Grecs, des origines au temps de Plutarque*, Paris, 1904 **LXVII**

CHIAPPELLI (Aless.), *L'Oriente e le origini della filosofia greca* (*Archiv f. Gesch. d. Philos.*, 1915) **LXVIIa**

REY (Abel), *Coup d'œil sur la mathématique égyptienne* (*Rev. de Synth. hist.*, 1926) **LXVIIb**

See also **XI**, bk. i, ch. 2 ; **XLII**, bk. i, bk. ii, ch. 10 ; **LXVIII**, ch. 66 to 73a. [MAIR (A. W.), *Hesiod . . . done into English prose*, Oxford, 1908.]

2. Pre-Socratic Philosophers

A. General Works [1]

Diels (Hermann), *Die Fragmente der Vorsokratiker*, in Greek and German (1903), 3rd ed., 2 vols., Berlin, 1912; 4th ed., 1923 [2]   **LXVIII**

Kranz (Walther), *Wortindex* (to the above), Berlin, 1923   **LXIX**

Tannery (Paul), *Pour l'histoire de la science hellène, de Thalès à Empédocle*,[3] Paris, 1887   **LXX**

Burnet (John), *Early Greek Philosophy*, (1892), 4th ed., London, 1920. French trans. by A. Reymond, *L'Aurore de la philosophie grecque*, Paris, 1919 [4]   **LXXI**

Goebel (H.), *Die vorsokratische Philosophie*, Bonn, 1910   **LXXII**

Diès (Aug.), *Le Cycle mystique*, Paris, 1909   **LXXIII**

See also especially **II**; **XI**; **XII**, pp. 1-101; **XX**; **XXIV**; **XXX**; **XLII**, bk. ii; **LIX**.

B. Special Studies

Tannery (Paul), *Une Nouvelle Hypothèse sur Anaximandre* (*Archiv für Gesch. d. Philosophie*, viii, pp. 443 ff.), 1895   **LXXIV**

Diels (Hermann), *Über Anaximanders Kosmos* (*ibid.*, x, pp. 228 ff.), 1897   **LXXV**

Heidel (William A.), *Anaximander's Book: the earliest known geographical treatise* (*Proceedings of the American Academy of Arts and Sciences*, lvi, 239-88), Boston, 1921   **LXXVI**

See also **II**, i, pp. 253-331; **XI**, bk. i, ch. 1; **LIV**; **LIX**; **LXI**, 1-2; **LXVIII**, ch. 1-3.

Delatte (Arm.), *Études sur la littérature pythagoricienne* (*Bibl. de l'École des Htes. Études Sciences histor. et phil.*, no. 217), Paris, 1915   **LXXVII**

—— *La Vie de Pythagore, de Diogène Laërce*, critical ed. with introduction and commentary, Brussels, 1922   **LXXVIII**

—— *Essai sur la politique pythagoricienne* (*Bibl. de la Fac. de Philosophie et lettres de l'Univ. de Liége*), Liége and Paris, 1922   **LXXIX**

Méautis (G.), *Recherches sur le pythagorisme*, Neufchâtel, 1922   **LXXIXa**

Frank (Erich), *Plato und die sogenannten Pythagoräer*, Halle, 1923   **LXXIXb**

Rostagni (A.), *Il Verbo di Pitagora*, Turin, 1924   **LXXIXc**

See also **II**, i, pp. 361-617; **XI**, bk. i, ch 3-5; **XXI**; **XXXIV**, ch. 3; **LXVIII**, ch. 4-10, 13-17, 32-45

Diels (Hermann), *Herakleitos von Ephesos*, 2nd ed., Berlin, 1909   **LXXX**

Bodrero (Em.), *Eraclito*, Turin, 1912   **LXXXI**

---

[1] I have also made use of the unpublished lectures of a course by O. Hamelin.
[2] A. Testimonies; B. Fragments; C. Imitations. Only the fragments are translated, except those in the Appendix (66-83). In the 3rd ed., which I have used, the critical apparatus and notes are at the foot of the page, and the pagination of the 2nd ed. is indicated in the margin. Vol. ii, pt. 2, contains two Indices (of authors quoted and of proper names). It should be used together with **LXII**, *Doxographi Graeci*.
[3] Trans. of fragments and testimonies in an Appendix.
[4] With trans. of the frags. and of parts of the doxography. My references are to the 2nd ed., 1908. The French translation is from the 2nd ed., but with corrections made by the author.

MACCHIORO (V.), *Eraclito*, Bari, 1922   **LXXXII**
See also **II**, ii, pp. 623-750 ; **XI**, bk. i, ch. 1 ; **LV** ; **LXVIII**, ch. 12 and 52.

DIELS (Hermann), *Parmenides Lehrgedicht*, Greek and German, with introduction and commentary, Berlin, 1897   **LXXXIII**

UNTERSTEINER (M.), *Parmenide* (with a trans. of the testimonies and fragments), Turin, 1925   **LXXXIIIa**
See also **II**, i, pp. 617-782 ; **XI**, bk. i, ch. 1-3 ; **XXI** : **XXXIV**, ch. 9 A ; **LII** ; **LXVI**, 2-3 ; **LXVIII**, ch. 11, 18-20

BIDEZ (J.), *La Biographie d'Empédocle* (*Travaux publiés par la Fac. de Philosophie et lettres de l'Univ. de Gand*), 1894   **LXXXIV**

MILLERD (Miss), *On the Interpretation of Empedocles*, Chicago, 1908   **LXXXV**

BIGNONE (Ettore), *Empedocle : studio critico ; traduzione e commentario delle testimonianze e dei frammenti*, Turin, 1916   **LXXXVI**
See also **II**, ii, pp. 750-837 ; **XI**, bk. ii, ch. 5 ; **LXI**, 5 ; **LXVIII**, ch. 21 ; **XCIII**.

HAMELIN (O.), *La Pesanteur de l'atome dans le système de Démocrite* (*Annales de la Fac. des Lettres de l'Univ. de Bordeaux*, N.S., v, pp. 194 ff.), 1888   **LXXXVII**

NATORP (P.), *Die Ethika des Demokritos : Text und Untersuchungen*, Marburg, 1893   **LXXXVIII**

DYROFF (A.), *Demokritstudien*, Munich, 1899   **LXXXIX**
See also **II**, ii, pp. 837-967 ; **XI**, bk. iii, ch. 2 and 4 ; **XII**, pp. 193-201 ; **XXXV**, ch. 12 ; **LII** ; **LIII** ; **LXVIII**, ch. 54-65.

For Anaxagoras, see **II**, ii, pp. 968-1031 ; **XI**, bk. ii, ch. 4 ; **LXVIII**, ch. 46.

3. ECLECTICS AND SOPHISTS

A. *The Eclectic Physicists*

KRAUSE (Ernst), *Diogenes von Apollonia* (*Beilage zum Jahresb. d. Gymnas. zu Gnesen*), Posen, 1908-9   **XC**
See also **II**, i, pp. 332-61, ii, pp. 1031-8 ; **XI**, bk. iii, ch. 3 ; **LXVIII**, ch. 26, 50-1, 53.

B. *The Sophists*

GOMPERZ (Heinrich), *Sophistik und Rhetorik : das Bildungsideal des εὖ λέγειν in seinem Verhältnis zur Philosophie des V. Jahrhunderts*, Leipzig, 1912   **XCI**

ARNIM (H. von), *Sophistik, Rhetorik, und Philosophie in ihrem Kampfe um die Jugendsbildung* (introduction to *Leben und Werke des Dion von Prusa*, Berlin, 1898)   **XCII**

DIELS (Hermann), *Gorgias und Empedokles* (*Sitzungsb. d. Akad. d. Wiss. zu Berlin*, 1884, 1, pp. 343 ff.)   **XCIII**
See also **II**, ii, pp. 1038-1164 ; **XI**, bk. iii, ch. 4-8 ; **LII** ; **LIII** ; **LXVIII**, ch. 73b-83

4. SOCRATES

FOUILLÉE (Alfred), *La Philosophie de Socrate*, 2 vols., Paris, 1874   **XCIV**

JOËL (Carl), *Der echte und der xenophontische Sokrates*, 3 vols., Berlin, 1901-3   **XCV**

TAYLOR (Alfred E.), *Varia Socratica*, 1st Series, Oxford, 1911   **XCVI**

MAIER (Heinrich), *Sokrates : sein werk und seine geschichtliche Stellung,*
Tübingen, 1913   **XCVII**
See also **III**, pp. 44-232 ; **XI**, bk. iv, ch. 3-5 ; **La** ; **LI** ; **LII** ; above, p. 156, nn. 1-2.

5. MEGARICS, CYNICS, CYRENAICS, ETC.

There are editions of the fragments of Antisthenes by A. W. WINCKELMANN,
Zurich, 1842, of Crates (**LXI**, 10), and of Teles by O. HENSE, Freiburg i. Br., 1889.

DUEMMLER (Ferd.), *Antisthenica*, Berlin, 1882   **XCVIII**

GEFFCKEN (J.), *Kynika und Verwandtes*, Heidelberg, 1909   **XCIX**

GILLESPIE (C. M.), *On the Megarians (Archiv. f. Gesch. d. Philosophie,*
xxiv, 218 ff.), 1911   **C**

—— *The Logic of Antisthenes (ibid.,* xxvi, 479 ; xxvii, 17), 1913   **CI**

RODIER (G.), *Conjecture sur le sens de la morale d'Antisthène (Année
philosophique,* xvi), 1906   **CII**

—— *Note sur la politique d'Antisthène (ibid.,* xxii), 1911   **CIII**

See also **III**, pp. 232-388 ; **V**, pp. 791-804 ; **XI**, bk. iv, ch. 6-9 ; **LVIa** ; **LXIII** ;
XCII ; **XCV** ; **XCVII** ; **CVII**, iii ; **CXII**, ii, ch. 18 ; **CXV**, ch. 1 and 8.

6. PLATO

A. *Writings* [1]

There is a very good edition of the text by J. BURNET, in *Bibl. Oxon.* Complete
edition, with introduction and notes in Latin, by G. STALLBAUM (Teubner, 1821,
etc.), many volumes of which have since been revised. There are several important editions of single works : *Phaedon* by BURNET, Oxford, 1911 ; *Republic*
by B. JOWETT and Lewis CAMPBELL, 3 vols., Oxford, 1894, and especially by
J. ADAM, 2 vols., London, 1902 ; *Theaetetos* by L. CAMPBELL, 2nd ed., Oxford,
1883 ; *Sophist* by O. APELT, Stallbaum's collection, 1897 ; *Sophist* and *Statesman*
by L. CAMPBELL, 1867 ; *Philebos* by R. G. BURY, Cambridge, 1897 ; *Timaeos*
by T. H. MARTIN (text, trans., comm.), 2 vols., Paris, 1841, and by A. E. TAYLOR,
Oxford, 1928 ; *Laws* by E. B. ENGLAND, London, 1921 ; *Letters* by Ernst HOWALD,
Zurich, 1923.

Pending the completion of the Plato in the *Collection Budé* (so far published :
i. *Hipp. Mi., Alcib., Apol., Euthyphr., Criton,* by M. CROISET ; ii. *Hipp. Ma.,
Charm., Laches, Lysis,* by A. CROISET ; iii. *Protag., Gorg., Menon,* by A. CROISET ;
iv. 1. *Phaedon,* by L. ROBIN ; viii. *Parmen., Theaet., Soph.,* by A. DIÈS ; x. *Tim.,
Critias,* by A. RIVAUD ; xiii. 1. *Letters,* by J. SOUILHÉ), there are only two
complete French translations, by Victor COUSIN (12 vols., 1822-40) and by A.
SAISSET and E. CHAUVET (*Bibl. Charpentier,* 10 vols., 1869, etc.). [*The Dialogues,
translated into English with analyses and introduction,* by B. JOWETT, 5 vols., 3rd
ed., Oxford, 1925.]

AST (Friedrich), *Lexicon Platonicum*, 3 vols., 1835-38 (anastatic repr.,
Berlin, 1908) [2]   **CIV**

ALLINE (H.), *Histoire du texte de Platon (Bibl. de l'École des Htes. études,
Sc. histor. et philol.,* no. 218), Paris, 1915   **CV**

B. *Works on Plato*

FOUILLÉE (Alfred), *La Philosophie de Platon* (1869), 2nd ed., 4 vols.,
Paris, 1888-89   **CVI**

GROTE (George), *Plato and the other Companions of Sokrates* (1865), 3rd
ed., 3 vols., London, 1875. [New ed., 4 vols., London, 1885]   **CVII**

---

[1] It has become traditional to refer to Plato's text by the pages (subdivided
from A to E) of Henri Estienne's ed., Paris, 1578.

[2] In 1909 Burnet and L. Campbell drew up the plan of a new lexicon, more
complete and more methodical.

LUTOSLAWSKI (Wincenty), *The Origin and Growth of Plato's Logic, with an account of Plato's style and of the chronology of his writings* (1897), 2nd ed., London, 1905   CVIII

NATORP (Paul), *Platons Ideenlehre* (1903), 2nd ed., Leipzig, 1921   CIX

RAEDER (Hans), *Platons philosophische Entwicklung*, Leipzig, 1905 [1]   CX

RITTER (Constantin), *Platon*, 2 vols., Munich, 1910-23   CXI

WILAMOWITZ-MŒLLENDORFF (Ulrich von), *Platon* (1919), 2 vols., 3rd ed., Berlin, 1920   CXII

ZELLER (Eduard), *Platonische Studien* (*Laws, Parmenides*, Aristotle's account of Plato's doctrine), Tübingen, 1839   CXIII

BONITZ (H.), *Platonische Studien* (*Gorgias, Theaetetos, Sophist, Euthydemos, Laches, Euthyphron, Charmides, Protagoras, Phaedros, Phaedon*), 3rd ed., Berlin, 1886   CXIV

DUEMMLER (Ferdinand), *Akademika*, Giessen, 1889   CXV

HALÉVY (Élie), *La Théorie platonicienne des sciences*, Paris, 1896   CXVI

RODIER (G.), *Remarques sur le Philèbe* (*Rev. des Études anciennes*), 1900   CXVII

—— *Les Mathématiques et la Dialectique dans le système de Platon* (*Archiv. f. Gesch. d. Philos.*, xv, 479 ff.), 1902   CXVIII

—— *L'Évolution de la Dialectique de Platon* (*Année philos.*, xvi), 1905   CXIX

SHOREY (Paul), *The Unity of Plato's Thought* (*Chicago Decennial Publications*, vol. vi), 1903   CXIXa

ROBIN (Léon), *La Théorie platonicienne des Idées et des Nombres d'après Aristote : étude historique et critique*, Paris, 1908   CXX

—— *La Théorie platonicienne de l'Amour*, Paris, 1908   CXXI

—— *Études sur la signification et la place de la physique dans la philosophie de Platon* (*Rev. Philos.*, ii, 1918), Paris, 1919   CXXII

MORE (Paul Elmer), *Platonism*, Princeton, 1917   CXXIII

SOUILHÉ (J.), *La Notion platonicienne d'intermédiaire dans la philosophie des Dialogues*, Paris, 1919   CXXIV

TAYLOR (A. E.), *Plato*, London, 1926   CXXV

See also **III**, pp. 389-982 ; **XI**, bk. v ; **XXI** ; **XXIII-XXV** ; **XXX** ; **XXXIV** ch. 4 , **XXXV**, ch. 13 ; **XLII**, bk. iii, pt. 1 ; **XLVI** ; **XLIX** ; **L** ; **La** ; **LII** ; **LIV** ; **LVI** ; **LVIa** ; **LXXIXb** ; above, p. 184 n. 1.

7. IMMEDIATE DISCIPLES OF PLATO

RAVAISSON (F.), *Speusippi de primis rerum principiis placita*, Paris, 1838   CXXVI

LANG (P.), *De Speusippi Acad. scriptis ; accedunt fragm.*, Bonn, 1911   CXXVII

HEINZE (Rich.), *Xenokrates : eine Darstellung der Lehre und Sammlung der Fragmente*, Leipzig, 1892   CXXVIII

VOSS (Otto), *De Heraclidis Pontici vita et scriptis*, Rostock, 1897   CXXIX

TANNERY (Paul), *Pseudonymes antiques* (*Rev. des Ét. gr.*, x), 1897   CXXX

—— *Sur Héraclide du Pont* (*ibid.*, xii), 1899   CXXXI

See also **III**, pp. 982-1049 ; **XI**, bk. vi, ch. 1 ; **XXIV**, ch. 16 and 18 ; **XXXIV**, ch. 4 ; **LXXIXb** ; **CXX**.

---

[1] Very useful for an introduction to the study of Plato's philosophy.

8. ARISTOTLE

A. *Writings*

The standard edition of the works of Aristotle is the " Berlin Academy " edition of Immanuel BEKKER, in 5 quarto vols., 1831-70.[1] Vol. iii contains the ancient Latin translations. Vol. iv, a collection of extracts from the Greek commentators by C. A. BRANDIS, did the greatest service before the complete publication, under the auspices of the Berlin Academy, from 1882 onwards, of 51 commentaries (in 23 vols.). Vol. v (1870) contains, in addition to Hermann BONITZ's admirable *Index Aristotelicus*, the Catalogues and Fragments, edited by Valentin ROSE (2nd ed., more complete, Teubner, 1886). A *Supplementum Aristotelicum* (3 vols., 1885-93) contains the *Constitution of Athens*, four important treatises by Alexander of Aphrodisias (*De Anima cum mantissa, De Fato, De Mixtione, Quaestiones et solutiones*), two by Priscian of Lydia (*Metaphrasis in Theophrastum* and his replies to the questions of Chosroës), Anonymus Londiniensis (extracts from Menon's ἰατρικά), etc.

Editions of single works, with commentaries : *Metaphysics*, by H. BONITZ, 1848-49 ; by W. D. Ross, 2 vols., Oxford, 1924 ; bks. i-iii, with French trans., by G. COLLE, Louvain and Paris, 1912-22 ; *Organon* by Th. WAITZ, 2 vols., 1844-46 ; *De Anima* by TRENDELENBURG, (1833), 2nd ed. by BELGER, 1877 ; by WALLACE (introd., Eng. trans., notes), 1892 ; by G. RODIER (trans. and comm.), 1900 ; by R. D. HICKS, 1907 ; *Meteorologica* by J. L. IDELER, 2 vols., 1834-36 ; *Nicomachean Ethics* by A. GRANT, 2 vols., 2nd ed., 1885 ; by STEWART, 2 vols., 2nd ed., 1892 ; by J. BURNET, 1900 ; *Politics* by NEWMAN, 4 vols., 1887-92, etc. ; *Physics*, bk. ii (trans and comm.), by O. HAMELIN, 1907 ; bks. i-iv, by H. CARTERON (text and trans.), *Coll. Budé*, 1926. G. RODIER has annotated *Nic. Eth.*, x (1897). Lastly, one must mention TRENDELENBURG's excellent *Elementa logices Aristoteleae* (1836 ; 9th ed., 1892), a collection of the essential logical texts, with trans. and comm. in Latin.

BARTHÉLÉMY SAINT-HILAIRE's French trans. merits no confidence. A good English trans., edited by J. A. SMITH and W. D. Ross, is in course of publication at Oxford ; it still lacks the *Organon, Physics, De Anima, Problems*.

B. *Works on Aristotle*

RAVAISSON (Félix), *Essai sur la Métaphysique d'Aristote*, 2 vols., Paris, 1837-46 (repr., 1913) — CXXXII

HAMELIN (Octave), *Le Système d'Aristote* (without his morals [2] and politics), published by L. ROBIN, Paris, 1920 — CXXXIII

PIAT (Cl.), *Aristote*, Paris, 1903 — CXXXIV

Ross (W. D.), *Aristotle*, London, 1923 — CXXXIVa

JAEGER (Werner), *Aristoteles : Grundlegung einer Geschichte seiner Entwicklung*, Berlin, 1923 — CXXXIVb

WERNER (C.), *Aristote et l'idéalisme platonicien*, Paris, 1910 — CXXXIVc

MAIER (Heinrich), *Die Syllogistik des Aristoteles*, 2 pts., Tübingen, 1896-1900 — CXXXV

MANSION (A.), *Introduction à la physique d'Aristote*, Louvain and Paris, 1913 — CXXXVI

OLLÉ-LAPRUNE (L.), *La Morale d'Aristote*, Paris, 1881 — CXXXVII

---

[1] The pagination of this edition, with the column (a, b) and the number of the line, is given in the margin of later partial editions.
[2] A lecture by Hamelin on *La Morale d'Aristote* has been published by L. Dugas in the *Rev. de Métaphysique*, 1923, pp. 497 ff.

DEFOURNY (M.), *Aristote : théorie économique et politique sociale* (*Annales de l'Inst. supér. de Philos.*, iii), Louvain, 1914   **CXXXVIII**

—— *Aristote et l'éducation* (*ibid.*, iv), Louvain, 1919   **CXXXIX**

POUCHET (G.), *La Biologie aristotélique*, Paris, 1885   **CXL**

    See also **IV**, pp. 1-806 ; **XI**, bk. vi, ch. 2-38 ; **XXIV**, ch. 16-17 ; **XXV** ; **XXX** ; **XXXIV**, ch. 5 ; **XXXV**, ch. 11, 14-16 ; **XLII**, bk. iii, pt. 2 ; **L** ; **La** ; **LI** ; **LIV** ; **LV** ; **LVIa** ; **LVIII** ; **CXX** ; **CXXIII** ; above, p. 258, n. 2.

9. IMMEDIATE DISCIPLES OF ARISTOTLE

    The *Characters* of Theophrastos has been translated into French and published by O. NAVARRE in the *Coll. Budé*. WIMMER has edited the botanical books and fragments (3 vols., Teubner) ; cf. **LXII**, 3. [*Characters*, ed. and trans. by R. C. JEBB, new ed. by SANDYS, London, 1909 ; *Enquiry into Plants*, trans. by Sir A. HORT, 2 vols., London 1916.]
    Fragments of Eudemos by L. SPENGEL, 1870.
    For Aristoxenos, see **LXVIII**, ch. 45 D.

RODIER (G.), *La Physique de Straton de Lampsaque*, Paris, 1891   **CXLI**

DIELS (Hermann), *Über das physikalische System des Stratons* (*Sitzungsb. d. Preuss. Akad. d. W.*, 1893, pp. 101-27)   **CXLII**

LALOY (L.), *Aristoxène de Tarente et la musique de l'antiquité*, Paris, 1904   **CXLIIa**

    See also **IV**, pp. 806-921 ; **XI**, iii, bk. vi, ch. 41-3 ; **LXXIXb**.

10. THE SCEPTICS

BROCHARD (Victor), *Les Sceptiques grecs*, Paris, 1887 (repr., 1923)   **CXLIII**

GOEDECKEMEYER (A), *Die Geschichte des griechischen Skeptizismus*, Leipzig, 1905   **CXLIV**

BRÉHIER (É.), *Le Mot νοητόν et Sextus Empiricus. Pour l'histoire du Scepticisme antique : les tropes d'Énésidème contre la logique inductive* (*Rev. des Études anciennes*, xvi, 269 ff. ; xx, 69 ff.), 1914, 1918   **CXLV**

COUISSIN (P.), *La Critique du réalisme des concepts chez Sextus Empiricus* (*Rev. d'Hist. de la philosophie*, 377-405), 1927   **CXLVa**

    See also **V**, pp. 494-507 ; **VI**, pp. 1-82 ; **LIII** ; **LXIII** ; **CLVIII**.

11. THE EPICUREANS

USENER (Hermann), *Epicurea*, Leipzig, 1887 (anastatic repr.)   **CXLVI**

    This important work, containing a collection of the fragments of Epicuros and the testimonies, should be supplemented by the *Gnomologium Vaticanum*, published by WOTKE (*Wiener Studien*, x, 1888), and by various papyrological fragments, particularly *Oxyrrhynch. Pap.*, 215 (1899 ; cf. H. DIELS, in *Sitzungsb. d. Preuss. Akad. d. W.*, 1916). New eds. of the three letters,[1] κύριαι δόξαι, and *Gnomologium* by Von der MÜHLL (Teubner, 1922), and by C. BAILEY, with a selection of fragments (text, trans., and comm., Oxford, 1926).
    Fragments of Metrodoros by A. KÖRTE (Teubner).
    Fragments of Demetrios the Laconian, see **CLI**.
    The most important philosophic fragments of Philodemos have been collected by T. GOMPERZ (Leipzig, 1865-6) ; cf. **LXII**, 4. His treatise *On the Gods* has been published by H. DIELS, Berlin, 1916-17.

---

    [1] Translated by O. Hamelin (*Rev. de Métaph. et de mor.*, xxiii, 1910 ; reprinted, Paris ; with the κύριαι δόξαι, by A. Ernout, *Lucr. Comment.*, i, pp. lix ff.

Lucretius has been edited and translated by A. ERNOUT (*Coll. Budé*, 2 vols., 2nd ed., 1924). Chief eds. with comm. : MUNRO (text, trans., comm.), 4th ed., 3 vols., Cambridge, 1886 ; C. GIUSSANI (text with notes), 3 vols., Turin, 1896-8 ; 2nd ed. by STAMPINI of bks. i-ii ; cf. **CL** ; W. A. MERRILL, N.Y., 1907 ; A. ERNOUT and L. ROBIN (comm. alone, without text), 3 vols., Paris, (i) 1925, (ii) 1926, (iii) 1928 ; *Index Lucretianus* by J. PAULSON, Göteborg, 1904. Fragments of Diogenes of Œnoanda, by H. WILLIAM, Teubner, 1906.

GUYAU (Marie Jean), *La Morale d'Épicure* (1878), 2nd ed., Paris, 1881   **CXLVII**

BIGNONE (Ettore), *Epicuro : opere, frammenti, testimonianze sulla sua vita, tradotti con introduzione e commento*, Bari, 1920   **CXLVIII**

ARNIM (H. von), *Epikur* (in **I**)   **CXLIX**

GIUSSANI (C.), *Studi lucreziani*,[1] Turin, 1906   **CL**

FALCO (Vitt. de), *L'Epicureo Demetrio Lacone*, Naples, 1923   **CLI**

CROENERT (Wilhelm), *Kolotes und Menedemos*, Leipzig, 1906   **CLII**

See also **V**, pp. 373-494, 565-72 ; **La** ; **LII** ; **LIII** ; **CLXVIII** ; above, p. 334, n. 3.

12. EARLY STOICISM

ARNIM (H. von), *Stoicorum veterum fragmenta*, 4 vols., Leipzig, 1903-5, 1924. i. Introd. on the sources (45 pp.) and fragments of Zenon, Ariston, Herillos, Cleanthes, Sphaeros ; ii. Chrysippos, logical and physical fragments ; iii. Chrysippos, moral fragments, and frags. of Diogenes of Babylon, Antipatros of Tarsos, etc. ; iv. *Indices* (Greek words, Latin words, proper names, sources), by Maximilian ADLER (PEARSON'S *The Fragments of Zeno and Cleanthes*, London, 1891, is excellent)   **CLIII**

RAVAISSON (F.), *Essai sur le Stoïcisme* (*Acad. des Inscr. et belles-lettres*, xxi, pt. i, 94 pp.), Paris, 1857   **CLIV**

OGEREAU (V.), *Essai sur le système philosophique des Stoïciens*, Paris, 1885   **CLV**

STEIN (Ludwig), *Die Psychologie der Stoa*, Berlin, 1886   **CLVI**

—— *Die Erkenntnistheorie der Stoa* (*Berliner Studien*, vii, 1), Berlin, 1888   **CLVII**

DYROFF (Ad.), *Die Ethik der alten Stoa* (*ibid.*, N.S., ii, 2-4), Berlin, 1897   **CLVIII**

HAMELIN (O.), *Sur la logique des Stoïciens* (*Année philos.*, xii), 1901   **CLIX**

RODIER (G.), *Sur la cohérence de la moral stoïcienne* (*ibid.*, xv), 1904   **CLX**

BRÉHIER (É.), *La Théorie des Incorporels dans l'ancien Stoïcisme*, Paris, 1908   **CLXI**

—— *Chrysippe*, Paris, 1910   **CLXII**

See also **V**, pp. 27-373 ; **La** ; **LII** ; **LVIa** ; **LXIII** ; **CLXVIII**.

13. THE NEW ACADEMY

CREDARO (L.), *Lo Scetticismo degli Academici*, 2 vols., Milan, 1889-93   **CLXIII**

ARNIM (H. von), *Arkesilaos, Karneades* (in **I**)   **CLXIV**

See also **III**, pp. 1045-9 ; **V**, pp. 507-46, 609-41 ; **LXIII** ; **XCII** ; **CXLIII** ; **CLXVIII**.

---

[1] First vol. of the edition of Lucretius, very important for the study of Epicuros.

14. MIDDLE STOICISM

SCHMEKEL (A.), *Die Philosophie der mittleren Stoa in ihrem geschichtlichen Zusammenhange*, Berlin, 1892 — **CLXV**

REINHARDT (C.), *Posidonios*, Munich, 1921 — **CLXVI**

HEINEMANN (J.), *Posidonios : Metaphys. Schriften*, i, Breslau, 1921 — **CLXVII**

See also **V**, pp. 572-609 ; **CLXVIII**.

15. ECLECTICISM. CICERO

There are very good editions of several philosophical works of Cicero : *De
Finibus* by MADVIG (Latin comm.), 3rd ed., 1876 ; bks. i-ii by J. S. REID, 1924 ;
De Natura Deorum by J. B. MAYOR (English), 3 vols., 1880-5 ; *De Divinatione*
by A. S. PEASE (4 nos. published by the University of Illinois, 1920, 3) ; *Academics*,
by J. S. REID, 1885. [*De Fin.*, trans. by H. RACKHAM, London, 1914 ; *De Off.*,
trans. by W. MILLER, London, 1913.] Useful lexicon of the philosophical works by
H. MERGUET, 3 vols., Jena, 1887-94.

HIRZEL (Rudolf), *Untersuchungen zu Ciceros philosophischen Schriften*
(i. *De Nat. deor.* ; ii. *De Fin.*, *De Off.* ; iii. *Acad.*, *Tusc.*), 3 vols.,
Leipzig, 1877-93 — **CLXVIII**

See also **V**, pp. 547-65, 671-99.

16. PHILON THE JEW

The best edition, not yet complete, is that of COHN and WENDLAND, Berlin
1896 ff. German trans., in progress, by COHN. Text and trans. of the *Commentary
on the Holy Laws* by É. BRÉHIER (in HEMMER and LEJAY'S *Textes et documents
pour l'histoire du Christianisme*), Paris, 1909.

BRÉHIER (É.), *Les Idées philosophiques et religieuses de Philon d'Alexandrie*, Paris, 1907 ; 2nd ed., 1924 — **CLXIX**

BILLINGS (T. H.), *The Platonism of Philo Judaeus*, Chicago, 1919 — **CLXX**

See also **VI**, pp. 261-467 ; **La**.

17. NEO-PYTHAGOREANS, SEXTIANS, NEO-STOICS, ECLECTIC PLATONISTS

See **VI**, pp. 92-175 ; **V**, pp. 699-706 ; **V**, 706-01 ; **VI**, pp. 175-261.

18. NEO-PLATONISTS AND GNOSTICS

Editions of Plotinus by R. VOLKMANN (Teubner) and H. F. MÜLLER (Weidmann).
German trans. by MÜLLER, 2 vols., 1878-80. Indifferent French trans. by M. N.
BOUILLET, 3 vols., 1857-61. [Eng. trans. by S. MCKENNA, in progress, London,
1917, etc.] The *Coll. Budé* has so far published 4 vols. (the first four *Enneads*)
of the new ed. with trans. by É. BRÉHIER.

SIMON (Jules), *Histoire de l'école d'Alexandrie*, 2 vols., Paris, 1843-45 — **CLXXI**

VACHEROT (Étienne), *Histoire critique de l'école d'Alexandrie*, 3 vols.,
Paris, 1846-51 — **CLXXII**

WHITTAKER (Thomas), *The Neoplatonists* (1901), 2nd ed., Cambridge,1918 — **CLXXIII**

KIRCHNER (Carl H.), *Die Philosophie des Plotin*, Halle, 1854 — **CLXXIV**

RICHTER (A.), *Neuplatonische Studien*, 5 pts., Halle, 1864-67 — **CLXXV**

INGE (William R.), *The Philosophy of Plotinus*, 2 vols., London, 1918 — **CLXXVI**

ARNOU (R.), *Le Désir de Dieu dans la philosophie de Plotin*, Paris, 1921 — **CLXXVII**

394 BIBLIOGRAPHY

Heinemann (Fr.), *Plotin*, Leipzig, 1921 **CLXXVIII**

Bréhier (É.), *La Philosophie de Plotin* (*Rev. des Cours et conférences*, 23rd year, 1st and 2nd series), 1922 **CLXXIX**

Bidez (J.), *Vie de Porphyre, le philosophe néoplatonicien* (*Travaux de la Fac. de Philos. et lettres de L'Univ. de Gand*, xliii), 1913 **CLXXX**

Stiglmayr (J.), *Der Neuplatoniker Proklus als Vorlage des sogenannten Dionysius Areopagita in der Lehre vom Bösen* (*Philologus*, liv), 1895 **CLXXXI**

Ruelle (C. E.), *Le Philosophe Damascius : études sur sa vie et ses écrits*, Paris, 1861 **CLXXXII**

Faye (E. de), *Introduction à l'histoire du Gnosticisme*, Paris, 1903 **CLXXXIIa**

—— *Gnostiques et Gnosticisme*, 2nd ed., Paris, 1925 **CLXXXIIb**

See also **VI**, pp. 468-519 (Neo-Platonism before Plotinus), 520-687 (Plotinus), 687-735 (Porphyry), 735-73 (Iamblichos), 834-90 (Proclos) ; **XII**, pp. 449-85 ; **La** ; **LVIa**.

INDEX

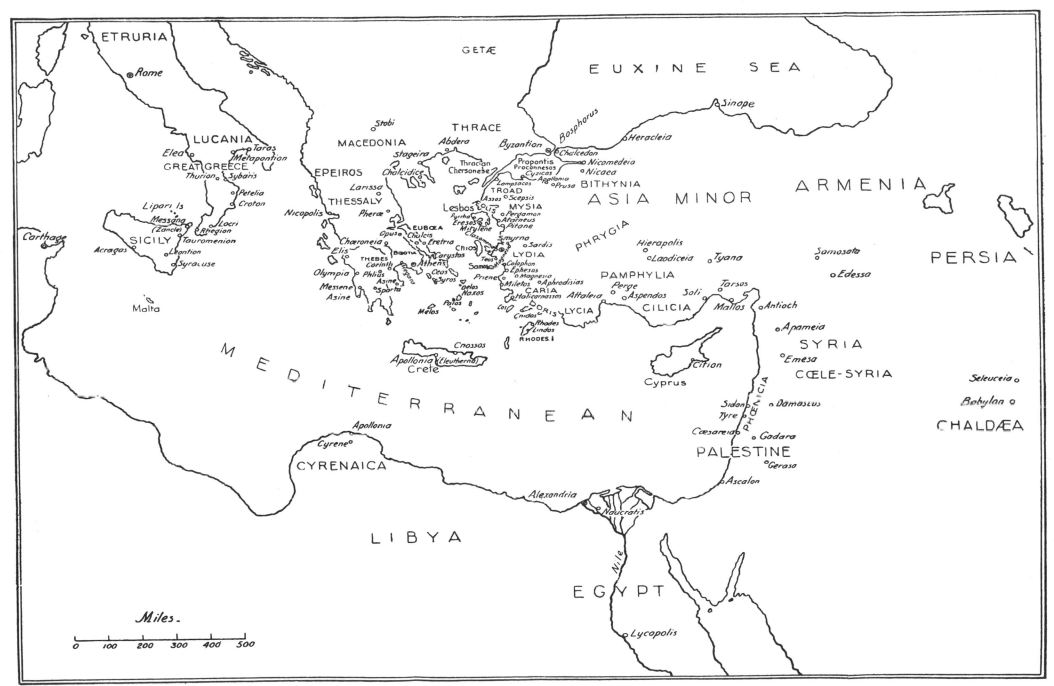

MAP OF THE EASTERN MEDITERRANEAN.

[*At End*